LAPACK

Users' Guide

E. Anderson
Z. Bai
C. Bischof
J. Demmel
J. Dongarra
J. Du Croz
A. Greenbaum
S. Hammarling
A. McKenney
S. Ostrouchov
D. Sorensen

Society for Industrial and Applied Mathematics

Philadelphia   1992

The royalties from the sales of this book are being placed in a fund to help students attend SIAM meetings and other SIAM related activities. This fund is administered by SIAM and qualified individuals are encouraged to write directly to SIAM for guidelines.

No warranties, express or implied, are made by the publisher, authors and their employers that the programs contained in this volume are free of error. They should not be relied on as the sole basis to solve a problem whose incorrect solution could result in injury to person or property. If the programs are employed in such a manner, it is at the user's own risk and the publisher, authors and their employers disclaim all liability for such misuse.

siam. is a registered trademark.

Library of Congress Cataloging-in-Publication Data

LAPACK users' guide / E. Anderson ... [et al.].
      p. cm.
    Includes bibliographical references and index.
    ISBN 0-89871-294-7
    1. FORTRAN (Computer program language)   2. Subroutines (Computer programs)   3. LAPACK.   4. Algebra, Linear—Data processing.
I. Anderson, E., 1962 - .
QA76.73.F25L36 1992
512 ' . 5 ' 02855133—dc20

                                                      92-14267

Dedication

This work is dedicated to Jim Wilkinson whose ideas and spirit have given us inspiration and influenced the project at every turn.

Authors' Affiliations:

E. Anderson
Cray Research, Inc.

Z. Bai
University of Kentucky

C. Bischof
Argonne National Laboratory

J. Demmel
University of California, Berkeley

J. Dongarra
University of Tennessee and
Oak Ridge National Laboratory

J. Du Croz
Numerical Algorithms Group Ltd.

A. Greenbaum
Courant Institute of Mathematical Sciences,
New York University

S. Hammarling
Numerical Algorithms Group Ltd.

A. McKenney
Courant Institute of Mathematical Sciences,
New York University

S. Ostrouchov
University of Tennessee

D. Sorensen
Rice University

Contents

List of Tables

Preface

The development of LAPACK was a natural step after specifications of the Level 2 and 3 BLAS were drawn up in 1984–86 and 1987–88. Research on block algorithms had been ongoing for several years, but agreement on the BLAS made it possible to construct a new software package to take the place of LINPACK and EISPACK, which would achieve much greater efficiency on modern high-performance computers. This also seemed to be a good time to implement a number of algorithmic advances that had been made since LINPACK and EISPACK were written in the 1970's. The proposal for LAPACK was submitted while the Level 3 BLAS were still being developed and funding was obtained from the National Science Foundation (NSF) beginning in 1987.

LAPACK is more than just a more efficient update of its popular predecessors. It extends the functionality of LINPACK and EISPACK by including: driver routines for linear systems; equilibration, iterative refinement and error bounds for linear systems; routines for computing and re-ordering the Schur factorization; and condition estimation routines for eigenvalue problems. LAPACK improves on the accuracy of the standard algorithms in EISPACK by including high accuracy algorithms for finding singular values and eigenvalues of bidiagonal and tridiagonal matrices, respectively, that arise in SVD and symmetric eigenvalue problems.

We have tried to be consistent with our documentation and coding style throughout LAPACK in the hope that LAPACK will serve as a model for other software development efforts. In particular, we hope that LAPACK and this guide will be of value in the classroom. But above all, LAPACK has been designed to be used for serious computation, especially as a source of building blocks for larger applications.

The LAPACK project has been a research project on achieving good performance in a portable way over a large class of modern computers. This goal has been achieved, subject to the following qualifications. For optimal performance, it is necessary, first, that the BLAS are implemented efficiently on the target machine, and second, that a small number of tuning parameters (such as the block size) have been set to suitable values (reasonable default values are provided). Most of the LAPACK code is written in standard Fortran 77, but the double precision complex data type is not part of the standard, so we have had to make some assumptions about the names of intrinsic functions that do not hold on all machines (see section 6.1). Finally, our rigorous testing suite included test problems scaled at the extremes of the arithmetic range, which can vary greatly from machine to machine. On some machines, we have had to restrict the range more than on others.

Since most of the performance improvements in LAPACK come from restructuring the algorithms to use the Level 2 and 3 BLAS, we benefited greatly by having access from the early stages of the project to a complete set of BLAS developed for the CRAY machines by Cray Research. Later, the BLAS library developed by IBM for the IBM RISC/6000 was very helpful in proving the worth of block algorithms and LAPACK on "super-scalar" workstations. Many of our test sites, both computer vendors and research institutions, also worked on optimizing the BLAS and thus helped to get good performance from LAPACK. We are very pleased at the extent to which the user community has embraced the BLAS, not only for performance reasons, but also because we feel developing software around a core set of common routines like the BLAS is good software engineering practice.

A number of technical reports were written during the development of LAPACK and published as LAPACK Working Notes, initially by Argonne National Laboratory and later by the University of Tennessee. Many of these reports later appeared as journal articles. Appendix E lists the LAPACK Working Notes, and the Bibliography gives the most recent published reference.

A follow-on project, LAPACK 2, has been funded in the U.S. by the NSF and DARPA. One of its aims will be to add a modest amount of additional functionality to the current LAPACK package — for example, routines for the generalized SVD and additional routines for generalized eigenproblems. These routines will be included in a future release of LAPACK when they are available. LAPACK 2 will also produce routines which implement LAPACK-type algorithms for distributed memory machines, routines which take special advantage of IEEE arithmetic, and versions of parts of LAPACK in C and Fortran 90. The precise form of these other software packages which will result from LAPACK 2 has not yet been decided.

As the successor to LINPACK and EISPACK, LAPACK has drawn heavily on both the software and documentation from those collections. The test and timing software for the Level 2 and 3 BLAS was used as a model for the LAPACK test and timing software, and in fact the LAPACK timing software includes the BLAS timing software as a subset. Formatting of the software and conversion from single to double precision was done using Toolpack/1 [40], which was indispensable to the project. We owe a great debt to our colleagues who have helped create the infrastructure of scientific computing on which LAPACK has been built.

The development of LAPACK was primarily supported by NSF grant ASC–8715728. Zhaojun Bai had partial support from DARPA grant F49620–87–C0065; Christian Bischof was supported by the Applied Mathematical Sciences subprogram of the Office of Energy Research, U.S. Department of Energy, under contract W–31–109–Eng–38; James Demmel had partial support from NSF grant DCR–8552474; and Jack Dongarra had partial support from the Applied Mathematical Sciences subprogram of the Office of Energy Research, U.S. Department of Energy, under Contract DE–AC05–84OR21400.

The cover was designed by Alan Edelman at UC Berkeley who discovered the matrix by performing Gaussian elimination on a certain 20-by-20 Hadamard matrix.

We acknowledge with gratitude the support which we have received from the following organizations, and the help of individual members of their staff: Cornell Theory Center; Cray Research Inc.; IBM ECSEC Rome; IBM Scientific Center, Bergen; NAG Ltd.

We also thank many, many people who have contributed code, criticism, ideas and encouragement. We wish especially to acknowledge the contributions of: Mario Arioli, Mir Assadullah, Jesse Barlow,

Mel Ciment, Percy Deift, Augustin Dubrulle, Iain Duff, Alan Edelman, Victor Eijkhout, Sam Figueroa, Pat Gaffney, Nick Higham, Liz Jessup, Bo Kågström, Velvel Kahan, Linda Kaufman, L.-C. Li, Bob Manchek, Peter Mayes, Cleve Moler, Beresford Parlett, Mick Pont, Giuseppe Radicati, Tom Rowan, Pete Stewart, Peter Tang, Carlos Tomei, Charlie Van Loan, Krešimir Veselić, Phuong Vu, and Reed Wade.

Finally we thank all the test sites who received three preliminary distributions of LAPACK software and who ran an extensive series of test programs and timing programs for us; their efforts have influenced the final version of the package in numerous ways.

The royalties from the sales of this book are being placed in a fund to help students attend SIAM meetings and other SIAM related activities. This fund is administered by SIAM and qualified individuals are encouraged to write directly to SIAM for guidelines.

Part 1

Guide

Chapter 1

Essentials

1.1 LAPACK

LAPACK is a library of Fortran 77 subroutines for solving the most commonly occurring problems in numerical linear algebra. It has been designed to be efficient on a wide range of modern high-performance computers. The name LAPACK is an acronym for Linear Algebra PACKage.

1.2 Problems that LAPACK can Solve

LAPACK can solve systems of linear equations, linear least squares problems, eigenvalue problems and singular value problems. LAPACK can also handle many associated computations such as matrix factorizations or estimating condition numbers.

LAPACK contains **driver routines** for solving standard types of problems, **computational routines** to perform a distinct computational task, and **auxiliary routines** to perform a certain subtask or common low-level computation. Each driver routine typically calls a sequence of computational routines. Taken as a whole, the computational routines can perform a wider range of tasks than are covered by the driver routines. Many of the auxiliary routines may be of use to numerical analysts or software developers, so we have documented the Fortran source for these routines with the same level of detail used for the LAPACK routines and driver routines.

Dense and band matrices are provided for, but not general sparse matrices. In all areas, similar functionality is provided for real and complex matrices. See Chapter 2 for a complete summary of the contents.

1.3 Computers for which LAPACK is Suitable

LAPACK is designed to give high efficiency on vector processors, high-performance "super-scalar" workstations, and shared memory multiprocessors. LAPACK in its present form is less likely to give good performance on other types of parallel architectures (for example, massively parallel SIMD machines, or distributed memory machines), but work has begun to try to adapt LAPACK to these new architectures. LAPACK can also be used satisfactorily on all types of scalar machines (PC's, workstations, mainframes). See Chapter 3 for some examples of the performance achieved by LAPACK routines.

1.4   LAPACK Compared with LINPACK and EISPACK

LAPACK has been designed to supersede LINPACK [15] and EISPACK [42, 28], principally by restructuring the software to achieve much greater efficiency, where possible, on modern high-performance computers; also by adding extra functionality, by using some new or improved algorithms, and by integrating the two sets of algorithms into a unified package.

Appendix D lists the LAPACK counterparts of LINPACK and EISPACK routines. Not all the facilities of LINPACK and EISPACK are covered by Release 1.0 of LAPACK.

1.5   LAPACK and the BLAS

LAPACK routines are written so that as much as possible of the computation is performed by calls to the Basic Linear Algebra Subprograms (BLAS) [38, 19, 17]. Highly efficient machine-specific implementations of the BLAS are available for many modern high-performance computers. The BLAS enable LAPACK routines to achieve high performance with portable code. The methodology for constructing LAPACK routines in terms of calls to the BLAS is described in Chapter 3.

The BLAS are not strictly speaking part of LAPACK, but Fortran 77 code for the BLAS is distributed with LAPACK, or can be obtained separately from *netlib* (see below). This code constitutes the "model implementation" [18, 16].

The model implementation is not expected to perform as well as a specially tuned implementation on most high-performance computers — on some machines it may give *much* worse performance — but it allows users to run LAPACK codes on machines that do not offer any other implementation of the BLAS.

1.6   Documentation for LAPACK

This **Users' Guide** gives an informal introduction to the design of the package, and a detailed description of its contents. Chapter 5 explains the conventions used in the software and documentation. Part 2 contains complete specifications of all the driver routines and computational routines. These specifications have been derived from the leading comments in the source text.

1.7   Availability of LAPACK

Individual routines from LAPACK are most easily obtained by electronic mail through *netlib* [21]. At the time of this writing, the e-mail addresses for *netlib* are

```
netlib@ornl.gov
netlib@research.att.com
```

General information about LAPACK can be obtained by sending mail to one of the above addresses with the message

```
send index from lapack
```

The complete package, including test code and timing programs in four different Fortran data types, constitutes some 600,000 lines of Fortran source and comments. It can be obtained on magnetic media from NAG for a cost-covering handling charge.

For further details contact NAG at one of the following addresses:

NAG Inc.
1400 Opus Place, Suite 200
Downers Grove, IL 60515-5702
USA
Tel: +1 708 971 2337
Fax: +1 708 971 2706

NAG Ltd.
Wilkinson House
Jordan Hill Road
Oxford OX2 8DR
England
Tel: +44 865 511245
Fax: +44 865 310139

NAG GmbH
Schleissheimerstrasse 5
W-8046 Garching bei München
Germany
Tel: +49 89 3207395
Fax: +49 89 3207396

1.8   Installation of LAPACK

A comprehensive Installation Guide [3] is distributed with the complete package. This includes descriptions of the test programs and timing programs, and detailed instructions on running them. See also Chapter 6.

1.9   Support for LAPACK

LAPACK has been thoroughly tested before release, on many different types of computers. The LAPACK project supports the package in the sense that reports of errors or poor performance will gain immediate attention from the developers. Such reports — and also descriptions of interesting applications and other comments — should be sent to:

LAPACK Project
c/o J. J. Dongarra
Computer Science Department
University of Tennessee
Knoxville, TN 37996-1301
USA
Email: lapack@cs.utk.edu

1.10   Known Problems in LAPACK

A list of known problems, bugs, and compiler errors for LAPACK is maintained on *netlib*. For a copy of this report, send email to netlib of the form:

    send release_notes from lapack

Chapter 2

Contents of LAPACK

2.1 Structure of LAPACK

2.1.1 Levels of Routines

The subroutines in LAPACK are classified as follows:

- **driver** routines, each of which solves a complete problem, for example solving a system of linear equations, or computing the eigenvalues of a real symmetric matrix. Users are recommended to use a driver routine if there is one that meets their requirements. They are listed in Section 2.2.

- **computational** routines, each of which performs a distinct computational task, for example an LU factorization, or the reduction of a real symmetric matrix to tridiagonal form. Each driver routine calls a sequence of computational routines. Users (especially software developers) may need to call computational routines directly to perform tasks, or sequences of tasks, that cannot conveniently be performed by the driver routines. They are listed in Section 2.3.

- **auxiliary** routines, which in turn can be classified as follows:

  - routines that perform subtasks of block algorithms — in particular, routines that implement unblocked versions of the algorithms;

  - routines that perform some commonly required low-level computations, for example scaling a matrix, computing a matrix-norm, or generating an elementary Householder matrix; some of these may be of interest to numerical analysts or software developers and could be considered for future additions to the BLAS;

  - a few extensions to the BLAS, such as routines for applying complex plane rotations, or matrix-vector operations involving complex symmetric matrices (the BLAS themselves are not strictly speaking part of LAPACK).

7

Both driver routines and computational routines are fully described in this Users' Guide, but not the auxiliary routines. A list of the auxiliary routines, with brief descriptions of their functions, is given in Appendix B.

2.1.2   Data Types and Precision

LAPACK provides the same range of functionality for **real** and **complex** data.

For most computations there are matching routines, one for real and one for complex data, but there are a few exceptions. For example, corresponding to the routines for real symmetric indefinite systems of linear equations, there are routines for complex Hermitian and complex symmetric systems, because both types of complex systems occur in practical applications. However, there is no complex analogue of the routine for finding selected eigenvalues of a real symmetric tridiagonal matrix, because a complex Hermitian matrix can always be reduced to a real symmetric tridiagonal matrix.

Matching routines for real and complex data have been coded to maintain a close correspondence between the two, wherever possible. However, in some areas (especially the nonsymmetric eigen-problem) the correspondence is necessarily weaker.

All routines in LAPACK are provided in both **single** and **double** precision versions. The double precision versions have been generated automatically, using Toolpack/1 [40].

Double precision routines for complex matrices require the non-standard Fortran data type COM-PLEX*16, which is available on most machines where double precision computation is usual.

2.1.3   Naming Scheme

The name of each LAPACK routine is a coded specification of its function (within the very tight limits of standard Fortran 77 6-character names).

All driver and computational routines have names of the form **XYYZZZ**, where for some driver routines the 6th character is blank.

The first letter, **X**, indicates the data type as follows:

S   REAL
D   DOUBLE PRECISION
C   COMPLEX
Z   COMPLEX*16 or DOUBLE COMPLEX

When we wish to refer to an LAPACK routine generically, regardless of data type, we replace the first letter by "x". Thus xGESV refers to any or all of the routines SGESV, CGESV, DGESV and ZGESV.

The next two letters, **YY**, indicate the type of matrix (or of the most significant matrix). Most of these two-letter codes apply to both real and complex matrices; a few apply specifically to one or the other, as indicated in Table 2.1.

Table 2.1: Matrix types in the LAPACK naming scheme

BD	bidiagonal
GB	general band
GE	general (i.e., unsymmetric, in some cases rectangular)
GG	general matrices, generalized problem (i.e., a pair of general matrices) (*not implemented in Release 1.0*)
GT	general tridiagonal
HB	(complex) Hermitian band
HE	(complex) Hermitian
HG	upper Hessenberg matrix, generalized problem (i.e a Hessenberg and a triangular matrix) (*not implemented in Release 1.0*)
HP	(complex) Hermitian, packed storage
HS	upper Hessenberg
OP	(real) orthogonal, packed storage
OR	(real) orthogonal
PB	symmetric or Hermitian positive definite band
PO	symmetric or Hermitian positive definite
PP	symmetric or Hermitian positive definite, packed storage
PT	symmetric or Hermitian positive definite tridiagonal
SB	(real) symmetric band
SP	symmetric, packed storage
ST	(real) symmetric tridiagonal
SY	symmetric
TB	triangular band
TG	triangular matrices, generalized problem (i.e., a pair of triangular matrices) (*not implemented in Release 1.0*)
TP	triangular, packed storage
TR	triangular (or in some cases quasi-triangular)
TZ	trapezoidal
UN	(complex) unitary
UP	(complex) unitary, packed storage

When we wish to refer to a class of routines that performs the same function on different types of matrices, we replace the first three letters by "xyy". Thus xyySVX refers to all the expert driver routines for systems of linear equations that are listed in Table 2.2.

The last three letters **ZZZ** indicate the computation performed. Their meanings will be explained in Section 2.3. For example, SGEBRD is a single precision routine that performs a bidiagonal reduction (BRD) of a real general matrix.

The names of auxiliary routines follow a similar scheme except that the 2nd and 3rd characters YY are usually LA (for example, SLASCL or CLARFG). There are two kinds of exception. Auxiliary routines that implement an unblocked version of a block algorithm have similar names to the routines that perform the block algorithm, with the sixth character being "2" (for example, SGETF2 is the unblocked version of SGETRF). A few routines that may be regarded as extensions to the BLAS are named according to the BLAS naming schemes (for example, CROT, CSYR).

2.2 Driver Routines

This section describes the driver routines in LAPACK. Further details on the terminology and the numerical operations they perform are given in Section 2.3, which describes the computational routines.

2.2.1 Linear Equations

Two types of driver routines are provided for solving systems of linear equations:

- a **simple** driver (name ending -SV), which solves the system $AX = B$ by factorizing A and overwriting B with the solution X;

- an **expert** driver (name ending -SVX), which can also perform the following functions (some of them optionally):

  - solve $A^T X = B$ or $A^H X = B$ (unless A is symmetric or Hermitian);
  - estimate the condition number of A and check for near-singularity;
  - refine the solution and compute forward and backward error bounds;
  - equilibrate the system if A is poorly scaled.

  The expert driver requires roughly twice as much storage as the simple driver in order to perform these extra functions.

Both types of driver routines can handle multiple right hand sides (the columns of B).

Different driver routines are provided to take advantage of special properties or storage schemes of the matrix A, as shown in Table 2.2.

These driver routines cover all the functionality of the computational routines for linear systems, except matrix inversion. It is seldom necessary to compute the inverse of a matrix explicitly, and it is certainly not recommended as a means of solving linear systems.

Table 2.2: Driver routines for linear equations

Type of matrix and storage scheme	Operation	Single precision		Double precision	
		real	complex	real	complex
general	simple driver	SGESV	CGESV	DGESV	ZGESV
	expert driver	SGESVX	CGESVX	DGESVX	ZGESVX
general band	simple driver	SGBSV	CGBSV	DGBSV	ZGBSV
	expert driver	SGBSVX	CGBSVX	DGBSVX	ZGBSVX
general tridiagonal	simple driver	SGTSV	CGTSV	DGTSV	ZGTSV
	expert driver	SGTSVX	CGTSVX	DGTSVX	ZGTSVX
symmetric/Hermitian positive definite	simple driver	SPOSV	CPOSV	DPOSV	ZPOSV
	expert driver	SPOSVX	CPOSVX	DPOSVX	ZPOSVX
symmetric/Hermitian positive definite (packed storage)	simple driver	SPPSV	CPPSV	DPPSV	ZPPSV
	expert driver	SPPSVX	CPPSVX	DPPSVX	ZPPSVX
symmetric/Hermitian positive definite band	simple driver	SPBSV	CPBSV	DPBSV	ZPBSV
	expert driver	SPBSVX	CPBSVX	DPBSVX	ZPBSVX
symmetric/Hermitian positive definite tridiagonal	simple driver	SPTSV	CPTSV	DPTSV	ZPTSV
	expert driver	SPTSVX	CPTSVX	DPTSVX	ZPTSVX
symmetric/Hermitian indefinite	simple driver	SSYSV	CHESV	DSYSV	ZHESV
	expert driver	SSYSVX	CHESVX	DSYSVX	ZHESVX
complex symmetric	simple driver		CSYSV		ZSYSV
	expert driver		CSYSVX		ZSYSVX
symmetric/Hermitian indefinite (packed storage)	simple driver	SSPSV	CHPSV	DSPSV	ZHPSV
	expert driver	SSPSVX	CHPSVX	DSPSVX	ZHPSVX
complex symmetric (packed storage)	simple driver		CSPSV		ZSPSV
	expert driver		CSPSVX		ZSPSVX

2.2.2 Linear Least Squares (LLS) Problems

The **linear least squares problem** is:

$$\underset{x}{\text{minimize}} \ \|b - Ax\|_2 \tag{2.1}$$

where A is an m-by-n matrix, b is a given m element vector and x is the n element solution vector.

In the most usual case $m \geq n$ and $\text{rank}(A) = n$, and in this case the solution to problem (2.1) is unique, and the problem is also referred to as finding a **least squares solution** to an **overdetermined** system of linear equations.

When $m < n$ and $\text{rank}(A) = m$, there are an infinite number of solutions x which exactly satisfy $b - Ax = 0$. In this case it is often useful to find the unique solution x which minimizes $\|x\|_2$, and the problem is referred to as finding a **minimum norm solution** to an **underdetermined** system of linear equations.

The driver routine xGELS solves problem (2.1) on the assumption that $\text{rank}(A) = \min(m, n)$ — in other words, A has **full rank** — finding a least squares solution of an overdetermined system when $m > n$, and a minimum norm solution of an underdetermined system when $m < n$. xGELS uses a QR or LQ factorization of A, and also allows A to be replaced by A^T in the statement of the problem (or by A^H if A is complex).

In the general case when we may have $\text{rank}(A) < \min(m, n)$ — in other words, A may be **rank-deficient** — we seek the **minimum norm least squares** solution x which minimizes both $\|x\|_2$ and $\|b - Ax\|_2$.

The driver routines xGELSX and xGELSS solve this general formulation of problem 2.1, allowing for the possibility that A is rank-deficient; xGELSX uses a **complete orthogonal factorization** of A, while xGELSS uses the **singular value decomposition** of A.

The LLS driver routines are listed in Table 2.3.

All three routines allow several right hand side vectors b and corresponding solutions x to be handled in a single call, storing these vectors as columns of matrices B and X, respectively. Note however that problem 2.1 is solved for each right hand side vector independently; this is *not* the same as finding a matrix X which minimizes $\|B - AX\|_2$.

Table 2.3: Driver routines for linear least squares problems

Operation	Single precision		Double precision	
	real	complex	real	complex
solve LLS using QR or LQ factorization	SGELS	CGELS	DGELS	ZGELS
solve LLS using complete orthogonal factorization	SGELSX	CGELSX	DGELSX	ZGELSX
solve LLS using SVD	SGELSS	CGELSS	DGELSS	ZGELSS

2.2.3 Standard Eigenvalue and Singular Value Problems

2.2.3.1 Symmetric Eigenproblems (SEP)

The **symmetric eigenvalue problem** is to find the **eigenvalues**, λ, and corresponding **eigenvectors**, $z \neq 0$, such that

$$Az = \lambda z, \quad A = A^T, \text{ where } A \text{ is real.}$$

For the **Hermitian eigenvalue problem** we have

$$Az = \lambda z, \quad A = A^H.$$

For both problems the eigenvalues λ are real.

When all eigenvalues and eigenvectors have been computed, we write:

$$A = Z\Lambda Z^T$$

where Λ is a diagonal matrix whose diagonal elements are the eigenvalues, and Z is an orthogonal (or unitary) matrix whose columns are the eigenvectors. This is the classical **spectral factorization** of A.

Two types of driver routines are provided for symmetric or Hermitian eigenproblems:

- a **simple** driver (name ending -EV), which computes all the eigenvalues and (optionally) the eigenvectors of a symmetric or Hermitian matrix A;

- an **expert** driver (name ending -EVX), which can compute either all or a selected subset of the eigenvalues, and (optionally) the corresponding eigenvectors.

Different driver routines are provided to take advantage of special structure or storage of the matrix A, as shown in Table 2.4.

2.2.3.2 Nonsymmetric Eigenproblems (NEP)

The **nonsymmetric eigenvalue problem** is to find the **eigenvalues**, λ, and corresponding **eigenvectors**, $v \neq 0$, such that

$$Av = \lambda v.$$

A real matrix A may have complex eigenvalues, occurring as complex conjugate pairs. More precisely, the vector v is called a **right eigenvector** of A, and a vector $u \neq 0$ satisfying

$$u^T A = \lambda u^T \quad (u^H A = \lambda u^H \text{ when } u \text{ is complex})$$

is called a **left eigenvector** of A.

This problem can be solved via the **Schur factorization** of A, defined in the real case as

$$A = ZTZ^T,$$

where Z is an orthogonal matrix and T is an upper quasi-triangular matrix with 1-by-1 and 2-by-2 diagonal blocks, the 2-by-2 blocks corresponding to complex conjugate pairs of eigenvalues of A. In the complex case the Schur factorization is

$$A = ZTZ^H,$$

where Z is unitary and T is a complex upper triangular matrix.

The columns of Z are called the **Schur vectors**. For each k ($1 \leq k \leq n$), the first k columns of Z form an orthonormal basis for the **invariant subspace** corresponding to the first k eigenvalues on the diagonal of T. Because this basis is orthonormal, it is preferable in many applications to compute Schur vectors rather than eigenvectors. It is possible to order the Schur factorization so that any desired set of k eigenvalues occupy the k leading positions on the diagonal of T.

Two pairs of drivers are provided, one pair focusing on the Schur factorization, and the other pair on the eigenvalues and eigenvectors as shown in Table 2.4:

- xGEES: a simple driver that computes all or part of the Schur factorization of A, with optional ordering of the eigenvalues;

- xGEESX: an expert driver that can additionally compute condition numbers for the average of a selected subset of the eigenvalues, and for the corresponding right invariant subspace;

- xGEEV: a simple driver that computes all the eigenvalues of A, and (optionally) the right or left eigenvectors (or both);

- xGEEVX: an expert driver that can additionally balance the matrix to improve the conditioning of the eigenvalues and eigenvectors, and compute condition numbers for the eigenvalues or right eigenvectors (or both).

2.2.3.3 Singular Value Decomposition (SVD)

The **singular value decomposition** of an m-by-n matrix A is given by

$$A = U\Sigma V^T, \quad (A = U\Sigma V^H \quad \text{in the complex case})$$

where U and V are orthogonal (unitary) and Σ is an m-by-n diagonal matrix with real diagonal elements, σ_i, such that

$$\sigma_1 \geq \sigma_2 \geq \ldots \sigma_{\min(m,n)} \geq 0.$$

The σ_i are the **singular values** of A and the first $\min(m,n)$ columns of U and V are the **left** and **right singular vectors** of A. The singular values and singular vectors satisfy:

$$Av_i = \sigma_i u_i \quad \text{and} \quad A^T u_i = \sigma_i v_i \quad (\text{or} \quad A^H u_i = \sigma_i v_i \quad)$$

where u_i and v_i are the ith columns of U and V respectively.

A single driver routine xGESVD computes all or part of the singular value decomposition of a general nonsymmetric matrix (see Table 2.4).

Table 2.4: Driver routines for standard eigenvalue and singular value problems

Type of problem	Function and storage scheme	Single precision		Double precision	
		real	complex	real	complex
SEP	simple driver	SSYEV	CHEEV	DSYEV	ZHEEV
	expert driver	SSYEVX	CHEEVX	DSYEVX	ZHEEVX
	simple driver (packed storage)	SSPEV	CHPEV	DSPEV	ZHPEV
	expert driver (packed storage)	SSPEVX	CHPEVX	DSPEVX	ZHPEVX
	simple driver (band matrix)	SSBEV	CHBEV	DSBEV	ZHBEV
	expert driver (band matrix)	SSBEVX	CHBEVX	DSBEVX	ZHBEVX
	simple driver (tridiagonal matrix)	SSTEV		DSTEV	
	expert driver (tridiagonal matrix)	SSTEVX		DSTEVX	
NEP	simple driver for Schur factorization	SGEES	CGEES	DGEES	ZGEES
	expert driver for Schur factorization	SGEESX	CGEESX	DGEESX	ZGEESX
	simple driver for eigenvalues/vectors	SGEEV	CGEEV	DGEEV	ZGEEV
	expert driver for eigenvalues/vectors	SGEEVX	CGEEVX	DGEEVX	ZGEEVX
SVD	singular values/vectors	SGESVD	CGESVD	DGESVD	ZGESVD

2.2.4 Generalized Eigenvalue Problems

2.2.4.1 Generalized Symmetric Definite Eigenproblems (GSEP)

Simple drivers are provided to compute all the eigenvalues and (optionally) the eigenvectors of the following types of problems:

1. $Az = \lambda Bz$

2. $ABz = \lambda z$

3. $BAz = \lambda z$

where A and B are symmetric or Hermitian and B is positive definite. For all these problems the eigenvalues λ are real. The matrices Z of computed eigenvectors satisfy $Z^T B Z = I$ (problem types 1 and 2) or $Z^T B^{-1} Z = I$ (problem type 3).

The routines are listed in Table 2.5

2.2.4.2 Generalized Nonsymmetric Eigenproblems (GNEP)

Routines for generalized nonsymmetric eigenproblems will be provided in a future release of LA-PACK.

Table 2.5: Driver routines for generalized eigenvalue problems

Type of problem	Function and storage scheme	Single precision		Double precision	
		real	complex	real	complex
GSEP	simple driver	SSYGV	CHEGV	DSYGV	ZHEGV
	simple driver (packed storage)	SSPGV	CHPGV	DSPGV	ZHPGV

2.3 Computational Routines

2.3.1 Linear Equations

We use the standard notation for a system of simultaneous linear equations:

$$Ax = b \tag{2.2}$$

where A is the **coefficient matrix**, b is the **right hand side**, and x is the **solution**. In (2.2) A is assumed to be a square matrix of order n, but some of the individual routines allow A to be rectangular. If there are several right hand sides, we write

$$AX = B \tag{2.3}$$

where the columns of B are the individual right hand sides, and the columns of X are the corresponding solutions. The basic task is to compute X, given A and B.

If A is upper or lower triangular, (2.2) can be solved by a straightforward process of backward or forward substitution. Otherwise, the solution is obtained after first factorizing A as a product of triangular matrices (and possibly also a diagonal matrix or permutation matrix).

The form of the factorization depends on the properties of the matrix A. LAPACK provides routines for the following types of matrices, based on the stated factorizations:

- **general** matrices (LU factorization with partial pivoting):

$$A = PLU$$

    where P is a permutation matrix, L is lower triangular with unit diagonal elements (lower trapezoidal if $m > n$), and U is upper triangular (upper trapezoidal if $m < n$).

- **general band** matrices including **tridiagonal** matrices (LU factorization with partial pivoting): If A is m-by-n with kl subdiagonals and ku superdiagonals, the factorization is

$$A = LU$$

    where L is a product of permutation and unit lower triangular matrices with kl subdiagonals, and U is upper triangular with $kl + ku$ superdiagonals.

- **symmetric and Hermitian positive definite** matrices including **band** matrices (Cholesky factorization):

$$A = U^T U \quad \text{or} \quad A = LL^T \text{(in the symmetric case)}$$

$$A = U^H U \quad \text{or} \quad A = LL^H \text{(in the Hermitian case)}$$

where U is an upper triangular matrix and L is lower triangular.

- **symmetric and Hermitian positive definite tridiagonal** matrices (LDL^T factorization):

$$A = UDU^T \quad \text{or} \quad A = LDL^T \text{(in the symmetric case)}$$

$$A = UDU^H \quad \text{or} \quad A = LDL^H \text{(in the Hermitian case)}$$

where U is a unit upper bidiagonal matrix, L is unit lower bidiagonal, and D is diagonal.

- **symmetric and Hermitian indefinite** matrices (symmetric indefinite factorization):

$$A = UDU^T \quad \text{or} \quad A = LDL^T \text{(in the symmetric case)}$$

$$A = UDU^H \quad \text{or} \quad A = LDL^H \text{(in the Hermitian case)}$$

where U (or L) is a product of permutation and unit upper (lower) triangular matrices, and D is symmetric and block diagonal with diagonal blocks of order 1 or 2.

The factorization for a general tridiagonal matrix is like that for a general band matrix with $kl = 1$ and $ku = 1$. The factorization for a symmetric positive definite band matrix with k superdiagonals (or subdiagonals) has the same form as for a symmetric positive definite matrix, but the factor U (or L) is a band matrix with k superdiagonals (subdiagonals). Band matrices use a compact band storage scheme described in section 5.3.3. LAPACK routines are also provided for symmetric matrices (whether positive definite or indefinite) using **packed** storage, as described in section 5.3.2.

While the primary use of a matrix factorization is to solve a system of equations, other related tasks are provided as well. Wherever possible, LAPACK provides routines to perform each of these tasks for each type of matrix and storage scheme (see Tables 2.6 and 2.7). The following list relates the tasks to the last 3 characters of the name of the corresponding computational routine:

xyyTRF: factorize (obviously not needed for triangular matrices);

xyyTRS: use the factorization (or the matrix A itself if it is triangular) to solve (2.3) by forward or backward substitution;

xyyCON: estimate the reciprocal of the condition number $\kappa(A) = \|A\|.\|A^{-1}\|$; Higham's modification [34] of Hager's method [31] is used to estimate $\|A^{-1}\|$, except for symmetric positive definite tridiagonal matrices for which it is computed directly with comparable efficiency [32];

xyyRFS: compute bounds on the error in the computed solution (returned by the xyyTRS routine), and refine the solution to reduce the backward error (see below);

xyyTRI: use the factorization (or the matrix A itself if it is triangular) to compute A^{-1} (not provided for band matrices, because the inverse does not in general preserve bandedness);

xyyEQU: compute scaling factors to equilibrate A (not provided for tridiagonal, symmetric indefinite, or triangular matrices). These routines do not actually scale the matrices: auxiliary routines xLAQyy may be used for that purpose — see the code of the driver routines xyySVX for sample usage.

Note that some of the above routines depend on the output of others:

xyyTRF: may work on an equilibrated matrix produced by xyyEQU and xLAQyy, if yy is one of {GE, GB, PO, PP, PB};

xyyTRS: requires the factorization returned by xyyTRF;

xyyCON: requires the norm of the original matrix A, and the factorization returned by xyyTRF;

xyyRFS: requires the original matrices A and B, the factorization returned by xyyTRF, and the solution X returned by xyyTRS;

xyyTRI: requires the factorization returned by xyyTRF.

The RFS ("refine solution") routines perform iterative refinement and compute backward and forward error bounds for the solution. Iterative refinement is done in the same precision as the input data. In particular, the residual is *not* computed with extra precision, as has been traditionally done. The benefit of this procedure is discussed in Section 4.6.

Table 2.6: Computational routines for linear equations

Type of matrix and storage scheme	Operation	Single precision		Double precision	
		real	complex	real	complex
general	factorize	SGETRF	CGETRF	DGETRF	ZGETRF
	solve using factorization	SGETRS	CGETRS	DGETRS	ZGETRS
	estimate condition number	SGECON	CGECON	DGECON	ZGECON
	error bounds for solution	SGERFS	CGERFS	DGERFS	ZGERFS
	invert using factorization	SGETRI	CGETRI	DGETRI	ZGETRI
	equilibrate	SGEEQU	CGEEQU	DGEEQU	ZGEEQU
general band	factorize	SGBTRF	CGBTRF	DGBTRF	ZGBTRF
	solve using factorization	SGBTRS	CGBTRS	DGBTRS	ZGBTRS
	estimate condition number	SGBCON	CGBCON	DGBCON	ZGBCON
	error bounds for solution	SGBRFS	CGBRFS	DGBRFS	ZGBRFS
	equilibrate	SGBEQU	CGBEQU	DGBEQU	ZGBEQU
general tridiagonal	factorize	SGTTRF	CGTTRF	DGTTRF	ZGTTRF
	solve using factorization	SGTTRS	CGTTRS	DGTTRS	ZGTTRS
	estimate condition number	SGTCON	CGTCON	DGTCON	ZGTCON
	error bounds for solution	SGTRFS	CGTRFS	DGTRFS	ZGTRFS
symmetric/Hermitian positive definite	factorize	SPOTRF	CPOTRF	DPOTRF	ZPOTRF
	solve using factorization	SPOTRS	CPOTRS	DPOTRS	ZPOTRS
	estimate condition number	SPOCON	CPOCON	DPOCON	ZPOCON
	error bounds for solution	SPORFS	CPORFS	DPORFS	ZPORFS
	invert using factorization	SPOTRI	CPOTRI	DPOTRI	ZPOTRI
	equilibrate	SPOEQU	CPOEQU	DPOEQU	ZPOEQU
symmetric/Hermitian positive definite (packed storage)	factorize	SPPTRF	CPPTRF	DPPTRF	ZPPTRF
	solve using factorization	SPPTRS	CPPTRS	DPPTRS	ZPPTRS
	estimate condition number	SPPCON	CPPCON	DPPCON	ZPPCON
	error bounds for solution	SPPRFS	CPPRFS	DPPRFS	ZPPRFS
	invert using factorization	SPPTRI	CPPTRI	DPPTRI	ZPPTRI
	equilibrate	SPPEQU	CPPEQU	DPPEQU	ZPPEQU
symmetric/Hermitian positive definite band	factorize	SPBTRF	CPBTRF	DPBTRF	ZPBTRF
	solve using factorization	SPBTRS	CPBTRS	DPBTRS	ZPBTRS
	estimate condition number	SPBCON	CPBCON	DPBCON	ZPBCON
	error bounds for solution	SPBRFS	CPBRFS	DPBRFS	ZPBRFS
	equilibrate	SPBEQU	CPBEQU	DPBEQU	ZPBEQU
symmetric/Hermitian positive definite tridiagonal	factorize	SPTTRF	CPTTRF	DPTTRF	ZPTTRF
	solve using factorization	SPTTRS	CPTTRS	DPTTRS	ZPTTRS
	estimate condition number	SPTCON	CPTCON	DPTCON	ZPTCON
	error bounds for solution	SPTRFS	CPTRFS	DPTRFS	ZPTRFS

Table 2.7: Computational routines for linear equations (continued)

Type of matrix and storage scheme	Operation	Single precision		Double precision	
		real	complex	real	complex
symmetric/Hermitian indefinite	factorize	SSYTRF	CHETRF	DSYTRF	ZHETRF
	solve using factorization	SSYTRS	CHETRS	DSYTRS	ZHETRS
	estimate condition number	SSYCON	CHECON	DSYCON	ZHECON
	error bounds for solution	SSYRFS	CHERFS	DSYRFS	ZHERFS
	invert using factorization	SSYTRI	CHETRI	DSYTRI	ZHETRI
complex symmetric	factorize		CSYTRF		ZSYTRF
	solve using factorization		CSYTRS		ZSYTRS
	estimate condition number		CSYCON		ZSYCON
	error bounds for solution		CSYRFS		ZSYRFS
	invert using factorization		CSYTRI		ZSYTRI
symmetric/Hermitian indefinite (packed storage)	factorize	SSPTRF	CHPTRF	DSPTRF	ZHPTRF
	solve using factorization	SSPTRS	CHPTRS	DSPTRS	ZHPTRS
	estimate condition number	SSPCON	CHPCON	DSPCON	ZHPCON
	error bounds for solution	SSPRFS	CHPRFS	DSPRFS	ZHPRFS
	invert using factorization	SSPTRI	CHPTRI	DSPTRI	ZHPTRI
complex symmetric (packed storage)	factorize		CSPTRF		ZSPTRF
	solve using factorization		CSPTRS		ZSPTRS
	estimate condition number		CSPCON		ZSPCON
	error bounds for solution		CSPRFS		ZSPRFS
	invert using factorization		CSPTRI		ZSPTRI
triangular	solve	STRTRS	CTRTRS	DTRTRS	ZTRTRS
	estimate condition number	STRCON	CTRCON	DTRCON	ZTRCON
	error bounds for solution	STRRFS	CTRRFS	DTRRFS	ZTRRFS
	invert	STRTRI	CTRTRI	DTRTRI	ZTRTRI
triangular (packed storage)	solve	STPTRS	CTPTRS	DTPTRS	ZTPTRS
	estimate condition number	STPCON	CTPCON	DTPCON	ZTPCON
	error bounds for solution	STPRFS	CTPRFS	DTPRFS	ZTPRFS
	invert	STPTRI	CTPTRI	DTPTRI	ZTPTRI
triangular band	solve	STBTRS	CTBTRS	DTBTRS	ZTBTRS
	estimate condition number	STBCON	CTBCON	DTBCON	ZTBCON
	error bounds for solution	STBRFS	CTBRFS	DTBRFS	ZTBRFS

2.3.2 Orthogonal Factorizations and Linear Least Squares Problems

LAPACK provides a number of routines for factorizing a general rectangular m-by-n matrix A, as the product of an **orthogonal** matrix (**unitary** if complex) and a **triangular** (or possibly trapezoidal) matrix.

A real matrix Q is **orthogonal** if $Q^T Q = I$; a complex matrix Q is **unitary** if $Q^H Q = I$. Orthogonal or unitary matrices have the important property that they leave the two-norm of a vector invariant:

$$\|x\|_2 = \|Qx\|_2, \quad \text{if } Q \text{ is orthogonal or unitary.}$$

As a result, they help to maintain numerical stability because they do not amplify rounding errors.

Orthogonal factorizations are used in the solution of linear least squares problems. They may also be used to perform preliminary steps in the solution of eigenvalue or singular value problems.

2.3.2.1 QR Factorization

The most common, and best known, of the factorizations is the **QR factorization** given by

$$A = Q \begin{pmatrix} R \\ 0 \end{pmatrix}, \quad \text{if } m \geq n,$$

where R is an n-by-n upper triangular matrix and Q is an m-by-m orthogonal (or unitary) matrix. If A is of full rank n, then R is non-singular. It is sometimes convenient to write the factorization as

$$A = \begin{pmatrix} Q_1 & Q_2 \end{pmatrix} \begin{pmatrix} R \\ 0 \end{pmatrix}$$

which reduces to

$$A = Q_1 R,$$

where Q_1 consists of the first n columns of Q, and Q_2 the remaining $m - n$ columns.

If $m < n$, R is trapezoidal, and the factorization can be written

$$A = Q \begin{pmatrix} R_1 & R_2 \end{pmatrix}, \quad \text{if } m < n,$$

where R_1 is upper triangular and R_2 is rectangular.

The routine xGEQRF computes the QR factorization. The matrix Q is not formed explicitly, but is represented as a product of elementary reflectors, as described in section 5.4. Users need not be aware of the details of this representation, because associated routines are provided to work with Q: xORGQR (or xUNGQR in the complex case) can generate all or part of Q, while xORMQR (or xUNMQR) can pre- or post-multiply a given matrix by Q or Q^T (Q^H if complex).

The QR factorization can be used to solve the linear least squares problem (2.1) when $m \geq n$ and A is of full rank, since

$$\|b - Ax\|_2 = \|Q^T b - Q^T Ax\|_2 = \left\| \begin{array}{c} c_1 - Rx \\ c_2 \end{array} \right\|_2, \quad \text{where } c \equiv \begin{pmatrix} c_1 \\ c_2 \end{pmatrix} = \begin{pmatrix} Q_1^T b \\ Q_2^T b \end{pmatrix} = Q^T b;$$

c can be computed by xORMQR (or xUNMQR), and c_1 consists of its first n elements. Then x is the solution of the upper triangular system

$$Rx = c_1$$

which can be computed by xTRTRS. The residual vector r is given by

$$r = b - Ax = Q \begin{pmatrix} 0 \\ c_2 \end{pmatrix},$$

and may be computed using xORMQR (or xUNMQR). The residual sum of squares $\|r\|_2^2$ may be computed without forming r explicitly, since

$$\|r\|_2 = \|b - Ax\|_2 = \|c_2\|_2.$$

2.3.2.2   *LQ* Factorization

The **LQ factorization** is given by

$$A = \begin{pmatrix} L & 0 \end{pmatrix} Q = \begin{pmatrix} L & 0 \end{pmatrix} \begin{pmatrix} Q_1 \\ Q_2 \end{pmatrix} = LQ_1, \quad \text{if } m \leq n,$$

where L is m-by-m lower triangular, Q is n-by-n orthogonal (or unitary), Q_1 consists of the first m rows of Q, and Q_2 the remaining $n - m$ rows.

This factorization is computed by the routine xGELQF, and again Q is represented as a product of elementary reflectors; xORGLQ (or xUNGLQ in the complex case) can generate all or part of Q, and xORMLQ (or xUNMLQ) can pre- or post-multiply a given matrix by Q or Q^T (Q^H if Q is complex).

The LQ factorization of A is essentially the same as the QR factorization of A^T (A^H if A is complex), since

$$A = \begin{pmatrix} L & 0 \end{pmatrix} Q \quad \Longleftrightarrow \quad A^T = Q^T \begin{pmatrix} L^T \\ 0 \end{pmatrix}.$$

The LQ factorization may be used to find a minimum norm solution of an underdetermined system of linear equations $Ax = b$ where A is m-by-n with $m < n$ and has rank m. The solution is given by

$$x = Q^T \begin{pmatrix} L^{-1}b \\ 0 \end{pmatrix}$$

and may be computed by calls to xTRTRS and xORMLQ.

2.3.2.3   *QR* Factorization with Column Pivoting

To solve a linear least squares problem (2.1) when A is not of full rank, or the rank of A is in doubt, we can perform either a QR factorization with column pivoting or a singular value decomposition (see subsection 2.3.5).

The **QR factorization with column pivoting** is given by

$$A = Q \begin{pmatrix} R \\ 0 \end{pmatrix} P^T, \quad m \geq n,$$

where Q and R are as before and P is a permutation matrix, chosen (in general) so that

$$|r_{11}| \geq |r_{22}| \geq \ldots \geq |r_{nn}|$$

and moreover, for each k,

$$|r_{kk}| \geq \|R_{k:j,j}\|_2 \quad \text{for } j = k+1, \ldots, n.$$

In exact arithmetic, if rank$(A) = k$, then the whole of the submatrix R_{22} in rows and columns $k+1$ to n would be zero. In numerical computation, the aim must be to determine an index k, such that the leading submatrix R_{11} in the first k rows and columns is well-conditioned, and R_{22} is negligible:

$$R = \begin{pmatrix} R_{11} & R_{12} \\ 0 & R_{22} \end{pmatrix} \simeq \begin{pmatrix} R_{11} & R_{12} \\ 0 & 0 \end{pmatrix}.$$

Then k is the effective rank of A. See Golub and Van Loan [29] for a further discussion of numerical rank determination.

The so-called basic solution to the linear least squares problem (2.1) can be obtained from this factorization as

$$x = P \begin{pmatrix} R_{11}^{-1} \hat{c}_1 \\ 0 \end{pmatrix},$$

where $\hat{c}_1$ consists of just the first k elements of $c = Q^T b$.

The routine xGEQPF computes the QR factorization with column pivoting, but does not attempt to determine the rank of A. The matrix Q is represented in exactly the same way as after a call of xGEQRF, and so the routines xORGQR and xORMQR can be used to work with Q (xUNGQR and xUNMQR if Q is complex).

2.3.2.4 Complete Orthogonal Factorization

The QR factorization with column pivoting does not enable us to compute a *minimum norm* solution to a rank-deficient linear least squares problem, unless $R_{12} = 0$. However, by applying further orthogonal (or unitary) transformations from the right to the upper trapezoidal matrix $\begin{pmatrix} R_{11} & R_{12} \end{pmatrix}$, using the routine xTZRQF, R_{12} can be eliminated:

$$\begin{pmatrix} R_{11} & R_{12} \end{pmatrix} Z = \begin{pmatrix} T_{11} & 0 \end{pmatrix}.$$

This gives the **complete orthogonal factorization**

$$AP = Q \begin{pmatrix} T_{11} & 0 \\ 0 & 0 \end{pmatrix} Z^T$$

from which the minimum norm solution can be obtained as

$$x = PZ \begin{pmatrix} T_{11}^{-1}\hat{c}_1 \\ 0 \end{pmatrix}.$$

2.3.2.5   Other Factorizations

The **QL** and **RQ** factorizations are given by

$$A = Q \begin{pmatrix} 0 \\ L \end{pmatrix}, \quad \text{if } m \geq n,$$

and

$$A = \begin{pmatrix} 0 & R \end{pmatrix} Q, \quad \text{if } m \leq n.$$

These factorizations are computed by xGEQLF and xGERQF, respectively; they are less commonly used than either the QR or LQ factorizations described above, but have applications in, for example, the computation of generalized QR factorizations [2].

All the factorization routines discussed here (except xTZRQF) allow arbitrary m and n, so that in some cases the matrices R or L are trapezoidal rather than triangular. A routine that performs pivoting is provided only for the QR factorization.

Table 2.8: Computational routines for orthogonal factorizations

Type of factorization and matrix	Operation	Single precision		Double precision	
		real	complex	real	complex
QR, general	factorize with pivoting	SGEQPF	CGEQPF	DGEQPF	ZGEQPF
	factorize, no pivoting	SGEQRF	CGEQRF	DGEQRF	ZGEQRF
	generate Q	SORGQR	CUNGQR	DORGQR	ZUNGQR
	multiply matrix by Q	SORMQR	CUNMQR	DORMQR	ZUNMQR
LQ, general	factorize, no pivoting	SGELQF	CGELQF	DGELQF	ZGELQF
	generate Q	SORGLQ	CUNGLQ	DORGLQ	ZUNGLQ
	multiply matrix by Q	SORMLQ	CUNMLQ	DORMLQ	ZUNMLQ
QL, general	factorize, no pivoting	SGEQLF	CGEQLF	DGEQLF	ZGEQLF
	generate Q	SORGQL	CUNGQL	DORGQL	ZUNGQL
	multiply matrix by Q	SORMQL	CUNMQL	DORMQL	ZUNMQL
RQ, general	factorize, no pivoting	SGERQF	CGERQF	DGERQF	ZGERQF
	generate Q	SORGRQ	CUNGRQ	DORGRQ	ZUNGRQ
	multiply matrix by Q	SORMRQ	CUNMRQ	DORMRQ	ZUNMRQ
RQ, trapezoidal	factorize, no pivoting	STZRQF	CTZRQF	DTZRQF	ZTZRQF

2.3.3 Symmetric Eigenproblems

Let A be a real symmetric or complex Hermitian n-by-n matrix. A scalar λ is called an **eigenvalue** and a nonzero column vector z the corresponding **eigenvector** if $Az = \lambda z$. λ is always real when A is real symmetric or complex Hermitian.

The basic task of the symmetric eigenproblem routines is to compute values of λ and, optionally, corresponding vectors z for a given matrix A.

This computation proceeds in the following stages:

1. The real symmetric or complex Hermitian matrix A is reduced to **real tridiagonal form** T. If A is real symmetric this decomposition is $A = QTQ^T$ with Q orthogonal and T symmetric tridiagonal. If A is complex Hermitian, the decomposition is $A = QTQ^H$ with Q unitary and T, as before, *real* symmetric tridiagonal.

2. Eigenvalues and eigenvectors of the real symmetric tridiagonal matrix T are computed. If all eigenvalues and eigenvectors are computed, this is equivalent to factorizing T as $T = S\Lambda S^T$, where S is orthogonal and Λ is diagonal. The diagonal entries of Λ are the eigenvalues of T, which are also the eigenvalues of A, and the columns of S are the eigenvectors of T; the eigenvectors of A are the columns of $Z = QS$, so that $A = Z\Lambda Z^T$ ($Z\Lambda Z^H$ when A is complex Hermitian).

In the real case, the decomposition $A = QTQ^T$ is computed by one of the routines xSYTRD, xSPTRD, or xSBTRD, depending on how the matrix is stored (see Table 2.9). The complex analogues of these routines are called xHETRD, xHPTRD, and xHBTRD.

The routine xSYTRD (or xHETRD) represents the matrix Q as a product of elementary reflectors, as described in section 5.4. The routine xORGTR (or in the complex case xUNMTR) is provided to form Q explicitly; this is needed in particular before calling xSTEQR to compute all the eigenvectors of A by the QR algorithm. The routine xORMTR (or in the complex case xUNMTR) is provided to multiply another matrix by Q without forming Q explicitly; this can be used to transform eigenvectors of T computed by xSTEIN, back to eigenvectors of A.

When packed storage is used, the corresponding routines for forming Q or multiplying another matrix by Q are xOPGTR and xOPMTR (in the complex case, xUPGTR and xUPMTR).

When A is banded and xSBTRD (or xHBTRD) is used to reduce it to tridiagonal form, Q is determined as a product of Givens rotations, not as a product of elementary reflectors; if Q is required, it must be formed explicitly by the reduction routine. xSBTRD is based on the vectorizable algorithm due to Kaufman [37].

There are several routines for computing eigenvalues and eigenvectors of T, to cover the cases of computing some or all of the eigenvalues, and some or all of the eigenvectors. In addition, some routines run faster in some computing environments or for some matrices than for others. Also, some routines are more accurate than other routines.

xSTEQR This routine uses the implicitly shifted QR algorithm. It switches between the QR and

QL variants in order to handle graded matrices more effectively than the simple QL variant that is provided by the EISPACK routines IMTQL1 and IMTQL2. See [30] for details.

xSTERF This routine uses a square-root free version of the QR algorithm, also switching between QR and QL variants, and can only compute all the eigenvalues. See [30] for details.

xPTEQR This routine applies to symmetric *positive definite* tridiagonal matrices only. It uses a combination of Cholesky factorization and bidiagonal QR iteration (see xBDSQR) and may be significantly more accurate than the other routines. See [9, 13, 10] for details.

xSTEBZ This routine uses bisection to compute some or all of the eigenvalues. Options provide for computing all the eigenvalues in a real interval or all the eigenvalues from the ith to the jth largest. It can be highly accurate, but may be adjusted to run faster if lower accuracy is acceptable.

xSTEIN Given accurate eigenvalues, this routine uses inverse iteration to compute some or all of the eigenvectors.

See Table 2.9.

Table 2.9: Computational routines for the symmetric eigenproblem

Type of matrix and storage scheme	Operation	Single precision		Double precision	
		real	complex	real	complex
dense symmetric (or Hermitian)	tridiagonal reduction	SSYTRD	CHETRD	DSYTRD	ZHETRD
packed symmetric (or Hermitian)	tridiagonal reduction	SSPTRD	CHPTRD	DSPTRD	ZHPTRD
band symmetric (or Hermitian)	tridiagonal reduction	SSBTRD	CHBTRD	DSBTRD	ZHBTRD
orthogonal/unitary	generate matrix after reduction by xSYTRD	SORGTR	CUNGTR	DORGTR	ZUNGTR
	multiply matrix after reduction by xSYTRD	SORMTR	CUNMTR	DORMTR	ZUNMTR
orthogonal/unitary (packed storage)	generate matrix after reduction by xSPTRD	SOPGTR	CUPGTR	DOPGTR	ZUPGTR
	multiply matrix after reduction by xSPTRD	SOPMTR	CUPMTR	DOPMTR	ZUPMTR
symmetric tridiagonal	eigenvalues/ eigenvectors	SSTEQR	CSTEQR	DSTEQR	ZSTEQR
	eigenvalues only via root-free QR	SSTERF		DSTERF	
	eigenvalues only via bisection	SSTEBZ		DSTEBZ	
	eigenvectors by inverse iteration	SSTEIN	CSTEIN	DSTEIN	ZSTEIN
symmetric tridiagonal positive definite	eigenvalues/ eigenvectors	SPTEQR	CPTEQR	DPTEQR	ZPTEQR

2.3.4   Nonsymmetric Eigenproblems

2.3.4.1   Eigenvalues, Eigenvectors and Schur Factorization

Let A be a square n-by-n matrix. A scalar λ is called an **eigenvalue** and a non-zero column vector v the corresponding **right eigenvector** if $Av = \lambda v$. A nonzero column vector u satisfying $u^H A = \lambda u^H$ ($u^T A = \lambda u^T$ if A and λ are real) is called the **left eigenvector**. The first basic task of the routines described in this section is to compute, for a given matrix A, all n values of λ and, if desired, their associated right eigenvectors v and/or left eigenvectors u.

A second basic task is to compute the **Schur factorization** of a matrix A. If A is complex, then its Schur factorization is $A = ZTZ^H$, where Z is unitary and T is upper triangular. If A is real, its Schur factorization is $A = ZTZ^T$, where Z is orthogonal. and T is upper quasi-triangular (1-by-1 and 2-by-2 blocks on its diagonal). The columns of Z are called the **Schur vectors** of A. The eigenvalues of A appear on the diagonal of T; complex conjugate eigenvalues of a real A correspond to 2-by-2 blocks on the diagonal of T.

These two basic tasks can be performed in the following stages:

1. A general matrix A is reduced to **upper Hessenberg form** H which is zero below the first subdiagonal. The reduction may be written $A = QHQ^T$ with Q orthogonal if A is real, or $A = QHQ^H$ with Q unitary if A is complex. The reduction is performed by subroutine xGEHRD, which represents Q in a factored form, as described in section 5.4. The routine xORGHR (or in the complex case xUNGHR) is provided to form Q explicitly. The routine xORMHR (or in the complex case xUNMHR) is provided to multiply another matrix by Q without forming Q explicitly.

2. The upper Hessenberg matrix H is reduced to Schur form T, giving the Schur factorization $H = STS^T$ (for H real) or $H = STS^H$ (for H complex). The matrix S (the Schur vectors of H) may optionally be computed as well. Alternatively S may be postmultiplied into the matrix Q determined in stage 1, to give the matrix $Z = QS$, the Schur vectors of A. The eigenvalues are obtained from the diagonal of T. All this is done by subroutine xHSEQR.

3. Given the eigenvalues, the eigenvectors may be computed in two different ways. xHSEIN performs inverse iteration on H to compute the eigenvectors of H; xORMHR can then be used to multiply the eigenvectors by the matrix Q in order to transform them to eigenvectors of A. xTREVC computes the eigenvectors of T, and optionally transforms them to those of H or A if the matrix S or Z is supplied. Both xHSEIN and xTREVC allow selected left and/or right eigenvectors to be computed.

Other subsidiary tasks may be performed before or after those just described.

2.3.4.2   Balancing

The routine xGEBAL may be used to **balance** the matrix A prior to reduction to Hessenberg form. Balancing involves two steps, either of which is optional:

- first, xGEBAL attempts to permute A by a similarity transformation to block upper triangular form:

$$PAP^T = A' = \begin{pmatrix} A'_{11} & A'_{12} & A'_{13} \\ 0 & A'_{22} & A'_{23} \\ 0 & 0 & A'_{33} \end{pmatrix}$$

  where P is a permutation matrix and A'_{11} and A'_{33} are *upper triangular*. Thus the matrix is already in Schur form outside the central diagonal block A'_{22} in rows and columns ILO to IHI. Subsequent operations by xGEBAL, xGEHRD or xHSEQR need only be applied to these rows and columns; therefore ILO and IHI are passed as arguments to xGEHRD and xHSEQR. This can save a significant amount of work if ILO > 1 or IHI < n. If no suitable permutation can be found (as is very often the case), xGEBAL sets ILO = 1 and IHI = n, and A'_{22} is the whole of A.

- secondly, xGEBAL applies a diagonal similarity transformation to A' to make the rows and columns of A'_{22} as close in norm in possible:

$$A'' = DA'D^{-1} = \begin{pmatrix} I & 0 & 0 \\ 0 & D_{22} & 0 \\ 0 & 0 & I \end{pmatrix} \begin{pmatrix} A'_{11} & A'_{12} & A'_{13} \\ 0 & A'_{22} & A'_{23} \\ 0 & 0 & A'_{33} \end{pmatrix} \begin{pmatrix} I & 0 & 0 \\ 0 & D_{22}^{-1} & 0 \\ 0 & 0 & I \end{pmatrix}$$

  This can improve the accuracy of later processing in some cases; see subsection 4.10.2.

If A was balanced by xGEBAL, then eigenvectors computed by subsequent operations are eigenvectors of the balanced matrix A''; xGEBAK must then be called to transform them back to eigenvectors of the original matrix A.

2.3.4.3 Invariant Subspaces and Condition Numbers

The Schur form depends on the order of the eigenvalues on the diagonal of T and this may optionally be chosen by the user. Suppose the user chooses that $\lambda_1, \ldots, \lambda_j, 0 < j < n$, appear in the upper left corner of T. Then the first j columns of Z span the **right invariant subspace** of A corresponding to $\lambda_1, \ldots, \lambda_j$.

The following routines perform this re-ordering and also compute condition numbers for eigenvalues, eigenvectors, and invariant subspaces:

1. xTREXC will move an eigenvalue (or 2-by-2 block) on the diagonal of the Schur form from its original position to any other position. It may be used to choose the order in which eigenvalues appear in the Schur form.

2. xTRSYL solves the Sylvester matrix equation $AX \pm XB = C$ for X, given matrices A, B and C, with A and B (quasi) triangular. It is used in the routines xTRSNA and xTRSEN, but it is also of independent interest.

3. xTRSNA computes the condition numbers of the eigenvalues and/or right eigenvectors of a matrix T in Schur form. These are the same as the condition numbers of the eigenvalues and

right eigenvectors of the original matrix A from which T is derived. The user may compute these condition numbers for all eigenvalue/eigenvector pairs, or for any selected subset. For more details, see section 4.10 and [8].

4. xTRSEN moves a selected subset of the eigenvalues of a matrix T in Schur form to the upper left corner of T, and optionally computes the condition numbers of their average value and of their right invariant subspace. These are the same as the condition numbers of the average eigenvalue and right invariant subspace of the original matrix A from which T is derived. For more details, see section 4.10 and [8]

See Table 2.10 for a complete list of the routines.

Table 2.10: Computational routines for the nonsymmetric eigenproblem

Type of matrix	Operation	Single precision		Double precision	
and storage scheme		real	complex	real	complex
general	Hessenberg reduction	SGEHRD	CGEHRD	DGEHRD	ZGEHRD
	balancing	SGEBAL	CGEBAL	DGEBAL	ZGEBAL
	backtransforming	SGEBAK	CGEBAK	DGEBAK	ZGEBAK
orthogonal/unitary	generate matrix after Hessenberg reduction	SORGHR	CUNGHR	DORGHR	ZUNGHR
	multiply matrix after Hessenberg reduction	SORMHR	CUNMHR	DORMHR	ZUNMHR
Hessenberg	Schur factorization	SHSEQR	CHSEQR	DHSEQR	ZHSEQR
	eigenvectors by inverse iteration	SHSEIN	CHSEIN	DHSEIN	ZHSEIN
(quasi)triangular	eigenvectors	STREVC	CTREVC	DTREVC	ZTREVC
	reordering Schur factorization	STREXC	CTREXC	DTREXC	ZTREXC
	Sylvester equation	STRSYL	CTRSYL	DTRSYL	ZTRSYL
	condition numbers of eigenvalues/vectors	STRSNA	CTRSNA	DTRSNA	ZTRSNA
	condition numbers of eigenvalue cluster/ invariant subspace	STRSEN	CTRSEN	DTRSEN	ZTRSEN

2.3.5 Singular Value Decomposition

Let A be a general real m-by-n matrix. The **singular value decomposition (SVD)** of A is the factorization $A = U\Sigma V^T$, where U and V are orthogonal, and $\Sigma = \text{diag}(\sigma_1, \ldots \sigma_r)$, $r = \min(m,n)$, with $\sigma_1 \geq \cdots \geq \sigma_r \geq 0$. If A is complex, then its SVD is $A = U\Sigma V^H$ where U and V are unitary, and Σ is as before with real diagonal elements. The σ_i are called the **singular values**, the first r columns of V the **right singular vectors** and the first r columns of U the **left singular vectors**.

The routines described in this section, and listed in Table 2.11, are used to compute this decomposition. The computation proceeds in the following stages:

1. The matrix A is reduced to bidiagonal form: $A = U_1 B V_1^T$ if A is real ($A = U_1 B V_1^H$ if A is complex), where U_1 and V_1 are orthogonal (unitary if A is complex), and B is real and upper-bidiagonal when $m \geq n$ and lower bidiagonal when $m < n$, so that B is nonzero only on the main diagonal and either on the first superdiagonal (if $m \geq n$) or the first subdiagonal (if $m < n$).

2. The SVD of the bidiagonal matrix B is computed: $B = U_2 \Sigma V_2^T$, where U_2 and V_2 are orthogonal and Σ is diagonal as described above. The singular vectors of A are then $U = U_1 U_2$ and $V = V_1 V_2$.

The reduction to bidiagonal form is performed by the subroutine xGEBRD, which represents U_1 and V_1 in factored form. If A is real, the matrices U_1 and V_1 may be computed explicitly using routine xORGBR, or multiplied by other matrices without forming U_1 and V_1 using routine xORMBR. If A is complex, one instead uses xUNGBR and xUNMBR, respectively. The SVD of the bidiagonal matrix is computed by the subroutine xBDSQR.

xBDSQR is more accurate than its counterparts in LINPACK and EISPACK: barring underflow and overflow, it computes all the singular values of B to nearly full relative precision, independent of their magnitudes. It also computes the singular vectors much more accurately. See section 4.8 and [13, 10] for details.

If $m \gg n$, it may be more efficient to first perform a QR factorization of A, using the routine xGEQRF, and then to compute the SVD of the n-by-n matrix R, since if $A = QR$ and $R = U\Sigma V^T$, then the SVD of A is given by $A = (QU)\Sigma V^T$.

Similarly, if $m \ll n$, it may be more efficient to first perform an LQ factorization of A, using xGELQF.

The SVD may be used to find a minimum norm solution to a (possibly) rank-deficient linear least squares problem (2.1). The effective rank, k, of A can be determined as the number of singular values which exceed a suitable threshold. Let $\hat{\Sigma}$ be the leading k-by-k submatrix of Σ, and $\hat{V}$ be the matrix consisting of the first k columns of V. Then the solution is given by:

$$x = \hat{V}\hat{\Sigma}^{-1}\hat{c}_1$$

where $\hat{c}_1$ consists of the first k elements of $c = U^T b = U_2^T U_1^T b$. $U_1^T b$ can be computed using xORMBR, and xBDSQR has an option to multiply a vector by U_2^T.

2.3.6 Generalized Symmetric Definite Eigenproblems

This section is concerned with the solution of the generalized eigenvalue problems $Az = \lambda Bz$, $ABz = \lambda z$, and $BAz = \lambda z$, where A and B are real symmetric or complex Hermitian and B

Table 2.11: Computational routines for the singular value decomposition

Type of matrix and storage scheme	Operation	Single precision		Double precision	
		real	complex	real	complex
general	bidiagonal reduction	SGEBRD	CGEBRD	DGEBRD	ZGEBRD
orthogonal/unitary	generate matrix after bidiagonal reduction	SORGBR	CUNGBR	DORGBR	ZUNGBR
	multiply matrix after bidiagonal reduction	SORMBR	CUNMBR	DORMBR	ZUNMBR
bidiagonal	singular values/ singular vectors	SBDSQR	CBDSQR	DBDSQR	ZBDSQR

is positive definite. Each of these problems can be reduced to a standard symmetric eigenvalue problem, using a Cholesky factorization of B as either $B = LL^T$ or $B = U^T U$ (LL^H or $U^H U$ in the Hermitian case).

With $B = LL^T$, we have

$$Az = \lambda Bz \quad \Rightarrow \quad (L^{-1}AL^{-T})(L^T z) = \lambda(L^T z).$$

Hence the eigenvalues of $Az = \lambda Bz$ are those of $Cy = \lambda y$, where C is the symmetric matrix $C = L^{-1}AL^{-T}$ and $y = L^T z$. In the complex case C is Hermitian with $C = L^{-1}AL^{-H}$ and $y = L^H z$.

Table 2.12 summarizes how each of the three types of problem may be reduced to standard form $Cy = \lambda y$, and how the eigenvectors z of the original problem may be recovered from the eigenvectors y of the reduced problem. The table applies to real problems; for complex problems, transposed matrices must be replaced by conjugate-transposes.

Table 2.12: Reduction of generalized symmetric definite eigenproblems to standard problems

	Type of problem	Factorization of B	Reduction	Recovery of eigenvectors
1.	$Az = \lambda Bz$	$B = LL^T$	$C = L^{-1}AL^{-T}$	$z = L^{-T}y$
		$B = U^T U$	$C = U^{-T}AU^{-1}$	$z = U^{-1}y$
2.	$ABz = \lambda z$	$B = LL^T$	$C = L^T AL$	$z = L^{-T}y$
		$B = U^T U$	$C = UAU^T$	$z = U^{-1}y$
3.	$BAz = \lambda z$	$B = LL^T$	$C = L^T AL$	$z = Ly$
		$B = U^T U$	$C = UAU^T$	$z = U^T y$

Given A and a Cholesky factorization of B, the routines xyyGST overwrite A with the matrix C of the corresponding standard problem $Cy = \lambda y$ (see Table 2.13). This may then be solved using the routines described in subsection 2.3.3. No special routines are needed to recover the eigenvectors z of the generalized problem from the eigenvectors y of the standard problem, because these computations are simple applications of Level 2 or Level 3 BLAS.

Table 2.13: Computational routines for the generalized symmetric definite eigenproblem

Type of matrix and storage scheme	Operation	Single precision		Double precision	
		real	complex	real	complex
symmetric/Hermitian	reduction	SSYGST	CHEGST	DSYGST	ZHEGST
symmetric/Hermitian (packed storage)	reduction	SSPGST	CHPGST	DSPGST	ZHPGST

Chapter 3

Performance of LAPACK

Note: this chapter presents some performance figures for LAPACK routines. The figures are provided for illustration only, and should not be regarded as a definitive up-to-date statement of performance. They have been selected from performance figures obtained in 1990–91 during the development of LAPACK. Performance is affected by many factors that may change from time to time, such as details of hardware (cycle time, cache size), compiler, and BLAS. To obtain up-to-date performance figures, use the timing programs provided with LAPACK.

3.1 Factors that Affect Performance

Can we provide **portable** software for computations in dense linear algebra that is **efficient** on a wide range of modern high-performance computers? If so, how? Answering these questions — and providing the desired software — has been the goal of the LAPACK project.

LINPACK [15] and EISPACK [42, 28] have for many years provided high-quality portable software for linear algebra; but on modern high-performance computers they often achieve only a small fraction of the peak performance of the machines. Therefore, LAPACK has been designed to supersede LINPACK and EISPACK, principally by achieving much greater efficiency — but at the same time also adding extra functionality, using some new or improved algorithms, and integrating the two sets of algorithms into a single package.

LAPACK was originally targeted to achieve good performance on single-processor vector machines and on shared memory multiprocessor machines with a modest number of powerful processors. Since the start of the project, another class of machines has emerged for which LAPACK software is equally well-suited—the high-performance "super-scalar" workstations. (LAPACK is intended to be used across the whole spectrum of modern computers, but when considering performance, the emphasis is on machines at the more powerful end of the spectrum.)

Here we discuss the main factors that affect the performance of linear algebra software on these classes of machines.

34

3.1.1   Vectorization

Designing vectorizable algorithms in linear algebra is usually straightforward. Indeed, for many computations there are several variants, all vectorizable, but with different characteristics in performance (see, for example, [22]). Linear algebra algorithms can come close to the peak performance of many machines — principally because peak performance depends on some form of chaining of vector addition and multiplication operations, and this is just what the algorithms require.

However, when the algorithms are realized in straightforward Fortran 77 code, the performance may fall well short of the expected level, usually because vectorizing Fortran compilers fail to minimize the number of memory references — that is, the number of vector load and store operations. This brings us to the next factor.

3.1.2   Data Movement

What often limits the actual performance of a vector—or scalar— floating-point unit is the rate of transfer of data between different levels of memory in the machine. Examples include: the transfer of vector operands in and out of vector registers, the transfer of scalar operands in and out of a high-speed scalar processor, the movement of data between main memory and a high-speed cache or local memory, and paging between actual memory and disk storage in a virtual memory system.

It is desirable to maximize the ratio of floating-point operations to memory references, and to re-use data as much as possible while it is stored in the higher levels of the memory hierarchy (for example, vector registers or high-speed cache).

A Fortran programmer has no explicit control over these types of data movement, although one can often influence them by imposing a suitable structure on an algorithm.

3.1.3   Parallelism

The nested loop structure of most linear algebra algorithms offers considerable scope for loop-based parallelism on shared memory machines. This is the principal type of parallelism that LAPACK at present aims to exploit. It can sometimes be generated automatically by a compiler, but often requires the insertion of compiler directives.

3.2   The BLAS as the Key to Portability

How then can we hope to be able to achieve sufficient control over vectorization, data movement, and parallelism in portable Fortran code, to obtain the levels of performance that machines can offer?

The LAPACK strategy for combining efficiency with portability is to construct the software as much as possible out of calls to the BLAS (Basic Linear Algebra Subprograms); the BLAS are used as building blocks.

Table 3.1: Speed in megaflops of Level 2 and Level 3 BLAS operations on a CRAY Y-MP

(all matrices are of order 500; U is upper triangular)

Number of processors:	1	2	4	8
Level 2: $y \leftarrow \alpha A x + \beta y$	311	611	1197	2285
Level 3: $C \leftarrow \alpha AB + \beta C$	312	623	1247	2425
Level 2: $x \leftarrow Ux$	293	544	898	1613
Level 3: $B \leftarrow UB$	310	620	1240	2425
Level 2: $x \leftarrow U^{-1}x$	272	374	479	584
Level 3: $B \leftarrow U^{-1}B$	309	618	1235	2398

The efficiency of LAPACK software depends on efficient implementations of the BLAS being provided by computer vendors (or others) for their machines. Thus the BLAS form a low-level interface between LAPACK software and different machine architectures. Above this level, almost all of the LAPACK software is truly portable.

There are now three levels of BLAS:

Level 1 BLAS [38]: for vector operations, such as $y \leftarrow \alpha x + y$

Level 2 BLAS [19]: for matrix-vector operations, such as $y \leftarrow \alpha A x + \beta y$

Level 3 BLAS [17]: for matrix-matrix operations, such as $C \leftarrow \alpha AB + \beta C$

Here, A, B and C are matrices, x and y are vectors, and α and β are scalars.

The Level 1 BLAS are used in LAPACK, but for convenience rather than for performance: they perform an insignificant fraction of the computation, and they cannot achieve high efficiency on most modern supercomputers.

The Level 2 BLAS can achieve near-peak performance on many vector processors, such as a single processor of a CRAY X-MP or Y-MP, or Convex C-2 machine. However on other vector processors, such as a CRAY-2 or an IBM 3090 VF, their performance is limited by the rate of data movement between different levels of memory.

This limitation is overcome by the Level 3 BLAS, which perform $O(n^3)$ floating-point operations on $O(n^2)$ data, whereas the Level 2 BLAS perform only $O(n^2)$ operations on $O(n^2)$ data.

The BLAS also allow us to exploit parallelism in a way that is transparent to the software that calls them. Even the Level 2 BLAS offer some scope for exploiting parallelism, but greater scope is provided by the Level 3 BLAS, as Table 3.1 illustrates.

3.3 Block Algorithms and their Derivation

It is comparatively straightforward to recode many of the algorithms in LINPACK and EISPACK so that they call Level 2 BLAS. Indeed, in the simplest cases the same floating-point operations are performed, possibly even in the same order: it is just a matter of reorganizing the software. To illustrate this point we derive the Cholesky factorization algorithm that is used in the LINPACK routine SPOFA, which factorizes a symmetric positive definite matrix as $A = U^T U$. Writing these equations as:

$$
\begin{pmatrix} A_{11} & a_j & A_{13} \\ \cdot & a_{jj} & \alpha_j^T \\ \cdot & \cdot & A_{33} \end{pmatrix} = \begin{pmatrix} U_{11}^T & 0 & 0 \\ u_j^T & u_{jj} & 0 \\ U_{13}^T & \mu_j & U_{33}^T \end{pmatrix} \begin{pmatrix} U_{11} & u_j & U_{13} \\ 0 & u_{jj} & \mu_j^T \\ 0 & 0 & U_{33} \end{pmatrix}
$$

and equating coefficients of the jth column, we obtain:

$$
\begin{aligned}
a_j &= U_{11}^T u_j \\
a_{jj} &= u_j^T u_j + u_{jj}^2.
\end{aligned}
$$

Hence, if U_{11} has already been computed, we can compute u_j and u_{jj} from the equations:

$$
\begin{aligned}
U_{11}^T u_j &= a_j \\
u_{jj}^2 &= a_{jj} - u_j^T u_j.
\end{aligned}
$$

Here is the body of the code of the LINPACK routine SPOFA, which implements the above method:

```
      DO 30 J = 1, N
         INFO = J
         S = 0.0E0
         JM1 = J - 1
         IF (JM1 .LT. 1) GO TO 20
         DO 10 K = 1, JM1
            T = A(K,J) - SDOT(K-1,A(1,K),1,A(1,J),1)
            T = T/A(K,K)
            A(K,J) = T
            S = S + T*T
   10    CONTINUE
   20    CONTINUE
         S = A(J,J) - S
C     ......EXIT
         IF (S .LE. 0.0E0) GO TO 40
         A(J,J) = SQRT(S)
   30 CONTINUE
```

And here is the same computation recoded in "LAPACK-style" to use the Level 2 BLAS routine STRSV (which solves a triangular system of equations). The call to STRSV has replaced the loop over K which made several calls to the Level 1 BLAS routine SDOT. (For reasons given below, this is not the actual code used in LAPACK — hence the term "LAPACK-style".)

```
      DO 10 J = 1, N
         CALL STRSV( 'Upper', 'Transpose', 'Non-unit', J-1, A, LDA,
     $               A(1,J), 1 )
         S = A(J,J) - SDOT( J-1, A(1,J), 1, A(1,J), 1 )
         IF( S.LE.ZERO ) GO TO 20
         A(J,J) = SQRT( S )
   10 CONTINUE
```

This change by itself is sufficient to make big gains in performance on a number of machines — for example, from 72 to 251 megaflops for a matrix of order 500 on one processor of a CRAY Y-MP. Since this is 81% of the peak speed of matrix-matrix multiplication on this processor, we cannot hope to do very much better by using Level 3 BLAS.

For example, on an IBM 3090E VF (using double precision) there is virtually no difference in performance between the LINPACK-style and the LAPACK-style code. Both run at about 23 megaflops. This is unsatisfactory on a machine on which matrix-matrix multiplication can run at 75 megaflops. To exploit the faster speed of Level 3 BLAS, the algorithms must undergo a deeper level of restructuring, and be re-cast as a **block algorithm** — that is, an algorithm that operates on **blocks** or submatrices of the original matrix.

To derive a block form of Cholesky factorization, we write the defining equation in partitioned form thus:

$$\begin{pmatrix} A_{11} & A_{12} & A_{13} \\ \cdot & A_{22} & A_{23} \\ \cdot & \cdot & A_{33} \end{pmatrix} = \begin{pmatrix} U_{11}^T & 0 & 0 \\ U_{12}^T & U_{22}^T & 0 \\ U_{13}^T & U_{23}^T & U_{33}^T \end{pmatrix} \begin{pmatrix} U_{11} & U_{12} & U_{13} \\ 0 & U_{22} & U_{23} \\ 0 & 0 & U_{33} \end{pmatrix}.$$

Equating submatrices in the second block of columns, we obtain:

$$\begin{aligned} A_{12} &= U_{11}^T U_{12} \\ A_{22} &= U_{12}^T U_{12} + U_{22}^T U_{22}. \end{aligned}$$

Hence, if U_{11} has already been computed, we can compute U_{12} as the solution to the equation

$$U_{11}^T U_{12} = A_{12}$$

by a call to the Level 3 BLAS routine STRSM; and then we can compute U_{22} from

$$U_{22}^T U_{22} = A_{22} - U_{12}^T U_{12}.$$

This involves first updating the symmetric submatrix A_{22} by a call to the Level 3 BLAS routine SSYRK, and then computing its Cholesky factorization. Since Fortran does not allow recursion, a separate routine must be called (using Level 2 BLAS rather than Level 3), named SPOTF2 in the code below. In this way successive blocks of columns of U are computed. Here is LAPACK-style code for the block algorithm. In this code-fragment NB denotes the width of the blocks.

Table 3.2: Speed in megaflops of Cholesky factorization $A = U^T U$ for $n = 500$

Machine:	IBM 3090 VF	CRAY Y-MP	CRAY Y-MP
Number of processors:	1	1	8
j-variant: LINPACK	23	72	72
j-variant: using Level 2 BLAS	24	251	378
j-variant: using Level 3 BLAS	49	287	1225
i-variant: using Level 3 BLAS	50	290	1414

```
   DO 10 J = 1, N, NB
      JB = MIN( NB, N-J+1 )
      CALL STRSM( 'Left', 'Upper', 'Transpose', 'Non-unit', J-1, JB,
   $              ONE, A, LDA, A(1,J), LDA )
      CALL SSYRK( 'Upper', 'Transpose', JB, J-1, -ONE, A(1,J), LDA,
   $              ONE, A(J,J), LDA )
      CALL SPOTF2( 'Upper', JB, A(J,J), LDA, INFO )
      IF( INFO.NE.0 ) GO TO 20
10 CONTINUE
```

This code runs at 49 megaflops on a 3090, more than double the speed of the LINPACK code. On a CRAY Y-MP, the use of Level 3 BLAS squeezes a little more performance out of one processor, but makes a large improvement when using all 8 processors.

But that is not the end of the story, and the code given above is not the code that is actually used in the LAPACK routine SPOTRF. We mentioned in subsection 3.1.1 that for many linear algebra computations there are several vectorizable variants, often referred to as i-, j- and k-variants, according to a convention introduced in [22] and used in [29]. The same is true of the corresponding block algorithms.

It turns out that the j-variant that was chosen for LINPACK, and used in the above examples, is not the fastest on many machines, because it is based on solving triangular systems of equations, which can be significantly slower than matrix-matrix multiplication. The variant actually used in LAPACK is the i-variant, which does rely on matrix-matrix multiplication.

Table 3.2 summarizes the results.

3.4   Examples of Block Algorithms in LAPACK

Having discussed in detail the derivation of one particular block algorithm, we now describe examples of the performance that has been achieved with a variety of block algorithms.

See Gallivan *et al.* [27] and Dongarra *et al.* [20] for an alternative survey of algorithms for dense linear algebra on high-performance computers.

Table 3.3: Speed in megaflops of SGETRF/DGETRF for square matrices of order n

	No. of processors	Block size	Values of n				
			100	200	300	400	500
IBM RISC/6000-530	1	32	19	25	29	31	33
Alliant FX/8	8	16	9	26	32	46	57
IBM 3090J VF	1	64	23	41	52	58	63
Convex C-240	4	64	31	60	82	100	112
CRAY Y-MP	1	1	132	219	254	272	283
CRAY-2	1	64	110	211	292	318	358
Siemens/Fujitsu VP 400-EX	1	64	46	132	222	309	397
NEC SX2	1	1	118	274	412	504	577
CRAY Y-MP	8	64	195	556	920	1188	1408

Table 3.4: Speed in megaflops of SPOTRF/DPOTRF for matrices of order n with UPLO = 'U'

	No. of processors	Block size	Values of n				
			100	200	300	400	500
IBM RISC/6000-530	1	32	21	29	34	36	38
Alliant FX/8	8	16	10	27	40	49	52
IBM 3090J VF	1	48	26	43	56	62	67
Convex C-240	4	64	32	63	82	96	103
CRAY Y-MP	1	1	126	219	257	275	285
CRAY-2	1	64	109	213	294	318	362
Siemens/Fujitsu VP 400-EX	1	1	53	145	237	312	369
NEC SX2	1	1	155	387	589	719	819
CRAY Y-MP	8	32	146	479	845	1164	1393

3.4.1 Factorizations for Solving Linear Equations

The well-known LU and Cholesky factorizations are the simplest block algorithms to derive. No extra floating-point operations nor extra working storage are required.

Table 3.3 illustrates the speed of the LAPACK routine for LU factorization of a real matrix, SGETRF in single precision on CRAY machines, and DGETRF in double precision on all other machines. Double precision corresponds to 64-bit floating-point arithmetic on all machines tested. A block size of 1 means that the unblocked algorithm is used, since it is faster than — or at least as fast as — a blocked algorithm.

Table 3.4 gives similar results for Cholesky factorization, extending the results given in Table 3.2.

LAPACK, like LINPACK, provides a factorization for symmetric indefinite matrices, so that A is factorized as $PUDU^T P^T$, where P is a permutation matrix, and D is block diagonal with blocks of

Table 3.5: Speed in megaflops of SSYTRF for matrices of order n with UPLO = 'U' on a CRAY-2

Block	Values of n				
size	100	200	300	400	500
1	75	128	154	164	176
64	78	160	213	249	281

order 1 or 2. A block form of this algorithm has been derived, and is implemented in the LAPACK routine SSYTRF/DSYTRF. It has to duplicate a little of the computation in order to "look ahead" to determine the necessary row and column interchanges, but the extra work can be more than compensated for by the greater speed of updating the matrix by blocks, as is illustrated in Table 3.5.

LAPACK, like LINPACK, provides *LU* and Cholesky factorizations of band matrices. The LIN-PACK algorithms can easily be restructured to use Level 2 BLAS, though that has little effect on performance for matrices of very narrow bandwidth. It is also possible to use Level 3 BLAS, at the price of doing some extra work with zero elements outside the band [26]. This becomes worthwhile for matrices of large order and semi-bandwidth greater than 100 or so.

3.4.2 QR Factorization

The traditional algorithm for QR factorization is based on the use of elementary Householder-Householder transformation - blocked form matrices of the general form

$$H = I - \tau v v^T$$

where v is a column vector and τ is a scalar. This leads to an algorithm with very good vector performance, especially if coded to use Level 2 BLAS.

The key to developing a block form of this algorithm is to represent a product of b elementary Householder matrices of order n as a block form of a Householder matrix. This can be done in various ways. LAPACK uses the following form [41]:

$$H_1 H_2 \ldots H_b = I - V T V^T$$

where V is an n-by-b matrix whose columns are the individual vectors $v_1, v_2, \ldots, v_b$ associated with the Householder matrices $H_1, H_2, \ldots, H_b$, and T is an upper triangular matrix of order b. Extra work is required to compute the elements of T, but once again this is compensated for by the greater speed of applying the block form. Table 3.6 summarizes results obtained with the LAPACK routine SGEQRF/DGEQRF.

3.4.3 Eigenvalue Problems

Eigenvalue problems have so far provided a less fertile ground for the development of block algorithms than the factorizations so far described. Nevertheless, useful improvements in performance have been obtained.

Table 3.6: Speed in megaflops of SGEQRF/DGEQRF for square matrices of order n

	No. of processors	Block size	Values of n				
			100	200	300	400	500
IBM RISC/6000-530	1	32	18	26	30	32	34
Alliant FX/8	8	16	11	28	39	47	50
IBM 3090J VF	1	32	28	54	68	75	80
Convex C-240	4	16	35	65	82	97	106
CRAY Y-MP	1	1	177	253	276	286	292
CRAY-2	1	32	105	208	269	303	326
Siemens/Fujitsu VP 400-EX	1	1	101	237	329	388	426
NEC SX2	1	1	217	498	617	690	768

The first step in solving many types of eigenvalue problems is to reduce the original matrix to a "condensed form" by orthogonal transformations.

In the reduction to condensed forms, the unblocked algorithms all use elementary Householder matrices and have good vector performance. Block forms of these algorithms have been developed [23], but all require additional operations, and a significant proportion of the work must still be performed by Level 2 BLAS, so there is less possibility of compensating for the extra operations.

The algorithms concerned are:

- reduction of a symmetric matrix to tridiagonal form to solve a symmetric eigenvalue problem: LAPACK routine SSYTRD applies a symmetric block update of the form

$$A \leftarrow A - UX^T - XU^T$$

  using the Level 3 BLAS routine SSYR2K; Level 3 BLAS account for at most half the work.

- reduction of a rectangular matrix to bidiagonal form to compute a singular value decomposition: LAPACK routine SGEBRD applies a block update of the form

$$A \leftarrow A - UX^T - YV^T$$

  using two calls to the Level 3 BLAS routine SGEMM; Level 3 BLAS account for at most half the work.

- reduction of a nonsymmetric matrix to Hessenberg form to solve a nonsymmetric eigenvalue problem: LAPACK routine SGEHRD applies a block update of the form

$$A \leftarrow (I - VT^TV^T)(A - XV^T).$$

Level 3 BLAS account for at most three-quarters of the work.

Table 3.7: Speed in megaflops of reductions to condensed forms on an IBM 3090E VF

(all matrices are square of order n)

	Block size	Values of n			
		128	256	384	512
SSYTRD	1	15	22	26	27
	16	15	26	32	34
SGEBRD	1	23	26	28	29
	12	23	33	38	41
SGEHRD	1	27	29	30	30
	24	36	51	57	58

Note that only in the reduction to Hessenberg form is it possible to use the block Householder representation described in subsection 3.4.2. Extra work must be performed to compute the n-by-b matrices X and Y that are required for the block updates (b is the block size) — and extra workspace is needed to store them.

Nevertheless, the performance gains can be worthwhile on some machines, for example, on an IBM 3090, as shown in Table 3.7.

Following the reduction to condensed form, there is no scope for using Level 2 or Level 3 BLAS in computing the eigenvalues and eigenvectors of a symmetric tridiagonal matrix, or in computing the singular values and vectors of a bidiagonal matrix.

However, for computing the eigenvalues and eigenvectors of a Hessenberg matrix—or rather for computing its Schur factorization— yet another flavour of block algorithm has been developed: a **multishift** QR iteration [7]. Whereas the traditional EISPACK routine HQR uses a double shift (and the corresponding complex routine COMQR uses a single shift), the multishift algorithm uses block shifts of higher order. It has been found that often the total number of operations *decreases* as the order of shift is increased until a minimum is reached typically between 4 and 8; for higher orders the number of operations increases quite rapidly. On many machines the speed of applying the shift increases steadily with the order, and the optimum order of shift is typically in the range 8–16. Note however that the performance can be very sensitive to the choice of the order of shift; it also depends on the numerical properties of the matrix. Dubrulle [24] has studied the practical performance of the algorithm, while Watkins and Elsner [46] discuss its theoretical asymptotic convergence rate.

Chapter 4

Accuracy and Stability

In addition to providing faster routines than previously available, LAPACK provides more comprehensive and better error bounds.

Our ultimate goal is to provide error bounds for all quantities computed by LAPACK, although this work is not yet complete. It is beyond the scope of this manual to prove all these error bounds are valid. Instead, we explain the overall approach, provide enough information to use the software, and give references for further explanation. The leading comments of the individual routines should be consulted for details. Much standard material on error analysis can be found in [29].

Traditional error bounds are based on the fact that the algorithms in LAPACK, like their predecessors in LINPACK and EISPACK, are **normwise backward stable**; the tighter error bounds provided by some LAPACK routines depend on algorithms which satisfy a stronger criterion called **componentwise relative backward stability**.

In section 4.1 we discuss roundoff error. Section 4.2 discusses the vector and matrix norms we need to measure errors, as well as other notation. Standard *normwise* error bounds satisfied by LAPACK (as well as LINPACK and EISPACK) routines are reviewed in section 4.3. Section 4.4 discusses the new *componentwise* approach to error analysis used in some LAPACK routines. Section 4.5 discusses how to read and understand the error bounds stated in the following sections, 4.6 through 4.11, which present bounds for linear equation solving, least squares problems, the singular value decomposition, the symmetric eigenproblem, the nonsymmetric eigenproblem, and the generalized symmetric definite eigenproblem, respectively. Section 4.12 discusses the impact of fast Level 3 BLAS on the accuracy of LAPACK routines.

4.1 Roundoff Errors in Floating-Point Arithmetic

We will let ϵ denote the *machine precision*, which is loosely described as the largest relative error in any floating-point operation which neither overflows nor underflows. In other words, it is the smallest number satisfying

$$|fl(a \oplus b) - (a \oplus b)| \le \epsilon \cdot |a \oplus b|$$

where a and b are floating-point numbers, $\oplus$ is one of the four operations $+$, $-$, $\times$ and $\div$, and $fl(a \oplus b)$ is the floating-point result of $a \oplus b$. A precise characterization of ϵ depends on the details of the machine arithmetic and even of the compiler. For example, if addition and subtraction are implemented without a guard digit[1] we must redefine ϵ to be the smallest number such that

$$|fl(a \pm b) - (a \pm b)| \leq \epsilon \cdot (|a| + |b|).$$

There are many other parameters required to specify computer arithmetic, such as the overflow threshold, underflow threshold, and so on. In order that LAPACK be portable, they are computed at runtime by the auxiliary routine xLAMCH[2].

Throughout our discussion, we will ignore overflow and significant underflow in discussing error bounds.

LAPACK routines are generally insensitive to the details of rounding, just as their counterparts in LINPACK and EISPACK. One newer algorithm (xLASV2) can return significantly more accurate results if addition and subtraction have a guard digit (see the end of section 4.8). Future releases of LAPACK will contain more routines whose performance depends strongly on having accurate and robust arithmetic, such as IEEE Standard Floating-Point Arithmeticfloating-point arithmetic, IEEE [4].

4.2 Vector and Matrix Norms

Loosely speaking, a norm of a vector or matrix measures the size of its largest entry. This is true for the norms we shall use, which are defined in Table 4.1.

Table 4.1: Vector and matrix norms

	Vector	Matrix
infinity-norm	$\|x\|_\infty = \max_i |x_i|$	$\|A\|_\infty = \max_i \sum_j |a_{ij}|$
one-norm	$\|x\|_1 = \sum_i |x_i|$	$\|A\|_1 = \max_j \sum_i |a_{ij}|$
two-norm	$\|x\|_2 = (\sum_i |x_i|^2)^{1/2}$	$\|A\|_2 = \max_{x \neq 0} \|Ax\|_2 / \|x\|_2$
Frobenius norm	$\|x\|_F = \|x\|_2$	$\|A\|_F = (\sum_{ij} |a_{ij}|^2)^{1/2}$

The two-norm of A, $\|A\|_2$, is the **largest singular value** $\sigma_{\max}(A)$ of A. The **smallest singular value**, $\min_{x \neq 0} \|Ax\|_2 / \|x\|_2$, is denoted $\sigma_{\min}(A)$. If A has more columns than rows, transpose A is used in the definition of $\sigma_{\min}$). The two-norm, Frobenius norm, and singular values of a matrix do not change if it is multiplied by a real orthogonal (or complex unitary) matrix.

$\kappa_p(A)$ will denote $\|A\|_p \cdot \|A^{-1}\|_p$ for $p = 1, 2, \infty$, and F, and A square and invertible.

We will denote the vector of absolute values of x by $|x|$ ($|x|_i = |x_i|$), and similarly for $|A|$ ($|A|_{ij} = |a_{ij}|$). The dimensions of A will be n-by-n if not otherwise specified.

---

[1]This is the case on Cybers and current Crays.
[2]See subsection 2.1.3 for explanation of the naming convention used for LAPACK routines.

4.3 Standard Error Analysis

We illustrate standard error analysis with the simple example of evaluating the scalar function $y = f(z)$. Let the output of the subroutine which implements $f(z)$ be denoted alg(z); this includes the effects of roundoff. If alg$(z) = f(z + \delta)$ where δ is small, then we say alg is a **backward stable** algorithm for f, or that the **backward error** δ is small. In other words, alg(z) is the exact value of f at a slightly perturbed input $z + \delta$.[3]

Suppose now that f is a smooth function, so that we may approximate it near z by a straight line: $f(z + \delta) \approx f(z) + f'(z) \cdot \delta$. Then we have the simple error estimate

$$\text{alg}(z) - f(z) = f(z + \delta) - f(z) \approx f'(z) \cdot \delta.$$

Thus, if δ is small, and the derivative $f'(z)$ is moderate, the error alg$(z) - f(z)$ will be small[4]. This is often written in the similar form

$$\left| \frac{\text{alg}(z) - f(z)}{f(z)} \right| \lesssim \left| \frac{f'(z) \cdot z}{f(z)} \right| \cdot \left| \frac{\delta}{z} \right| \equiv \kappa(f, z) \cdot \left| \frac{\delta}{z} \right|.$$

This approximately bounds the **relative error** $\frac{\text{alg}(z) - f(z)}{f(z)}$ by the product of the **condition number of** f at z, $\kappa(f, z)$, and the **relative backward error** $|\frac{\delta}{z}|$. Thus we get an error bound by multiplying a condition number and a backward error (or bounds for these quantities). We call a problem **ill-conditioned** if its condition number is large, and **ill-posed** if its condition number is infinite (or does not exist)[5].

If f and z are vector quantities, then $f'(z)$ is a matrix (the Jacobian). So instead of using absolute values as before, we now measure δ by a vector norm $\|\delta\|$ and $f'(z)$ by a matrix norm $\|f'(z)\|$. The conventional (and coarsest) error analysis uses the a norm such as the infinity norm. We therefore call this **normwise backward stability**. For example, a normwise stable method for solving a system of linear equations $Ax = b$ will produce a solution $\hat{x}$ satisfying $(A + E)\hat{x} = b + f$ where $\|E\|_\infty / \|A\|_\infty$ and $\|f\|_\infty / \|b\|_\infty$ are both small (close to ϵ). In this case the condition number is $\kappa_\infty(A) = \|A\|_\infty \cdot \|A^{-1}\|_\infty$ (see section 4.6 below).

Almost all the algorithms in LAPACK (as well as LINPACK and EISPACK) are stable in the sense just described[6]: when applied to a matrix A they produce the exact result for a slightly different matrix $A + E$, where $\|E\|_\infty / \|A\|_\infty$ is near ϵ.

---

[3]Sometimes our algorithms satisfy only alg$(z) = f(z + \delta) + \eta$ where both δ and η are small. This does not significantly change the following analysis.

[4]More generally, we only need Lipschitz continuity of f, and may use the Lipschitz constant in place of f' in deriving error bounds.

[5]This is a different use of the term ill-posed than used in other contexts. For example, to be well-posed (not ill-posed) in the sense of Hadamard, it is sufficient for f to be continuous, whereas we require Lipschitz continuity.

[6]There are some caveats to this statement. When computing the inverse of a matrix, the backward error E is small taking the columns of the computed inverse one at a time, with a different E for each column [25]. The same is true when computing the eigenvectors of a nonsymmetric matrix. When computing the eigenvalues and eigenvectors of $A - \lambda B$, $AB - \lambda I$ or $BA - \lambda I$, with A symmetric and B symmetric and positive definite (using xSYGV or xHEGV) then the method may not be backward normwise stable if B has a large condition number $\kappa_\infty(B)$, although it has useful error bounds in this case too (see section 4.11). Solving the Sylvester equation $AX + XB = C$ for the matrix X may not be backward stable, although there are again useful error bounds for X.

Condition numbers may be expensive to compute exactly. For example, it costs $O(n^3)$ operations to solve $Ax = b$ for a general matrix A, and computing $\kappa_\infty(A)$ exactly is at least three times as expensive. But $\kappa_\infty(A)$ can be estimated in only $O(n^2)$ operations beyond those necessary for solution. Therefore, most of LAPACK's condition numbers and error bounds are based on estimated condition numbers, using the method of [31, 33, 34]. The price one pays for using an estimator is occasional (but very rare) underestimates; years of experience attest to the reliability of our estimators, although examples where they badly underestimate can be constructed [35]. In particular, once an estimate is large enough (usually $O(1/\epsilon)$) it means that the computed answer may be completely incorrect, but the condition estimate itself may be a serious underestimate.

4.4   Improved Error Bounds

The standard error analysis just outlined has a drawback: by using the infinity norm $\|\delta\|_\infty$ to measure the backward error, entries of equal magnitude in δ contribute equally to the final error bound $\kappa(f, z)(\|\delta\|/\|z\|)$. This means that if z is sparse or has some very tiny entries, a normwise backward stable algorithm may make very large changes in these entries compared to their original values. If these tiny values are known accurately by the user, these errors may be unacceptable, or the error bounds may be unacceptably large.

For example, consider solving a diagonal system of linear equations $Ax = b$. Each component of the solution is computed accurately by Gaussian elimination: $x_i = b_i/a_{ii}$. The usual error bound is approximately $\epsilon \cdot \kappa_\infty(A) = \epsilon \cdot \max_i |a_{ii}| / \min_i |a_{ii}|$, which can arbitrarily overestimate the true error.

LAPACK addresses this inadequacy by providing some algorithms whose backward error δ is a tiny relative change in each component of z: $|\delta_i| = O(\epsilon)|z_i|$. This backward error retains both the sparsity structure of z as well as the information in tiny entries. These algorithms are therefore called **componentwise relatively backward stable**. Furthermore, computed error bounds reflect this tinier backward error[7].

If the input data has independent uncertainty in each component, each component must have at least a small *relative* uncertainty, since each is a floating-point number. In this case, the extra uncertainty contributed by the algorithm is not much worse than the uncertainty in the input data, so one could say the answer provided by a componentwise relatively backward stable algorithm is as accurate as the data warrants[1].

When solving $Ax = b$ using expert driver xyySVX or computational routine xyyRFS, for example, this means that we (almost always) compute $\hat{x}$ satisfying $(A + E)\hat{x} = b + f$, where e_{ij} is a small relative change in a_{ij} and f_k is a small relative change in b_k. In particular, if A is diagonal, the corresponding error bound is always tiny, as one would expect (see the next section).

LAPACK can achieve this accuracy for linear equation solving, the bidiagonal singular value decomposition, the symmetric tridiagonal eigenproblem, and provides facilities for achieving this accuracy

---

[7]For other algorithms, the answers (and computed error bounds) are as accurate as though the algorithms were componentwise relatively backward stable, even though they are not. These algorithms are called *componentwise relatively forward stable*.

for least squares problems. Future versions of LAPACK will also achieve this accuracy for other linear algebra problems, as discussed below.

4.5 How to Read Error Bounds

Here we discuss some notation used in all the error bounds of later subsections.

All our bounds will contain the factor $p(n)$ (or $p(m,n)$), which grows as a function of matrix dimension n (or matrix dimensions m and n). It measures how errors can grow as a function of matrix dimension, and represents a potentially different function for each problem. In practice, it usually grows just linearly; $p(n) \leq 10n$ is often true. But we can generally only prove much weaker bounds of the form $p(n) = O(n^3)$, since we can not rule out the extremely unlikely possibility of rounding errors all adding together instead of cancelling on average. Using $p(n) = O(n^3)$ would give very pessimistic and unrealistic bounds, especially for large n, so we content ourselves with describing $p(n)$ as a "modestly growing" function of n. For detailed derivations of various $p(n)$, see [29, 47].

There is also one situation where $p(n)$ can grow as large as 2^{n-1}: Gaussian elimination. This only occurs on specially constructed matrices presented in numerical analysis courses [47, p. 212]. Thus we can assume $p(n) \leq 10n$ in practice for Gaussian elimination too.

For linear equation and least squares solvers for $Ax = b$, we will bound the relative error $\|x - \hat{x}\|/\|x\|$ in the computed solution $\hat{x}$ where x is the true solution (the choice of norm $\|\cdot\|$ will differ). For eigenvalue problems we bound the error $|\lambda_i - \hat{\lambda}_i|$ in the ith computed eigenvalue $\hat{\lambda}_i$, where λ_i is the true i^{th} eigenvalue. For singular value problems we similarly bound $|\sigma_i - \hat{\sigma}_i|$.

Bounding the error in computed eigenvectors and singular vectors $\hat{v}_i$ is more subtle because these vectors are not unique: even though we restrict $\|\hat{v}_i\|_2 = 1$ and $\|v_i\|_2 = 1$, we may still multiply them by arbitrary constants of absolute value 1. So to avoid ambiguity we bound the *angular difference* between $\hat{v}_i$ and the true vector v_i:

$$\begin{aligned}\theta(v_i, \hat{v}_i) &= \text{acute angle between } v_i \text{ and } \hat{v}_i \\ &= \arccos |v_i^H \hat{v}_i|.\end{aligned} \tag{4.1}$$

When $\theta(v_i, \hat{v}_i)$ is small, one can choose a constant α with absolute value 1 so that $\|\alpha v_i - \hat{v}_i\|_2 \approx \theta(v_i, \hat{v}_i)$.

In addition to bounds for individual eigenvectors, we supply bounds for the spaces spanned by collections of eigenvectors, because these may be much more accurately determined than the individual eigenvectors which span them. These spaces are called *invariant subspaces* in the case of eigenvectors, because if v is any vector in the space, Av is also in the space, where A is the matrix. Again, we will use angle to measure the difference between a computed space $\hat{S}$ and the true space S:

$$\begin{aligned}\theta(S, \hat{S}) &= \text{acute angle between } S \text{ and } \hat{S} \\ &= \max_{\substack{s \in S \\ s \neq 0}} \min_{\substack{\hat{s} \in \hat{S} \\ \hat{s} \neq 0}} \theta(s, \hat{s}) \text{ or } \max_{\substack{\hat{s} \in \hat{S} \\ \hat{s} \neq 0}} \min_{\substack{s \in S \\ s \neq 0}} \theta(s, \hat{s}).\end{aligned} \tag{4.2}$$

We may compute $\theta(\mathcal{S}, \hat{\mathcal{S}})$ as follows. Let S be a matrix whose columns are orthonormal and span $\mathcal{S}$. Similarly let $\hat{S}$ be an orthonormal matrix with columns spanning $\hat{\mathcal{S}}$. Then

$$\theta(\mathcal{S}, \hat{\mathcal{S}}) = \arccos \sigma_{\min}(S^H \hat{S}).$$

Finally, we remark on the accuracy of our bounds when they are large. Relative errors like $\|\hat{x} - x\|/\|x\|$ and angular errors like $\theta(\hat{v}_i, v_i)$ are only of interest when they are much less than 1. We have correspondingly stated some bounds so that they are not strictly true when they are close to 1, since rigorous bounds would have been more complicated and supplied little extra information in the interesting case of small errors. We have indicated these bounds by using the symbol $\lesssim$, or "approximately less than", instead of the usual $\leq$. Thus, when these bounds are close to 1 or greater, they indicate that the computed answer may have no significant digits at all, but do not otherwise bound the error.

4.6 Error Bounds for Linear Equation Solving

The conventional error analysis of linear equation solving goes as follows. Let $Ax = b$ be the system to be solved. Let $\hat{x}$ be the solution computed by LAPACK (or LINPACK) using any of their linear equation solvers. Let r be the residual $r = b - A\hat{x}$. In the absence of rounding error r would be zero and $\hat{x}$ would equal x; with rounding error one can only say the following:

The normwise backward error ω_∞, measured using the infinity norm, is the smallest value of

$$\max \left(\frac{\|E\|_\infty}{\|A\|_\infty}, \frac{\|f\|_\infty}{\|b\|_\infty} \right)$$

such that the computed solution $\hat{x}$ exactly satisfies $(A + E)\hat{x} = b + f$. The normwise backward error is given by

$$\omega_\infty = \frac{\|r\|_\infty}{\|A\|_\infty \cdot \|\hat{x}\|_\infty + \|b\|_\infty} \leq p(n) \cdot \epsilon$$

where $p(n)$ is a modestly growing function of n. The corresponding condition number is $\kappa_\infty(A) \equiv \|A\|_\infty \cdot \|A^{-1}\|_\infty$. The error $x - \hat{x}$ is bounded by

$$\frac{\|x - \hat{x}\|_\infty}{\|x\|_\infty} \lesssim 2 \cdot \omega_\infty \cdot \kappa_\infty(A).$$

Approximations of $\kappa_\infty(A)$ — or, strictly speaking, its reciprocal — are returned by computational routines xyyCON (subsection 2.3.1) or driver routines xyySVX (subsection 2.2.1).

As stated in the last section, this approach does not respect the presence of zero or tiny entries in A. In contrast, the LAPACK computational routines xyyRFS (subsection 2.3.1) or driver routines xyySVX (subsection 2.2.1) will (except in rare cases) compute a solution $\hat{x}$ with the following properties:

The componentwise backward error ω_c is the smallest value of

$$\max_{i,j,k}\left(\frac{|e_{ij}|}{|a_{ij}|}, \frac{|f_k|}{|b_k|}\right)$$

(where we interpret $0/0$ as 0) such that the computed solution $\hat{x}$ exactly satisfies $(A + E)\hat{x} = b + f$. The componentwise backward error is given by

$$\omega_c = \max_i \frac{|r_i|}{(|A| \cdot |\hat{x}| + |b|)_i} \leq p(n) \cdot \epsilon$$

where $p(n)$ is a modestly growing function of n. In other words, $\hat{x}$ is the exact solution of the perturbed problem $(A + E)\hat{x} = b + f$ where E and f are small relative perturbations in each entry of A and b, respectively. The corresponding condition number is $\kappa_c(A, b, \hat{x}) \equiv \| |A^{-1}|(|A| \cdot |\hat{x}| + |b|) \|_\infty / \|\hat{x}\|_\infty$. The error $x - \hat{x}$ is bounded by

$$\frac{\|x - \hat{x}\|_\infty}{\|\hat{x}\|_\infty} \leq \omega_c \cdot \kappa_c(A, b, \hat{x}).$$

The routines xyyRFS and xyySVX return bounds on the componentwise relative backward error ω_c (called BERR) and the actual error $\|x - \hat{x}\|_\infty / \|\hat{x}\|_\infty$ (called FERR).

Even in the rare cases where xyyRFS fails to make ω_c close to its minimum ϵ, the error bound computed by the routine may remain small. See [5] for details.

4.7   Error Bounds for Linear Least Squares Problems

The conventional error analysis of linear least squares problems goes as follows. The problem is to find the x minimizing $\|Ax - b\|_2$. Let $\hat{x}$ be the solution computed by LAPACK using one of the least squares drivers xGELS, xGELSS or xGELSX (see subsection 2.2.2). We discuss the most common case, where A is overdetermined (i.e., has more rows than columns) and has full rank [29]:

The computed solution $\hat{x}$ has a small normwise backward error. In other words $\hat{x}$ minimizes $\|(A + E)\hat{x} - (b + f)\|_2$, where

$$\max\left(\frac{\|E\|_2}{\|A\|_2}, \frac{\|f\|_2}{\|b\|_2}\right) \leq p(n)\epsilon$$

and $p(n)$ is a modestly growing function of n. Let $\kappa_2(A) = \sigma_{\max}(A)/\sigma_{\min}(A)$, $\rho = \|Ax - b\|_2$, and $\sin(\theta) = \rho/\|b\|_2$. Then if $p(n)\epsilon$ is small enough, the error $\hat{x} - x$ is bounded by

$$\frac{\|x - \hat{x}\|_2}{\|x\|_2} \lesssim p(n)\epsilon\left\{\frac{2\kappa_2(A)}{\cos(\theta)} + \tan(\theta)\kappa_2^2(A)\right\}.$$

$\kappa_2(A) = \sigma_{\max}(A)/\sigma_{\min}(A)$ may be computed from the singular values of A returned by xGELSS or xGESVD. $\|b\|_2$ and $\rho = \|A\hat{x} - b\|_2$ (and then $\sin(\theta) = \rho/\|b\|_2$, $\cos(\theta)$ and $\tan(\theta)$) may be easily computed from the arguments of xGELSS.

If A is rank-deficient, xGELSS and xGELSX can be used to **regularize** the problem by treating all singular values less than a user-specified threshold (RCOND $\cdot \sigma_{\max}(A)$) as exactly zero. The number of singular values treated as nonzero is returned in RANK. See [29] for error bounds in this case, as well as [11, 29] for the underdetermined case.

The solution of the overdetermined, full-rank problem may also be characterized as the solution of the linear system of equations

$$\begin{pmatrix} I & A \\ A^T & 0 \end{pmatrix} \begin{pmatrix} r \\ x \end{pmatrix} = \begin{pmatrix} b \\ 0 \end{pmatrix}.$$

By solving this linear system using xyyRFS or xyySVX (see section 4.6) componentwise error bounds can also be obtained [6].

4.8 Error Bounds for the Singular Value Decomposition

The singular value decomposition (SVD) of a real m-by-n matrix is the factorization $A = U\Sigma V^T$ ($A = U\Sigma V^H$ in the complex case), where U and V are orthogonal (unitary) matrices and $\Sigma = \mathrm{diag}(\sigma_1, \ldots, \sigma_{\min(m,n)})$ is diagonal, with $\sigma_1 \geq \sigma_2 \geq \cdots \geq \sigma_{\min(m,n)} \geq 0$. The σ_i are the **singular values** of A and the leading $\min(m, n)$ columns u_i of U and v_i of V the **left and right singular vectors,** respectively.

The usual error analysis of the SVD algorithm xGESVD in LAPACK (see subsection 2.2.3) or the routines in LINPACK and EISPACK is as follows [29]:

The computed SVD, $\hat{U}\hat{\Sigma}\hat{V}^T$, is nearly the exact SVD of $A + E$, i.e., $A + E = (\hat{U} + \delta\hat{U})\hat{\Sigma}(\hat{V} + \delta\hat{V})$ is the true SVD, so that $\hat{U} + \delta\hat{U}$ and $\hat{V} + \delta\hat{V}$ are both orthogonal, where $\|E\|_2/\|A\|_2 \leq p(m,n)\epsilon$, $\|\delta\hat{U}\| \leq p(m,n)\epsilon$, and $\|\delta\hat{V}\| \leq p(m,n)\epsilon$. Here $p(m,n)$ is a modestly growing function of m and n. Each computed singular value $\hat{\sigma}_i$ differs from the true σ_i by at most

$$|\hat{\sigma}_i - \sigma_i| \leq p(m,n) \cdot \epsilon \cdot \sigma_1.$$

Thus large singular values (those near σ_1) are computed to high relative accuracy and small ones may not be.

The angular difference between the computed left singular vector $\hat{u}_i$ and the true u_i satisfies the approximate bound

$$\theta(\hat{u}_i, u_i) \lesssim \frac{p(m,n)\epsilon\|A\|_2}{\mathrm{gap}_i}$$

where $\mathrm{gap}_i = \min_{j \neq i} |\sigma_i - \sigma_j|$ is the **absolute gap** between σ_i and the nearest other singular value. Thus, if σ_i is close to other singular values, its corresponding singular vector u_i may be inaccurate. The same bound applies to the computed right singular vector $\hat{v}_i$ and the true vector v_i. The gaps may be easily computed from the array of computed singular values.

Let $\hat{\mathcal{S}}$ be the space spanned by a collection of computed left singular vectors $\{\hat{u}_i\,,\ i \in \mathcal{I}\}$, where $\mathcal{I}$ is a subset of the integers from 1 to n. Let $\mathcal{S}$ be the corresponding true space. Then

$$\theta(\hat{\mathcal{S}}, \mathcal{S}) \lesssim \frac{p(m,n)\epsilon\|A\|_2}{\mathrm{gap}_{\mathcal{I}}}.$$

where

$$\mathrm{gap}_{\mathcal{I}} = \min_{\substack{i \in \mathcal{I} \\ j \notin \mathcal{I}}} |\sigma_i - \sigma_j|$$

is the absolute gap between the singular values in $\mathcal{I}$ and the nearest other singular value. Thus, a cluster of close singular values which is far away from any other singular value may have a well determined space $\hat{\mathcal{S}}$ even if its individual singular vectors are ill-conditioned. The same bound applies to a set of right singular vectors $\{\hat{v}_i\,,\ i \in \mathcal{I}\}$[8].

In the special case of bidiagonal matrices, the singular values and singular vectors may be computed much more accurately. A bidiagonal matrix B has nonzero entries only on the main diagonal and the diagonal immediately above it (or immediately below it). xGESVD computes the SVD of a general matrix by first reducing it to bidiagonal form B, and then calling xBDSQR (subsection 2.3.5) to compute the SVD of B. Reduction of a dense matrix to bidiagonal form B can introduce additional errors, so the following bounds for the bidiagonal case do not apply to the dense case[9].

Each computed singular value of a bidiagonal matrix is accurate to nearly full relative accuracy, no matter how tiny it is:

$$|\hat{\sigma}_i - \sigma_i| \leq p(m,n) \cdot \epsilon \cdot \sigma_i.$$

The computed left singular vector $\hat{u}_i$ has an angular error at most about

$$\theta(\hat{u}_i, u_i) \lesssim \frac{p(m,n)\epsilon}{\mathrm{relgap}_i}$$

where $\mathrm{relgap}_i = \min_{j \neq i} |\sigma_i - \sigma_j|/(\sigma_i + \sigma_j)$ is the **relative gap** between σ_i and the nearest other singular value. The same bound applies to the right singular vector $\hat{v}_i$ and v_i. Since the relative gap may be much larger than the absolute gap, this error bound may be much smaller than the previous one. The relative gaps may be easily computed from the array of computed singular values.

In the very special case of 2-by-2 bidiagonal matrices, xBDSQR calls auxiliary routine xLASV2 to compute the SVD. xLASV2 will actually compute nearly correctly rounded singular vectors independent of the relative gap, but this requires accurate computer arithmetic: if leading digits cancel during floating-point subtraction, the resulting difference must be exact. On machines without guard digits one has the slightly weaker result that the algorithm is componentwise relatively backward stable.

---

[8]These bounds are special cases of those in sections 4.9 and 4.10, since the singular values and vectors of A are simply related to the eigenvalues and eigenvectors of the Hermitian matrix $\begin{pmatrix} 0 & A^H \\ A & 0 \end{pmatrix}$ [29, p. 427].

[9]Recent work has extended some of these results to dense matrices [14]. This work will appear in a later version of LAPACK.

4.9 Error Bounds for the Symmetric Eigenproblem

The eigendecomposition of an n-by-n real symmetric matrix is the factorization $A = Z\Lambda Z^T$ ($A = Z\Lambda Z^H$ in the complex Hermitian case), where Z is orthogonal (unitary) and $\Lambda = \text{diag}(\lambda_1, \ldots, \lambda_n)$ is real and diagonal. The λ_i are the **eigenvalues** of A and the columns z_i of Z are the **eigenvectors**. This is also often written $Az_i = \lambda_i z_i$.

The usual error analysis of the symmetric eigenproblem (using any LAPACK routine in subsection 2.2.3 such as drivers xSYEV and xSYEVX, or any EISPACK routine) is as follows [39]:

> The computed eigendecomposition $\hat{Z}\hat{\Lambda}\hat{Z}^T$ is nearly the exact eigendecomposition of $A + E$, i.e., $A + E = (\hat{Z} + \delta\hat{Z})\hat{\Lambda}(\hat{Z} + \delta\hat{Z})^T$ is the true eigendecomposition so that $\hat{Z} + \delta\hat{Z}$ is orthogonal, where $\|E\|_2/\|A\|_2 \leq p(n)\epsilon$ and $\|\delta\hat{Z}\|_2 \leq p(n)\epsilon$. Here $p(n)$ is a modestly growing function of n. Each computed eigenvalue $\hat{\lambda}_i$ differs from the true λ_i by at most

$$|\hat{\lambda}_i - \lambda_i| \leq p(n) \cdot \epsilon \cdot \|A\|_2$$

Thus large eigenvalues (those near $\max_i |\lambda_i| = \|A\|_2$) are computed to high relative accuracy and small ones may not be.

The angular difference between the computed unit singular vector $\hat{z}_i$ and the true z_i by at most about

$$\theta(\hat{z}_i, z_i) \lesssim \frac{p(n)\epsilon\|A\|_2}{\text{gap}_i}$$

if $p(n)\epsilon$ is small enough, where $\text{gap}_i = \min_{j \neq i} |\lambda_i - \lambda_j|$ is the **absolute gap** between λ_i and the nearest other eigenvalue. Thus, if λ_i is close to other eigenvalues, its corresponding eigenvector z_i may be inaccurate. The gaps may be easily computed from the array of computed eigenvalues.

Let $\hat{S}$ be the invariant subspace spanned by a collection of eigenvectors $\{\hat{z}_i, i \in \mathcal{I}\}$, where $\mathcal{I}$ is a subset of the integers from 1 to n. Let S be the corresponding true subspace. Then

$$\theta(\hat{S}, S) \lesssim \frac{p(n)\epsilon\|A\|_2}{\text{gap}_{\mathcal{I}}}$$

where

$$\text{gap}_{\mathcal{I}} = \min_{\substack{i \in \mathcal{I} \\ j \notin \mathcal{I}}} |\lambda_i - \lambda_j|$$

is the absolute gap between the eigenvalues in $\mathcal{I}$ and the nearest other eigenvalue. Thus, a cluster of close eigenvalues which is far away from any other eigenvalue may have a well determined invariant subspace $\hat{S}$ even if its individual eigenvectors are ill-conditioned[10].

In the special case of a real symmetric tridiagonal matrix T, the eigenvalues and eigenvectors can be computed much more accurately. xSYEV (and the other symmetric eigenproblem drivers) computes the eigenvalues and eigenvectors of a dense symmetric matrix by first reducing it to

---

[10]These bounds are special cases of those in section 4.10.

tridiagonal form T, and then finding the eigenvalues and eigenvectors of T. Reduction of a dense matrix to tridiagonal form T can introduce additional errors, so the following bounds for the tridiagonal case do not apply to the dense case[11].

The eigenvalues of T may be computed with small componentwise relative backward error ($O(\epsilon)$) by using subroutine xSTEBZ (subsection 2.3.3) or driver xSTEVX (subsection 2.2.3). If T is also positive definite, they may also be computed at least as accurately by xPTEQR (subsection 2.3.3). To compute error bounds for the computed eigenvalues $\hat{\lambda}_i$ we must make some assumptions about T. The bounds discussed here are from [9]. Suppose T is positive definite, and write $T = DHD$ where $D = \mathrm{diag}(t_{11}^{1/2}, \ldots, t_{nn}^{1/2})$ and $h_{ii} = 1$. Then the computed eigenvalues $\hat{\lambda}_i$ can differ from the true eigenvalues λ_i by

$$|\hat{\lambda}_i - \lambda_i| \le p(n) \cdot \epsilon \cdot \kappa_2(H) \cdot \lambda_i$$

where $p(n)$ is a modestly growing function of n. Thus if $\kappa_2(H)$ is moderate, each eigenvalue will be computed to high relative accuracy, no matter how tiny it is. The eigenvectors $\hat{z}_i$ computed by xPTEQR can differ from the true eigenvectors z_i by at most about

$$\theta(\hat{z}_i, z_i) \lesssim \frac{p(n) \cdot \epsilon \cdot \kappa_2(H)}{\mathrm{relgap}_i}$$

if $p(n)\epsilon$ is small enough, where $\mathrm{relgap}_i = \min_{j \ne i} |\lambda_i - \lambda_j| / (\lambda_i + \lambda_j)$ is the **relative gap** between λ_i and the nearest other eigenvalue. Since the relative gap may be much larger than the absolute gap, this error bound may be much smaller than the previous one.

$\kappa_2(H)$ could be computed by applying xPTCON (subsection 2.3.1) to H. The relative gaps are easily computed from the array of computed eigenvalues.

For further results, including error bounds appropriate to indefinite matrices, see [9].

4.10   Error Bounds for the Nonsymmetric Eigenproblem

4.10.1   Summary

The nonsymmetric eigenvalue problem is more complicated than the symmetric eigenvalue problem. In this subsection, as in previous sections, we will just summarize the bounds; in later subsections we provide some further details.

Bounds for individual eigenvalues and eigenvectors are provided by driver xGEEVX (subsection 2.2.3) or computational routine xTRSNA (subsection 2.3.4). Bounds for clusters of eigenvalues and their associated invariant subspace are provided by driver xGEESX (subsection 2.2.3) or computational routine xTRSEN (subsection 2.3.4). Further details can be found in [8].

We let $\hat{\lambda}_i$ be the ith computed eigenvalue and λ_i the ith true eigenvalue. Let $\hat{v}_i$ be the corresponding computed right eigenvector, and v_i the true right eigenvector (so $Av_i = \lambda_i v_i$). If $\mathcal{I}$ is

---

[11]Recent work has extended some of these results to dense symmetric positive definite matrices [14]. This work will appear in a later version of LAPACK.

a subset of the integers from 1 to n, we let $\lambda_{\mathcal{I}}$ denote the average of the selected eigenvalues: $\lambda_{\mathcal{I}} = (\sum_{i \in \mathcal{I}} \lambda_i)/(\sum_{i \in \mathcal{I}} 1)$, and similarly for $\hat{\lambda}_{\mathcal{I}}$. We also let $\mathcal{S}_{\mathcal{I}}$ denote the subspace spanned by $\{v_i, i \in \mathcal{I}\}$; it is called a right invariant subspace because if v is any vector in $\mathcal{S}_{\mathcal{I}}$ then Av is also in $\mathcal{S}_{\mathcal{I}}$. $\hat{\mathcal{S}}_{\mathcal{I}}$ is the corresponding computed subspace.

The algorithms for the nonsymmetric eigenproblem are normwisebackward stable: they compute the exact eigenvalues, eigenvectors and invariant subspaces of slightly perturbed matrices $A + E$, where $\|E\| \leq p(n)\epsilon$. Some of the bounds are stated in terms of $\|E\|_2$ and others in terms of $\|E\|_F$; one may use $p(n)\epsilon$ for either quantity.

xGEEVX (or xTRSNA) returns two quantities for each $\hat{\lambda}_i$, $\hat{v}_i$ pair: s_i and sep_i. xGEESX (or xTRSEN) returns two quantities for a selected subset $\mathcal{I}$ of eigenvalues: $s_{\mathcal{I}}$ and $\text{sep}_{\mathcal{I}}$. The error bounds in the Table 4.2 are true for sufficiently small $\|E\|$, which is why they are called asymptotic:

Table 4.2: Asymptotic error bounds for the nonsymmetric eigenproblem

Simple eigenvalue	$\|\hat{\lambda}_i - \lambda_i\| \lesssim \|E\|_2/s_i$
Eigenvalue cluster	$\|\hat{\lambda}_{\mathcal{I}} - \lambda_{\mathcal{I}}\| \lesssim \|E\|_2/s_{\mathcal{I}}$
Eigenvector	$\theta(\hat{v}_i, v_i) \lesssim \|E\|_F/\text{sep}_i$
Invariant subspace	$\theta(\hat{\mathcal{S}}_{\mathcal{I}}, \mathcal{S}_{\mathcal{I}}) \lesssim \|E\|_F/\text{sep}_{\mathcal{I}}$

If the problem is ill-conditioned, the asymptotic bounds may only hold for extremely small $\|E\|$. Therefore, we also provide global bounds which are guaranteed to hold for all $\|E\|_F < s \cdot \text{sep}/4$:

Table 4.3: Global error bounds for the nonsymmetric eigenproblem

Simple eigenvalue	$\|\hat{\lambda}_i - \lambda_i\| \leq n\|E\|_2/s_i$	Holds for all E
Eigenvalue cluster	$\|\hat{\lambda}_{\mathcal{I}} - \lambda_{\mathcal{I}}\| \leq 2\|E\|_2/s_{\mathcal{I}}$	Requires $\|E\|_F < s_{\mathcal{I}} \cdot \text{sep}_{\mathcal{I}}/4$
Eigenvector	$\theta(\hat{v}_i, v_i) \leq \arctan(2\|E\|_F/(\text{sep}_i - 4\|E\|_F/s_i))$	Requires $\|E\|_F < s_i \cdot \text{sep}_i/4$
Invariant subspace	$\theta(\hat{\mathcal{S}}_{\mathcal{I}}, \mathcal{S}_{\mathcal{I}}) \leq \arctan(2\|E\|_F/(\text{sep}_{\mathcal{I}} - 4\|E\|_F/s_{\mathcal{I}}))$	Requires $\|E\|_F < s_{\mathcal{I}} \cdot \text{sep}_{\mathcal{I}}/4$

Finally, the quantities s and sep tell use how we can best (block) diagonalize a matrix A by a similarity, $V^{-1}AV = \text{diag}(A_{11}, \ldots, A_{bb})$, where each diagonal block A_{ii} has a selected subset of the eigenvalues of A. The goal is to choose a V with a nearly minimum condition number $\kappa_2(V)$ which performs this decomposition. This may be done as follows. Let A_{ii} be n_i-by-n_i. Then columns $1 + \sum_{j=1}^{i-1} n_j$ through $\sum_{j=1}^{i} n_j$ of V span the invariant subspace of A corresponding to the eigenvalues of A_{ii}; these columns should be chosen to be any orthonormal basis of this space (as computed by xGEESX, for example). Let s_i be the value corresponding to the cluster of eigenvalues of A_{ii}, as computed by xGEESX or xTRSEN. Then $\kappa_2(V) \leq b/\min_i s_i$, and no other choice of V can make its condition number smaller than $1/\min_i s_i$. Thus choosing orthonormal subblocks of V gets $\kappa_2(V)$ to within a factor b of its minimum value.

In the case of a real symmetric (or complex Hermitian) matrix, $s = 1$ and sep is the absolute gap, as defined in subsection 4.9.

4.10.2   Balancing and Conditioning

There are two preprocessing steps one may perform on a matrix A in order to make its eigenproblem easier. The first is **permutation**, or reordering the rows and columns to make A more nearly upper triangular (closer to Schur form): $A' = PAP^T$, where P is a permutation matrix. If A' is permutable to upper triangular form (or close to it), then no floating-point operations (or very few) are needed to reduce it to Schur form. The second is **scaling** by a diagonal matrix D to make the rows and columns of A' more nearly equal in norm: $A'' = DA'D^{-1}$. Scaling can make the matrix norm smaller with respect to the eigenvalues, and so possibly reduce the inaccuracy contributed by roundoff [48, Chap. II/11]. We refer to these two operations as **balancing**.

Balancing is performed by driver xGEEVX, which calls computational routine xGEBAL. The user may tell xGEEVX to optionally permute, scale, do both, or do neither; this is specified by input parameter BALANC. Permuting has no effect on the condition numbers or their interpretation as described in previous subsections. Scaling, however, does change their interpretation, as we now describe.

The output parameters of xGEEVX – SCALE (real array of length N), ILO (integer), IHI (integer) and ABNRM (real) – describe the result of balancing a matrix A into A'', where N is the dimension of A. The matrix A'' is block upper triangular, with at most three blocks: from 1 to ILO−1, from ILO to IHI, and from IHI+1 to N. The first and last blocks are upper triangular, and so already in Schur form. These are not scaled; only the block from ILO to IHI is scaled. Details of the scaling and permutation are described in SCALE (see the specification of xGEEVX or xGEBAL for details). The one norm of A'' is returned in ABNRM.

The condition numbers described in earlier subsections are computed for the balanced matrix A'', and so some interpretation is needed to apply them to the eigenvalues and eigenvectors of the original matrix A. To use the bounds for eigenvalues in Tables 4.2 and 4.3, we must replace $\|E_2\|$ and $\|E_F\|$ by $O(\epsilon)\|A''\| = O(\epsilon) \cdot$ ABNRM. To use the bounds for eigenvectors, we also need to take into account that bounds on rotations of eigenvectors are for the eigenvectors x'' of A'', which are related to the eigenvectors x of A by $DPx = x''$, or $x = P^T D^{-1} x''$. One coarse but simple way to do this is as follows: let θ'' be the bound on rotations of x'' from the Perturbation Table, and let θ be the desired bound on rotation of x. Let

$$\kappa(D) = \frac{\max_{\text{ILO} \leq i \leq \text{IHI}} \text{SCALE}(i)}{\min_{\text{ILO} \leq i \leq \text{IHI}} \text{SCALE}(i)}$$

be the condition number of D. Then

$$\theta \leq \arccos\left(\frac{\cos\theta''}{\kappa^2(D)}\right).$$

4.10.3 Computing s and sep

To explain s and sep, we need to introduce the **spectral projector** P [43, 36], and the **separation of two matrices** A and B, sep(A, B) [43, 45].

We may assume the matrix A is in Schur form, because reducing it to this form does not change the values of s and sep. Consider a cluster of $m \geq 1$ eigenvalues, counting multiplicities. Further assume the n-by-n matrix A is

$$A = \begin{pmatrix} A_{11} & A_{12} \\ 0 & A_{22} \end{pmatrix} \tag{4.3}$$

where the eigenvalues of the m-by-m matrix A_{11} are exactly those in which we are interested. In practice, if the eigenvalues on the diagonal of A are in the wrong order, routine xTREXC can be used to put the desired ones in the upper left corner as shown.

We define the **spectral projector**, or simply projector P belonging to the eigenvalues of A_{11} as

$$P = \begin{pmatrix} I_m & R \\ 0 & 0 \end{pmatrix} \tag{4.4}$$

where R satisfies the system of linear equations

$$A_{11}R - RA_{22} = A_{12}. \tag{4.5}$$

Equation (4.5) is called a Sylvester equation. Given the Schur form (4.3), we solve equation (4.5) for R using the subroutine xTRSYL.

We can now define s for the eigenvalues of A_{11}:

$$s = \frac{1}{\|P\|_2} = \frac{1}{\sqrt{1 + \|R\|_2^2}}. \tag{4.6}$$

In practice we do not use this expression since $\|R\|_2$ is hard to compute. Instead we use the more easily computed underestimate

$$\frac{1}{\sqrt{1 + \|R\|_F^2}} \tag{4.7}$$

which can underestimate the true value of s by no more than a factor $\sqrt{\min(m, n - m)}$. This underestimation makes our error bounds more conservative.

The **separation** sep(A_{11}, A_{22}) of the matrices A_{11} and A_{22} is defined as the smallest singular value of the linear map in (4.5) which takes X to $A_{11}X - XA_{22}$, i.e.,

$$\text{sep}(A_{11}, A_{22}) = \min_{X \neq 0} \frac{\|A_{11}X - XA_{22}\|_F}{\|X\|_F}. \tag{4.8}$$

This formulation lets us estimate sep(A_{11}, A_{22}) using the condition estimator xLACON [31, 33, 34], which estimates the norm of a linear operator $\|T\|_1 = \max_j \sum_i |t_{ij}|$ given the ability to compute Tx and $T^T x$ quickly for arbitrary x. In our case, multiplying an arbitrary vector by T means solving the Sylvester equation (4.5) with an arbitrary right hand side using xTRSYL, and multiplying by T^T means solving the same equation with A_{11} replaced by A_{11}^T and A_{22} replaced by A_{22}^T. Solving either equation costs at most $O(n^3)$ operations, or as few as $O(n^2)$ if $m \ll n$. Since the true value of sep is $\|T\|_2$ but we use $\|T\|_1$, our estimate of sep may differ from the true value by as much as $\sqrt{m(n-m)}$.

Another formulation which in principle permits an exact evaluation of $\text{sep}(A_{11}, A_{22})$ is

$$\text{sep}(A_{11}, A_{22}) = \sigma_{\min}(I_{n-m} \otimes A_{11} - A_{22}^T \otimes I_m) \tag{4.9}$$

where $X \otimes Y \equiv [x_{ij} Y]$ is the Kronecker product of X and Y. This method is generally impractical, however, because the matrix whose smallest singular value we need is $m(n-m)$ dimensional, which can be as large as $n^2/4$. Thus we would require as much as $O(n^4)$ extra workspace and $O(n^6)$ operations, much more than the estimation method of the last paragraph.

The expression $\text{sep}(A_{11}, A_{22})$ measures the "separation" of the spectra of A_{11} and A_{22} in the following sense. It is zero if and only if A_{11} and A_{22} have a common eigenvalue, and small if there is a small perturbation of either one that makes them have a common eigenvalue. If A_{11} and A_{22} are both Hermitian matrices, then $\text{sep}(A_{11}, A_{22})$ is just the gap, or minimum distance between an eigenvalue of A_{11} and an eigenvalue of A_{22}. On the other hand, if A_{11} and A_{22} are non-Hermitian, $\text{sep}(A_{11}, A_{22})$ may be much smaller than this gap.

4.11   Error Bounds for the Generalized Symmetric Definite Eigenproblem

There are three types of problems to consider. In all cases A and B are real symmetric (or complex Hermitian) and B is positive definite.

1. $A - \lambda B$. The eigendecomposition may be written $A = Z\Lambda Z^T$ and $B = ZZ^T$ (or $A = Z\Lambda Z^H$ and $B = ZZ^H$ if A and B are complex). Here Λ is real and diagonal, and the columns z_i of Z are linearly independent vectors. The diagonal entries $\lambda_i = \Lambda_{ii}$ are called **eigenvalues** and the z_i are **eigenvectors**. This may also be written $Az_i = \lambda_i Bz_i$.

2. $AB - \lambda I$. The eigendecomposition may be written $A = Z\Lambda Z^T$ and $B = Z^{-T}Z^{-1}$ ($A = Z\Lambda Z^H$ and $B = Z^{-H}Z^{-1}$ if A and B are complex). Here Λ is real diagonal with diagonal entries λ_i, and the columns z_i of Z are linearly independent vectors. The λ_i are called **eigenvalues** and the z_i are **eigenvectors**. This may also be written $ABz_i = \lambda_i z_i$.

3. $BA - \lambda I$. The eigendecomposition may be written $A = Z^T\Lambda Z^{-1}$ and $B = ZZ^T$ ($A = Z^H\Lambda Z^{-1}$ and $B = ZZ^H$ if A and B are complex). Here Λ is real diagonal with diagonal entries λ_i, and the columns z_i of Z are linearly independent vectors. The λ_i are called **eigenvalues** and the z_i are **eigenvectors**. This may also be written $BAz_i = \lambda_i z_i$.

The error analysis of the driver routine xSYGV, or xHEGV in the complex case (see subsection 2.2.4), goes as follows. In all cases $\text{gap}_i = \min_{j \neq i} |\lambda_i - \lambda_j|$ is the **absolute gap** between λ_i and the nearest other eigenvalue.

1. $A - \lambda B$. The computed eigenvalues $\hat{\lambda}_i$ can differ from the true eigenvalues λ_i by at most about

$$|\hat{\lambda}_i - \lambda_i| \lesssim p(n)\epsilon \|B^{-1}\|_2 \|A\|_2.$$

The angular difference between the computed eigenvector $\hat{z}_i$ and the true eigenvector z_i is

$$\theta(\hat{z}_i, z_i) \lesssim \frac{p(n)\epsilon \|B^{-1}\|_2 \|A\|_2 (\kappa_2(B))^{1/2}}{\text{gap}_i}.$$

2. $AB - \lambda I$ or $BA - \lambda I$. The computed eigenvalues $\hat{\lambda}_i$ can differ from the true eigenvalues λ_i by at most about

$$|\hat{\lambda}_i - \lambda_i| \lesssim p(n)\epsilon \|B\|_2 \|A\|_2.$$

The angular difference between the computed eigenvector $\hat{z}_i$ and the true eigenvector z_i is

$$\theta(\hat{z}_i, z_i) \lesssim \frac{q(n)\epsilon \|B\|_2 \|A\|_2 (\kappa_2(B))^{1/2}}{\text{gap}_i}.$$

These error bounds are large when B is ill-conditioned with respect to inversion ($\kappa_2(B)$ is large). It is often the case that the eigenvalues and eigenvectors are much better conditioned than indicated here. We mention two ways to get tighter bounds. The first way is effective when the diagonal entries of B differ widely in magnitude[12]:

1. $A - \lambda B$. Let $D = \text{diag}(b_{11}^{-1/2}, \ldots, b_{nn}^{-1/2})$ be a diagonal matrix. Then replace B by DBD and A by DAD in the above bounds.

2. $AB - \lambda I$ or $BA - \lambda I$. Let $D = \text{diag}(b_{11}^{-1/2}, \ldots, b_{nn}^{-1/2})$ be a diagonal matrix. Then replace B by DBD and A by $D^{-1}AD^{-1}$ in the above bounds.

The second way to get tighter bounds does not actually supply guaranteed bounds, but its estimates are often better in practice. It is not guaranteed because it assumes the algorithm is backward stable, which is not necessarily true when B is ill-conditioned. It estimates the **chordal distance** between a true eigenvalue λ_i and a computed eigenvalue $\hat{\lambda}_i$:

$$\chi(\hat{\lambda}_i, \lambda_i) = \frac{|\hat{\lambda}_i - \lambda_i|}{\sqrt{1 + \hat{\lambda}_i^2} \cdot \sqrt{1 + \lambda_i^2}}.$$

To interpret this measure we write $\lambda_i = \tan\theta$ and $\hat{\lambda}_i = \tan\hat{\theta}$. Then $\chi(\hat{\lambda}_i, \lambda_i) = |\sin(\hat{\theta} - \theta)|$. Thus χ is bounded by one, and is small when both arguments are large[13]. It applies only to the first problem, $A - \lambda B$.

---

[12]This is true only if the Level 3 BLAS are implemented in a conventional way, not in a fast way as described in section 4.12.

[13]Another interpretation of chordal distance is as half the usual Euclidean distance between the projections of $\hat{\lambda}_i$ and λ_i on the Riemann sphere, i.e., half the length of the chord connecting the projections.

Suppose a computed eigenvalue $\hat{\lambda}_i$ of $A - \lambda B$ is the exact eigenvalue of a perturbed problem $(A + E) - \lambda(B + F)$. Let x_i be the unit eigenvector ($\|x_i\|_2 = 1$) for the exact eigenvalue λ_i. Then if $\|E\|$ is small compared to $\|A\|$, and if $\|F\|$ is small compared to $\|B\|$, we have

$$\chi(\hat{\lambda}_i, \lambda_i) \lesssim \frac{\|E\| + \|F\|}{\sqrt{(x_i^H A x_i)^2 + (x_i^H B x_i)^2}}.$$

Thus $1/\sqrt{(x_i^H A x_i)^2 + (x_i^H B x_i)^2}$ is a condition number for eigenvalue λ_i.

Other yet more refined algorithms and error bounds are discussed in [9, 44, 47], and will be available in future releases.

4.12   Error Bounds for Fast Level 3 BLAS

The Level 3 BLAS specifications [17] specify the input, output and call sequence for each routine, but allow freedom of implementation, subject to the requirement that the routines be numerically stable. Level 3 BLAS implementations can therefore be built using matrix multiplication algorithms that achieve a more favorable operation count (for suitable dimensions) than the standard multiplication technique, provided that these "fast" algorithms are numerically stable. The best known fast matrix multiplication technique is Strassen's method, which can multiply two n-by-n matrices in fewer than $4.7n^{\log_2 7}$ operations, where $\log_2 7 \approx 2.807$.

The effect on the results in this chapter of using a fast Level 3 BLAS implementation can be explained as follows. In general, reasonably implemented fast Level 3 BLAS preserve all the bounds presented here (except those at the end of subsection 4.11), but the constant $p(n)$ may increase somewhat. Also, the iterative refinement routine xyyRFS may take more steps to converge.

This is what we mean by reasonably implemented fast Level 3 BLAS. Here, c_i denotes a constant depending on the specified matrix dimensions.

(1) If A is m-by-n, B is n-by-p and $\widehat{C}$ is the computed approximation to $C = AB$, then

$$\|\widehat{C} - AB\|_\infty \leq c_1(m, n, p)\epsilon\|A\|_\infty\|B\|_\infty + O(\epsilon^2).$$

(2) The computed solution $\widehat{X}$ to the triangular systems $TX = B$, where T is m-by-m and B is m-by-p, satisfies

$$\|T\widehat{X} - B\|_\infty \leq c_2(m, p)\epsilon\|T\|_\infty\|\widehat{X}\|_\infty + O(\epsilon^2).$$

For conventional Level 3 BLAS implementations these conditions hold with $c_1(m, n, p) = n^2$ and $c_2(m, p) = m(m + 1)$. Strassen's method satisfies these bounds for slightly larger c_1 and c_2.

For further details, and references to fast multiplication techniques, see [12].

Chapter 5

Documentation and Software Conventions

5.1 Design and Documentation of Argument Lists

The argument lists of all LAPACK routines conform to a single set of conventions for their design and documentation.

Specifications of all LAPACK driver and computational routines are given in Part 2. These are derived from the specifications given in the leading comments in the code, but in Part 2 the specifications for real and complex versions of each routine have been merged, in order to save space.

5.1.1 Structure of the Documentation

The documentation of each LAPACK routine includes:

- the SUBROUTINE or FUNCTION statement, followed by statements declaring the type and dimensions of the arguments;

- a summary of the **Purpose** of the routine;

- descriptions of each of the **Arguments** in the order of the argument list;

- (optionally) **Further Details** (only in the code, not in Part 2);

- (optionally) **Internal Parameters** (only in the code, not in Part 2).

5.1.2 Order of Arguments

Arguments of an LAPACK routine appear in the following order:

- arguments specifying options;

- problem dimensions;

- array or scalar arguments defining the input data; some of them may be overwritten by results;

- other array or scalar arguments returning results;

- work arrays (and associated array dimensions);

- diagnostic argument INFO.

5.1.3   Argument Descriptions

The style of the argument descriptions is illustrated by the following example:

N　　　　　(input) INTEGER
　　　　　　The number of columns of the matrix A. $N \geq 0$.

A　　　　　(input/output) REAL array, dimension (LDA,N)
　　　　　　On entry, the m-by-n matrix to be factored.
　　　　　　On exit, the factors L and U from the factorization $A = P*L*U$; the unit diagonal elements of L are not stored.

The description of each argument gives:

- a classification of the argument as input, output, input/output or workspace;

- the type of the argument;

- (for an array) its dimension(s);

- a specification of the value(s) that must be supplied for the argument (if it's an input argument), or of the value(s) returned by the routine (if it's an output argument), or both (if it's an input/output argument). In the last case, the two parts of the description are introduced by the phrases "On entry" and "On exit".

- (for a scalar input argument) any constraints that the supplied values must satisfy (such as "$N \geq 0$" in the example above).

5.1.4   Option Arguments

Arguments specifying options are usually of type CHARACTER*1. The meaning of each valid value is given, as in this example:

UPLO　　(input) CHARACTER*1
　　　　　= 'U': Upper triangle of A is stored;
　　　　　= 'L': Lower triangle of A is stored.

The corresponding lower-case characters may be supplied (with the same meaning), but any other value is illegal (see subsection 5.1.8).

A longer character string can be passed as the actual argument, making the calling program more readable, but only the first character is significant; this is a standard feature of Fortran 77. For example:

```
CALL SPOTRS ('upper', . . . )
```

5.1.5 Problem Dimensions

It is permissible for the problem dimensions to be passed as zero, in which case the computation (or part of it) is skipped. Negative dimensions are regarded as erroneous.

5.1.6 Array Arguments

Each two-dimensional array argument is immediately followed in the argument list by its leading dimension, whose name has the form LD<array-name>. For example:

A	(input/output) REAL/COMPLEX array, dimension (LDA,N)
	. . .
LDA	(input) INTEGER
	The leading dimension of the array A. LDA $\geq$ max(1,M).

It should be assumed, unless stated otherwise, that vectors and matrices are stored in one- and two-dimensional arrays in the conventional manner. That is, if an array X of dimension (N) holds a vector x, then X(i) holds x_i for $i = 1, \ldots, n$. If a two-dimensional array A of dimension (LDA,N) holds an m-by-n matrix A, then A(i, j) holds a_{ij} for $i = 1, \ldots, m$ and $j = 1, \ldots, n$ (LDA must be at least m). See Section 5.3 for more about storage of matrices.

Note that array arguments are usually declared in the software as assumed-size arrays (last dimension *), for example:

```
REAL A( LDA, * )
```

although the documentation gives the dimensions as (LDA,N). The latter form is more informative since it specifies the required minimum value of the last dimension. However an assumed-size array declaration has been used in the software, in order to overcome some limitations in the Fortran 77 standard. In particular it allows the routine to be called when the relevant dimension (N, in this case) is zero. However actual array dimensions in the calling program must be at least 1 (LDA in this example).

5.1.7   Work Arrays

Many LAPACK routines require one or more work arrays to be passed as arguments. The name of a work array is usually WORK — sometimes IWORK, RWORK or BWORK to distinguish work arrays of integer, real or logical (Boolean) type.

A number of routines implementing block algorithms require workspace sufficient to hold one block of rows or columns of the matrix, for example, workspace of size n-by-nb, where nb is the block size. In such cases, the actual declared length of the work array must be passed as a separate argument LWORK, which immediately follows WORK in the argument-list.

See Section 5.2 for further explanation.

5.1.8   Error Handling and the Diagnostic Argument INFO

All documented routines have a diagnostic argument INFO that indicates the success or failure of the computation, as follows:

- INFO = 0: successful termination

- INFO < 0: illegal value of one or more arguments — no computation performed

- INFO > 0: failure in the course of computation

All driver and auxiliary routines check that input arguments such as N or LDA or option arguments of type character have permitted values. If an illegal value of the ith argument is detected, the routine sets INFO = $-i$, and then calls an error-handling routine XERBLA.

The standard version of XERBLA issues an error message and halts execution, so that no LAPACK routine would ever return to the calling program with INFO < 0. However, this might occur if a non-standard version of XERBLA is used.

5.2   Determining the Block Size for Block Algorithms

LAPACK routines that implement block algorithms need to determine what block size to use. The intention behind the design of LAPACK is that the choice of block size should be hidden from users as much as possible, but at the same time easily accessible to installers of the package when tuning LAPACK for a particular machine.

LAPACK routines call an auxiliary enquiry function ILAENV, which returns the optimal block size to be used, as well as other parameters. The version of ILAENV supplied with the package contains default values that led to good behavior over a reasonable number of our test machines, but to achieve optimal performance, it may be beneficial to tune ILAENV for your particular machine environment. Ideally a distinct implementation of ILAENV is needed for each machine environment (see also Chapter 6). The optimal block size may also depend on the routine, the combination of option arguments (if any), and the problem dimensions.

If ILAENV returns a block size of 1, then the routine performs the unblocked algorithm, calling Level 2 BLAS, and makes no calls to Level 3 BLAS.

Some LAPACK routines require a work array whose size is proportional to the block size (see subsection 5.1.7). The actual length of the work array is supplied as an argument LWORK. The description of the arguments WORK and LWORK typically goes as follows:

> WORK (workspace) REAL array, dimension (LWORK)
> On exit, if INFO = 0, then WORK(1) returns the optimal LWORK.
>
> LWORK (input) INTEGER
> The dimension of the array WORK. LWORK $\geq$ max(1,N).
> For optimal performance LWORK $\geq$ N*NB, where NB is the optimal block size returned by ILAENV.

The routine determines the block size to be used by the following steps:

1. the optimal block size is determined by calling ILAENV;

2. if the value of LWORK indicates that enough workspace has been supplied, the routine uses the optimal block size;

3. otherwise, the routine determines the largest block size that can be used with the supplied amount of workspace;

4. if this new block size does not fall below a threshold value (also returned by ILAENV), the routine uses the new value;

5. otherwise, the routine uses the unblocked algorithm.

The minimum value of LWORK that would be needed to use the optimal block size, is returned in WORK(1).

Thus, the routine uses the largest block size allowed by the amount of workspace supplied, as long as this is likely to give better performance than the unblocked algorithm. WORK(1) is not always a simple formula in terms of N and NB.

The specification of LWORK gives the minimum value for the routine to return correct results. If the supplied value is less than the minimum — indicating that there is insufficient workspace to perform the unblocked algorithm — the value of LWORK is regarded as an illegal value, and is treated like any other illegal argument value (see subsection 5.1.8).

If in doubt about how much workspace to supply, users should supply a generous amount (assume a block size of 64, say), and then examine the value of WORK(1) on exit.

5.3 Matrix Storage Schemes

LAPACK allows the following different storage schemes for matrices:

- conventional storage in a two-dimensional array;

- packed storage for symmetric, Hermitian or triangular matrices;

- band storage for band matrices;

- the use of two or three one-dimensional arrays to store tridiagonal or bidiagonal matrices.

These storage schemes are compatible with those used in LINPACK and the BLAS, but EISPACK uses incompatible schemes for band and tridiagonal matrices.

In the examples below, ∗ indicates an array element that need not be set and is not referenced by LAPACK routines. Elements that "need not be set" are never read, written to, or otherwise accessed by the LAPACK routines. The examples illustrate only the relevant part of the arrays; array arguments may of course have additional rows or columns, according to the usual rules for passing array arguments in Fortran 77.

5.3.1 Conventional Storage

The default scheme for storing matrices is the obvious one described in subsection 5.1.6: a matrix A is stored in a two-dimensional array A, with matrix element a_{ij} stored in array element $\mathrm{A}(i,j)$.

If a matrix is **triangular** (upper or lower, as specified by the argument UPLO), only the elements of the relevant triangle are accessed. The remaining elements of the array need not be set. Such elements are indicated by ∗ in the examples below. For example, when $n = 4$:

UPLO	Triangular matrix A				Storage in array A			
'U'	a_{11}	a_{12}	a_{13}	a_{14}	a_{11}	a_{12}	a_{13}	a_{14}
		a_{22}	a_{23}	a_{24}	∗	a_{22}	a_{23}	a_{24}
			a_{33}	a_{34}	∗	∗	a_{33}	a_{34}
				a_{44}	∗	∗	∗	a_{44}
'L'	a_{11}				a_{11}	∗	∗	∗
	a_{21}	a_{22}			a_{21}	a_{22}	∗	∗
	a_{31}	a_{32}	a_{33}		a_{31}	a_{32}	a_{33}	∗
	a_{41}	a_{42}	a_{43}	a_{44}	a_{41}	a_{42}	a_{43}	a_{44}

Similarly, if the matrix is upper Hessenberg, elements below the first subdiagonal need not be set.

Routines that handle **symmetric** or **Hermitian** matrices allow for either the upper or lower triangle of the matrix (as specified by UPLO) to be stored in the corresponding elements of the array; the remaining elements of the array need not be set. For example, when $n = 4$:

UPLO	Hermitian matrix A				Storage in array A			
'U'	a_{11}	a_{12}	a_{13}	a_{14}	a_{11}	a_{12}	a_{13}	a_{14}
	$\bar{a}_{12}$	a_{22}	a_{23}	a_{24}	$*$	a_{22}	a_{23}	a_{24}
	$\bar{a}_{13}$	$\bar{a}_{23}$	a_{33}	a_{34}	$*$	$*$	a_{33}	a_{34}
	$\bar{a}_{14}$	$\bar{a}_{24}$	$\bar{a}_{34}$	a_{44}	$*$	$*$	$*$	a_{44}
'L'	a_{11}	$\bar{a}_{21}$	$\bar{a}_{31}$	$\bar{a}_{41}$	a_{11}	$*$	$*$	$*$
	a_{21}	a_{22}	$\bar{a}_{32}$	$\bar{a}_{42}$	a_{21}	a_{22}	$*$	$*$
	a_{31}	a_{32}	a_{33}	$\bar{a}_{43}$	a_{31}	a_{32}	a_{33}	$*$
	a_{41}	a_{42}	a_{43}	a_{44}	a_{41}	a_{42}	a_{43}	a_{44}

5.3.2 Packed Storage

Symmetric, Hermitian or triangular matrices may be stored more compactly, if the relevant triangle (again as specified by UPLO) is packed **by columns** in a one-dimensional array. In LAPACK, arrays that hold matrices in packed storage, have names ending in 'P'. So:

- if UPLO = 'U', a_{ij} is stored in $AP(i + j(j-1)/2)$ for $i \leq j$;

- if UPLO = 'L', a_{ij} is stored in $AP(i + (2n - j)(j-1)/2)$ for $j \leq i$.

For example:

UPLO	Triangular matrix A				Packed storage in array AP
'U'	a_{11}	a_{12}	a_{13}	a_{14}	$a_{11}\ \underbrace{a_{12}\ a_{22}}\ \underbrace{a_{13}\ a_{23}\ a_{33}}\ \underbrace{a_{14}\ a_{24}\ a_{34}\ a_{44}}$
		a_{22}	a_{23}	a_{24}	
			a_{33}	a_{34}	
				a_{44}	
'L'	a_{11}				$\underbrace{a_{11}\ a_{21}\ a_{31}\ a_{41}}\ \underbrace{a_{22}\ a_{32}\ a_{42}}\ \underbrace{a_{33}\ a_{43}}\ a_{44}$
	a_{21}	a_{22}			
	a_{31}	a_{32}	a_{33}		
	a_{41}	a_{42}	a_{43}	a_{44}	

Note that for real or complex symmetric matrices, packing the upper triangle by columns is equivalent to packing the lower triangle by rows; packing the lower triangle by columns is equivalent to packing the upper triangle by rows. For complex Hermitian matrices, packing the upper triangle by columns is equivalent to packing the conjugate of the lower triangle by rows; packing the lower triangle by columns is equivalent to packing the conjugate of the upper triangle by rows.

5.3.3 Band Storage

A band matrix with kl subdiagonals and ku superdiagonals may be stored compactly in a two-dimensional array with $kl + ku + 1$ rows and n columns. Columns of the matrix are stored in corresponding columns of the array, and diagonals of the matrix are stored in rows of the array.

This storage scheme should be used in practice only if $kl, ku \ll n$, although LAPACK routines work correctly for all values of kl and ku. In LAPACK, arrays that hold matrices in band storage have names ending in 'B'.

To be precise, a_{ij} is stored in $AB(ku + 1 + i - j, j)$ for $\max(1, j - ku) \leq i \leq \min(n, j + kl)$. For example, when $n = 5$, $kl = 2$ and $ku = 1$:

Band matrix A	Band storage in array AB
$\begin{pmatrix} a_{11} & a_{12} & & & \\ a_{21} & a_{22} & a_{23} & & \\ a_{31} & a_{32} & a_{33} & a_{34} & \\ & a_{42} & a_{43} & a_{44} & a_{45} \\ & & a_{53} & a_{54} & a_{55} \end{pmatrix}$	$\begin{array}{ccccc} * & a_{12} & a_{23} & a_{34} & a_{45} \\ a_{11} & a_{22} & a_{33} & a_{44} & a_{55} \\ a_{21} & a_{32} & a_{43} & a_{54} & * \\ a_{31} & a_{42} & a_{53} & * & * \end{array}$

The elements marked $*$ in the upper left and lower right corners of the array AB need not be set, and are not referenced by LAPACK routines.

Note: when a band matrix is supplied for LU factorization, space must be allowed to store an additional kl superdiagonals, generated by fill-in as a result of row interchanges. This means that the matrix is stored according to the above scheme, but with $kl + ku$ superdiagonals.

Triangular band matrices are stored in the same format, with either $kl = 0$ if upper triangular, or $ku = 0$ if lower triangular.

For symmetric or Hermitian band matrices with kd subdiagonals or superdiagonals, only the upper or lower triangle (as specified by UPLO) need be stored:

- if UPLO = 'U', a_{ij} is stored in $AB(kd + 1 + i - j, j)$ for $\max(1, j - kd) \leq i \leq j$;

- if UPLO = 'L', a_{ij} is stored in $AB(1 + i - j, j)$ for $j \leq i \leq \min(n, j + kd)$.

For example, when $n = 5$ and $kd = 2$:

UPLO	Hermitian band matrix A	Band storage in array AB
'U'	$\begin{pmatrix} a_{11} & a_{12} & a_{13} & & \\ \bar{a}_{12} & a_{22} & a_{23} & a_{24} & \\ \bar{a}_{13} & \bar{a}_{23} & a_{33} & a_{34} & a_{35} \\ & \bar{a}_{24} & \bar{a}_{34} & a_{44} & a_{45} \\ & & \bar{a}_{35} & \bar{a}_{45} & a_{55} \end{pmatrix}$	$\begin{array}{ccccc} * & * & a_{13} & a_{24} & a_{35} \\ * & a_{12} & a_{23} & a_{34} & a_{45} \\ a_{11} & a_{22} & a_{33} & a_{44} & a_{55} \end{array}$
'L'	$\begin{pmatrix} a_{11} & \bar{a}_{21} & \bar{a}_{31} & & \\ a_{21} & a_{22} & \bar{a}_{32} & \bar{a}_{42} & \\ a_{31} & a_{32} & a_{33} & \bar{a}_{43} & \bar{a}_{53} \\ & a_{42} & a_{43} & a_{44} & \bar{a}_{54} \\ & & a_{53} & a_{54} & a_{55} \end{pmatrix}$	$\begin{array}{ccccc} a_{11} & a_{22} & a_{33} & a_{44} & a_{55} \\ a_{21} & a_{32} & a_{43} & a_{54} & * \\ a_{31} & a_{42} & a_{53} & * & * \end{array}$

EISPACK routines use a different storage scheme for band matrices, in which rows of the matrix are stored in corresponding rows of the array, and diagonals of the matrix are stored in columns of the array (see Appendix D).

5.3.4 Tridiagonal and Bidiagonal Matrices

An unsymmetric tridiagonal matrix of order n is stored in three one-dimensional arrays, one of length n containing the diagonal elements, and two of length $n-1$ containing the subdiagonal and superdiagonal elements in elements $1 : n - 1$.

A symmetric tridiagonal or bidiagonal matrix is stored in two one-dimensional arrays, one of length n containing the diagonal elements, and one of length $n-1$ containing the off-diagonal elements. (EISPACK routines store the off-diagonal elements in elements $2 : n$ of a vector of length n.)

5.3.5 Unit Triangular Matrices

Some LAPACK routines have an option to handle unit triangular matrices (that is, triangular matrices with diagonal elements = 1). This option is specified by an argument DIAG. If DIAG = 'U' (Unit triangular), the diagonal elements of the matrix need not be stored, and the corresponding array elements are not referenced by the LAPACK routines. The storage scheme for the rest of the matrix (whether conventional, packed or band) remains unchanged, as described in subsections 5.3.1, 5.3.2 and 5.3.3.

5.3.6 Real Diagonal Elements of Complex Matrices

Complex Hermitian matrices have diagonal matrices that are by definition purely real. In addition, some complex triangular matrices computed by LAPACK routines are defined by the algorithm to have real diagonal elements — in Cholesky or QR factorization, for example.

If such matrices are supplied as input to LAPACK routines, the imaginary parts of the diagonal elements are not referenced, but are assumed to be zero. If such matrices are returned as output by LAPACK routines, the computed imaginary parts are explicitly set to zero.

5.4 Representation of Orthogonal or Unitary Matrices

A real orthogonal or complex unitary matrix (usually denoted Q) is often represented in LAPACK as a product of **elementary reflectors** — also referred to as **elementary Householder matrices** (usually denoted H_i). For example,

$$Q = H_1 H_2 \ldots H_k.$$

Most users need not be aware of the details, because LAPACK routines are provided to work with this representation:

- routines whose names begin SORG- (real) or CUNG- (complex) can generate all or part of Q explicitly;

- routines whose name begin SORM- (real) or CUNM- (complex) can multiply a given matrix by Q or Q^H without forming Q explicitly.

The following further details may occasionally be useful.

An elementary reflector (or elementary Householder matrix) H of order n is a unitary matrix of the form

$$H = I - \tau v v^H \tag{5.1}$$

where τ is a scalar, and v is an n-vector, with $|\tau|^2 \|v\|_2^2 = 2\text{Re}(\tau)$; v is often referred to as the **Householder vector** . Often v has several leading or trailing zero elements, but for the purpose of this discussion assume that H has no such special structure.

There is some redundancy in the representation (5.1), which can be removed in various ways. The representation used in LAPACK (which differs from those used in LINPACK or EISPACK) sets $v_1 = 1$; hence v_1 need not be stored. In real arithmetic, $1 \leq \tau \leq 2$, except that $\tau = 0$ implies $H = I$.

In complex arithmetic, τ may be complex, and satisfies $1 \leq \text{Re}(\tau) \leq 2$ and $|\tau - 1| \leq 1$. Thus a complex H is not Hermitian (as it is in other representations), but it is unitary, which is the important property. The advantage of allowing τ to be complex is that, given an arbitrary complex vector x, H can be computed so that

$$Hx = \beta(1, 0, \ldots, 0)^T$$

with *real* β. This is useful, for example, when reducing a complex Hermitian matrix to real symmetric tridiagonal form, or a complex rectangular matrix to real bidiagonal form.

Chapter 6

Installing LAPACK Routines

6.1 Points to Note

For anyone who obtains the complete LAPACK package from NAG (see Chapter 1), a comprehensive installation guide is provided. We recommend installation of the complete package as the most convenient and reliable way to make LAPACK available.

People who obtain copies of a few LAPACK routines from *netlib* need to be aware of the following points:

1. Double precision complex routines (names beginning Z-) use a COMPLEX*16 data type. This is an extension to the Fortran 77 standard, but is provided by many Fortran compilers on machines where double precision computation is usual. The following related extensions are also used:

   - the intrinsic function DCONJG, with argument and result of type COMPLEX*16;
   - the intrinsic functions DBLE and DIMAG, with COMPLEX*16 argument and DOUBLE PRECISION result, returning the real and imaginary parts, respectively;
   - the intrinsic function DCMPLX, with DOUBLE PRECISION argument(s) and COMPLEX*16 result;
   - COMPLEX*16 constants, formed from a pair of double precision constants in parentheses.

   Some compilers provide DOUBLE COMPLEX as an alternative to COMPLEX*16, and an intrinsic function DREAL instead of DBLE to return the real part of a COMPLEX*16 argument. If the compiler does not accept the constructs used in LAPACK, the installer will have to modify the code: for example, globally change COMPLEX*16 to DOUBLE COMPLEX, or selectively change DBLE to DREAL.[1]

---

[1] Changing DBLE to DREAL must be selective, because instances of DBLE with an *integer* argument must *not* be changed. The compiler should flag any instances of DBLE with a COMPLEX*16 argument if it does not accept them.

2. For optimal performance, a small set of tuning parameters must be set for each machine, or even for each configuration of a given machine (for example, different parameters may be optimal for different numbers of processors). These values, such as the block size, minimum block size, crossover point below which an unblocked routine should be used, and others, are set by calls to an inquiry function ILAENV. The default version of ILAENV provided with LAPACK uses generic values which often give satisfactory performance, but users who are particularly interested in performance may wish to modify this subprogram or substitute their own version. Further details on setting ILAENV for a particular environment are provided in section 6.2.

3. SLAMCH/DLAMCH determines properties of the floating-point arithmetic at run-time, such as the machine epsilon, underflow threshold, overflow threshold, and related parameters. It works satisfactorily on all commercially important machines of which we are aware, but will necessarily be updated from time to time as new machines and compilers are produced.

6.2   Installing ILAENV

Machine-dependent parameters such as the block size are set by calls to an inquiry function which may be set with different values on each machine. The declaration of the environment inquiry function is

```
INTEGER FUNCTION ILAENV( ISPEC, NAME, OPTS, N1, N2, N3, N4 )
```

where ISPEC, N1, N2, N3, and N4 are integer variables and NAME and OPTS are CHARACTER*(*). NAME specifies the subroutine name: OPTS is a character string of options to the subroutine; and N1–N4 are the problem dimensions. ISPEC specifies the parameter to be returned; the following values are currently used in LAPACK:

ISPEC = 1:   NB, optimal block size
 = 2:   NBMIN, minimum block size for the block routine to be used
 = 3:   NX, crossover point (in a block routine, for $N < NX$, an unblocked routine should be used)
 = 4:   NS, number of shifts
 = 6:   NXSVD is the threshold point for which the QR factorization is performed prior to reduction to bidiagonal form. If $M > NXSVD \cdot N$, then a QR factorization is performed.
 = 8:   MAXB, crossover point for block multishift QR

The three block size parameters, NB, NBMIN, and NX, are used in many different subroutines (see Table 6.1). NS and MAXB are used in the block multishift QR algorithm, xHSEQR. NXSVD is used in the driver routines xGELSS and xGESVD.

The LAPACK testing and timing programs use a special version of ILAENV where the parameters are set via a COMMON block interface. This is convenient for experimenting with different values

real	complex	NB	NBMIN	NX
SGBTRF	CGBTRF	•		
SGEBRD	CGEBRD	•	•	•
SGEHRD	CGEHRD	•	•	•
SGELQF	CGELQF	•	•	•
SGEQLF	CGEQLF	•	•	•
SGEQRF	CGEQRF	•	•	•
SGERQF	CGERQF	•	•	•
SGETRF	CGETRF	•		
SGETRI	CGETRI	•	•	
SORGLQ	CUNGLQ	•	•	•
SORGQL	CUNGQL	•	•	•
SORGQR	CUNGQR	•	•	•
SORGRQ	CUNGRQ	•	•	•
SORMLQ	CUNMLQ	•	•	
SORMQL	CUNMQL	•	•	
SORMQR	CUNMQR	•	•	
SORMRQ	CUNMRQ	•	•	
SPBTRF	CPBTRF	•		
SPOTRF	CPOTRF	•		
SPOTRI	CPOTRI	•		
SSTEBZ		•		
SSYGST	CHEGST	•		
SSYTRD	CHETRD	•	•	•
SSYTRF	CHETRF	•	•	
	CSYTRF	•	•	
STRTRI	CTRTRI	•		

Table 6.1: Use of the block parameters NB, NBMIN, and NX in LAPACK

of, say, the block size in order to exercise different parts of the code and to compare the relative performance of different parameter values.

The LAPACK timing programs were designed to collect data for all the routines in Table 6.1. The range of problem sizes needed to determine the optimal block size or crossover point is machine-dependent, but the input files provided with the LAPACK test and timing package can be used as a starting point. For subroutines that require a crossover point, it is best to start by finding the best block size with the crossover point set to 0, and then to locate the point at which the performance of the unblocked algorithm is beaten by the block algorithm. The best crossover point will be somewhat smaller than the point where the curves for the unblocked and blocked methods cross.

For example, for SGEQRF on a single processor of a CRAY-2, NB = 32 was observed to be a good block size, and the performance of the block algorithm with this block size surpasses the unblocked algorithm for square matrices between $N = 176$ and $N = 192$. Experiments with crossover points from 64 to 192 found that NX = 128 was a good choice, although the results for NX from 3*NB

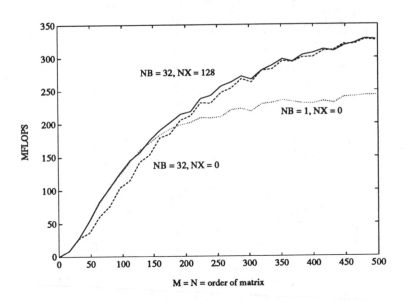

Figure 6.1: QR factorization on CRAY-2 (1 processor)

to 5*NB are broadly similar. This means that matrices with $N \leq 128$ should use the unblocked algorithm, and for $N > 128$ block updates should be used until the remaining submatrix has order less than 128. The performance of the unblocked (NB = 1) and blocked (NB = 32) algorithms for SGEQRF and for the blocked algorithm with a crossover point of 128 are compared in Figure 6.1.

By experimenting with small values of the block size, it should be straightforward to choose NBMIN, the smallest block size that gives a performance improvement over the unblocked algorithm. Note that on some machines, the optimal block size may be 1 (the unblocked algorithm gives the best performance); in this case, the choice of NBMIN is arbitrary. The prototype version of ILAENV sets NBMIN to 2, so that blocking is always done, even though this could lead to poor performance from a block routine if insufficient workspace is supplied (see chapter 7).

Complicating the determination of optimal parameters is the fact that the orthogonal factorization routines and SGEBRD accept non-square matrices as input. The LAPACK timing program allows M and N to be varied independently. We have found the optimal block size to be generally insensitive to the shape of the matrix, but the crossover point is more dependent on the matrix shape. For example, if $M \gg N$ in the QR factorization, block updates may always be faster than unblocked updates on the remaining submatrix, so one might set NX = NB if $M \geq 2N$.

Parameter values for the number of shifts, etc. used to tune the block multishift QR algorithm can be varied from the input files to the eigenvalue timing program. In particular, the performance of xHSEQR is particularly sensitive to the correct choice of block parameters. Setting NS = 2 will give essentially the same performance as EISPACK. Interested users should consult [3] for a description of the timing program input files.

Chapter 7

Troubleshooting

7.1 Common Errors in Calling LAPACK Routines

For the benefit of less experienced programmers, we give here a list of common programming errors in calling an LAPACK routine. These errors may cause the LAPACK routine to report a failure, as described in Section 7.2; they may cause an error to be reported by the system; or they may lead to wrong results — see also Section 7.3.

- wrong number of arguments

- arguments in the wrong order

- an argument of the wrong type (especially real and complex arguments of the wrong precision)

- wrong dimensions for an array argument

- insufficient space in a workspace argument

- failure to assign a value to an input argument

Some modern compilation systems, as well as software tools such as the portability checker in Toolpack [40], can check that arguments agree in number and type; and many compilation systems offer run-time detection of errors such as an array element out-of-bounds or use of an unassigned variable.

7.2 Failures Detected by LAPACK Routines

There are two ways in which an LAPACK routine may report a failure to complete a computation successfully.

7.2.1   Invalid Arguments and XERBLA

If an illegal value is supplied for one of the input arguments to an LAPACK routine, it will call the error handler XERBLA to write a message to the standard output unit of the form:

```
** On entry to SGESV  parameter number  4 had an illegal value
```

This particular message would be caused by passing to SGESV a value of LDA which was less than the value of the argument N. The documentation for SGESV in Part 2 states the set of acceptable input values: "LDA $\geq$ max(1,N)." This is required in order that the array A with leading dimension LDA can store an n-by-n matrix.[1] The arguments are checked in order, beginning with the first. In the above example, it may — from the user's point of view — be the value of N which is in fact wrong. Invalid arguments are often caused by the kind of error listed in Section 7.1.

In the model implementation of XERBLA which is supplied with LAPACK, execution stops after the message; but the call to XERBLA is followed by a RETURN statement in the LAPACK routine, so that if the installer removes the STOP statement in XERBLA, the result will be an immediate exit from the LAPACK routine with a negative value of INFO. It is good practice always to check for a non-zero value of INFO on return from an LAPACK routine. (We recommend however that XERBLA should not be modified to return control to the calling routine, unless absolutely necessary, since this would remove one of the built-in safety-features of LAPACK.)

7.2.2   Computational Failures and INFO > 0

A positive value of INFO on return from an LAPACK routine indicates a failure in the course of the algorithm. Common causes are:

- a matrix is singular (to working precision);

- a symmetric matrix is not positive definite;

- an iterative algorithm for computing eigenvalues or eigenvectors fails to converge in the permitted number of iterations.

For example, if SGESVX is called to solve a system of equations with a coefficient matrix that is approximately singular, it may detect exact singularity at the ith stage of the LU factorization, in which case it returns INFO $= i$; or (more probably) it may compute an estimate of the reciprocal condition number that is less than machine precision, in which case it returns INFO $= n+1$. Again, the documentation in Part 2 should be consulted for a description of the error.

When a failure with INFO > 0 occurs, control is *always* returned to the calling program; XERBLA is *not* called, and no error message is written. It is worth repeating that it is good practice always to check for a non-zero value of INFO on return from an LAPACK routine.

---

[1]The requirement is stated "LDA $\geq$ max(1,N)" rather than simply "LDA $\geq$ N" because LDA must always be at least 1, even if N = 0, to satisfy the requirements of standard Fortran; on some systems, a zero or negative value of LDA would cause a run-time fault.

A failure with INFO > 0 may indicate any of the following:

- an inappropriate routine was used: for example, if a routine fails because a symmetric matrix turns out not to be positive definite, consider using a routine for symmetric indefinite matrices.

- a single precision routine was used when double precision was needed: for example, if SGESVX reports approximate singularity (as illustrated above), the corresponding double precision routine DGESVX may be able to solve the problem (but nevertheless the problem is ill-conditioned).

- a programming error occurred in generating the data supplied to a routine: for example, even though theoretically a matrix should be well-conditioned and positive-definite, a programming error in generating the matrix could easily destroy either of those properties.

- a programming error occurred in calling the routine, of the kind listed in Section 7.1.

7.3 Wrong Results

Wrong results from LAPACK routines are most often caused by incorrect usage.

It is also possible that wrong results are caused by a bug outside of LAPACK, in the compiler or in one of the library routines, such as the BLAS, that are linked with LAPACK. Test procedures are available for both LAPACK and the BLAS, and the LAPACK installation guide [3] should be consulted for descriptions of the tests and for advice on resolving problems.

A list of known problems, compiler errors, and bugs in LAPACK routines is maintained on *netlib*; see Chapter 1.

Users who suspect they have found a new bug in an LAPACK routine are encouraged to report it promptly to the developers as directed in Chapter 1. The bug report should include a test case, a description of the problem and expected results, and the actions, if any, that the user has already taken to fix the bug.

7.4 Poor Performance

We have tried to make the performance of LAPACK "transportable" by performing most of the computation within the Level 1, 2, and 3 BLAS, and by isolating all of the machine-dependent tuning parameters in a single integer function ILAENV. To avoid poor performance from LAPACK routines, note the following recommendations:

BLAS: One should use BLAS that have been optimized for the machine being used if they are available. Many manufacturers and research institutions have developed, or are developing, efficient versions of the BLAS for particular machines. A portable set of Fortran BLAS is supplied with LAPACK and can always be used if no other BLAS are available or if there is a suspected problem in the local BLAS library, but no attempt has been made to structure the Fortran BLAS for high performance.

ILAENV: For best performance, the LAPACK routine ILAENV should be set with optimal tuning parameters for the machine being used. The version of ILAENV provided with LAPACK supplies default values for these parameters that give good, but not optimal, average case performance on a range of existing machines. In particular, the performance of xHSEQR is particularly sensitive to the correct choice of block parameters; the same applies to the driver routines which call xHSEQR, namely xGEES, xGEESX, xGEEV and xGEEVX. Further details on setting parameters in ILAENV are found in section 6.

LWORK ≥ WORK(1): The performance of some routines depends on the amount of workspace supplied. In such cases, an argument, usually called WORK, is provided, accompanied by an integer argument LWORK specifying its length as a linear array. On exit, WORK(1) returns the amount of workspace required to use the optimal tuning parameters. If LWORK < WORK(1), then insufficient workspace was provided to use the optimal parameters, and the performance may be less than possible. One should check that LWORK ≥ WORK(1) on return from an LAPACK routine requiring user-supplied workspace to see if enough workspace has been provided. Note that the computation is performed correctly, even if the amount of workspace is less than optimal, unless LWORK is reported as an invalid value by a call to XERBLA as described in Section 7.2.

xLAMCH: Users should beware of the high cost of the *first* call to the LAPACK auxiliary routine xLAMCH, which computes machine characteristics such as epsilon and the smallest invertible number. The first call dynamically determines a set of parameters defining the machine's arithmetic, but these values are saved and subsequent calls incur only a trivial cost. For performance testing, the initial cost can be hidden by including a call to xLAMCH in the main program, before any calls to LAPACK routines that will be timed. A sample use of SLAMCH is

```
XXXXXX = SLAMCH( 'P' )
```

or in double precision:

```
XXXXXX = DLAMCH( 'P' )
```

A cleaner but less portable solution is for the installer to save the values computed by xLAMCH for a specific machine and create a new version of xLAMCH with these constants set in DATA statements, taking care that no accuracy is lost in the translation.

Appendix A

Index of Driver and Computational Routines

Notes

1. This index lists related pairs of real and complex routines together, for example, SBDSQR and CBDSQR.

2. Driver routines are listed in bold type, for example **SGBSV** and **CGBSV**.

3. Routines are listed in alphanumeric order of the real (single precision) routine name (which always begins with S-). (See subsection 2.1.3 for details of the LAPACK naming scheme.)

4. Double precision routines are not listed here; they have names beginning with D- instead of S-, or Z- instead of C-.

5. This index gives only a brief description of the purpose of each routine. For a precise description, consult the specifications in Part 2, where the routines appear in the same order as here.

6. The text of the descriptions applies to both real and complex routines, except where alternative words or phrases are indicated, for example "symmetric/Hermitian", "orthogonal/unitary" or "quasi-triangular/triangular". For the real routines A^H is equivalent to A^T. (The same convention is used in Part 2.)

7. In a few cases, three routines are listed together, one for real symmetric, one for complex symmetric, and one for complex Hermitian matrices (for example SSPCON, CSPCON and CHPCON).

8. A few routines for real matrices have no complex equivalent (for example SSTEBZ).

Routine		Description
real	complex	
SBDSQR	CBDSQR	Computes the singular value decomposition (SVD) of a real bidiagonal matrix, using the bidiagonal QR algorithm.
SGBCON	CGBCON	Estimates the reciprocal of the condition number of a general band matrix, in either the 1-norm or the infinity-norm, using the LU factorization computed by SGBTRF/CGBTRF.
SGBEQU	CGBEQU	Computes row and column scalings to equilibrate a general band matrix and reduce its condition number.
SGBRFS	CGBRFS	Improves the computed solution to a general banded system of linear equations $AX = B$, $A^T X = B$ or $A^H X = B$, and provides forward and backward error bounds for the solution.
SGBSV	**CGBSV**	Solves a general banded system of linear equations $AX = B$.
SGBSVX	**CGBSVX**	Solves a general banded system of linear equations $AX = B$, $A^T X = B$ or $A^H X = B$, and provides an estimate of the condition number and error bounds on the solution.
SGBTRF	CGBTRF	Computes an LU factorization of a general band matrix, using partial pivoting with row interchanges.
SGBTRS	CGBTRS	Solves a general banded system of linear equations $AX = B$, $A^T X = B$ or $A^H X = B$, using the LU factorization computed by SGBTRF/CGBTRF.
SGEBAK	CGEBAK	Transforms eigenvectors of a balanced matrix to those of the original matrix supplied to SGEBAL/CGEBAL.
SGEBAL	CGEBAL	Balances a general matrix in order to improve the accuracy of computed eigenvalues.
SGEBRD	CGEBRD	Reduces a general rectangular matrix to real bidiagonal form by an orthogonal/unitary transformation.
SGECON	CGECON	Estimates the reciprocal of the condition number of a general matrix, in either the 1-norm or the infinity-norm, using the LU factorization computed by SGETRF/CGETRF.
SGEEQU	CGEEQU	Computes row and column scalings to equilibrate a general rectangular matrix and reduce its condition number.
SGEES	**CGEES**	Computes the eigenvalues and Schur factorization of a general matrix, and orders the factorization so that selected eigenvalues are at the top left of the Schur form.
SGEESX	**CGEESX**	Computes the eigenvalues and Schur factorization of a general matrix, orders the factorization so that selected eigenvalues are at the top left of the Schur form, and computes reciprocal condition numbers for the average of the selected eigenvalues, and for the associated right invariant subspace.
SGEEV	**CGEEV**	Computes the eigenvalues and left and right eigenvectors of a general matrix.
SGEEVX	**CGEEVX**	Computes the eigenvalues and left and right eigenvectors of a general matrix, with preliminary balancing of the matrix, and computes reciprocal condition numbers for the eigenvalues and right eigenvectors.

Routine		Description
real	complex	
SGEHRD	CGEHRD	Reduces a general matrix to upper Hessenberg form by an orthogonal/unitary similarity transformation.
SGELQF	CGELQF	Computes an LQ factorization of a general rectangular matrix.
SGELS	**CGELS**	Computes the least squares solution to an overdetermined system of linear equations, $AX = B$ or $A^H X = B$, or the minimum norm solution of an underdetermined system, where A is a general rectangular matrix of full rank, using a QR or LQ factorization of A.
SGELSS	**CGELSS**	Computes the inimum norm least squares solution to an over- or underdetermined system of linear equations $AX = B$, using the singular value decomposition of A.
SGELSX	**CGELSX**	Computes the minimum norm least squares solution to an over- or underdetermined system of linear equations $AX = B$, using a complete orthogonal factorization of A.
SGEQLF	CGEQLF	Computes a QL factorization of a general rectangular matrix.
SGEQPF	CGEQPF	Computes a QR factorization with column pivoting of a general rectangular matrix.
SGEQRF	CGEQRF	Computes a QR factorization of a general rectangular matrix.
SGERFS	CGERFS	Improves the computed solution to a general system of linear equations $AX = B$, $A^T X = B$ or $A^H X = B$, and provides forward and backward error bounds for the solution.
SGERQF	CGERQF	Computes an RQ factorization of a general rectangular matrix.
SGESV	**CGESV**	Solves a general system of linear equations $AX = B$.
SGESVD	**CGESVD**	Computes the singular value decomposition (SVD) of a general rectangular matrix.
SGESVX	**CGESVX**	Solves a general system of linear equations $AX = B$, $A^T X = B$ or $A^H X = B$, and provides an estimate of the condition number and error bounds on the solution.
SGETRF	CGETRF	Computes an LU factorization of a general matrix, using partial pivoting with row interchanges.
SGETRI	CGETRI	Computes the inverse of a general matrix, using the LU factorization computed by SGETRF/CGETRF.
SGETRS	CGETRS	Solves a general system of linear equations $AX = B$, $A^T X = B$ or $A^H X = B$, using the LU factorization computed by SGETRF/CGETRF.
SGTCON	CGTCON	Estimates the reciprocal of the condition number of a general tridiagonal matrix, in either the 1-norm or the infinity-norm, using the LU factorization computed by SGTTRF/CGTTRF.
SGTRFS	CGTRFS	Improves the computed solution to a general tridiagonal system of linear equations $AX = B$, $A^T X = B$ or $A^H X = B$, and provides forward and backward error bounds for the solution.
SGTSV	**CGTSV**	Solves a general tridiagonal system of linear equations $AX = B$.

Routine		Description
real	complex	
SGTSVX	**CGTSVX**	Solves a general tridiagonal system of linear equations $AX = B$, $A^T X = B$ or $A^H X = B$, and provides an estimate of the condition number and error bounds on the solution.
SGTTRF	CGTTRF	Computes an LU factorization of a general tridiagonal matrix, using partial pivoting with row interchanges.
SGTTRS	CGTTRS	Solves a general tridiagonal system of linear equations $AX = B$, $A^T X = B$ or $A^H X = B$, using the LU factorization computed by SGTTRF/CGTTRF.
SHSEIN	CHSEIN	Computes specified right and/or left eigenvectors of an upper Hessenberg matrix by inverse iteration.
SHSEQR	CHSEQR	Computes the eigenvalues and Schur factorization of an upper Hessenberg matrix, using the multishift QR algorithm.
SOPGTR	CUPGTR	Generates the orthogonal/unitary transformation matrix from a reduction to tridiagonal form determined by SSPTRD/CHPTRD.
SOPMTR	CUPMTR	Multiplies a general matrix by the orthogonal/unitary transformation matrix from a reduction to tridiagonal form determined by SSPTRD/CHPTRD.
SORGBR	CUNGBR	Generates the orthogonal/unitary transformation matrices from a reduction to bidiagonal form determined by SGEBRD/CGEBRD.
SORGHR	CUNGHR	Generates the orthogonal/unitary transformation matrix from a reduction to Hessenberg form determined by SGEHRD/CGEHRD.
SORGLQ	CUNGLQ	Generates all or part of the orthogonal/unitary matrix Q from an LQ factorization determined by SGELQF/CGELQF.
SORGQL	CUNGQL	Generates all or part of the orthogonal/unitary matrix Q from a QL factorization determined by SGEQLF/CGEQLF.
SORGQR	CUNGQR	Generates all or part of the orthogonal/unitary matrix Q from a QR factorization determined by SGEQRF/CGEQRF.
SORGRQ	CUNGRQ	Generates all or part of the orthogonal/unitary matrix Q from an RQ factorization determined by SGERQF/CGERQF.
SORGTR	CUNGTR	Generates the orthogonal/unitary transformation matrix from a reduction to tridiagonal form determined by SSYTRD/CHETRD.
SORMBR	CUNMBR	Multiplies a general matrix by one of the orthogonal/unitary transformation matrices from a reduction to bidiagonal form determined by SGEBRD/CGEBRD.
SORMHR	CUNMHR	Multiplies a general matrix by the orthogonal/unitary transformation matrix from a reduction to Hessenberg form determined by SGEHRD/CGEHRD.
SORMLQ	CUNMLQ	Multiplies a general matrix by the orthogonal/unitary matrix from an LQ factorization determined by SGELQF/CGELQF.
SORMQL	CUNMQL	Multiplies a general matrix by the orthogonal/unitary matrix from a QL factorization determined by SGEQLF/CGEQLF.
SORMQR	CUNMQR	Multiplies a general matrix by the orthogonal/unitary matrix from a QR factorization determined by SGEQRF/CGEQRF.

| Routine | | Description |
real	complex	
SORMRQ	CUNMRQ	Multiplies a general matrix by the orthogonal/unitary matrix from an *RQ* factorization determined by SGERQF/CGERQF.
SORMTR	CUNMTR	Multiplies a general matrix by the orthogonal/unitary transformation matrix from a reduction to tridiagonal form determined by SSYTRD/CHETRD.
SPBCON	CPBCON	Estimates the reciprocal of the condition number of a symmetric/Hermitian positive definite band matrix, using the Cholesky factorization computed by SPBTRF/CPBTRF.
SPBEQU	CPBEQU	Computes row and column scalings to equilibrate a symmetric/Hermitian positive definite band matrix and reduce its condition number.
SPBRFS	CPBRFS	Improves the computed solution to a symmetric/Hermitian positive definite banded system of linear equations $AX = B$, and provides forward and backward error bounds for the solution.
SPBSV	**CPBSV**	Solves a symmetric/Hermitian positive definite banded system of linear equations $AX = B$.
SPBSVX	**CPBSVX**	Solves a symmetric/Hermitian positive definite banded system of linear equations $AX = B$, and provides an estimate of the condition number and error bounds on the solution.
SPBTRF	CPBTRF	Computes the Cholesky factorization of a symmetric/Hermitian positive definite band matrix.
SPBTRS	CPBTRS	Solves a symmetric/Hermitian positive definite banded system of linear equations $AX = B$, using the Cholesky factorization computed by SPBTRF/CPBTRF.
SPOCON	CPOCON	Estimates the reciprocal of the condition number of a symmetric/Hermitian positive definite matrix, using the Cholesky factorization computed by SPOTRF/CPOTRF.
SPOEQU	CPOEQU	Computes row and column scalings to equilibrate a symmetric/Hermitian positive definite matrix and reduce its condition number.
SPORFS	CPORFS	Improves the computed solution to a symmetric/Hermitian positive definite system of linear equations $AX = B$, and provides forward and backward error bounds for the solution.
SPOSV	**CPOSV**	Solves a symmetric/Hermitian positive definite system of linear equations $AX = B$.
SPOSVX	**CPOSVX**	Solves a symmetric/Hermitian positive definite system of linear equations $AX = B$, and provides an estimate of the condition number and error bounds on the solution.
SPOTRF	CPOTRF	Computes the Cholesky factorization of a symmetric/Hermitian positive definite matrix.
SPOTRI	CPOTRI	Computes the inverse of a symmetric/Hermitian positive definite matrix, using the Cholesky factorization computed by SPOTRF/CPOTRF.

Routine		Description
real	complex	
SPOTRS	CPOTRS	Solves a symmetric/Hermitian positive definite system of linear equations $AX = B$, using the Cholesky factorization computed by SPOTRF/CPOTRF.
SPPCON	CPPCON	Estimates the reciprocal of the condition number of a symmetric/Hermitian positive definite matrix in packed storage, using the Cholesky factorization computed by SPPTRF/CPPTRF.
SPPEQU	CPPEQU	Computes row and column scalings to equilibrate a symmetric/Hermitian positive definite matrix in packed storage and reduce its condition number.
SPPRFS	CPPRFS	Improves the computed solution to a symmetric/Hermitian positive definite system of linear equations $AX = B$, where A is held in packed storage, and provides forward and backward error bounds for the solution.
SPPSV	**CPPSV**	Solves a symmetric/Hermitian positive definite system of linear equations $AX = B$, where A is held in packed storage.
SPPSVX	**CPPSVX**	Solves a symmetric/Hermitian positive definite system of linear equations $AX = B$, where A is held in packed storage, and provides an estimate of the condition number and error bounds on the solution.
SPPTRF	CPPTRF	Computes the Cholesky factorization of a symmetric/Hermitian positive definite matrix in packed storage.
SPPTRI	CPPTRI	Computes the inverse of a symmetric/Hermitian positive definite matrix in packed storage, using the Cholesky factorization computed by SPPTRF/CPPTRF.
SPPTRS	CPPTRS	Solves a symmetric/Hermitian positive definite system of linear equations $AX = B$, where A is held in packed storage, using the Cholesky factorization computed by SPPTRF/CPPTRF.
SPTCON	CPTCON	Computes the reciprocal of the condition number of a symmetric/Hermitian positive definite tridiagonal matrix, using the LDL^H factorization computed by SPTTRF/CPTTRF.
SPTEQR	CPTEQR	Computes all eigenvalues and eigenvectors of a real symmetric positive definite tridiagonal matrix, by computing the SVD of its bidiagonal Cholesky factor.
SPTRFS	CPTRFS	Improves the computed solution to a symmetric/Hermitian positive definite tridiagonal system of linear equations $AX = B$, and provides forward and backward error bounds for the solution.
SPTSV	**CPTSV**	Solves a symmetric/Hermitian positive definite tridiagonal system of linear equations $AX = B$.
SPTSVX	**CPTSVX**	Solves a symmetric/Hermitian positive definite tridiagonal system of linear equations $AX = B$, and provides an estimate of the condition number and error bounds on the solution.
SPTTRF	CPTTRF	Computes the LDL^H factorization of a symmetric/Hermitian positive definite tridiagonal matrix.

Routine		Description
real	**complex**	
SPTTRS	CPTTRS	Solves a symmetric/Hermitian positive definite tridiagonal system of linear equations, using the LDL^H factorization computed by SPTTRF/CPTTRF.
SSBEV	**CHBEV**	Computes all eigenvalues and eigenvectors of a symmetric/Hermitian band matrix.
SSBEVX	**CHBEVX**	Computes selected eigenvalues and eigenvectors of a symmetric/Hermitian band matrix.
SSBTRD	CHBTRD	Reduces a symmetric/Hermitian band matrix to real symmetric tridiagonal form by an orthogonal/unitary similarity transformation.
SSPCON	CSPCON CHPCON	Estimates the reciprocal of the condition number of a real symmetric/complex symmetric/complex Hermitian indefinite matrix in packed storage, using the factorization computed by SSPTRF/CSPTRF/CHPTRF.
SSPEV	**CHPEV**	Computes all eigenvalues and eigenvectors of a symmetric/Hermitian matrix in packed storage.
SSPEVX	**CHPEVX**	Computes selected eigenvalues and eigenvectors of a symmetric/Hermitian matrix in packed storage.
SSPGST	CHPGST	Reduces a symmetric/Hermitian definite generalized eigenproblem $Ax = \lambda Bx$, $ABx = \lambda x$, or $BAx = \lambda x$, to standard form, where A and B are held in packed storage, and B has been factorized by SPPTRF/CPPTRF.
SSPGV	**CHPGV**	Computes all eigenvalues and eigenvectors of a generalized symmetric/Hermitian definite generalized eigenproblem, $Ax = \lambda Bx$, $ABx = \lambda x$, or $BAx = \lambda x$, where A and B are in packed storage.
SSPRFS	CSPRFS CHPRFS	Improves the computed solution to a real symmetric/complex symmetric/complex Hermitian indefinite system of linear equations $AX = B$, where A is held in packed storage, and provides forward and backward error bounds for the solution.
SSPSV	**CSPSV CHPSV**	Solves a real symmetric/complex symmetric/complex Hermitian indefinite system of linear equations $AX = B$, where A is held in packed storage.
SSPSVX	**CSPSVX CHPSVX**	Solves a real symmetric/complex symmetric/complex Hermitian indefinite system of linear equations $AX = B$, where A is held in packed storage, and provides an estimate of the condition number and error bounds on the solution.
SSPTRD	CHPTRD	Reduces a symmetric/Hermitian matrix in packed storage to real symmetric tridiagonal form by an orthogonal/unitary similarity transformation.
SSPTRF	CSPTRF CHPTRF	Computes the factorization of a real symmetric/complex symmetric/complex Hermitian indefinite matrix in packed storage, using the diagonal pivoting method.

| Routine | | Description |
real	complex	
SSPTRI	CSPTRI CHPTRI	Computes the inverse of a real symmetric/complex symmetric/complex Hermitian indefinite matrix in packed storage, using the factorization computed by SSPTRF/CSPTRF/CHPTRF.
SSPTRS	CSPTRS CHPTRS	Solves a real symmetric/complex symmetric/complex Hermitian indefinite system of linear equations $AX = B$, where A is held in packed storage, using the factorization computed by SSPTRF/CSPTRF/CHPTRF.
SSTEBZ		Computes selected eigenvalues of a real symmetric tridiagonal matrix by bisection.
SSTEIN	CSTEIN	Computes selected eigenvectors of a real symmetric tridiagonal matrix by inverse iteration.
SSTEQR	CSTEQR	Computes all eigenvalues and eigenvectors of a real symmetric tridiagonal matrix, using the implicit QL or QR algorithm.
SSTERF		Computes all eigenvalues of a real symmetric tridiagonal matrix, using a root-free variant of the QL or QR algorithm.
SSTEV		Computes all eigenvalues and eigenvectors of a real symmetric tridiagonal matrix.
SSTEVX		Computes selected eigenvalues and eigenvectors of a real symmetric tridiagonal matrix.
SSYCON	CSYCON CHECON	Estimates the reciprocal of the condition number of a real symmetric/complex symmetric/complex Hermitian indefinite matrix, using the factorization computed by SSYTRF/CSYTRF/CHETRF.
SSYEV	**CHEEV**	Computes all eigenvalues and eigenvectors of a symmetric/Hermitian matrix.
SSYEVX	**CHEEVX**	Computes selected eigenvalues and eigenvectors of a symmetric/Hermitian matrix.
SSYGST	CHEGST	Reduces a symmetric/Hermitian definite generalized eigenproblem $Ax = \lambda Bx$, $ABx = \lambda x$, or $BAx = \lambda x$, to standard form, where B has been factorized by SPOTRF/CPOTRF.
SSYGV	**CHEGV**	Computes all eigenvalues and the eigenvectors of a generalized symmetric/Hermitian definite generalized eigenproblem, $Ax = \lambda Bx$, $ABx = \lambda x$, or $BAx = \lambda x$.
SSYRFS	CSYRFS CHERFS	Improves the computed solution to a real symmetric/complex symmetric/complex Hermitian indefinite system of linear equations $AX = B$, and provides forward and backward error bounds for the solution.
SSYSV	**CSYSV** **CHESV**	Solves a real symmetric/complex symmetric/complex Hermitian indefinite system of linear equations $AX = B$.
SSYSVX	**CSYSVX** **CHESVX**	Solves a real symmetric/complex symmetric/complex Hermitian indefinite system of linear equations $AX = B$, and provides an estimate of the condition number and error bounds on the solution.
SSYTRD	CHETRD	Reduces a symmetric/Hermitian matrix to real symmetric tridiagonal form by an orthogonal/unitary similarity transformation.

Routine		Description
real	complex	
SSYTRF	CSYTRF CHETRF	Computes the factorization of a real symmetric/complex symmetric/complex Hermitian indefinite matrix, using the diagonal pivoting method.
SSYTRI	CSYTRI CHETRI	Computes the inverse of a real symmetric/complex symmetric/complex Hermitian indefinite matrix, using the factorization computed by SSYTRF/CSYTRF/CHETRF.
SSYTRS	CSYTRS CHETRS	Solves a real symmetric/complex symmetric/complex Hermitian indefinite system of linear equations $AX = B$, using the factorization computed by SSPTRF/CSPTRF/CHPTRF.
STBCON	CTBCON	Estimates the reciprocal of the condition number of a triangular band matrix, in either the 1-norm or the infinity-norm.
STBRFS	CTBRFS	Provides forward and backward error bounds for the solution of a triangular banded system of linear equations $AX = B$, $A^T X = B$ or $A^H X = B$.
STBTRS	CTBTRS	Solves a triangular banded system of linear equations $AX = B$, $A^T X = B$ or $A^H X = B$.
STPCON	CTPCON	Estimates the reciprocal of the condition number of a triangular matrix in packed storage, in either the 1-norm or the infinity-norm.
STPRFS	CTPRFS	Provides forward and backward error bounds for the solution of a triangular system of linear equations $AX = B$, $A^T X = B$ or $A^H X = B$, where A is held in packed storage.
STPTRI	CTPTRI	Computes the inverse of a triangular matrix in packed storage.
STPTRS	CTPTRS	Solves a triangular system of linear equations $AX = B$, $A^T X = B$ or $A^H X = B$, where A is held in packed storage.
STRCON	CTRCON	Estimates the reciprocal of the condition number of a triangular matrix, in either the 1-norm or the infinity-norm.
STREVC	CTREVC	Computes left and right eigenvectors of an upper quasi-triangular/triangular matrix.
STREXC	CTREXC	Reorders the Schur factorization of a matrix by a unitary similarity transformation.
STRRFS	CTRRFS	Provides forward and backward error bounds for the solution of a triangular system of linear equations $AX = B$, $A^T X = B$ or $A^H X = B$.
STRSEN	CTRSEN	Reorders the Schur factorization of a matrix in order to find an orthonormal basis of a right invariant subspace corresponding to selected eigenvalues, and returns reciprocal condition numbers (sensitivities) of the average of the cluster of eigenvalues and of the invariant subspace.
STRSNA	CTRSNA	Estimates the reciprocal condition numbers (sensitivities) of selected eigenvalues and eigenvectors of an upper quasi-triangular/triangular matrix.
STRSYL	CTRSYL	Solves the Sylvester matrix equation $AX \pm XB = C$ where A and B are upper quasi-triangular/triangular, and may be transposed.

Routine		Description
real	complex	
STRTRI	CTRTRI	Computes the inverse of a triangular matrix.
STRTRS	CTRTRS	Solves a triangular system of linear equations $AX = B$, $A^T X = B$ or $A^H X = B$.
STZRQF	CTZRQF	Computes an RQ factorization of an upper trapezoidal matrix.

Appendix B

Index of Auxiliary Routines

Notes

1. This index lists related pairs of real and complex routines together, in the same style as in Appendix A.

2. Routines are listed in alphanumeric order of the real (single precision) routine name (which always begins with S-). (See subsection 2.1.3 for details of the LAPACK naming scheme.)

3. A few complex routines have no real equivalents, and they are listed first; routines listed in italics (for example, *CROT*), have real equivalents in the Level 1 or Level 2 BLAS.

4. Double precision routines are not listed here; they have names beginning with D- instead of S-, or Z- instead of C-. The only exceptions to this simple rule are that the double precision versions of ICMAX1, SCSUM1 and CSRSCL are named IZMAX1, DZSUM1 and ZDRSCL.

5. A few routines in the list have names that are independent of data type: ILAENV, LSAME, LSAMEN and XERBLA.

6. This index gives only a brief description of the purpose of each routine. For a precise description consult the leading comments in the code, which have been written in the same style as for the driver and computational routines.

Routine		Description
real	complex	
	CLACGV	Conjugates a complex vector.
	CLACRT	Applies a plane rotation with complex cosine and sine to a pair of complex vectors.
	CLAESY	Computes the eigenvalues and eigenvectors of a 2-by-2 complex symmetric matrix, and checks that the norm of the matrix of eigenvectors is larger than a threshold value.
	CROT	Applies a plane rotation with real cosine and complex sine to a pair of complex vectors.
	CSPMV	Computes the matrix-vector product $y = \alpha Ax + \beta y$, where α and β are complex scalars, x and y are complex vectors and A is a complex symmetric matrix in packed storage.
	CSPR	Performs the symmetric rank-1 update $A = \alpha xx^T + A$, where α is a complex scalar, x is a complex vector and A is a complex symmetric matrix in packed storage.
	CSROT	Applies a plane rotation with real cosine and sine to a pair of complex vectors.
	CSYMV	Computes the matrix-vector product $y = \alpha Ax + \beta y$, where α and β are complex scalars, x and y are complex vectors and A is a complex symmetric matrix.
	CSYR	Performs the symmetric rank-1 update $A = \alpha xx^T + A$, where α is a complex scalar, x is a complex vector and A is a complex symmetric matrix.
	ICMAX1	Finds the index of the element whose real part has maximum absolute value (similar to the Level 1 BLAS ICAMAX, but using the absolute value of the real part).
ILAENV		Environmental enquiry function which returns values for tuning algorithmic performance.
LSAME		Tests two characters for equality regardless of case.
LSAMEN		Tests two character strings for equality regardless of case.
	SCSUM1	Forms the 1-norm of a complex vector (similar to the Level 1 BLAS SCASUM, but using the true absolute value).
SGBTF2	CGBTF2	Computes an LU factorization of a general band matrix, using partial pivoting with row interchanges (unblocked algorithm).
SGEBD2	CGEBD2	Reduces a general rectangular matrix to real bidiagonal form by an orthogonal/unitary transformation (unblocked algorithm).
SGEHD2	CGEHD2	Reduces a general matrix to upper Hessenberg form by an orthogonal/unitary similarity transformation (unblocked algorithm).
SGELQ2	CGELQ2	Computes an LQ factorization of a general rectangular matrix (unblocked algorithm).
SGEQL2	CGEQL2	Computes a QL factorization of a general rectangular matrix (unblocked algorithm).
SGEQR2	CGEQR2	Computes a QR factorization of a general rectangular matrix (unblocked algorithm).

Routine		Description
real	complex	
SGERQ2	CGERQ2	Computes an RQ factorization of a general rectangular matrix (unblocked algorithm).
SGETF2	CGETF2	Computes an LU factorization of a general matrix, using partial pivoting with row interchanges (unblocked algorithm).
SLABAD		Returns the square root of the underflow and overflow thresholds if the exponent-range is very large.
SLABRD	CLABRD	Reduces the first nb rows and columns of a general rectangular matrix A to real bidiagonal form by an orthogonal/unitary transformation, and returns auxiliary matrices which are needed to apply the transformation to the unreduced part of A.
SLACON	CLACON	Estimates the 1-norm of a square matrix, using reverse communication for evaluating matrix-vector products.
SLACPY	CLACPY	Copies all or part of one two-dimensional array to another.
SLADIV	CLADIV	Performs complex division in real arithmetic, avoiding unnecessary overflow.
SLAE2		Computes the eigenvalues of a 2-by-2 symmetric matrix.
SLAEBZ		Computes the number of eigenvalues of a real symmetric tridiagonal matrix which are less than or equal to a given value, and performs other tasks required by the routine SSTEBZ.
SLAEIN	CLAEIN	Computes a specified right or left eigenvector of an upper Hessenberg matrix by inverse iteration.
SLAEV2	CLAEV2	Computes the eigenvalues and eigenvectors of a 2-by-2 symmetric/Hermitian matrix.
SLAEXC		Swaps adjacent diagonal blocks of a real upper quasi-triangular matrix in Schur canonical form, by an orthogonal similarity transformation.
SLAGTF		Computes an LU factorization of a matrix $(T - \lambda I)$, where T is a general tridiagonal matrix, and λ a scalar, using partial pivoting with row interchanges.
SLAGTM	CLAGTM	Performs a matrix-matrix product of the form $C = \alpha AB + \beta C$, where A is a tridiagonal matrix, B and C are rectangular matrices, and α and β are scalars, which may be 0, 1, or -1.
SLAGTS		Solves the system of equations $(T - \lambda I)x = y$ or $(T - \lambda I)^T x = y$, where T is a general tridiagonal matrix and λ a scalar, using the LU factorization computed by SLAGTF.
SLAHQR	CLAHQR	Computes the eigenvalues and Schur factorization of an upper Hessenberg matrix, using the double-shift/single-shift QR algorithm.
SLAHRD	CLAHRD	Reduces the first nb columns of a general rectangular matrix A so that elements below the kth subdiagonal are zero, by an orthogonal/unitary transformation, and returns auxiliary matrices which are needed to apply the transformation to the unreduced part of A.
SLAIC1	CLAIC1	Applies one step of incremental condition estimation.

Routine		Description
real	complex	
SLALN2		Solves a 1-by-1 or 2-by-2 system of equations of the form $(\gamma A - \lambda D)x = \sigma b$ or $(\gamma A^T - \lambda D)x = \sigma b$, where D is a diagonal matrix, λ, b and x may be complex, and σ is a scale factor set to avoid overflow.
SLAMCH		Determines machine parameters for floating-point arithmetic.
SLANGB	CLANGB	Returns the value of the 1-norm, Frobenius norm, infinity-norm, or the largest absolute value of any element, of a general band matrix.
SLANGE	CLANGE	Returns the value of the 1-norm, Frobenius norm, infinity-norm, or the largest absolute value of any element, of a general rectangular matrix.
SLANGT	CLANGT	Returns the value of the 1-norm, Frobenius norm, infinity-norm, or the largest absolute value of any element, of a general tridiagonal matrix.
SLANHS	CLANHS	Returns the value of the 1-norm, Frobenius norm, infinity-norm, or the largest absolute value of any element, of an upper Hessenberg matrix.
SLANSB	CLANSB CLANHB	Returns the value of the 1-norm, Frobenius norm, infinity-norm, or the largest absolute value of any element, of a real symmetric/complex symmetric/complex Hermitian band matrix.
SLANSP	CLANSP CLANHP	Returns the value of the 1-norm, Frobenius norm, infinity-norm, or the largest absolute value of any element, of a real symmetric/complex symmetric/complex Hermitian matrix in packed storage.
SLANST	CLANST	Returns the value of the 1-norm, Frobenius norm, infinity-norm, or the largest absolute value of any element, of a symmetric/Hermitian tridiagonal matrix.
SLANSY	CLANSY CLANHE	Returns the value of the 1-norm, Frobenius norm, infinity-norm, or the largest absolute value of any element, of a real symmetric/complex symmetric/complex Hermitian matrix.
SLANTB	CLANTB	Returns the value of the 1-norm, Frobenius norm, infinity-norm, or the largest absolute value of any element, of a triangular band matrix.
SLANTP	CLANTP	Returns the value of the 1-norm, Frobenius norm, infinity-norm, or the largest absolute value of any element, of a triangular matrix in packed storage.
SLANTR	CLANTR	Returns the value of the 1-norm, Frobenius norm, infinity-norm, or the largest absolute value of any element, of a triangular matrix.
SLANV2		Computes the Schur factorization of a real 2-by-2 nonsymmetric matrix in Schur canonical form.
SLAPY2		Returns $\sqrt{x^2 + y^2}$, avoiding unnecessary overflow or harmful underflow.
SLAPY3		Returns $\sqrt{x^2 + y^2 + z^2}$, avoiding unnecessary overflow or harmful underflow.
SLAQGB	CLAQGB	Scales a general band matrix, using row and column scaling factors computed by SGBEQU/CGBEQU.

Routine		Description
real	complex	
SLAQGE	CLAQGE	Scales a general rectangular matrix, using row and column scaling factors computed by SGEEQU/CGEEQU.
SLAQSB	CLAQSB	Scales a symmetric/Hermitian band matrix, using scaling factors computed by SPBEQU/CPBEQU.
SLAQSP	CLAQSP	Scales a symmetric/Hermitian matrix in packed storage, using scaling factors computed by SPPEQU/CPPEQU.
SLAQSY	CLAQSY	Scales a symmetric/Hermitian matrix, using scaling factors computed by SPOEQU/CPOEQU.
SLAQTR		Solves a real quasi-triangular system of equations, or a complex quasi-triangular system of special form, in real arithmetic.
SLAR2V	CLAR2V	Applies a vector of plane rotations with real cosines and real/complex sines from both sides to a sequence of 2-by-2 symmetric/Hermitian matrices.
SLARF	CLARF	Applies an elementary reflector to a general rectangular matrix.
SLARFB	CLARFB	Applies a block reflector or its transpose/conjugate-transpose to a general rectangular matrix.
SLARFG	CLARFG	Generates an elementary reflector (Householder matrix).
SLARFT	CLARFT	Forms the triangular factor T of a block reflector $H = I - VTV^H$.
SLARFX	CLARFX	Applies an elementary reflector to a general rectangular matrix, with loop unrolling when the reflector has order ≤ 10.
SLARGV	CLARGV	Generates a vector of plane rotations with real cosines and real/complex sines.
SLARNV	CLARNV	Returns a vector of random numbers from a uniform or normal distribution.
SLARTG	CLARTG	Generates a plane rotation with real cosine and real/complex sine.
SLARTV	CLARTV	Applies a vector of plane rotations with real cosines and real/complex sines to the elements of a pair of vectors.
SLARUV		Returns a vector of n random real numbers from a uniform (0,1) distribution ($n \leq 128$).
SLAS2		Computes the singular values of a 2-by-2 triangular matrix.
SLASCL	CLASCL	Multiplies a general rectangular matrix by a real scalar defined as c_{to}/c_{from}.
SLASET	CLASET	Initializes the off-diagonal elements of a matrix to α and the diagonal elements to β.
SLASR	CLASR	Applies a sequence of plane rotations to a general rectangular matrix.
SLASSQ	CLASSQ	Updates a sum of squares represented in scaled form.
SLASV2		Computes the singular value decomposition of a 2-by-2 triangular matrix.
SLASWP	CLASWP	Performs a sequence of row interchanges on a general rectangular matrix.
SLASY2		Solves the Sylvester matrix equation $AX \pm XB = \sigma C$ where A and B are of order 1 or 2, and may be transposed, and σ is a scale factor.

Routine		Description
real	complex	
SLASYF	CLASYF CLAHEF	Computes a partial factorization of a real symmetric/complex symmetric/complex Hermitian indefinite matrix, using the diagonal pivoting method.
SLATBS	CLATBS	Solves a triangular banded system of equations $Ax = \sigma b$, $A^T x = \sigma b$, or $A^H x = \sigma b$, where σ is a scale factor set to prevent overflow.
SLATPS	CLATPS	Solves a triangular system of equations $Ax = \sigma b$, $A^T x = \sigma b$, or $A^H x = \sigma b$, where A is held in packed storage, and σ is a scale factor set to prevent overflow.
SLATRD	CLATRD	Reduces the first nb rows and columns of a symmetric/Hermitian matrix A to real tridiagonal form by an orthogonal/unitary similarity transformation, and returns auxiliary matrices which are needed to apply the transformation to the unreduced part of A.
SLATRS	CLATRS	Solves a triangular system of equations $Ax = \sigma b$, $A^T x = \sigma b$, or $A^H x = \sigma b$, where σ is a scale factor set to prevent overflow.
SLATZM	CLATZM	Applies an elementary reflector generated by STZRQF/CTZRQF to a general rectangular matrix.
SLAUU2	CLAUU2	Computes the product UU^H or $L^H L$, where U and L are upper or lower triangular matrices (unblocked algorithm).
SLAUUM	CLAUUM	Computes the product UU^H or $L^H L$, where U and L are upper or lower triangular matrices.
SLAZRO	CLAZRO	Initializes the off-diagonal elements of a matrix to α and the diagonal elements to β.
SORG2L	CUNG2L	Generates all or part of the orthogonal/unitary matrix Q from a QL factorization determined by SGEQLF/CGEQLF (unblocked algorithm).
SORG2R	CUNG2R	Generates all or part of the orthogonal/unitary matrix Q from a QR factorization determined by SGEQRF/CGEQRF (unblocked algorithm).
SORGL2	CUNGL2	Generates all or part of the orthogonal/unitary matrix Q from an LQ factorization determined by SGELQF/CGELQF (unblocked algorithm).
SORGR2	CUNGR2	Generates all or part of the orthogonal/unitary matrix Q from an RQ factorization determined by SGERQF/CGERQF (unblocked algorithm).
SORM2L	CUNM2L	Multiplies a general matrix by the orthogonal/unitary matrix from a QL factorization determined by SGEQLF/CGEQLF (unblocked algorithm).
SORM2R	CUNM2R	Multiplies a general matrix by the orthogonal/unitary matrix from a QR factorization determined by SGEQRF/CGEQRF (unblocked algorithm).
SORML2	CUNML2	Multiplies a general matrix by the orthogonal/unitary matrix from an LQ factorization determined by SGELQF/CGELQF (unblocked algorithm).

Routine		Description
real	complex	
SORMR2	CUNMR2	Multiplies a general matrix by the orthogonal/unitary matrix from an RQ factorization determined by SGERQF/CGERQF (unblocked algorithm).
SPBTF2	CPBTF2	Computes the Cholesky factorization of a symmetric/Hermitian positive definite band matrix (unblocked algorithm).
SPOTF2	CPOTF2	Computes the Cholesky factorization of a symmetric/Hermitian positive definite matrix (unblocked algorithm).
SRSCL	CSRSCL	Multiplies a vector by the reciprocal of a real scalar.
SSYGS2	CHEGS2	Reduces a symmetric/Hermitian definite generalized eigenproblem $Ax = \lambda Bx$, $ABx = \lambda x$, or $BAx = \lambda x$, to standard form, where B has been factorized by SPOTRF/CPOTRF (unblocked algorithm).
SSYTD2	CHETD2	Reduces a symmetric/Hermitian matrix to real symmetric tridiagonal form by an orthogonal/unitary similarity transformation (unblocked algorithm).
SSYTF2	CSYTF2	Computes the factorization of a real symmetric/complex symmetric/complex Hermitian indefinite matrix, using the diagonal pivoting method (unblocked algorithm).
	CHETF2	
STRTI2	CTRTI2	Computes the inverse of a triangular matrix (unblocked algorithm).
XERBLA		Error handling routine called by LAPACK routines if an input parameter has an invalid value.

Appendix C

Quick Reference Guide to the BLAS

Level 1 BLAS

	dim	scalar	vector	vector	scalars	5-element array	prefixes
SUBROUTINE _ROTG (					A, B, C, S)		S, D
SUBROUTINE _ROTMG(					D1, D2, A, B,	PARAM)	S, D
SUBROUTINE _ROT (	N,		X, INCX, Y, INCY,		C, S)		S, D
SUBROUTINE _ROTM (	N,		X, INCX, Y, INCY,			PARAM)	S, D
SUBROUTINE _SWAP (	N,		X, INCX, Y, INCY)				S, D, C, Z
SUBROUTINE _SCAL (	N,	ALPHA,	X, INCX)				S, D, C, Z, CS, ZD
SUBROUTINE _COPY (	N,		X, INCX, Y, INCY)				S, D, C, Z
SUBROUTINE _AXPY (	N,	ALPHA,	X, INCX, Y, INCY)				S, D, C, Z
FUNCTION _DOT (	N,		X, INCX, Y, INCY)				S, D, DS
FUNCTION _DOTU (	N,		X, INCX, Y, INCY)				C, Z
FUNCTION _DOTC (	N,		X, INCX, Y, INCY)				C, Z
FUNCTION __DOT (	N,	ALPHA,	X, INCX, Y, INCY)				SDS
FUNCTION _NRM2 (	N,		X, INCX)				S, D, SC, DZ
FUNCTION _ASUM (	N,		X, INCX)				S, D, SC, DZ
FUNCTION I_AMAX(	N,		X, INCX)				S, D, C, Z

Name	Operation	Prefixes
_ROTG	Generate plane rotation	S, D
_ROTMG	Generate modified plane rotation	S, D
_ROT	Apply plane rotation	S, D
_ROTM	Apply modified plane rotation	S, D
_SWAP	$x \leftrightarrow y$	S, D, C, Z
_SCAL	$x \leftarrow \alpha x$	S, D, C, Z, CS, ZD
_COPY	$y \leftarrow x$	S, D, C, Z
_AXPY	$y \leftarrow \alpha x + y$	S, D, C, Z
_DOT	$dot \leftarrow x^T y$	S, D, DS
_DOTU	$dot \leftarrow x^T y$	C, Z
_DOTC	$dot \leftarrow x^H y$	C, Z
__DOT	$dot \leftarrow \alpha + x^T y$	SDS
_NRM2	$nrm2 \leftarrow \|x\|_2$	S, D, SC, DZ
_ASUM	$asum \leftarrow \|re(x)\|_1 + \|im(x)\|_1$	S, D, SC, DZ
I_AMAX	$amax \leftarrow 1^{st} k \ni \|re(x_k)\| + \|im(x_k)\|$ $= max(\|re(x_i)\| + \|im(x_i)\|)$	S, D, C, Z

Level 2 BLAS

	options		dim	b-width	scalar	matrix	vector	scalar	vector	prefixes
_GEMV (		TRANS,	M, N,		ALPHA,	A, LDA,	X, INCX,	BETA,	Y, INCY)	S, D, C, Z
_GBMV (		TRANS,	M, N,	KL, KU,	ALPHA,	A, LDA,	X, INCX,	BETA,	Y, INCY)	S, D, C, Z
_HEMV (	UPLO,		N,		ALPHA,	A, LDA,	X, INCX,	BETA,	Y, INCY)	C, Z
_HBMV (	UPLO,		N, K,		ALPHA,	A, LDA,	X, INCX,	BETA,	Y, INCY)	C, Z
_HPMV (	UPLO,		N,		ALPHA,	AP,	X, INCX,	BETA,	Y, INCY)	C, Z
_SYMV (	UPLO,		N,		ALPHA,	A, LDA,	X, INCX,	BETA,	Y, INCY)	S, D
_SBMV (	UPLO,		N, K,		ALPHA,	A, LDA,	X, INCX,	BETA,	Y, INCY)	S, D
_SPMV (	UPLO,		N,		ALPHA,	AP,	X, INCX,	BETA,	Y, INCY)	S, D
_TRMV (	UPLO, TRANS, DIAG,		N,			A, LDA,	X, INCX)			S, D, C, Z
_TBMV (	UPLO, TRANS, DIAG,		N, K,			A, LDA,	X, INCX)			S, D, C, Z
_TPMV (	UPLO, TRANS, DIAG,		N,			AP,	X, INCX)			S, D, C, Z
_TRSV (	UPLO, TRANS, DIAG,		N,			A, LDA,	X, INCX)			S, D, C, Z
_TBSV (	UPLO, TRANS, DIAG,		N, K,			A, LDA,	X, INCX)			S, D, C, Z
_TPSV (	UPLO, TRANS, DIAG,		N,			AP,	X, INCX)			S, D, C, Z

	options	dim	scalar	vector	vector	matrix	prefixes
_GER (		M, N,	ALPHA,	X, INCX,	Y, INCY,	A, LDA)	S, D
_GERU (		M, N,	ALPHA,	X, INCX,	Y, INCY,	A, LDA)	C, Z
_GERC (		M, N,	ALPHA,	X, INCX,	Y, INCY,	A, LDA)	C, Z
_HER (	UPLO,	N,	ALPHA,	X, INCX,		A, LDA)	C, Z
_HPR (	UPLO,	N,	ALPHA,	X, INCX,		AP)	C, Z
_HER2 (	UPLO,	N,	ALPHA,	X, INCX,	Y, INCY,	A, LDA)	C, Z
_HPR2 (	UPLO,	N,	ALPHA,	X, INCX,	Y, INCY,	AP)	C, Z
_SYR (	UPLO,	N,	ALPHA,	X, INCX,		A, LDA)	S, D
_SPR (	UPLO,	N,	ALPHA,	X, INCX,		AP)	S, D
_SYR2 (	UPLO,	N,	ALPHA,	X, INCX,	Y, INCY,	A, LDA)	S, D
_SPR2 (	UPLO,	N,	ALPHA,	X, INCX,	Y, INCY,	AP)	S, D

Level 3 BLAS

	options		dim	scalar	matrix	matrix	scalar	matrix	prefixes
_GEMM (		TRANSA, TRANSB,	M, N, K,	ALPHA,	A, LDA,	B, LDB,	BETA,	C, LDC)	S, D, C, Z
_SYMM (	SIDE, UPLO,		M, N,	ALPHA,	A, LDA,	B, LDB,	BETA,	C, LDC)	S, D, C, Z
_HEMM (	SIDE, UPLO,		M, N,	ALPHA,	A, LDA,	B, LDB,	BETA,	C, LDC)	C, Z
_SYRK (	UPLO, TRANS,		N, K,	ALPHA,	A, LDA,		BETA,	C, LDC)	S, D, C, Z
_HERK (	UPLO, TRANS,		N, K,	ALPHA,	A, LDA,		BETA,	C, LDC)	C, Z
_SYR2K(	UPLO, TRANS,		N, K,	ALPHA,	A, LDA,	B, LDB,	BETA,	C, LDC)	S, D, C, Z
_HER2K(	UPLO, TRANS,		N, K,	ALPHA,	A, LDA,	B, LDB,	BETA,	C, LDC)	C, Z
_TRMM (	SIDE, UPLO, TRANSA,	DIAG,	M, N,	ALPHA,	A, LDA,	B, LDB)			S, D, C, Z
_TRSM (	SIDE, UPLO, TRANSA,	DIAG,	M, N,	ALPHA,	A, LDA,	B, LDB)			S, D, C, Z

Name	Operation	Prefixes
_GEMV	$y \leftarrow \alpha A x + \beta y, y \leftarrow \alpha A^T x + \beta y, y \leftarrow \alpha A^H x + \beta y, A - m \times n$	S, D, C, Z
_GBMV	$y \leftarrow \alpha A x + \beta y, y \leftarrow \alpha A^T x + \beta y, y \leftarrow \alpha A^H x + \beta y, A - m \times n$	S, D, C, Z
_HEMV	$y \leftarrow \alpha A x + \beta y$	C, Z
_HBMV	$y \leftarrow \alpha A x + \beta y$	C, Z
_HPMV	$y \leftarrow \alpha A x + \beta y$	C, Z
_SYMV	$y \leftarrow \alpha A x + \beta y$	S, D
_SBMV	$y \leftarrow \alpha A x + \beta y$	S, D
_SPMV	$y \leftarrow \alpha A x + \beta y$	S, D
_TRMV	$x \leftarrow A x, x \leftarrow A^T x, x \leftarrow A^H x$	S, D, C, Z
_TBMV	$x \leftarrow A x, x \leftarrow A^T x, x \leftarrow A^H x$	S, D, C, Z
_TPMV	$x \leftarrow A x, x \leftarrow A^T x, x \leftarrow A^H x$	S, D, C, Z
_TRSV	$x \leftarrow A^{-1} x, x \leftarrow A^{-T} x, x \leftarrow A^{-H} x$	S, D, C, Z
_TBSV	$x \leftarrow A^{-1} x, x \leftarrow A^{-T} x, x \leftarrow A^{-H} x$	S, D, C, Z
_TPSV	$x \leftarrow A^{-1} x, x \leftarrow A^{-T} x, x \leftarrow A^{-H} x$	S, D, C, Z
_GER	$A \leftarrow \alpha x y^T + A, A - m \times n$	S, D
_GERU	$A \leftarrow \alpha x y^T + A, A - m \times n$	C, Z
_GERC	$A \leftarrow \alpha x y^H + A, A - m \times n$	C, Z
_HER	$A \leftarrow \alpha x x^H + A$	C, Z
_HPR	$A \leftarrow \alpha x x^H + A$	C, Z
_HER2	$A \leftarrow \alpha x y^H + y(\alpha x)^H + A$	C, Z
_HPR2	$A \leftarrow \alpha x y^H + y(\alpha x)^H + A$	C, Z
_SYR	$A \leftarrow \alpha x x^T + A$	S, D
_SPR	$A \leftarrow \alpha x x^T + A$	S, D
_SYR2	$A \leftarrow \alpha x y^T + \alpha y x^T + A$	S, D
_SPR2	$A \leftarrow \alpha x y^T + \alpha y x^T + A$	S, D

Name	Operation	Prefixes
_GEMM	$C \leftarrow \alpha op(A) op(B) + \beta C, op(X) = X, X^T, X^H, C - m \times n$	S, D, C, Z
_SYMM	$C \leftarrow \alpha A B + \beta C, C \leftarrow \alpha B A + \beta C, C - m \times n, A = A^T$	S, D, C, Z
_HEMM	$C \leftarrow \alpha A B + \beta C, C \leftarrow \alpha B A + \beta C, C - m \times n, A = A^H$	C, Z
_SYRK	$C \leftarrow \alpha A A^T + \beta C, C \leftarrow \alpha A^T A + \beta C, C - n \times n$	S, D, C, Z
_HERK	$C \leftarrow \alpha A A^H + \beta C, C \leftarrow \alpha A^H A + \beta C, C - n \times n$	C, Z
_SYR2K	$C \leftarrow \alpha A B^T + \alpha B A^T + \beta C, C \leftarrow \alpha A^T B + \alpha B^T A + \beta C, C - n \times n$	S, D, C, Z
_HER2K	$C \leftarrow \alpha A B^H + \alpha B A^H + \beta C, C \leftarrow \alpha A^H B + \alpha B^H A + \beta C, C - n \times n$	C, Z
_TRMM	$B \leftarrow \alpha op(A) B, B \leftarrow \alpha B op(A), op(A) = A, A^T, A^H, B - m \times n$	S, D, C, Z
_TRSM	$B \leftarrow \alpha op(A^{-1}) B, B \leftarrow \alpha B op(A^{-1}), op(A) = A, A^T, A^H, B - m \times n$	S, D, C, Z

Notes

Meaning of prefixes

S - REAL	C - COMPLEX
D - DOUBLE PRECISION	Z - COMPLEX*16 (this may not be supported by all machines)

For the Level 2 BLAS a set of extended-precision routines with the prefixes ES, ED, EC, EZ may also be available.

Level 1 BLAS

In addition to the listed routines there are two further extended-precision dot product routines DQDOTI and DQDOTA.

Level 2 and Level 3 BLAS

Matrix types

GE - GEneral	GB - General Band	
SY - SYmmetric	SB - Symmetric Band	SP - Symmetric Packed
HE - HErmitian	HB - Hermitian Band	HP - Hermitian Packed
TR - TRiangular	TB - Triangular Band	TP - Triangular Packed

Options

Arguments describing options are declared as CHARACTER*1 and may be passed as character strings.

TRANS	= 'No transpose', 'Transpose', 'Conjugate transpose' (X, X^T, X^C)
UPLO	= 'Upper triangular', 'Lower triangular'
DIAG	= 'Non-unit triangular', 'Unit triangular'
SIDE	= 'Left', 'Right' (A or op(A) on the left, or A or op(A) on the right)

For real matrices, TRANS = 'T' and TRANS = 'C' have the same meaning.
For Hermitian matrices, TRANS = 'T' is not allowed.
For complex symmetric matrices, TRANS = 'H' is not allowed.

Appendix D

Converting from LINPACK or EISPACK

This appendix is designed to assist people to convert programs that currently call LINPACK or EISPACK routines, to call LAPACK routines instead.

Notes

1. The appendix consists mainly of indexes giving the nearest LAPACK equivalents of LINPACK and EISPACK routines. These indexes should not be followed blindly or rigidly, especially when two or more LINPACK or EISPACK routines are being used together: in many such cases one of the LAPACK driver routines may be a suitable replacement.

2. When two or more LAPACK routines are given in a single entry, these routines must be combined to achieve the equivalent function.

3. For LINPACK, an index is given for equivalents of the real LINPACK routines; these equivalences apply also to the corresponding complex routines. For EISPACK, an index is given for all real and complex routines, since there is no direct 1-to-1 correspondence between real and complex routines in EISPACK.

4. A few of the less commonly used routines in LINPACK and EISPACK have no equivalents in Release 1.0 of LAPACK; equivalents for some of these (but not all) are planned for a future release.

5. For some EISPACK routines, there are LAPACK routines providing similar functionality, but using a significantly different method; such routines are marked by a reference to this note. For example, the EISPACK routine ELMHES uses non-orthogonal transformations, whereas the nearest equivalent LAPACK routine, SGEHRD, uses orthogonal transformations.

6. In some cases the LAPACK equivalents require matrices to be stored in a different storage scheme. For example:

- EISPACK routines BANDR, BANDV, BQR and the driver routine RSB require the lower triangle of a symmetric band matrix to be stored in a different storage scheme to that used in LAPACK, which is illustrated in subsection 5.3.3. The corresponding storage scheme used by the EISPACK routines is:

symmetric band matrix A					EISPACK band storage		
a_{11}	a_{21}	a_{31}			$*$	$*$	a_{11}
a_{21}	a_{22}	a_{32}	a_{42}		$*$	a_{21}	a_{22}
a_{31}	a_{32}	a_{33}	a_{43}	a_{53}	a_{31}	a_{32}	a_{33}
	a_{42}	a_{43}	a_{44}	a_{54}	a_{42}	a_{43}	a_{44}
		a_{53}	a_{54}	a_{55}	a_{53}	a_{54}	a_{55}

- EISPACK routines TRED1, TRED2, TRED3, HTRID3, HTRIDI, TQL1, TQL2, IMTQL1, IMTQL2, RATQR, TQLRAT and the driver routine RST store the off-diagonal elements of a symmetric tridiagonal matrix in elements $2 : n$ of the array E, whereas LAPACK routines use elements $1 : n - 1$.

7. The EISPACK and LINPACK routines for the singular value decomposition return the matrix of right singular vectors, V, whereas the corresponding LAPACK routines return the transposed matrix V^T.

8. In general, the argument lists of the LAPACK routines are different from those of the corresponding EISPACK and LINPACK routines, and the workspace requirements are often different.

LAPACK equivalents of LINPACK routines for real matrices		
LINPACK	LAPACK	Function of LINPACK routine
SCHDC		Cholesky factorization with diagonal pivoting option
SCHDD		Rank-1 downdate of a Cholesky factorization or the triangular factor of a QR factorization
SCHEX		Rank-1 update of a Cholesky factorization or the triangular factor of a QR factorization
SCHUD		Modifies a Cholesky factorization under permutations of the original matrix
SGBCO	SLANGB SGBTRF SGBCON	LU factorization and condition estimation of a general band matrix
SGBDI		Determinant of a general band matrix, after factorization by SGBCO or SGBFA
SGBFA	SGBTRF	LU factorization of a general band matrix
SGBSL	SGBTRS	Solves a general band system of linear equations, after factorization by SGBCO or SGBFA
SGECO	SLANGE SGETRF SGECON	LU factorization and condition estimation of a general matrix
SGEDI	SGETRI	Determinant and inverse of a general matrix, after factorization by SGECO or SGEFA
SGEFA	SGETRF	LU factorization of a general matrix
SGESL	SGETRS	Solves a general system of linear equations, after factorization by SGECO or SGEFA
SGTSL	SGTSV	Solves a general tridiagonal system of linear equations
SPBCO	SLANSB SPBTRF SPBCON	Cholesky factorization and condition estimation of a symmetric positive definite band matrix
SPBDI		Determinant of a symmetric positive definite band matrix, after factorization by SPBCO or SPBFA
SPBFA	SPBTRF	Cholesky factorization of a symmetric positive definite band matrix
SPBSL	SPBTRS	Solves a symmetric positive definite band system of linear equations, after factorization by SPBCO or SPBFA
SPOCO	SLANSY SPOTRF SPOCON	Cholesky factorization and condition estimation of a symmetric positive definite matrix
SPODI	SPOTRI	Determinant and inverse of a symmetric positive definite matrix, after factorization by SPOCO or SPOFA
SPOFA	SPOTRF	Cholesky factorization of a symmetric positive definite matrix
SPOSL	SPOTRS	Solves a symmetric positive definite system of linear equations, after factorization by SPOCO or SPOFA
SPPCO	SLANSY SPPTRF SPPCON	Cholesky factorization and condition estimation of a symmetric positive definite matrix (packed storage)

LAPACK equivalents of LINPACK routines for real matrices (continued)		
LINPACK	LAPACK	Function of LINPACK routine
SPPDI	SPPTRI	Determinant and inverse of a symmetric positive definite matrix, after factorization by SPPCO or SPPFA (packed storage)
SPPFA	SPPTRF	Cholesky factorization of a symmetric positive definite matrix (packed storage)
SPPSL	SPPTRS	Solves a symmetric positive definite system of linear equations, after factorization by SPPCO or SPPFA (packed storage)
SPTSL	SPTSV	Solves a symmetric positive definite tridiagonal system of linear equations
SQRDC	SGEQPF or SGEQRF	QR factorization with optional column pivoting
SQRSL	SORMQR STRSV	Solves linear least squares problems after factorization by SQRDC
SSICO	SLANSY SSYTRF SSYCON	Symmetric indefinite factorization and condition estimation of a symmetric indefinite matrix
SSIDI	SSYTRI	Determinant, inertia and inverse of a symmetric indefinite matrix, after factorization by SSICO or SSIFA
SSIFA	SSYTRF	Symmetric indefinite factorization of a symmetric indefinite matrix
SSISL	SSYTRS	Solves a symmetric indefinite system of linear equations, after factorization by SSICO or SSIFA
SSPCO	SLANSP SSPTRF SSPCON	Symmetric indefinite factorization and condition estimation of a symmetric indefinite matrix (packed storage)
SSPDI	SSPTRI	Determinant, inertia and inverse of a symmetric indefinite matrix, after factorization by SSPCO or SSPFA (packed storage)
SSPFA	SSPTRF	Symmetric indefinite factorization of a symmetric indefinite matrix (packed storage)
SSPSL	SSPTRS	Solves a symmetric indefinite system of linear equations, after factorization by SSPCO or SSPFA (packed storage)
SSVDC	SGESVD	All or part of the singular value decomposition of a general matrix
STRCO	STRCON	Condition estimation of a triangular matrix
STRDI	STRTRI	Determinant and inverse of a triangular matrix
STRSL	STRTRS	Solves a triangular system of linear equations

LAPACK equivalents of EISPACK routines		
EISPACK	LAPACK	Function of EISPACK routine
BAKVEC		Backtransform eigenvectors after transformation by FIGI
BALANC	SGEBAL	Balance a real matrix
BALBAK	SGEBAK	Backtransform eigenvectors of a real matrix after balancing by BALANC
BANDR	SSBTRD	Reduce a real symmetric band matrix to tridiagonal form
BANDV		Selected eigenvectors of a real band matrix by inverse iteration
BISECT	SSTEBZ	Eigenvalues in a specified interval of a real symmetric tridiagonal matrix
BQR	SSBEVX (note 5)	Some eigenvalues of a real symmetric band matrix
CBABK2	CGEBAK	Backtransform eigenvectors of a complex matrix after balancing by CBAL
CBAL	CGEBAL	Balance a complex matrix
CG	CGEEV	All eigenvalues and optionally eigenvectors of a complex general matrix (driver routine)
CH	CHEEV	All eigenvalues and optionally eigenvectors of a complex Hermitian matrix (driver routine)
CINVIT	CHSEIN	Selected eigenvectors of a complex upper Hessenberg matrix by inverse iteration
COMBAK	CUNMHR (note 5)	Backtransform eigenvectors of a complex matrix after reduction by COMHES
COMHES	CGEHRD (note 5)	Reduce a complex matrix to upper Hessenberg form by a non-unitary transformation
COMLR	CHSEQR (note 5)	All eigenvalues of a complex upper Hessenberg matrix, by the LR algorithm
COMLR2	CUNGHR CHSEQR CTREVC (note 5)	All eigenvalues/vectors of a complex matrix by the LR algorithm, after reduction by COMHES
COMQR	CHSEQR	All eigenvalues of a complex upper Hessenberg matrix by the QR algorithm
COMQR2	CUNGHR CHSEQR CTREVC	All eigenvalues/vectors of a complex matrix by the QR algorithm, after reduction by CORTH
CORTB	CUNMHR	Backtransform eigenvectors of a complex matrix, after reduction by CORTH
CORTH	CGEHRD	Reduce a complex matrix to upper Hessenberg form by a unitary transformation
ELMBAK	SORMHR (note 5)	Backtransform eigenvectors of a real matrix after reduction by ELMHES
ELMHES	SGEHRD (note 5)	Reduce a real matrix to upper Hessenberg form by a non-orthogonal transformation
ELTRAN	SORGHR (note 5)	Generate transformation matrix used by ELMHES

LAPACK equivalents of EISPACK routines (continued)		
EISPACK	LAPACK	Function of EISPACK routine
FIGI		Transform a nonsymmetric tridiagonal matrix of special form to a symmetric matrix
FIGI2		As FIGI, with generation of the transformation matrix
HQR	SHSEQR	All eigenvalues of a complex upper Hessenberg matrix by the QR algorithm
HQR2	SHSEQR STREVC	All eigenvalues/vectors of a real upper Hessenberg matrix by the QR algorithm
HTRIB3	CUPMTR	Backtransform eigenvectors of a complex Hermitian matrix after reduction by HTRID3
HTRIBK	CUNMTR	Backtransform eigenvectors of a complex Hermitian matrix after reduction by HTRIDI
HTRID3	CHPTRD	Reduce a complex Hermitian matrix to tridiagonal form (packed storage)
HTRIDI	CHETRD	Reduce a complex Hermitian matrix to tridiagonal form
IMTQL1	SSTEQR	All eigenvalues of a symmetric tridiagonal matrix, by the implicit QL algorithm
IMTQL2	SSTEQR	All eigenvalues/vectors of a symmetric tridiagonal matrix, by the implicit QL algorithm
IMTQLV	SSTEQR	As IMTQL1, preserving the input matrix
INVIT	SHSEIN	Selected eigenvectors of a real upper Hessenberg matrix, by inverse iteration
MINFIT	SGELSS	Minimum norm solution of a linear least squares problem, using the singular value decomposition
ORTBAK	SORMHR	Backtransform eigenvectors of a real matrix after reduction to upper Hessenberg form by ORTHES
ORTHES	SGEHRD	Reduce a real matrix to upper Hessenberg form by an orthogonal transformation
ORTRAN	SORGHR	Generate orthogonal transformation matrix used by ORTHES
QZHES		Reduce a real generalized eigenproblem $Ax = \lambda Bx$ to a form in which A is upper Hessenberg and B is upper triangular
QZIT QZVAL		Generalized Schur factorization of a real generalized eigenproblem, after reduction by QZHES
QZVEC		All eigenvectors of a real generalized eigenproblem from generalized Schur factorization
RATQR	SSTEBZ (note 5)	Extreme eigenvalues of a symmetric tridiagonal matrix using the rational QR algorithm with Newton corrections
REBAK	STRSM	Backtransform eigenvectors of a symmetric definite generalized eigenproblem $Ax = \lambda Bx$ or $ABx = \lambda x$ after reduction by REDUC or REDUC2
REBAKB	STRMM	Backtransform eigenvectors of a symmetric definite generalized eigenproblem $BAx = \lambda x$ after reduction by REDUC2
REDUC	SSYGST	Reduce the symmetric definite generalized eigenproblem $Ax = \lambda Bx$ to a standard symmetric eigenproblem

LAPACK equivalents of EISPACK routines (continued)		
EISPACK	LAPACK	Function of EISPACK routine
REDUC2	SSYGST	Reduce the symmetric definite generalized eigenproblem $ABx = \lambda x$ or $BAx = \lambda x$ to a standard symmetric eigenproblem
RG	SGEEV	All eigenvalues and optionally eigenvectors of a real general matrix (driver routine)
RGG		All eigenvalues and optionally eigenvectors or a real generalized eigenproblem (driver routine)
RS	SSYEV	All eigenvalues and optionally eigenvectors of a real symmetric matrix (driver routine)
RSB	SSBEV	All eigenvalues and optionally eigenvectors of a real symmetric band matrix (driver routine)
RSG	SSYGV	All eigenvalues and optionally eigenvectors of a real symmetric definite generalized eigenproblem $Ax = \lambda Bx$ (driver routine)
RSGAB	SSYGV	All eigenvalues and optionally eigenvectors of a real symmetric definite generalized eigenproblem $ABx = \lambda x$ (driver routine)
RSGBA	SSYGV	All eigenvalues and optionally eigenvectors of a real symmetric definite generalized eigenproblem $BAx = \lambda x$ (driver routine)
RSM	SSYEVX	Selected eigenvalues and optionally eigenvectors of a real symmetric matrix (driver routine)
RSP	SSPEV	All eigenvalues and optionally eigenvectors of a real symmetric matrix (packed storage) (driver routine)
RST	SSTEV	All eigenvalues and optionally eigenvectors of a real symmetric tridiagonal matrix (driver routine)
RT		All eigenvalues and optionally eigenvectors of a real tridiagonal matrix of special form (driver routine)
SVD	SGESVD	Singular value decomposition of a real matrix
TINVIT	SSTEIN	Selected eigenvectors of a symmetric tridiagonal matrix by inverse iteration
TQL1	SSTEQR (note 5)	All eigenvalues of a symmetric tridiagonal matrix by the explicit QL algorithm
TQL2	SSTEQR (note 5)	All eigenvalues/vectors of a symmetric tridiagonal matrix by the explicit QL algorithm
TQLRAT	SSTERF	All eigenvalues of a symmetric tridiagonal matrix by a rational variant of the QL algorithm
TRBAK1	SORMTR	Backtransform eigenvectors of a real symmetric matrix after reduction by TRED1
TRBAK3	SOPMTR	Backtransform eigenvectors of a real symmetric matrix after reduction by TRED3 (packed storage)
TRED1	SSYTRD	Reduce a real symmetric matrix to tridiagonal form
TRED2	SSYTRD SORGTR	As TRED1, but also generating the orthogonal transformation matrix
TRED3	SSPTRD	Reduce a real symmetric matrix to tridiagonal form (packed storage)
TRIDIB	SSTEBZ	Eigenvalues between specified indices of a symmetric tridiagonal matrix

LAPACK equivalents of EISPACK routines (continued)		
EISPACK	LAPACK	Function of EISPACK routine
TSTURM	SSTEBZ SSTEIN	Eigenvalues in a specified interval of a symmetric tridiagonal matrix, and corresponding eigenvectors by inverse iteration

Appendix E

LAPACK Working Notes

Most of these working notes are available from *netlib*, where they can only be obtained in postscript form. To receive a list of available postscript reports, send email to `netlib@ornl.gov` of the form: `send index from lapack/lawns`

1. J. W. Demmel, J. J. Dongarra, J. Du Croz, A. Greenbaum, S. Hammarling, and D. Sorensen, *Prospectus for the Development of a Linear Algebra Library for High-Performance Computers*, ANL, MCS-TM-97, September 1987.

2. J. J. Dongarra, S. Hammarling, and D. Sorensen, *Block Reduction of Matrices to Condensed Forms for Eigenvalue Computations*, ANL, MCS-TM-99, September 1987.

3. J. W. Demmel and W. Kahan, *Computing Small Singular Values of Bidiagonal Matrices with Guaranteed High Relative Accuracy*, ANL, MCS-TM-110, February 1988.

4. J. W. Demmel, J. Du Croz, S. Hammarling, and D. Sorensen, *Guidelines for the Design of Symmetric Eigenroutines, SVD, and Iterative Refinement and Condition Estimation for Linear Systems*, ANL, MCS-TM-111, March 1988.

5. C. Bischof, J. W. Demmel, J. J. Dongarra, J. Du Croz, A. Greenbaum, S. Hammarling, and D. Sorensen, *Provisional Contents*, ANL, MCS-TM-38, September 1988.

6. O. Brewer, J. J. Dongarra, and D. Sorensen, *Tools to Aid in the Analysis of Memory Access Patterns for FORTRAN Programs*, ANL, MCS-TM-120, June 1988.

7. J. Barlow and J. W. Demmel, *Computing Accurate Eigensystems of Scaled Diagonally Dominant Matrices*, ANL, MCS-TM-126, December 1988.

8. Z. Bai and J. W. Demmel, *On a Block Implementation of Hessenberg Multishift QR Iteration*, ANL, MCS-TM-127, January 1989.

9. J. W. Demmel and A. McKenney, *A Test Matrix Generation Suite*, ANL, MCS-P69-0389, March 1989.

10. E. ANDERSON AND J. J. DONGARRA, *Installing and Testing the Initial Release of LAPACK – Unix and Non-Unix Versions*, ANL, MCS-TM-130, May 1989.

11. P. DEIFT, J. W. DEMMEL, L.-C. LI, AND C. TOMEI, *The Bidiagonal Singular Value Decomposition and Hamiltonian Mechanics*, ANL, MCS-TM-133, August 1989.

12. P. MAYES AND G. RADICATI, *Banded Cholesky Factorization Using Level 3 BLAS*, ANL, MCS-TM-134, August 1989.

13. Z. BAI, J. W. DEMMEL, AND A. MCKENNEY, *On the Conditioning of the Nonsymmetric Eigenproblem: Theory and Software*, UT, CS-89-86, October 1989.

14. J. W. DEMMEL, *On Floating-Point Errors in Cholesky*, UT, CS-89-87, October 1989.

15. J. W. DEMMEL AND K. VESELIĆ, *Jacobi's Method is More Accurate than QR*, UT, CS-89-88, October 1989.

16. E. ANDERSON AND J. J. DONGARRA, *Results from the Initial Release of LAPACK*, UT, CS-89-89, November 1989.

17. A. GREENBAUM AND J. J. DONGARRA, *Experiments with QR/QL Methods for the Symmetric Tridiagonal Eigenproblem*, UT, CS-89-92, November 1989.

18. E. ANDERSON AND J. J. DONGARRA, *Implementation Guide for LAPACK*, UT, CS-90-101, April 1990.

19. E. ANDERSON AND J. J. DONGARRA, *Evaluating Block Algorithm Variants in LAPACK*, UT, CS-90-103, April 1990.

20. E. ANDERSON, Z. BAI, C. BISCHOF, J. W. DEMMEL, J. J. DONGARRA, J. DU CROZ, A. GREENBAUM, S. HAMMARLING, A. MCKENNEY, AND D. SORENSEN, *LAPACK: A Portable Linear Algebra Library for High-Performance Computers*, UT, CS-90-105, May 1990.

21. J. DU CROZ, P. MAYES, AND G. RADICATI, *Factorizations of Band Matrices Using Level 3 BLAS*, UT, CS-90-109, July 1990.

22. J. W. DEMMEL AND N. J. HIGHAM, *Stability of Block Algorithms with Fast Level 3 BLAS*, UT, CS-90-110, July 1990.

23. J. W. DEMMEL AND N. J. HIGHAM, *Improved Error Bounds for Underdetermined System Solvers*, UT, CS-90-113, August 1990.

24. J. J. DONGARRA AND S. OSTROUCHOV, *LAPACK Block Factorization Algorithms on the Intel iPSC/860*, UT, CS-90-115, October, 1990.

25. J. J. DONGARRA, S. HAMMARLING, AND J. H. WILKINSON, *Numerical Considerations in Computing Invariant Subspaces*, UT, CS-90-117, October, 1990.

26. E. ANDERSON, C. BISCHOF, J. W. DEMMEL, J. J. DONGARRA, J. DU CROZ, S. HAMMARLING, AND W. KAHAN, *Prospectus for an Extension to LAPACK: A Portable Linear Algebra Library for High-Performance Computers*, UT, CS-90-118, November 1990.

27. J. DU CROZ AND N. J. HIGHAM, *Stability of Methods for Matrix Inversion*, UT, CS-90-119, October, 1990.

28. J. J. DONGARRA, P. MAYES, AND G. RADICATI, *The IBM RISC System/6000 and Linear Algebra Operations*, UT, CS-90-122, December 1990.

29. R. VAN DE GEIJN, *On Global Combine Operations*, UT, CS-91-129, April 1991.

30. J. J. DONGARRA AND R. VAN DE GEIJN, *Reduction to Condensed Form for the Eigenvalue Problem on Distributed Memory Architectures*, UT, CS-91-130, April 1991.

31. E. ANDERSON, Z. BAI, AND J. J. DONGARRA, *Generalized QR Factorization and its Applications*, UT, CS-91-131, April 1991.

32. C. BISCHOF AND P. TANG, *Generalized Incremental Condition Estimation*, UT, CS-91-132, May 1991.

33. C. BISCHOF AND P. TANG, *Robust Incremental Condition Estimation*, UT, CS-91-133, May 1991.

34. J. J. DONGARRA, *Workshop on the BLACS*, UT, CS-91-134, May 1991.

35. E. ANDERSON, J. J. DONGARRA, AND S. OSTROUCHOV, *Implementation guide for LAPACK*, UT, CS-91-138, August 1991. (*replaced by Working Note 41*)

36. E. ANDERSON, *Robust Triangular Solves for Use in Condition Estimation*, UT, CS-91-142, August 1991.

37. J. J. DONGARRA AND R. VAN DE GEIJN, *Two Dimensional Basic Linear Algebra Communication Subprograms*, UT, CS-91-138, October 1991.

38. Z. BAI AND J. W. DEMMEL, *On a Direct Algorithm for Computing Invariant Subspaces with Specified Eigenvalues*, UT, CS-91-139, November 1991.

39. J. W. DEMMEL, J. J. DONGARRA, AND W. KAHAN, *On Designing Portable High Performance Numerical Libraries*, UT, CS-91-141, July 1991.

40. J. W. DEMMEL, N. J. HIGHAM, AND R. SCHREIBER, *Block LU Factorization*, UT, CS-92-149, February 1992.

41. E. ANDERSON, J. J. DONGARRA, AND S. OSTROUCHOV, *Installation Guide for LAPACK*, UT, CS-92-151, February 1992.

Bibliography

[1] E. ANDERSON, Z. BAI, C. BISCHOF, J. W. DEMMEL, J. J. DONGARRA, J. DU CROZ, A. GREENBAUM, S. HAMMARLING, A. MCKENNEY, AND D. SORENSEN, *LAPACK: A portable linear algebra library for high-performance computers*, Computer Science Dept. Technical Report CS-90-105, University of Tennessee, Knoxville, 1990. (LAPACK Working Note 20).

[2] E. ANDERSON, Z. BAI, AND J. J. DONGARRA, *Generalized QR Factorization and its Applications*, Computer Science Dept. Technical Report CS-91-131, University of Tennessee, Knoxville, 1991. (LAPACK Working Note 31).

[3] E. ANDERSON, J. J. DONGARRA, AND S. OSTROUCHOV, *Installation guide for LAPACK*, Computer Science Dept. Technical Report CS-92-151, University of Tennessee, Knoxville, 1992. (LAPACK Working Note 41).

[4] ANSI/IEEE, *IEEE Standard for Binary Floating-Point Arithmetic*, New York, Std 754-1985 ed., 1985.

[5] M. ARIOLI, J. W. DEMMEL, AND I. S. DUFF, *Solving sparse linear systems with sparse backward error*, SIAM J. Matrix Anal. Appl., 10 (1989), pp. 165–190.

[6] M. ARIOLI, I. S. DUFF, AND P. P. M. DE RIJK, *On the augmented system approach to sparse least squares problems*, Num. Math., 55 (1989), pp. 667–684.

[7] Z. BAI AND J. W. DEMMEL, *On a block implementation of Hessenberg multishift QR iteration*, Int. J. of High Speed Comput., 1 (1989), pp. 97–112. (LAPACK Working Note 8).

[8] Z. BAI, J. W. DEMMEL, AND A. MCKENNEY, *On the conditioning of the nonsymmetric eigenproblem: Theory and software*, Computer Science Dept. Technical Report 469, Courant Institute, New York, NY, 1989. (LAPACK Working Note 13).

[9] J. BARLOW AND J. DEMMEL, *Computing accurate eigensystems of scaled diagonally dominant matrices*, SIAM J. Num. Anal., 27 (1990), pp. 762–791. (LAPACK Working Note 7).

[10] P. DEIFT, J. W. DEMMEL, L.-C. LI, AND C. TOMEI, *The bidiagonal singular value decomposition and Hamiltonian mechanics*, SIAM J. Num. Anal., 28 (1991), pp. 1463–1516. (LAPACK Working Note 11).

112

[11] J. W. DEMMEL AND N. J. HIGHAM, *Improved error bounds for underdetermined systems solvers*, Computer Science Dept. Technical Report CS-90-113, University of Tennessee, Knoxville, 1990. (LAPACK Working Note 23), to appear in SIAM J. Mat. Anal. Appl..

[12] ——, *Stability of block algorithms with fast level 3 BLAS*, Computer Science Dept. Technical Report CS-90-110, University of Tennessee, Knoxville, 1990. (LAPACK Working Note 22), to appear in ACM Trans. Math. Soft..

[13] J. W. DEMMEL AND W. KAHAN, *Accurate singular values of bidiagonal matrices*, SIAM J. Sci. Stat. Comput., 11 (1990), pp. 873–912. (LAPACK Working Note 3).

[14] J. W. DEMMEL AND K. VESELIĆ, *Jacobi's method is more accurate than QR*, Computer Science Dept. Technical Report 468, Courant Institute, New York, NY, October 1989. (LAPACK Working Note 15), to appear in SIAM J. Matrix Anal. Appl.

[15] J. J. DONGARRA, J. R. BUNCH, C. B. MOLER, AND G. W. STEWART, *LINPACK Users' Guide*, SIAM, Philadelphia, PA, 1979.

[16] J. J. DONGARRA, J. DU CROZ, I. S. DUFF, AND S. HAMMARLING, *Algorithm 679: A set of Level 3 Basic Linear Algebra Subprograms*, ACM Trans. Math. Soft., 16 (1990), pp. 18–28.

[17] ——, *A set of Level 3 Basic Linear Algebra Subprograms*, ACM Trans. Math. Soft., 16 (1990), pp. 1–17.

[18] J. J. DONGARRA, J. DU CROZ, S. HAMMARLING, AND R. J. HANSON, *Algorithm 656: An extended set of FORTRAN Basic Linear Algebra Subprograms*, ACM Trans. Math. Soft., 14 (1988), pp. 18–32.

[19] ——, *An extended set of FORTRAN Basic Linear Algebra Subprograms*, ACM Trans. Math. Soft., 14 (1988), pp. 1–17.

[20] J. J. DONGARRA, I. S. DUFF, D. C. SORENSEN, AND H. A. VAN DER VORST, *Solving Linear Systems on Vector and Shared Memory Computers*, SIAM Publications, 1991.

[21] J. J. DONGARRA AND E. GROSSE, *Distribution of mathematical software via electronic mail*, Communications of the ACM, 30 (1987), pp. 403–407.

[22] J. J. DONGARRA, F. G. GUSTAFSON, AND A. KARP, *Implementing linear algebra algorithms for dense matrices on a vector pipeline machine*, SIAM Review, 26 (1984), pp. 91–112.

[23] J. J. DONGARRA, S. HAMMARLING, AND D. C. SORENSEN, *Block reduction of matrices to condensed forms for eigenvalue computations*, JCAM, 27 (1989), pp. 215–227. (LAPACK Working Note 2).

[24] A. DUBRULLE, *The multishift QR algorithm: is it worth the trouble?*, Palo Alto Scientific Center Report G320-3558x, IBM Corp., Palo Alto, 1991.

[25] J. DU CROZ AND N. J. HIGHAM, *Stability of methods for matrix inversion*, IMA J. Num. Anal., 12 (1992), pp. 1–19. (LAPACK Working Note 27).

[26] J. DU CROZ, P. J. D. MAYES, AND G. RADICATI DI BROZOLO, *Factorizations of band matrices using Level 3 BLAS*, Computer Science Dept. Technical Report CS-90-109, University of Tennessee, Knoxville, 1990. (LAPACK Working Note 21).

[27] K. A. GALLIVAN, R. J. PLEMMONS, AND A. H. SAMEH, *Parallel algorithms for dense linear algebra computations*, SIAM Review, 32 (1990), pp. 54–135.

[28] B. S. GARBOW, J. M. BOYLE, J. J. DONGARRA, AND C. B. MOLER, *Matrix Eigensystem Routines – EISPACK Guide Extension*, vol. 51 of Lecture Notes in Computer Science, Springer-Verlag, Berlin, 1977.

[29] G. GOLUB AND C. F. VAN LOAN, *Matrix Computations*, Johns Hopkins University Press, Baltimore, MD, 2nd ed., 1989.

[30] A. GREENBAUM AND J. J. DONGARRA, *Experiments with QL/QR methods for the symmetric tridiagonal eigenproblem*, Computer Science Dept. Technical Report CS-89-92, University of Tennessee, Knoxville, 1989. (LAPACK Working Note 17).

[31] W. W. HAGER, *Condition estimators*, SIAM J. Sci. Stat. Comput., 5 (1984), pp. 311–316.

[32] N. J. HIGHAM, *Efficient algorithms for computing the condition number of a tridiagonal matrix*, SIAM J. Sci. Stat. Comput., 7 (1986), pp. 150–165.

[33] ——, *A survey of condition number estimation for triangular matrices*, SIAM Review, 29 (1987), pp. 575–596.

[34] ——, *FORTRAN codes for estimating the one-norm of a real or complex matrix, with applications to condition estimation*, ACM Trans. Math. Soft., 14 (1988), pp. 381–396.

[35] ——, *Experience with a matrix norm estimator*, SIAM J. Sci. Stat. Comput., 11 (1990), pp. 804–809.

[36] T. KATO, *Perturbation Theory for Linear Operators*, Springer Verlag, Berlin, 2 ed., 1980.

[37] L. KAUFMAN, *Banded eigenvalue solvers on vector machines*, ACM Trans. Math. Soft., 10 (1984), pp. 73–86.

[38] C. L. LAWSON, R. J. HANSON, D. KINCAID, AND F. T. KROGH, *Basic Linear Algebra Subprograms for FORTRAN usage*, ACM Trans. Math. Soft., 5 (1979), pp. 308–323.

[39] B. PARLETT, *The Symmetric Eigenvalue Problem*, Prentice Hall, Englewood Cliffs, NJ, 1980.

[40] A. A. POLLICINI, ed., *Using Toolpack Software Tools*, Kluwer Academic, 1989.

[41] R. SCHREIBER AND C. F. VAN LOAN, *A storage efficient WY representation for products of Householder transformations*, SIAM J. Sci. Stat. Comput., 10 (1989), pp. 53–57.

[42] B. T. SMITH, J. M. BOYLE, J. J. DONGARRA, B. S. GARBOW, Y. IKEBE, V. C. KLEMA, AND C. B. MOLER, *Matrix Eigensystem Routines – EISPACK Guide*, vol. 6 of Lecture Notes in Computer Science, Springer-Verlag, Berlin, 2 ed., 1976.

[43] G. W. STEWART, *Error and perturbation bounds for subspaces associated with certain eigenvalue problems*, SIAM Review, 15 (1973), pp. 727–764.

[44] G. W. STEWART AND J.-G. SUN, *Matrix Perturbation Theory*, Academic Press, New York, 1990.

[45] J. VARAH, *On the separation of two matrices*, SIAM J. Num. Anal., 16 (1979), pp. 216–222.

[46] D. S. WATKINS AND L. ELSNER, *Convergence of algorithms of decomposition type for the eigenvalue problem*, Linear Algebra Appl. 143 (1991), pp. 19–47.

[47] J. H. WILKINSON, *The Algebraic Eigenvalue Problem*, Oxford University Press, Oxford, 1965.

[48] J. H. WILKINSON AND C. REINSCH, eds., *Handbook for Automatic Computation, vol 2.: Linear Algebra*, Springer-Verlag, Heidelberg, 1971.

Index

Part 2

Specifications of Routines

Notes

1. The specifications that follow give the calling sequence, purpose, and descriptions of the arguments of each LAPACK driver and computational routine (but not of auxiliary routines).

2. Specifications of pairs of real and complex routines have been merged (for example SBD-SQR/CBDSQR). In a few cases, specifications of three routines have been merged, one for real symmetric, one for complex symmetric, and one for complex Hermitian matrices (for example SSYTRF/CSYTRF/CHETRF). A few routines for real matrices have no complex equivalent (for example SSTEBZ).

3. Specifications are given only for *single precision* routines. To adapt them for the double precision version of the software, simply interpret REAL as DOUBLE PRECISION, COMPLEX as COMPLEX*16 (or DOUBLE COMPLEX), and the initial letters S- and C- of LAPACK routine names as D- and Z-.

4. Specifications are arranged in alphabetical order of the real routine name.

5. The text of the specifications has been derived from the leading comments in the source-text of the routines. It makes only a limited use of mathematical typesetting facilities. To eliminate redundancy, A^H has been used throughout the specifications. Thus, the reader should note that A^H is equivalent to A^T in the real case.

```
SUBROUTINE SBDSQR( UPLO, N, NCVT, NRU, NCC, D, E, VT, LDVT, U,
$                  LDU, C, LDC, WORK, INFO )
CHARACTER         UPLO
INTEGER           INFO, LDC, LDU, LDVT, N, NCC, NCVT, NRU
REAL              C( LDC, * ), D( * ), E( * ), U( LDU, * ),
$                  VT( LDVT, * ), WORK( * )

SUBROUTINE CBDSQR( UPLO, N, NCVT, NRU, NCC, D, E, VT, LDVT, U,
$                  LDU, C, LDC, WORK, INFO )
CHARACTER         UPLO
INTEGER           INFO, LDC, LDU, LDVT, N, NCC, NCVT, NRU
REAL              D( * ), E( * ), WORK( * )
COMPLEX           C( LDC, * ), U( LDU, * ), VT( LDVT, * )
```

Purpose

SBDSQR/CBDSQR computes the singular value decomposition (SVD) of a real n-by-n (upper or lower) bidiagonal matrix B: B = $Q*S*P^T$, where S is a diagonal matrix with non-negative diagonal elements (the singular values of B), and Q and P are orthogonal matrices.

The routine computes S, and optionally computes $U*Q$, P^T*VT, or Q^T*C, for given real/complex input matrices U, VT and C.

Arguments

UPLO   (input) CHARACTER*1
        = 'U': B is upper bidiagonal;
        = 'L': B is lower bidiagonal.

N   (input) INTEGER
        The order of the matrix B. N ≥ 0.

NCVT   (input) INTEGER
        The number of columns of the matrix VT. NCVT ≥ 0.

NRU   (input) INTEGER
        The number of rows of the matrix U. NRU ≥ 0.

NCC   (input) INTEGER
        The number of columns of the matrix C. NCC ≥ 0.

D   (input/output) REAL array, dimension (N)
        On entry, the n diagonal elements of the bidiagonal matrix B.
        On exit, if INFO = 0, the singular values of B in decreasing order.

E   (input/output) REAL array, dimension (N−1)
        On entry, the (n−1) off-diagonal elements of the bidiagonal matrix B.
        On exit, E is destroyed.

VT   (input/output) REAL/COMPLEX array, dimension (LDVT, NCVT)
        On entry, an n-by-ncvt matrix VT.
        On exit, VT is overwritten by P^T*VT.
        VT is not referenced if NCVT = 0.

LDVT   (input) INTEGER
        The leading dimension of the array VT.
        LDVT ≥ max(1,N) if NCVT > 0; LDVT ≥ 1 if NCVT = 0.

U   (input/output) REAL/COMPLEX array, dimension (LDU, N)
        On entry, an nru-by-n matrix U.
        On exit, U is overwritten by $U*Q$.
        U is not referenced if NRU = 0.

LDU   (input) INTEGER
        The leading dimension of the array U. LDU ≥ max(1,NRU).

C   (input/output) REAL/COMPLEX array, dimension (LDC, NCC)
        On entry, an n-by-ncc matrix C.
        On exit, C is overwritten by Q^T*C.
        C is not referenced if NCC = 0.

LDC   (input) INTEGER
        The leading dimension of the array C.
        LDC ≥ max(1,N) if NCC > 0; LDC ≥ 1 if NCC = 0.

WORK   (workspace) REAL array, dimension (max(1,4*N−4))
        WORK is not referenced if NCVT = NRU = NCC = 0.

INFO   (output) INTEGER
        = 0: successful exit
        < 0: if INFO = −i, the ith argument had an illegal value
        > 0: the algorithm did not converge; D and E contain the elements
              of a bidiagonal matrix which is orthogonally similar to the input
              matrix B; if INFO = i, i elements of E have not converged to
              zero.

```
SUBROUTINE SGBCON( NORM, N, KL, KU, AB, LDAB, IPIV, ANORM, RCOND,
$                  WORK, IWORK, INFO )
CHARACTER         NORM
INTEGER           INFO, KL, KU, LDAB, N
REAL              ANORM, RCOND
INTEGER           IPIV( * ), IWORK( * )
REAL              AB( LDAB, * ), WORK( * )
```

```
SUBROUTINE CGBCON( NORM, N, KL, KU, AB, LDAB, IPIV, ANORM, RCOND,
$                  WORK, RWORK, INFO )
    CHARACTER     NORM
    INTEGER       INFO, KL, KU, LDAB, N
    REAL          ANORM, RCOND
    INTEGER       IPIV( * )
    REAL          RWORK( * )
    COMPLEX       AB( LDAB, * ), WORK( * )
```

Purpose

SGBCON/CGBCON estimates the reciprocal of the condition number of a general real/complex band matrix A, in either the 1-norm or the infinity-norm, using the LU factorization computed by SGBTRF/CGBTRF.

An estimate is obtained for $\|A^{-1}\|$, and RCOND is computed as RCOND $= 1/(\|A\|\cdot\|A^{-1}\|)$.

Arguments

NORM   (input) CHARACTER*1
        Specifies whether the 1-norm condition number or the infinity-norm condition number is required:
        = '1' or 'O': 1-norm;
        = 'I': Infinity-norm.

N   (input) INTEGER
        The order of the matrix A. N $\geq$ 0.

KL   (input) INTEGER
        The number of subdiagonals within the band of A. KL $\geq$ 0.

KU   (input) INTEGER
        The number of superdiagonals within the band of A. KU $\geq$ 0.

AB   (input) REAL/COMPLEX array, dimension (LDAB,N)
        Details of the LU factorization of the band matrix A, as computed by SGBTRF/CGBTRF. U is stored as an upper triangular band matrix with kl+ku superdiagonals in rows 1 to kl+ku+1, and the multipliers used during the factorization are stored in rows kl+ku+2 to 2*kl+ku+1.

LDAB   (input) INTEGER
        The leading dimension of the array AB. LDAB $\geq$ 2*KL+KU+1.

IPIV   (input) INTEGER array, dimension (N)
        The pivot indices; for $1 \leq i \leq N$, row i of the matrix was interchanged with row IPIV(i).

ANORM   (input) REAL
        If NORM = '1' or 'O', the 1-norm of the original matrix A.
        If NORM = 'I', the infinity-norm of the original matrix A.

RCOND   (output) REAL
        The reciprocal of the condition number of the matrix A, computed as RCOND $= 1/(\|A\|\cdot\|A^{-1}\|)$.

WORK   *SGBCON* (workspace) REAL array, dimension (3*N)
        CGBCON (workspace) COMPLEX array, dimension (2*N)

IWORK   *SGBCON only* (workspace) INTEGER array, dimension (N)

RWORK   *CGBCON only* (workspace) REAL array, dimension (N)

INFO   (output) INTEGER
        = 0: successful exit
        < 0: if INFO = −i, the ith argument had an illegal value

---

SGBEQU/CGBEQU

```
SUBROUTINE SGBEQU( M, N, KL, KU, AB, LDAB, R, C, ROWCND, COLCND,
$                  AMAX, INFO )
    INTEGER       INFO, KL, KU, LDAB, M, N
    REAL          AMAX, COLCND, ROWCND
    REAL          AB( LDAB, * ), C( * ), R( * )

SUBROUTINE CGBEQU( M, N, KL, KU, AB, LDAB, R, C, ROWCND, COLCND,
$                  AMAX, INFO )
    INTEGER       INFO, KL, KU, LDAB, M, N
    REAL          AMAX, COLCND, ROWCND
    REAL          C( * ), R( * )
    COMPLEX       AB( LDAB, * )
```

Purpose

SGBEQU/CGBEQU computes row and column scalings intended to equilibrate an m-by-n band matrix A and reduce its condition number. R returns the row scale factors and C the column scale factors, chosen to try to make the largest element in each row and column of the matrix B with elements B(i,j) = R(i)*A(i,j)*C(j) have absolute value 1.

R(i) and C(j) are restricted to be between SMLNUM = smallest safe number and BIGNUM = largest safe number. Use of these scaling factors is not guaranteed to reduce the condition number of A but works well in practice.

Arguments

M   (input) INTEGER
        The number of rows of the matrix A. M $\geq$ 0.

N   (input) INTEGER
        The number of columns of the matrix A. N $\geq$ 0.

KL   (input) INTEGER
        The number of subdiagonals within the band of A. KL $\geq$ 0.

KU   (input) INTEGER
        The number of superdiagonals within the band of A. KU $\geq$ 0.

AB   (input) REAL/COMPLEX array, dimension (LDAB,N)
The band matrix A, stored in rows 1 to kl+ku+1. The jth column of A is stored in the jth column of the array AB as follows:
$AB(ku+1+i-j,j) = A(i,j)$ for $max(1,j-ku)\leq i\leq min(m,j+kl)$.

LDAB   (input) INTEGER
The leading dimension of the array AB. LDAB $\geq$ KL+KU+1.

R   (output) REAL array, dimension (M)
If INFO = 0 or INFO > M, R contains the row scale factors for A.

C   (output) REAL array, dimension (N)
If INFO = 0, C contains the column scale factors for A.

ROWCND   (output) REAL
If INFO = 0 or INFO > M, RCOND contains the ratio of the smallest R(i) to the largest R(i). If ROWCND $\geq$ 0.1 and AMAX is neither too large nor too small, it is not worth scaling by R.

COLCND   (output) REAL
If INFO = 0, COLCND contains the ratio of the smallest C(i) to the largest C(i). If COLCND $\geq$ 0.1, it is not worth scaling by C.

AMAX   (output) REAL
Absolute value of largest matrix element. If AMAX is very close to overflow or very close to underflow, the matrix should be scaled.

INFO   (output) INTEGER
= 0:   successful exit
< 0:   if INFO = $-i$, the ith argument had an illegal value
> 0:   if INFO = i, and i is
    $\leq$ M: the ith row of A is exactly zero
    > M: the $(i-M)^{th}$ column of A is exactly zero

SGBRFS/CGBRFS

```
SUBROUTINE SGBRFS( TRANS, N, KL, KU, NRHS, AB, LDAB, AFB, LDAFB,
$                  IPIV, B, LDB, X, LDX, FERR, BERR, WORK, IWORK,
$                  INFO )
CHARACTER          TRANS
INTEGER            INFO, KL, KU, LDAB, LDAFB, LDB, LDX, N, NRHS
INTEGER            IPIV( * ), IWORK( * )
REAL               AB( LDAB, * ), AFB( LDAFB, * ), B( LDB, * ),
$                  BERR( * ), FERR( * ), WORK( * ), X( LDX, * )
```

```
SUBROUTINE CGBRFS( TRANS, N, KL, KU, NRHS, AB, LDAB, AFB, LDAFB,
$                  IPIV, B, LDB, X, LDX, FERR, BERR, WORK, RWORK,
$                  INFO )
CHARACTER          TRANS
INTEGER            INFO, KL, KU, LDAB, LDAFB, LDB, LDX, N, NRHS
INTEGER            IPIV( * )
REAL               BERR( * ), FERR( * ), RWORK( * )
COMPLEX            AB( LDAB, * ), AFB( LDAFB, * ), B( LDB, * ),
$                  WORK( * ), X( LDX, * )
```

Purpose

SGBRFS/CGBRFS improves the computed solution to a system of linear equations when the coefficient matrix is banded, and provides error bounds and backward error estimates for the solution.

Arguments

TRANS   (input) CHARACTER*1
Specifies the form of the system of equations:
= 'N': $A*X = B$ (No transpose)
= 'T': $A^T*X = B$ (Transpose)
= 'C': $A^H*X = B$ (Conjugate transpose)

N   (input) INTEGER
The order of the matrix A. N $\geq$ 0.

KL   (input) INTEGER
The number of subdiagonals within the band of A. KL $\geq$ 0.

KU   (input) INTEGER
The number of superdiagonals within the band of A. KU $\geq$ 0.

NRHS   (input) INTEGER
The number of right hand sides, i.e., the number of columns of the matrices B and X. NRHS $\geq$ 0.

AB   (input) REAL/COMPLEX array, dimension (LDAB,N)
The original band matrix A, stored in rows 1 to kl+ku+1. The jth column of A is stored in the jth column of the array AB as follows:
$AB(ku+1+i-j,j) = A(i,j)$ for $max(1,j-ku)\leq i\leq min(n,j+kl)$.

LDAB   (input) INTEGER
The leading dimension of the array AB. LDAB $\geq$ KL+KU+1.

AFB   (input) REAL/COMPLEX array, dimension (LDAFB,N)
Details of the LU factorization of the band matrix A, as computed by SGBTRF/CGBTRF. U is stored as an upper triangular band matrix with kl+ku superdiagonals in rows 1 to kl+ku+1, and the multipliers used during the factorization are stored in rows kl+ku+2 to 2*kl+ku+1.

LDAFB   (input) INTEGER
The leading dimension of the array AFB. LDAFB $\geq$ 2*KL+KU+1.

Purpose

SGBSV/CGBSV computes the solution to a real/complex system of linear equations $A*X = B$, where A is a band matrix of order n with kl subdiagonals and ku superdiagonals, and X and B are n-by-nrhs matrices.

The LU decomposition with partial pivoting and row interchanges is used to factor A as $A = LU$, where L is a product of permutation and unit lower triangular matrices with kl subdiagonals, and U is upper triangular with kl+ku superdiagonals. The factored form of A is then used to solve the system of equations $A*X = B$.

Arguments

N   (input) INTEGER
The number of linear equations, i.e., the order of the matrix A. $N \geq 0$.

KL   (input) INTEGER
The number of subdiagonals within the band of A. $KL \geq 0$.

KU   (input) INTEGER
The number of superdiagonals within the band of A. $KU \geq 0$.

NRHS   (input) INTEGER
The number of right hand sides, i.e., the number of columns of the matrix B. $NRHS \geq 0$.

AB   (input/output) REAL/COMPLEX array, dimension (LDAB,N)
On entry, the matrix A in band storage, in rows kl+1 to 2*kl+ku+1; rows 1 to kl of the array need not be set. The jth column of A is stored in the jth column of the array AB as follows:
$AB(kl+ku+1+i-j,j) = A(i,j)$ for $\max(1,j-ku)\leq i\leq\min(n,j+kl)$
On exit, details of the factorization: U is stored as an upper triangular band matrix with kl+ku superdiagonals in rows 1 to kl+ku+1, and the multipliers used during the factorization are stored in rows kl+ku+2 to 2*kl+ku+1.

LDAB   (input) INTEGER
The leading dimension of the array AB. $LDAB \geq 2*KL+KU+1$.

IPIV   (output) INTEGER array, dimension (N)
The pivot indices that define the permutation matrix P; row i of the matrix was interchanged with row IPIV(i).

B   (input/output) REAL/COMPLEX array, dimension (LDB,NRHS)
On entry, the n-by-nrhs right hand side matrix B.
On exit, if INFO = 0, the n-by-nrhs solution matrix X.

LDB   (input) INTEGER
The leading dimension of the array B. $LDB \geq \max(1,N)$.

INFO   (output) INTEGER
= 0:   successful exit
< 0:   if INFO = $-i$, the ith argument had an illegal value
> 0:   if INFO = i, U(i,i) is exactly zero. The factorization has been completed, but the factor U is exactly singular, and the solution has not been computed.

IPIV   (input) INTEGER array, dimension (N)
The pivot indices from SGBTRF/CGBTRF; for $1\leq i\leq N$, row i of the matrix was interchanged with row IPIV(i).

B   (input) REAL/COMPLEX array, dimension (LDB,NRHS)
The right hand side matrix B.

LDB   (input) INTEGER
The leading dimension of the array B. $LDB \geq \max(1,N)$.

X   (input/output) REAL/COMPLEX array, dimension (LDX,NRHS)
On entry, the solution matrix X, as computed by SGBTRS/CGBTRS.
On exit, the improved solution matrix X.

LDX   (input) INTEGER
The leading dimension of the array X. $LDX \geq \max(1,N)$.

FERR   (output) REAL array, dimension (NRHS)
The estimated forward error bound for each solution vector X(j) (the jth column of the solution matrix X). If XTRUE is the true solution corresponding to X(j), FERR(j) bounds the magnitude of the largest element in (X(j) – XTRUE) divided by the magnitude of the largest element in X(j). The quality of the error bound depends on the quality of the estimate of $\|A^{-1}\|$ computed in the code; if the estimate of $\|A^{-1}\|$ is accurate, the error bound is guaranteed.

BERR   (output) REAL array, dimension (NRHS)
The componentwise relative backward error of each solution vector X(j) (i.e., the smallest relative change in any element of A or B that makes X(j) an exact solution).

WORK   *SGBRFS* (workspace) REAL array, dimension (3*N)
         CGBRFS (workspace) COMPLEX array, dimension (2*N)

IWORK   *SGBRFS only* (workspace) INTEGER array, dimension (N)

RWORK   *CGBRFS only* (workspace) REAL array, dimension (N)

INFO   (output) INTEGER
= 0:   successful exit
< 0:   if INFO = $-i$, the ith argument had an illegal value

SGBSV/CGBSV

```
SUBROUTINE SGBSV( N, KL, KU, NRHS, AB, LDAB, IPIV, B, LDB, INFO )
INTEGER        INFO, KL, KU, LDAB, LDB, N, NRHS
INTEGER        IPIV( * )
REAL           AB( LDAB, * ), B( LDB, * )

SUBROUTINE CGBSV( N, KL, KU, NRHS, AB, LDAB, IPIV, B, LDB, INFO )
INTEGER        INFO, KL, KU, LDAB, LDB, N, NRHS
INTEGER        IPIV( * )
COMPLEX        AB( LDAB, * ), B( LDB, * )
```

SGBSVX/CGBSVX

```
SUBROUTINE SGBSVX( FACT, TRANS, N, KL, KU, NRHS, AB, LDAB, AFB,
$                   LDAFB, IPIV, EQUED, R, C, B, LDB, X, LDX,
$                   RCOND, FERR, BERR, WORK, IWORK, INFO )
CHARACTER          EQUED, FACT, TRANS
INTEGER            INFO, KL, KU, LDAB, LDAFB, LDB, LDX, N, NRHS
REAL               RCOND
INTEGER            IPIV( * ), IWORK( * )
REAL               AB( LDAB, * ), AFB( LDAFB, * ), B( LDB, * ),
$                   BERR( * ), C( * ), FERR( * ), R( * ),
$                   WORK( * ), X( LDX, * )

SUBROUTINE CGBSVX( FACT, TRANS, N, KL, KU, NRHS, AB, LDAB, AFB,
$                   LDAFB, IPIV, EQUED, R, C, B, LDB, X, LDX,
$                   RCOND, FERR, BERR, WORK, RWORK, INFO )
CHARACTER          EQUED, FACT, TRANS
INTEGER            INFO, KL, KU, LDAB, LDAFB, LDB, LDX, N, NRHS
REAL               RCOND
INTEGER            IPIV( * )
REAL               BERR( * ), C( * ), FERR( * ), R( * ),
$                   RWORK( * )
COMPLEX            AB( LDAB, * ), AFB( LDAFB, * ), B( LDB, * ),
$                   WORK( * ), X( LDX, * )
```

Purpose

SGBSVX/CGBSVX uses the LU factorization to compute the solution to a real/complex system of linear equations $A*X = B$, $A^T*X = B$, or $A^H*X = B$, where A is a band matrix of order n with kl subdiagonals and ku superdiagonals, and X and B are n-by-nrhs matrices.

Error bounds on the solution and a condition estimate are also provided.

Description

The following steps are performed:

1. If FACT = 'E', real scaling factors are computed to equilibrate the system:

$$\begin{aligned}
\text{TRANS} = \text{'N'}: \quad &\text{diag}(R)*A*\text{diag}(C)*\text{diag}(C)^{-1}*X = \text{diag}(R)*B \\
\text{TRANS} = \text{'T'}: \quad &(\text{diag}(R)*A*\text{diag}(C))^T*\text{diag}(R)^{-1}*X = \text{diag}(C)*B \\
\text{TRANS} = \text{'C'}: \quad &(\text{diag}(R)*A*\text{diag}(C))^H*\text{diag}(R)^{-1}*X = \text{diag}(C)*B
\end{aligned}$$

Whether or not the system will be equilibrated depends on the scaling of the matrix A, but if equilibration is used, A is overwritten by $\text{diag}(R)*A*\text{diag}(C)$ and B by $\text{diag}(R)*B$ (if TRANS='N') or $\text{diag}(C)*B$ (if TRANS = 'T' or 'C').

2. If FACT = 'N' or 'E', the LU decomposition is used to factor the matrix A (after equilibration if FACT = 'E') as $A = LU$, where L is a product of permutation and unit lower triangular matrices with kl subdiagonals, and U is upper triangular with kl+ku superdiagonals.

3. The factored form of A is used to estimate the condition number of the matrix A. If the reciprocal of the condition number is less than machine precision, steps 4–6 are skipped.

4. The system of equations is solved for X using the factored form of A.

5. Iterative refinement is applied to improve the computed solution vectors and calculate error bounds and backward error estimates for them.

6. If FACT = 'E' and equilibration was used, the vectors X are premultiplied by $\text{diag}(C)$ (if TRANS = 'N') or $\text{diag}(R)$ (if TRANS = 'T' or 'C') so that they solve the original system before equilibration.

Arguments

FACT	(input) CHARACTER*1

Specifies whether or not the factored form of the matrix A is supplied on entry, and if not, whether the matrix A should be equilibrated before it is factored.

= 'F': On entry, AFB and IPIV contain the factored form of A. AB, AFB, and IPIV will not be modified.

= 'N': The matrix A will be copied to AFB and factored.

= 'E': The matrix A will be equilibrated if necessary, then copied to AFB and factored.

TRANS	(input) CHARACTER*1

Specifies the form of the system of equations:

= 'N': $A*X = B$ (No transpose)

= 'T': $A^T*X = B$ (Transpose)

= 'C': $A^H*X = B$ (Conjugate transpose)

N	(input) INTEGER

The number of linear equations, i.e., the order of the matrix A. $N \geq 0$.

KL	(input) INTEGER

The number of subdiagonals within the band of A. $KL \geq 0$.

KU	(input) INTEGER

The number of superdiagonals within the band of A. $KU \geq 0$.

NRHS	(input) INTEGER

The number of right hand sides, i.e., the number of columns of the matrices B and X. $NRHS \geq 0$.

AB	(input/output) REAL/COMPLEX array, dimension (LDAB,N)

On entry, the matrix A in band storage, in rows 1 to kl+ku+1. The jth column of A is stored in the jth column of the array AB as follows:

$AB(ku+1+i-j,j) = A(i,j)$ for $\max(1,j-ku) \leq i \leq \min(n,j+kl)$

On exit, if EQUED $\neq$ 'N', A is scaled as follows:

EQUED = 'R': A := diag(R)*A;
EQUED = 'C': A := A*diag(C);
EQUED = 'B': A := diag(R)*A*diag(C).

LDAB   (input) INTEGER
The leading dimension of the array AB. LDAB $\geq$ KL+KU+1.

AFB   (input or output) REAL/COMPLEX array, dimension (LDAFB,N)
If FACT = 'F', then AFB is an input argument and on entry contains details of the LU factorization of the band matrix A, as computed by SGBTRF/CGBTRF. U is stored as an upper triangular band matrix with kl+ku superdiagonals in rows 1 to kl+ku+1, and the multipliers used during the factorization are stored in rows kl+ku+2 to 2*kl+ku+1.
If FACT = 'N', then AFB is an output argument and on exit returns details of the LU factorization of A.
If FACT = 'E', then AFB is an output argument and on exit returns details of the LU factorization of the equilibrated matrix A (see the description of AB for the form of the equilibrated matrix).

LDAFB   (input) INTEGER
The leading dimension of the array AFB. LDAFB $\geq$ 2*KL+KU+1.

IPIV   (input or output) INTEGER array, dimension (N)
If FACT = 'F', then IPIV is an input argument and on entry contains the pivot indices from the factorization A = LU as computed by SGBTRF/CGBTRF; row i of the matrix was interchanged with row IPIV(i).
If FACT = 'N', then IPIV is an output argument and on exit contains the pivot indices from the factorization A = LU of the original matrix A.
If FACT = 'E', then IPIV is an output argument and on exit contains the pivot indices from the factorization A = LU of the equilibrated matrix A.

EQUED   (output) CHARACTER*1
Specifies the form of equilibration that was done.
= 'N':   No equilibration (always true if FACT = 'F' or 'N').
= 'R':   Row equilibration, i.e., A has been premultiplied by diag(R).
= 'C':   Column equilibration, i.e., A has been postmultiplied by diag(C).
= 'B':   Both row and column equilibration, i.e., A has been replaced by diag(R)*A*diag(C).

R   (output) REAL array, dimension (N)
The row scale factors for A.
If EQUED = 'R' or 'B', A is multiplied on the left by diag(R).
R is not assigned if FACT = 'F' or 'N'.

C   (output) REAL array, dimension (N)
The column scale factors for A.
If EQUED = 'C' or 'B', A is multiplied on the right by diag(C).
C is not assigned if FACT = 'F' or 'N'.

B   (input/output) REAL/COMPLEX array, dimension (LDB,NRHS)
On entry, the n-by-nrhs right hand side matrix B.
On exit, if EQUED = 'N', B is not modified; if TRANS = 'N' and EQUED = 'R' or 'B', B is overwritten by diag(R)*B; if TRANS = 'T' or 'C' and EQUED = 'C' or 'B', B is overwritten by diag(C)*B.

LDB   (input) INTEGER
The leading dimension of the array B. LDB $\geq$ max(1,N).

X   (output) REAL/COMPLEX array, dimension (LDX,NRHS)
If INFO = 0, the n-by-nrhs solution matrix X to the original system of equations. Note that A and B are modified on exit if EQUED $\neq$ 'N', and the solution to the equilibrated system is diag(C)$^{-1}$*X if TRANS = 'N' and EQUED = 'C' or 'B', or diag(R)$^{-1}$*X if TRANS = 'T' or 'C' and EQUED = 'R' or 'B'.

LDX   (input) INTEGER
The leading dimension of the array X. LDX $\geq$ max(1,N).

RCOND   (output) REAL
The estimate of the reciprocal condition number of the matrix A. If RCOND is less than the machine precision (in particular, if RCOND = 0), the matrix is singular to working precision. This condition is indicated by a return code of INFO > 0, and the solution and error bounds are not computed.

FERR   (output) REAL array, dimension (NRHS)
The estimated forward error bound for each solution vector X(j) (the jth column of the solution matrix X). If XTRUE is the true solution corresponding to X(j), FERR(j) bounds the magnitude of the largest element in (X(j) − XTRUE) divided by the magnitude of the largest element in X(j). The quality of the error bound depends on the quality of the estimate of $||A^{-1}||$ computed in the code; if the estimate of $||A^{-1}||$ is accurate, the error bound is guaranteed.

BERR   (output) REAL array, dimension (NRHS)
The componentwise relative backward error of each solution vector X(j) (i.e., the smallest relative change in any element of A or B that makes X(j) an exact solution).

WORK   SGBSVX   (workspace) REAL array, dimension (3*N)
CGBSVX   (workspace) COMPLEX array, dimension (2*N)

IWORK   SGBSVX only   (workspace) INTEGER array, dimension (N)

RWORK   CGBSVX only   (workspace) REAL array, dimension (N)

INFO   (output) INTEGER
= 0:   successful exit
< 0:   if INFO = −i, the ith argument had an illegal value
> 0:   if INFO = i, and i is
$\leq$ N: if INFO = i, U(i,i) is exactly zero. The factorization has been completed, but the factor U is exactly singular, so the solution and error bounds could not be computed.

= N+1: RCOND is less than machine precision. The factorization has been completed, but the matrix is singular to working precision, and the solution and error bounds have not been computed.

SGBTRF/CGBTRF

```
SUBROUTINE SGBTRF( M, N, KL, KU, AB, LDAB, IPIV, INFO )
INTEGER    INFO, KL, KU, LDAB, M, N
INTEGER    IPIV( * )
REAL       AB( LDAB, * )

SUBROUTINE CGBTRF( M, N, KL, KU, AB, LDAB, IPIV, INFO )
INTEGER    INFO, KL, KU, LDAB, M, N
INTEGER    IPIV( * )
COMPLEX    AB( LDAB, * )
```

Purpose

SGBTRF/CGBTRF computes an LU factorization of a real/complex m-by-n band matrix A using partial pivoting with row interchanges.

Arguments

M   (input) INTEGER
The number of rows of the matrix A. $M \geq 0$.

N   (input) INTEGER
The number of columns of the matrix A. $N \geq 0$.

KL   (input) INTEGER
The number of subdiagonals within the band of A. $KL \geq 0$.

KU   (input) INTEGER
The number of superdiagonals within the band of A. $KU \geq 0$.

AB   (input/output) REAL/COMPLEX array, dimension (LDAB,N)
On entry, the matrix A in band storage, in rows kl+1 to 2*kl+ku+1; rows 1 to kl of the array need not be set. The jth column of A is stored in the jth column of the array AB as follows:
AB(kl+ku+1+i-j,j)=A(i,j) for $\max(1,j-ku) \leq i \leq \min(m,j+kl)$
On exit, details of the factorization: U is stored as an upper triangular band matrix with kl+ku superdiagonals in rows 1 to kl+ku+1, and the multipliers used during the factorization are stored in rows kl+ku+2 to 2*kl+ku+1.

LDAB   (input) INTEGER
The leading dimension of the array AB. $LDAB \geq 2*KL+KU+1$.

IPIV   (output) INTEGER array, dimension (min(M,N))
The pivot indices; for $1 \leq i \leq \min(M,N)$, row i of the matrix was interchanged with row IPIV(i).

INFO   (output) INTEGER
= 0: successful exit
< 0: if INFO = −i, the ith argument had an illegal value
> 0: if INFO = i, U(i,i) is exactly zero. The factorization has been completed, but the factor U is exactly singular, and division by zero will occur if it is used to solve a system of equations.

SGBTRS/CGBTRS

```
SUBROUTINE SGBTRS( TRANS, N, KL, KU, NRHS, AB, LDAB, IPIV, B, LDB,
$                  INFO )
CHARACTER  TRANS
INTEGER    INFO, KL, KU, LDAB, LDB, N, NRHS
INTEGER    IPIV( * )
REAL       AB( LDAB, * ), B( LDB, * )

SUBROUTINE CGBTRS( TRANS, N, KL, KU, NRHS, AB, LDAB, IPIV, B, LDB,
$                  INFO )
CHARACTER  TRANS
INTEGER    INFO, KL, KU, LDAB, LDB, N, NRHS
INTEGER    IPIV( * )
COMPLEX    AB( LDAB, * ), B( LDB, * )
```

Purpose

SGBTRS/CGBTRS solves a system of linear equations $A*X = B$, $A^T*X = B$, or $A^H*X = B$, with a general band matrix A using the LU factorization computed by SGBTRF/CGBTRF.

Arguments

TRANS   (input) CHARACTER*1
Specifies the form of the system of equations:
= 'N': $A*X = B$ (No transpose)
= 'T': $A^T*X = B$ (Transpose)
= 'C': $A^H*X = B$ (Conjugate transpose)

N   (input) INTEGER
The order of the matrix A. $N \geq 0$.

KL   (input) INTEGER
The number of subdiagonals within the band of A. $KL \geq 0$.

KU   (input) INTEGER
The number of superdiagonals within the band of A. $KU \geq 0$.

NRHS   (input) INTEGER
The number of right hand sides, i.e., the number of columns of the matrix B. $NRHS \geq 0$.

AB: (input) REAL/COMPLEX array, dimension (LDAB,N)
Details of the LU factorization of the band matrix A, as computed by SGBTRF/CGBTRF. U is stored as an upper triangular band matrix with kl+ku superdiagonals in rows 1 to kl+ku+1, and the multipliers used during the factorization are stored in rows kl+ku+2 to 2*kl+ku+1.

LDAB: (input) INTEGER
The leading dimension of the array AB. LDAB $\geq$ 2*KL+KU+1.

IPIV: (input) INTEGER array, dimension (N)
The pivot indices; for $1 \leq i \leq N$, row i of the matrix was interchanged with row IPIV(i).

B: (input/output) REAL/COMPLEX array, dimension (LDB,NRHS)
On entry, the right hand side matrix B.
On exit, the solution matrix X.

LDB: (input) INTEGER
The leading dimension of the array B. LDB $\geq$ max(1,N).

INFO: (output) INTEGER
= 0: successful exit
< 0: if INFO = $-i$, the ith argument had an illegal value

SGEBAK/CGEBAK

```
SUBROUTINE SGEBAK( JOB, SIDE, N, ILO, IHI, SCALE, M, V, LDV,
$                  INFO )
        CHARACTER      JOB, SIDE
        INTEGER        IHI, ILO, INFO, LDV, M, N
        REAL           V( LDV, * ), SCALE( * )

SUBROUTINE CGEBAK( JOB, SIDE, N, ILO, IHI, SCALE, M, V, LDV,
$                  INFO )
        CHARACTER      JOB, SIDE
        INTEGER        IHI, ILO, INFO, LDV, M, N
        REAL           SCALE( * )
        COMPLEX        V( LDV, * )
```

Purpose

SGEBAK/CGEBAK forms the left or right eigenvectors of a general real/complex matrix by backward transformation on the computed eigenvectors of the balanced matrix output by SGEBAL/CGEBAL.

Arguments

JOB: (input) CHARACTER*1
Specifies the type of backward transformation required:
= 'N': do nothing, return immediately;

= 'P': do backward transformation for permutation only;
= 'S': do backward transformation for scaling only;
= 'B': do backward transformations for both permutation and scaling.
JOB must be the same as the argument JOB supplied to SGEBAL/CGEBAL.

SIDE: (input) CHARACTER*1
= 'R': V contains right eigenvectors;
= 'L': V contains left eigenvectors.

N: (input) INTEGER
The number of rows of the matrix V. N $\geq$ 0.

ILO, IHI: (input) INTEGER
The integers ILO and IHI determined by SGEBAL/CGEBAL.

SCALE: (input) REAL array, dimension (N)
Details of the permutations and scaling factors, as returned by SGEBAL/CGEBAL.

M: (input) INTEGER
The number of columns of the matrix V.

V: (input/output) REAL/COMPLEX array, dimension (LDV,M)
On entry, the matrix of right or left eigenvectors to be transformed, as returned by SHSEIN/CHSEIN or STREVC/CTREVC.
On exit, V is overwritten by the transformed eigenvectors.

LDV: (input) INTEGER
The leading dimension of the array V. LDV $\geq$ max(1,N).

INFO: (output) INTEGER
= 0: successful exit
< 0: if INFO = $-i$, the ith argument had an illegal value.

SGEBAL/CGEBAL

```
SUBROUTINE SGEBAL( JOB, N, A, LDA, ILO, IHI, SCALE, INFO )
        CHARACTER      JOB
        INTEGER        IHI, ILO, INFO, LDA, N
        REAL           A( LDA, * ), SCALE( * )

SUBROUTINE CGEBAL( JOB, N, A, LDA, ILO, IHI, SCALE, INFO )
        CHARACTER      JOB
        INTEGER        IHI, ILO, INFO, LDA, N
        REAL           SCALE( * )
        COMPLEX        A( LDA, * )
```

Purpose

SGEBAL/CGEBAL balances a general real/complex matrix A. This involves, first, permuting A by a similarity transformation to isolate eigenvalues in the first 1 to

ILO−1 and last IHI+1 to N elements on the diagonal; and second, applying a diagonal similarity transformation to rows and columns ILO to IHI to make the rows and columns as close in norm as possible. Both steps are optional.

Balancing may reduce the 1-norm of the matrix, and improve the accuracy of the computed eigenvalues and/or eigenvectors.

Arguments

JOB (input) CHARACTER*1
    Specifies the operations to be performed on A:
    = 'N': none: simply set ILO = 1, IHI = N, SCALE(i) = 1.0 for i = 1,...,N;
    = 'P': permute only;
    = 'S': scale only;
    = 'B': both permute and scale.

N (input) INTEGER
    The order of the matrix A. $N \geq 0$.

A (input/output) REAL/COMPLEX array, dimension (LDA,N)
    On entry, the input matrix A.
    On exit, A is overwritten by the balanced matrix.
    If JOB = 'N', A is not referenced.

LDA (input) INTEGER
    The leading dimension of the array A. $LDA \geq \max(1,N)$.

ILO, IHI (output) INTEGER
    ILO and IHI are set to integers such that on exit A(i,j) = 0 if i > j and j = 1,...,ilo−1 or i = ihi+1,...,n.
    If JOB = 'N' or 'S', ILO = 1 and IHI = N.

SCALE (output) REAL array, dimension (N)
    Details of the permutations and scaling factors applied to A. If P(j) is the index of the row and column interchanged with row and column j, and D(j) is the scaling factor applied to row and column j, then
    SCALE(j) = P(j)   for j = 1,...,ilo−1
            = D(j)   for j = ilo,...,ihi
            = P(j)   for j = ihi+1,...,n.
    The order in which the interchanges are made is n to ihi+1, then 1 to ilo−1.

INFO (output) INTEGER
    = 0: successful exit
    < 0: if INFO = −i, the ith argument had an illegal value.

SGEBRD/CGEBRD

```
SUBROUTINE SGEBRD( M, N, A, LDA, D, E, TAUQ, TAUP, WORK, LWORK,
$                  INFO )
INTEGER    INFO, LDA, LWORK, M, N
REAL       A( LDA, * ), D( * ), E( * ), TAUP( * ),
$          TAUQ( * ), WORK( LWORK )

SUBROUTINE CGEBRD( M, N, A, LDA, D, E, TAUQ, TAUP, WORK, LWORK,
$                  INFO )
INTEGER    INFO, LDA, LWORK, M, N
REAL       D( * ), E( * )
COMPLEX    A( LDA, * ), TAUP( * ), TAUQ( * ),
$          WORK( LWORK )
```

Purpose

SGEBRD/CGEBRD reduces a general real/complex m-by-n matrix A to upper or lower bidiagonal form B by an orthogonal/unitary transformation: $Q^H * A * P = B$.

If $m \geq n$, B is upper bidiagonal; if $m < n$, B is lower bidiagonal.

Arguments

M (input) INTEGER
    The number of rows in the matrix A. $M \geq 0$.

N (input) INTEGER
    The number of columns in the matrix A. $N \geq 0$.

A (input/output) REAL/COMPLEX array, dimension (LDA,N)
    On entry, the m-by-n general matrix to be reduced.
    On exit, if $m \geq n$, the diagonal and the first superdiagonal are overwritten with the upper bidiagonal matrix B; the elements below the diagonal, with the array TAUQ, represent the orthogonal/unitary matrix Q as a product of elementary reflectors, and the elements above the first superdiagonal, with the array TAUP, represent the orthogonal/unitary matrix P as a product of elementary reflectors; if $m < n$, the diagonal and the first subdiagonal are overwritten with the lower bidiagonal matrix B; the elements below the first subdiagonal, with the array TAUQ, represent the orthogonal/unitary matrix Q as a product of elementary reflectors, and the elements above the diagonal, with the array TAUP, represent the orthogonal/unitary matrix P as a product of elementary reflectors.

LDA (input) INTEGER
    The leading dimension of the array A. $LDA \geq \max(1,M)$.

D (output) REAL array, dimension (min(M,N))
    The diagonal elements of the bidiagonal matrix B: $D(i) = A(i,i)$.

E (output) REAL array, dimension (min(M,N)−1)
    The off-diagonal elements of the bidiagonal matrix B:

if m ≥ n, E(i) = A(i,i+1) for i = 1,2,...,n−1;
if m < n, E(i) = A(i+1,i) for i = 1,2,...,m−1.

TAUQ   (output) REAL/COMPLEX array dimension (min(M,N))
The scalar factors of the elementary reflectors which represent the orthogonal/unitary matrix Q.

TAUP   (output) REAL/COMPLEX array, dimension (min(M,N))
The scalar factors of the elementary reflectors which represent the orthogonal/unitary matrix P.

WORK   (workspace) REAL/COMPLEX array, dimension (LWORK)
On exit, if INFO = 0, WORK(1) returns the optimal LWORK.

LWORK   (input) INTEGER
The length of the array WORK. LWORK ≥ max(1,M,N).
For optimum performance LWORK ≥ (M+N)*NB, where NB is the optimal block size.

INFO   (output) INTEGER
= 0: successful exit
< 0: if INFO = −i, the ith argument had an illegal value.

SGECON/CGECON

```
SUBROUTINE SGECON( NORM, N, A, LDA, ANORM, RCOND, WORK, IWORK,
$                   INFO )
   CHARACTER  NORM
   INTEGER    INFO, LDA, N
   REAL       ANORM, RCOND
   INTEGER    IWORK( * )
   REAL       A( LDA, * ), WORK( * )

SUBROUTINE CGECON( NORM, N, A, LDA, ANORM, RCOND, WORK, RWORK,
$                   INFO )
   CHARACTER  NORM
   INTEGER    INFO, LDA, N
   REAL       ANORM, RCOND
   REAL       RWORK( * )
   COMPLEX    A( LDA, * ), WORK( * )
```

Purpose

SGECON/CGECON estimates the reciprocal of the condition number of a general real/complex matrix A, in either the 1-norm or the infinity-norm, using the LU factorization computed by SGETRF/CGETRF.

An estimate is obtained for $||A^{-1}||$, and the reciprocal of the condition number is computed as RCOND $= 1/(||A|| \cdot ||A^{-1}||)$.

Arguments

NORM   (input) CHARACTER*1
Specifies whether the 1-norm condition number or the infinity-norm condition number is required:
= '1' or 'O': 1-norm;
= 'I': Infinity-norm.

N   (input) INTEGER
The order of the matrix A. N ≥ 0.

A   (input) REAL/COMPLEX array, dimension (LDA,N)
The factors L and U from the factorization A = P*L*U as computed by SGETRF/CGETRF.

LDA   (input) INTEGER
The leading dimension of the array A. LDA ≥ max(1,N).

ANORM   (input) REAL
If NORM = '1' or 'O', the 1-norm of the original matrix A.
If NORM = 'I', the infinity-norm of the original matrix A.

RCOND   (output) REAL
The reciprocal of the condition number of the matrix A, computed as RCOND $= 1/(||A|| \cdot ||A^{-1}||)$.

WORK   SGECON (workspace) REAL array, dimension (4*N)
        CGECON (workspace) COMPLEX array, dimension (2*N)

IWORK   SGECON only (workspace) INTEGER array, dimension (N)

RWORK   CGECON only (workspace) REAL array, dimension (2*N)

INFO   (output) INTEGER
= 0: successful exit
< 0: if INFO = −i, the ith argument had an illegal value

SGEEQU/CGEEQU

```
SUBROUTINE SGEEQU( M, N, A, LDA, R, C, ROWCND, COLCND, AMAX,
$                   INFO )
   INTEGER    INFO, LDA, M, N
   REAL       AMAX, COLCND, ROWCND
   REAL       A( LDA, * ), C( * ), R( * )

SUBROUTINE CGEEQU( M, N, A, LDA, R, C, ROWCND, COLCND, AMAX,
$                   INFO )
   INTEGER    INFO, LDA, M, N
   REAL       AMAX, COLCND, ROWCND
   REAL       C( * ), R( * )
   COMPLEX    A( LDA, * )
```

Purpose

SGEEQU/CGEEQU computes row and column scalings intended to equilibrate an m-by-n matrix A and reduce its condition number. R returns the row scale factors and C the column scale factors, chosen to try to make the largest element in each row and column of the matrix B with elements $B(i,j) = R(i)*A(i,j)*C(j)$ have absolute value 1.

$R(i)$ and $C(j)$ are restricted to be between SMLNUM = smallest safe number and BIGNUM = largest safe number. Use of these scaling factors is not guaranteed to reduce the condition number of A but works well in practice.

Arguments

M   (input) INTEGER
The number of rows of the matrix A. $M \geq 0$.

N   (input) INTEGER
The number of columns of the matrix A. $N \geq 0$.

A   (input) REAL/COMPLEX array, dimension (LDA,N)
The m-by-n matrix whose equilibration factors are to be computed.

LDA   (input) INTEGER
The leading dimension of the array A. $LDA \geq \max(1,M)$.

R   (output) REAL array, dimension (M)
If INFO = 0 or INFO > M, R contains the row scale factors for A.

C   (output) REAL array, dimension (N)
If INFO = 0, C contains the column scale factors for A.

ROWCND   (output) REAL
If INFO = 0 or INFO > M, RCOND contains the ratio of the smallest R(i) to the largest R(i). If ROWCND $\geq$ 0.1 and AMAX is neither too large nor too small, it is not worth scaling by R.

COLCND   (output) REAL
If INFO = 0, COLCND contains the ratio of the smallest C(i) to the largest C(i). If COLCND $\geq$ 0.1, it is not worth scaling by C.

AMAX   (output) REAL
Absolute value of largest matrix element. If AMAX is very close to overflow or very close to underflow, the matrix should be scaled.

INFO   (output) INTEGER
= 0:   successful exit
< 0:   if INFO = -i, the ith argument had an illegal value
> 0:   if INFO = i, and i is
    $\leq$ M: the ith row of A is exactly zero
    > M: the i-Mth column of A is exactly zero

SGEES/CGEES

```
SUBROUTINE SGEES( JOBVS, SORT, SELECT, N, A, LDA, SDIM, WR, WI,
$                 VS, LDVS, WORK, LWORK, BWORK, INFO )
     CHARACTER       JOBVS, SORT
     INTEGER         INFO, LDA, LDVS, LWORK, N, SDIM
     LOGICAL         BWORK( * )
     REAL            A( LDA, * ), VS( LDVS, * ), WI( * ), WORK( * ),
$                    WR( * )
     LOGICAL         SELECT
     EXTERNAL        SELECT
```

```
SUBROUTINE CGEES( JOBVS, SORT, SELECT, N, A, LDA, SDIM, W, VS,
$                 LDVS, WORK, LWORK, RWORK, BWORK, INFO )
     CHARACTER       JOBVS, SORT
     INTEGER         INFO, LDA, LDVS, LWORK, N, SDIM
     LOGICAL         BWORK( * )
     REAL            RWORK( * )
     COMPLEX         A( LDA, * ), VS( LDVS, * ), W( * ), WORK( * )
     LOGICAL         SELECT
     EXTERNAL        SELECT
```

Purpose

SGEES/CGEES computes for an n-by-n real/complex nonsymmetric matrix A, the eigenvalues, the real-Schur/Schur form T, and, optionally, the matrix of Schur vectors Z. This gives the Schur factorization $A = Z*T*Z^H$.

Optionally, it also orders the eigenvalues on the diagonal of the real-Schur/Schur form so that selected eigenvalues are at the top left. The leading columns of Z then form an orthonormal basis for the invariant subspace corresponding to the selected eigenvalues.

A real matrix is in real-Schur form if it is upper quasi-triangular with 1-by-1 and 2-by-2 diagonal blocks. 2-by-2 diagonal blocks will be standardized in the form
$$\begin{bmatrix} a & b \\ c & a \end{bmatrix}$$
where $b*c < 0$. The eigenvalues of such a block are $a \pm \sqrt{bc}$.

A complex matrix is in Schur form if it is upper triangular.

Arguments

JOBVS   (input) CHARACTER*1
= 'N':   Schur vectors are not computed;
= 'V':   Schur vectors are computed.

SORT   (input) CHARACTER*1
Specifies whether or not to order the eigenvalues on the diagonal of the Schur form.
= 'N':   Eigenvalues are not ordered;

= 'S':   Eigenvalues are ordered (see SELECT).

SELECT   *SGEES* (input) LOGICAL FUNCTION of two REAL variables
CGEES (input) LOGICAL FUNCTION of one COMPLEX variable
SELECT must be declared EXTERNAL in the calling subroutine.
If SORT = 'S', SELECT is used to select eigenvalues to sort to the top left of the Schur form.
If SORT = 'N', SELECT is not referenced.
SGEES
An eigenvalue $WR(j) + i*WI(j)$ is selected if $SELECT(WR(j),WI(j))$ is true. A complex eigenvalue is selected if either $SELECT(WR(j),WI(j))$ or $SELECT(WR(j),-WI(j))$ is true: i.e., if either one of a complex conjugate pair of eigenvalues is selected, then both are. Note that a selected complex eigenvalue may no longer satisfy $SELECT(WR(j),WI(j))$ =.TRUE. after ordering, since ordering may change the value of complex eigenvalues (especially if the eigenvalue is ill-conditioned); in this case INFO may be set to N+2 (see INFO below).
CGEES
An eigenvalue $W(j)$ is selected if $SELECT(W(j))$ is true.

N   (input) INTEGER
The order of the matrix A. $N \geq 0$.

A   (input/output) REAL/COMPLEX array, dimension (LDA, N)
On entry, the n-by-n matrix A.
On exit, A is overwritten by its real-Schur/Schur form T.

LDA   (input) INTEGER
The leading dimension of the array A. $LDA \geq \max(1,N)$.

SDIM   (output) INTEGER
If SORT = 'N', SDIM = 0.
If SORT = 'S', SDIM = number of eigenvalues (after sorting) for which SELECT is true.
SGEES only
(Complex conjugate pairs for which SELECT is true for either eigenvalue count as 2.)

WR, WI   *SGEES only* (output) REAL array, dimension (N)
WR and WI contain the real and imaginary parts, respectively, of the computed eigenvalues, in the same order that they appear on the diagonal of the output Schur form T. Complex conjugate pairs of eigenvalues appear consecutively with the eigenvalue having the positive imaginary part first.

W   *CGEES only* (output) COMPLEX array, dimension (N)
W contains the computed eigenvalues, in the same order that they appear on the diagonal of the output Schur form T.

VS   (output) REAL/COMPLEX array, dimension (LDVS,N)
If JOBVS = 'V', VS contains the orthogonal/unitary matrix Z of Schur vectors.
If JOBVS = 'N', VS is not referenced.

LDVS   (input) INTEGER
The leading dimension of the array VS. $LDVS \geq 1$; if JOBVS = 'V', $LDVS \geq N$.

WORK   (workspace) REAL/COMPLEX array, dimension (LWORK)
On exit, if INFO = 0, WORK(1) returns the optimal LWORK.

LWORK   (input) INTEGER
The dimension of the array WORK.
$LWORK \geq \max(1,3*N)$ *(SGEES)*
$LWORK \geq \max(1,2*N)$ *(CGEES)*.
For good performance, LWORK must generally be larger.

RWORK   *CGEES only* (workspace) REAL array, dimension (N)

BWORK   (workspace) LOGICAL array, dimension (N)
Not referenced if SORT = 'N'.

INFO   (output) INTEGER
= 0:   successful exit
< 0:   if INFO = $-i$, the ith argument had an illegal value.
> 0:   if INFO = i, and i is
$\leq N$:   the QR algorithm failed to compute all the eigenvalues; elements i+1:n of WR and WI *(SGEES)* or W *(CGEES)* contain those eigenvalues which have converged; if JOBVS = 'V', VS contains the matrix which reduces A to its partially converged Schur form.
= N+1:   the eigenvalues could not be reordered because some eigenvalues were too close to separate (the problem is very ill-conditioned);
= N+2:   after reordering, roundoff changed values of some complex eigenvalues so that leading eigenvalues in the Schur form no longer satisfy SELECT=.TRUE. This could also be caused by underflow due to scaling.

SGEESX/CGEESX

```
SUBROUTINE SGEESX( JOBVS, SORT, SELECT, SENSE, N, A, LDA, SDIM,
     $                   WR, WI, VS, LDVS, RCONDE, RCONDV, WORK, LWORK,
     $                   IWORK, LIWORK, BWORK, INFO )
      CHARACTER          JOBVS, SENSE, SORT
      INTEGER            INFO, LDA, LDVS, LIWORK, LWORK, N, SDIM
      REAL               RCONDE, RCONDV
      LOGICAL            BWORK( * )
      INTEGER            IWORK( * )
      REAL               A( LDA, * ), VS( LDVS, * ), WI( * ), WORK( * ),
     $                   WR( * )
      LOGICAL            SELECT
      EXTERNAL           SELECT
```

```
SUBROUTINE CGEESX( JOBVS, SORT, SELECT, SENSE, N, A, LDA, SDIM,
     $                   W, VS, LDVS, RCONDE, RCONDV, WORK, LWORK,
     $                   RWORK, BWORK, INFO )
      CHARACTER          JOBVS, SENSE, SORT
      INTEGER            INFO, LDA, LDVS, LWORK, N, SDIM
      REAL               RCONDE, RCONDV
      LOGICAL            BWORK( * )
      REAL               RWORK( * )
      COMPLEX            A( LDA, * ), VS( LDVS, * ), W( * ), WORK( * )
      LOGICAL            SELECT
      EXTERNAL           SELECT
```

Purpose

SGEESX/CGEESX computes for an n-by-n real/complex nonsymmetric matrix A, the eigenvalues, the real-Schur/Schur form T, and, optionally, the matrix of Schur vectors Z. This gives the Schur factorization $A = Z*T*Z^H$.

Optionally, it also orders the eigenvalues on the diagonal of the real-Schur/Schur form so that selected eigenvalues are at the top left; computes a reciprocal condition number for the average of the selected eigenvalues (RCONDE); and computes a reciprocal condition number for the right invariant subspace corresponding to the selected eigenvalues (RCONDV). The leading columns of Z form an orthonormal basis for this invariant subspace.

For further explanation of the reciprocal condition numbers RCONDE and RCONDV, see Section 4.10 (where these quantities are called s and sep respectively).

A real matrix is in real-Schur form if it is upper quasi-triangular with 1-by-1 and 2-by-2 diagonal blocks. 2-by-2 diagonal blocks will be standardized in the form
$$\begin{bmatrix} a & b \\ c & a \end{bmatrix}$$
where $b*c < 0$. The eigenvalues of such a block are $a \pm \sqrt{bc}$.

A complex matrix is in Schur form if it is upper triangular.

Arguments

JOBVS   (input) CHARACTER*1
   = 'N':   Schur vectors are not computed;
   = 'V':   Schur vectors are computed.

SORT   (input) CHARACTER*1
   Specifies whether or not to order the eigenvalues on the diagonal of the Schur form.
   = 'N':   Eigenvalues are not ordered;
   = 'S':   Eigenvalues are ordered (see SELECT).

SELECT   *SGEESX* (input) LOGICAL FUNCTION of two REAL variables
   CGEESX (input) LOGICAL FUNCTION of one COMPLEX variable
   SELECT must be declared EXTERNAL in the calling subroutine.
   If SORT = 'S', SELECT is used to select eigenvalues to sort to the top

left of the Schur form.
If SORT = 'N', SELECT is not referenced.
SGEESX
An eigenvalue WR(j) + i*WI(j) is selected if SELECT(WR(j),WI(j)) is true. A complex eigenvalue is selected if either SELECT(WR(j),WI(j)) or SELECT(WR(j),–WI(j)) is true: i.e., if either one of a complex conjugate pair of eigenvalues is selected, then both are. Note that a selected complex eigenvalue may no longer satisfy SELECT(WR(j),WI(j)) = .TRUE. after ordering, since ordering may change the value of complex eigenvalues (especially if the eigenvalue is ill-conditioned); in this case INFO may be set to N+2 (see INFO below).
CGEESX
An eigenvalue W(j) is selected if SELECT(W(j)) is true.

SENSE   (input) CHARACTER*1
   Determines which reciprocal condition numbers are computed.
   = 'N':   None are computed;
   = 'E':   Computed for average of selected eigenvalues only;
   = 'V':   Computed for selected right invariant subspace only;
   = 'B':   Computed for both.
   If SENSE = 'E', 'V' or 'B', SORT must equal 'S'.

N   (input) INTEGER
   The order of the matrix A. N $\geq$ 0.

A   (input/output) REAL/COMPLEX array, dimension (LDA,N)
   On entry, the n-by-n matrix A.
   On exit, A is overwritten by its real-Schur/Schur form T.

LDA   (input) INTEGER
   The leading dimension of the array A. LDA $\geq$ max(1,N).

SDIM   (output) INTEGER
   If SORT = 'N', SDIM = 0.
   If SORT = 'S', SDIM = number of eigenvalues (after sorting) for which SELECT is true.
   SGEESX only
   (Complex conjugate pairs for which SELECT is true for either eigenvalue count as 2.)

WR, WI   *SGEESX only* (output) REAL array, dimension (N)
   WR and WI contain the real and imaginary parts, respectively, of the computed eigenvalues, in the same order that they appear on the diagonal of the output Schur form T. Complex conjugate pairs of eigenvalues appear consecutively with the eigenvalue having the positive imaginary part first.

W   *CGEESX only* (output) COMPLEX array, dimension (N)
   W contains the computed eigenvalues, in the same order that they appear on the diagonal of the output Schur form T.

VS   (output) REAL/COMPLEX array, dimension (LDVS,N)
   If JOBVS = 'V', VS contains the orthogonal/unitary matrix Z of Schur

vectors.
If JOBVS = 'N', VS is not referenced.

LDVS   (input) INTEGER
The leading dimension of the array VS. LDVS ≥ 1; if JOBVS = 'V', LDVS ≥ N.

RCONDE   (output) REAL
If SENSE = 'E' or 'B', RCONDE contains the reciprocal condition number for the average of the selected eigenvalues.
Not referenced if SENSE = 'N' or 'V'.

RCONDV   (output) REAL
If SENSE = 'V' or 'B', RCONDV contains the reciprocal condition number for the selected right invariant subspace.
Not referenced if SENSE = 'N' or 'E'.

WORK   (workspace) REAL/COMPLEX array, dimension (LWORK)
On exit, if INFO = 0, WORK(1) returns the optimal LWORK.

LWORK   (input) INTEGER
The dimension of the array WORK.
LWORK ≥ max(1,3*N) (SGEESX)
LWORK ≥ max(1,2*N) (CGEESX).
Also, if SENSE = 'E' or 'V' or 'B',
LWORK ≥ N+2*SDIM*(N−SDIM) (SGEESX)
LWORK ≥ 2*SDIM*(N−SDIM) (CGEESX),
where SDIM is the number of selected eigenvalues computed by this routine. Note that 2*SDIM*(N−SDIM) ≤ N*N/2.
For good performance, LWORK must generally be larger.

IWORK   SGEESX only (workspace) INTEGER array, dimension (LIWORK)
Not referenced if SENSE = 'N' or 'E'.

LIWORK   SGEESX only (input) INTEGER The dimension of the array IWORK.
LIWORK ≥ 1; if SENSE = 'V' or 'B', LIWORK ≥ SDIM*(N−SDIM).

RWORK   CGEESX only (workspace) REAL array, dimension (N)

BWORK   (workspace) LOGICAL array, dimension (N)
Not referenced if SORT = 'N'.

INFO   (output) INTEGER
= 0:   successful exit
< 0:   if INFO = −i, the i-th argument had an illegal value.
> 0:   if INFO = i, and i is
≤ N: the QR algorithm failed to compute all the eigenvalues; elements i+1:n of WR and WI (SGEESX) or W (CGEESX) contain those eigenvalues which have converged; if JOBVS = 'V', VS contains the transformation which reduces A to its partially converged Schur form.
= N+1: the eigenvalues could not be reordered because some eigenvalues were too close to separate (the problem is very ill-conditioned);

= N+2: after reordering, roundoff changed values of some complex eigenvalues so that leading eigenvalues in the Schur form no longer satisfy SELECT=.TRUE. This could also be caused by underflow due to scaling.

SGEEV/CGEEV

```
SUBROUTINE SGEEV( JOBVL, JOBVR, N, A, LDA, WR, WI, VL, LDVL, VR,
$                 LDVR, WORK, LWORK, INFO )
CHARACTER         JOBVL, JOBVR
INTEGER           INFO, LDA, LDVL, LDVR, LWORK, N
REAL              A( LDA, * ), VL( LDVL, * ), VR( LDVR, * ),
$                 WI( * ), WORK( * ), WR( * )
```

```
SUBROUTINE CGEEV( JOBVL, JOBVR, N, A, LDA, W, VL, LDVL, VR,
$                 LDVR, WORK, LWORK, RWORK, INFO )
CHARACTER         JOBVL, JOBVR
INTEGER           INFO, LDA, LDVL, LDVR, LWORK, N
REAL              RWORK( * )
COMPLEX           A( LDA, * ), VL( LDVL, * ), VR( LDVR, * ),
$                 W( * ), WORK( * )
```

Purpose

SGEEV/CGEEV computes for an n-by-n real/complex nonsymmetric matrix A, the eigenvalues and, optionally, the left and/or right eigenvectors.

The left eigenvectors of A are the same as the right eigenvectors of A^H. If u(j) and v(j) are the left and right eigenvectors, respectively, corresponding to the eigenvalue $\lambda(j)$, then $u(j)^H*A = \lambda(j)*u(j)^H$ and $A*v(j) = \lambda(j)*v(j)$.

The computed eigenvectors are normalized to have Euclidean norm equal to 1 and largest component real.

Arguments

JOBVL   (input) CHARACTER*1
= 'N':   left eigenvectors of A are not computed.
= 'V':   left eigenvectors of A are computed.

JOBVR   (input) CHARACTER*1
= 'N':   right eigenvectors of A are not computed.
= 'V':   right eigenvectors of A are computed.

N   (input) INTEGER
The order of the matrix A. N ≥ 0.

SGEEV/CGEEV

A   (input/output) REAL/COMPLEX array, dimension (LDA,N)
On entry, the n-by-n matrix A.
On exit, A has been overwritten.

LDA   (input) INTEGER
The leading dimension of A. LDA ≥ max(1,N).

WR, WI   *SGEEV only* (output) REAL array, dimension (N)
WR and WI contain the real and imaginary parts, respectively, of the computed eigenvalues. Complex conjugate pairs of eigenvalues appear consecutively with the eigenvalue having the positive imaginary part first.

W   *CGEEV only* (output) COMPLEX array, dimension (N)
W contains the computed eigenvalues.

VL   (output) REAL/COMPLEX array, dimension (LDVL,N)
If JOBVL = 'V', the left eigenvectors u(j) are stored one after another in the columns of VL, in the same order as their eigenvalues.
If JOBVL = 'N', VL is not referenced.
SGEEV
If the jth eigenvalue is real, then u(j) = VL(:,j), the jth column of VL.
If the jth and $(j+1)^{th}$ eigenvalues form a complex conjugate pair, then u(j) = VL(:,j) + i*VL(:,j+1) and u(j+1) = VL(:,j) − i*VL(:,j+1).
CGEEV
u(j) = VL(:,j), the jth column of VL.

LDVL   (input) INTEGER
The leading dimension of the array VL. LDVL ≥ 1; if JOBVL = 'V', LDVL ≥ N.

VR   (output) REAL/COMPLEX array, dimension (LDVR,N)
If JOBVR = 'V', the right eigenvectors v(j) are stored one after another in the columns of VR, in the same order as their eigenvalues.
If JOBVR = 'N', VR is not referenced.
SGEEV
If the jth eigenvalue is real, then v(j) = VR(:,j), the jth column of VR.
If the jth and $(j+1)^{th}$ eigenvalues form a complex conjugate pair, then v(j) = VR(:,j) + i*VR(:,j+1) and v(j+1) = VR(:,j) − i*VR(:,j+1).
CGEEV
v(j) = VR(:,j), the jth column of VR.

LDVR   (input) INTEGER
The leading dimension of the matrix VR. LDVR ≥ 1; if JOBVR = 'V', LDVR ≥ N.

WORK   (workspace) REAL/COMPLEX array, dimension (LWORK)
On exit, if INFO = 0, WORK(1) returns the optimal LWORK.

LWORK   (input) INTEGER
The dimension of the array WORK.
LWORK ≥ max(1,3*N), and if JOBVL = 'V' or JOBVR = 'V', LWORK ≥ max(1,4*N) (*SGEEV*)

LWORK ≥ max(1,2*N) (*CGEEV*).
For good performance, LWORK must generally be larger.

RWORK   *CGEEV only* (workspace) REAL array, dimension (2*N)

INFO   (output) INTEGER
= 0: successful exit
< 0: if INFO = −i, the ith argument had an illegal value.
> 0: if INFO = i, the QR algorithm failed to compute all the eigenvalues, and no eigenvectors have been computed; elements i+1:n of WR and WI (*SGEEV*) or W (*CGEEV*) contain eigenvalues which have converged.

SGEEVX/CGEEVX

```
SUBROUTINE SGEEVX( BALANC, JOBVL, JOBVR, SENSE, N, A, LDA, WR,
$                  WI, VL, LDVL, VR, LDVR, ILO, IHI, SCALE, ABNRM,
$                  RCONDE, RCONDV, WORK, LWORK, IWORK, INFO )
CHARACTER          BALANC, JOBVL, JOBVR, SENSE
INTEGER            IHI, ILO, INFO, LDA, LDVL, LDVR, LWORK, N
REAL               ABNRM
INTEGER            IWORK( * )
REAL               A( LDA, * ), RCONDE( * ), RCONDV( * ),
$                  SCALE( * ), VL( LDVL, * ), VR( LDVR, * ),
$                  WI( * ), WORK( * ), WR( * )
```

```
SUBROUTINE CGEEVX( BALANC, JOBVL, JOBVR, SENSE, N, A, LDA, W,
$                  VL, LDVL, VR, LDVR, ILO, IHI, SCALE, ABNRM,
$                  RCONDE, RCONDV, WORK, LWORK, RWORK, INFO )
CHARACTER          BALANC, JOBVL, JOBVR, SENSE
INTEGER            IHI, ILO, INFO, LDA, LDVL, LDVR, LWORK, N
REAL               ABNRM
REAL               RCONDE( * ), RCONDV( * ), RWORK( * ),
$                  SCALE( * )
COMPLEX            A( LDA, * ), VL( LDVL, * ), VR( LDVR, * ),
$                  W( * ), WORK( * )
```

Purpose

SGEEVX/CGEEVX computes for an n-by-n real/complex nonsymmetric matrix A, the eigenvalues and, optionally, the left and/or right eigenvectors.

Optionally also, it computes a balancing transformation to improve the conditioning of the eigenvalues and eigenvectors (ILO, IHI, SCALE, and ABNRM), reciprocal condition numbers for the eigenvalues (RCONDE), and reciprocal condition numbers for the right eigenvectors (RCONDV).

SGEEVX/CGVEEX

The left eigenvectors of A are the same as the right eigenvectors of A^H. If $u(j)$ and $v(j)$ are the left and right eigenvectors, respectively, corresponding to the eigenvalue $\lambda(j)$, then $u(j)^H * A = \lambda(j) * u(j)^H$ and $A * v(j) = \lambda(j) * v(j)$.

The computed eigenvectors are normalized to have Euclidean norm equal to 1 and largest component real.

Balancing a matrix means permuting the rows and columns to make it more nearly upper triangular, and applying a diagonal similarity transformation $D*A*D^{-1}$, where D is a diagonal matrix, to make its rows and columns closer in norm and the condition numbers of its eigenvalues and eigenvectors smaller. The computed reciprocal condition numbers correspond to the balanced matrix. Permuting rows and columns will not change the condition numbers (in exact arithmetic) but diagonal scaling will. For further explanation of balancing, see section 4.10.2.

For further explanation of the reciprocal condition numbers RCONDE and RCONDV, see Section 4.10 (where these quantities are called s and sep respectively).

Arguments

BALANC (input) CHARACTER*1
Indicates how the input matrix should be diagonally scaled and/or permuted to improve the conditioning of its eigenvalues.
= 'N':   Do not diagonally scale or permute;
= 'P':   Perform permutations to make the matrix more nearly upper triangular. Do not diagonally scale;
= 'S':   Diagonally scale the matrix, ie. replace A by $D*A*D^{-1}$, where D is a diagonal matrix chosen to make the rows and columns of A more equal in norm. Do not permute;
= 'B':   Both diagonally scale and permute A.
Computed reciprocal condition numbers will be for the matrix after balancing and/or permuting. Permuting does not change condition numbers (in exact arithmetic), but balancing does.

JOBVL   (input) CHARACTER*1
= 'N':   left eigenvectors of A are not computed;
= 'V':   left eigenvectors of A are computed.
If SENSE = 'E' or 'B', JOBVL must = 'V'.

JOBVR   (input) CHARACTER*1
= 'N':   right eigenvectors of A are not computed;
= 'V':   right eigenvectors of A are computed.
If SENSE = 'E' or 'B', JOBVR must = 'V'.

SENSE   (input) CHARACTER*1
Determines which reciprocal condition numbers are computed.
= 'N':   None are computed;
= 'E':   Computed for eigenvalues only;
= 'V':   Computed for right eigenvectors only;
= 'B':   Computed for eigenvalues and right eigenvectors.

If SENSE = 'E' or 'B', both left and right eigenvectors must also be computed (JOBVL = 'V' and JOBVR = 'V').

N   (input) INTEGER
The order of the matrix A. N $\geq$ 0.

A   (input/output) REAL/COMPLEX array, dimension (LDA,N)
On entry, the n-by-n matrix A.
On exit, A has been overwritten. If JOBVL = 'V' or JOBVR = 'V', A contains the real-Schur/Schur form of the balanced version of the input matrix A.

LDA   (input) INTEGER
The leading dimension of the array A. LDA $\geq$ max(1,N).

WR, WI SGEEVX only (output) REAL array, dimension (N)
WR and WI contain the real and imaginary parts, respectively, of the computed eigenvalues. Complex conjugate pairs of eigenvalues appear consecutively with the eigenvalue having the positive imaginary part first.

W   CGEEVX only (output) COMPLEX array, dimension (N)
W contains the computed eigenvalues.

VL   (output) REAL/COMPLEX array, dimension (LDVL,N)
If JOBVL = 'V', the left eigenvectors $u(j)$ are stored one after another in the columns of VL, in the same order as their eigenvalues.
If JOBVL = 'N', VL is not referenced.
SGEEV
If the jth eigenvalue is real, then $u(j) = VL(:,j)$, the jth column of VL.
If the jth and $(j+1)^{th}$ eigenvalues form a complex conjugate pair, then $u(j) = VL(:,j) + i*VL(:,j+1)$ and $u(j+1) = VL(:,j) - i*VL(:,j+1)$.
CGEEV
$u(j) = VL(:,j)$, the jth column of VL.

LDVL   (input) INTEGER
The leading dimension of the array VL. LDVL $\geq$ 1; if JOBVL = 'V', LDVL $\geq$ N.

VR   (output) REAL/COMPLEX array, dimension (LDVR,N)
If JOBVR = 'V', the right eigenvectors $v(j)$ are stored one after another in the columns of VR, in the same order as their eigenvalues.
If JOBVR = 'N', VR is not referenced.
SGEEV
If the jth eigenvalue is real, then $v(j) = VR(:,j)$, the jth column of VR.
If the jth and $(j+1)^{th}$ eigenvalues form a complex conjugate pair, then $v(j) = VR(:,j) + i*VR(:,j+1)$ and $v(j+1) = VR(:,j) - i*VR(:,j+1)$.
CGEEV
$v(j) = VR(:,j)$, the jth column of VR.

LDVR   (input) INTEGER
The leading dimension of the matrix VR. LDVR $\geq$ 1; if JOBVR = 'V', LDVR $\geq$ N.

SGEHRD/CGEHRD

```
SUBROUTINE SGEHRD( N, ILO, IHI, A, LDA, TAU, WORK, LWORK, INFO )
INTEGER              IHI, ILO, INFO, LDA, LWORK, N
REAL                 A( LDA, * ), TAU( * ), WORK( * )

SUBROUTINE CGEHRD( N, ILO, IHI, A, LDA, TAU, WORK, LWORK, INFO )
INTEGER              IHI, ILO, INFO, LDA, LWORK, N
COMPLEX              A( LDA, * ), TAU( * ), WORK( * )
```

Purpose

SGEHRD/CGEHRD reduces a general real/complex matrix A to upper Hessenberg form H by an orthogonal/unitary similarity transformation: $Q^H * A * Q = H$.

Arguments

N   (input) INTEGER
The order of the matrix A. N ≥ 0.

ILO, IHI   (input) INTEGER
It is assumed that A is already upper triangular in rows and columns 1:ilo−1 and ihi+1:n. ILO and IHI are normally set by a previous call to SGEBAL/CGEBAL; otherwise they should be set to 1 and N respectively. If N > 0, 1 ≤ ILO ≤ IHI ≤ N; otherwise set ILO = 1, IHI = N.

A   (input/output) REAL/COMPLEX array, dimension (LDA,N)
On entry, the n-by-n general matrix to be reduced.
On exit, the upper triangle and the first subdiagonal of A are overwritten with the upper Hessenberg matrix H, and the elements below the first subdiagonal, with the array TAU, represent the orthogonal/unitary matrix Q as a product of elementary reflectors.

LDA   (input) INTEGER
The leading dimension of the array A. LDA ≥ max(1,N).

TAU   (output) REAL/COMPLEX array, dimension (N)
The scalar factors of the elementary reflectors. Elements 1:ilo−1 and ihi:n of TAU are set to zero.

WORK   (workspace) REAL/COMPLEX array, dimension (LWORK)
On exit, if INFO = 0, WORK(1) returns the optimal LWORK.

LWORK   (input) INTEGER
The length of the array WORK. LWORK ≥ max(1,N).
For optimum performance LWORK ≥ N*NB, where NB is the optimal block size.

INFO   (output) INTEGER
= 0:   successful exit

ILO, IHI   (output) INTEGER
ILO and IHI are integer values determined when A was balanced. The balanced A(i,j) = 0 if i > j and j = 1,...,ilo−1 or i = ihi+1,...,n.
If BALANC = 'N' or 'S', ILO = 1 and IHI = N.

SCALE   (output) REAL array, dimension (N)
Details of the permutations and scaling factors applied when balancing A. If P(j) is the index of the row and column interchanged with row and column j, and D(j) is the scaling factor applied to row and column j, then

SCALE(j) = P(j)   for j = 1,...,ilo−1
         = D(j)   for j = ilo,...,ihi
         = P(j)   for j = ihi+1,...,n.

The order in which the interchanges are made is n to ihi+1, then 1 to ilo−1.

ABNRM   (output) REAL
The one-norm of the balanced matrix (the maximum of the sum of absolute values of elements of any column).

RCONDE   (output) REAL array, dimension (N)
RCONDE(j) is the reciprocal condition number of the jth eigenvalue.

RCONDV   (output) REAL array, dimension (N)
RCONDV(j) is the reciprocal condition number of the jth right eigenvector.

WORK   (workspace) REAL/COMPLEX array, dimension (LWORK)
On exit, if INFO = 0, WORK(1) returns the optimal LWORK.

LWORK   (input) INTEGER
The dimension of the array WORK.
SGEEVX
If SENSE = 'N' or 'E', LWORK ≥ max(1,2*N), and
if JOBVL = 'V' or JOBVR = 'V', LWORK ≥ 3*N.
If SENSE = 'V' or 'B', LWORK ≥ N*(N+6).
For good performance, LWORK must generally be larger.
CGEEVX
If SENSE = 'N' or 'E', LWORK ≥ max(1,2*N), and
if SENSE = 'V' or 'B', LWORK ≥ N*N+2*N.
For good performance, LWORK must generally be larger.

IWORK   SGEEVX only   (workspace) INTEGER array, dimension (2*N−2)

RWORK   CGEEVX only   (workspace) REAL array, dimension (2*N)

INFO   (output) INTEGER
= 0:   successful exit
< 0:   if INFO = −i, the ith argument had an illegal value.
> 0:   if INFO = i, the QR algorithm failed to compute all the eigenvalues, and no eigenvectors or condition numbers have been computed; elements 1:ilo−1 and i+1:n of WR and WI (SGEEVX) or W (CGEEVX) contain eigenvalues which have converged.

< 0:   if INFO = −i, the ith argument had an illegal value.

SGELQF/CGELQF

```
SUBROUTINE SGELQF( M, N, A, LDA, TAU, WORK, LWORK, INFO )
           INTEGER        INFO, LDA, LWORK, M, N
           REAL           A( LDA, * ), TAU( * ), WORK( LWORK )

SUBROUTINE CGELQF( M, N, A, LDA, TAU, WORK, LWORK, INFO )
           INTEGER        INFO, LDA, LWORK, M, N
           COMPLEX        A( LDA, * ), TAU( * ), WORK( LWORK )
```

Purpose

SGELQF/CGELQF computes an LQ factorization of a real/complex m-by-n matrix A: A = L*Q.

Arguments

M   (input) INTEGER
The number of rows of the matrix A. $M \geq 0$.

N   (input) INTEGER
The number of columns of the matrix A. $N \geq 0$.

A   (input/output) REAL/COMPLEX array, dimension (LDA,N)
On entry, the m-by-n matrix A.
On exit, the elements on and below the diagonal of the array contain the m-by-min(m,n) lower trapezoidal matrix L (L is lower triangular if $m \leq n$); the elements above the diagonal, with the array TAU, represent the orthogonal/unitary matrix Q as a product of min(m,n) elementary reflectors).

LDA   (input) INTEGER
The leading dimension of the array A. $LDA \geq \max(1,M)$.

TAU   (output) REAL/COMPLEX array, dimension (min(M,N))
The scalar factors of the elementary reflectors.

WORK   (workspace) REAL/COMPLEX array, dimension (LWORK)
On exit, if INFO = 0, WORK(1) returns the optimal LWORK.

LWORK   (input) INTEGER
The dimension of the array WORK. $LWORK \geq \max(1,M)$. For optimum performance $LWORK \geq M*NB$, where NB is the optimal block size.

INFO   (output) INTEGER
= 0:   successful exit
< 0:   if INFO = −i, the ith argument had an illegal value

---

SGELS/CGELS

```
SUBROUTINE SGELS( TRANS, M, N, NRHS, A, LDA, B, LDB, WORK, LWORK,
     $                 INFO )
           CHARACTER      TRANS
           INTEGER        INFO, LDA, LDB, LWORK, M, N, NRHS
           REAL           A( LDA, * ), B( LDB, * ), WORK( LWORK )

SUBROUTINE CGELS( TRANS, M, N, NRHS, A, LDA, B, LDB, WORK, LWORK,
     $                 INFO )
           CHARACTER      TRANS
           INTEGER        INFO, LDA, LDB, LWORK, M, N, NRHS
           COMPLEX        A( LDA, * ), B( LDB, * ), WORK( LWORK )
```

Purpose

SGELS/CGELS solves overdetermined or underdetermined real/complex linear systems involving an m-by-n matrix A or its transpose/conjugate-transpose, using a QR or LQ factorization of A. It is assumed that A has full rank.

The following options are provided:

1. If TRANS = 'N' and $m \geq n$: find the least squares solution of an overdetermined system, i.e., solve the least squares problem

   minimize $\| b - A*x \|_2$.

2. If TRANS = 'N' and $m < n$: find the minimum norm solution of an underdetermined system $A*x = b$.

3. If TRANS = 'T' or 'C' and $m \geq n$: find the minimum norm solution of an underdetermined system $A^H*x = b$.

4. If TRANS = 'T' or 'C' and $m < n$: find the least squares solution of an overdetermined system, i.e., solve the least squares problem

   minimize $\| b - A^H*x \|_2$.

Several right hand side vectors b and solution vectors x can be handled in a single call; they are stored as the columns of the m-by-nrhs right hand side matrix B and the n-by-nrhs solution matrix X.

Arguments

TRANS   (input) CHARACTER*1
= 'N':   the linear system involves A;
= 'T':   the linear system involves A^T (*SGELS*);
= 'C':   the linear system involves A^H (*CGELS*).

M (input) INTEGER
The number of rows of the matrix A. $M \geq 0$.

N (input) INTEGER
The number of columns of the matrix A. $N \geq 0$.

NRHS (input) INTEGER
The number of right hand sides, i.e., the number of columns of the matrices B and X. $NRHS \geq 0$.

A (input/output) REAL/COMPLEX array, dimension (LDA,N)
On entry, the m-by-n matrix A.
On exit,
if $m \geq n$, A is overwritten by details of its QR factorization as returned by SGEQRF;
if $m < n$, A is overwritten by details of its LQ factorization as returned by SGELQF.

LDA (input) INTEGER
The leading dimension of the array A. $LDA \geq \max(1,M)$.

B (input/output) REAL/COMPLEX array, dimension (LDB,NRHS)
On entry, the matrix B of right hand side vectors, stored columnwise; B is m-by-nrhs if TRANS = 'N', or n-by-nrhs if TRANS = 'T' or 'C'.
On exit, B is overwritten by the solution vectors, stored columnwise:
if TRANS = 'N' and $m \geq n$, rows 1 to n of B contain the least squares solution vectors; the residual sum of squares for the solution in each column is given by the sum of squares of elements n+1 to m in that column;
if TRANS = 'N' and $m < n$, rows 1 to n of B contain the minimum norm solution vectors;
if TRANS = 'T' or 'C' and $m \geq n$, rows 1 to m of B contain the minimum norm solution vectors;
if TRANS = 'T' or 'C' and $m < n$, rows 1 to m of B contain the least squares solution vectors; the residual sum of squares for the solution in each column is given by the sum of squares of elements m+1 to n in in that column.

LDB (input) INTEGER
The leading dimension of the array B. $LDB \geq \max(1,M,N)$.

WORK (workspace) REAL/COMPLEX array, dimension (LWORK)
On exit, if INFO = 0, WORK(1) returns the optimal LWORK.

LWORK (input) INTEGER
The dimension of the array WORK.
$LWORK \geq \min(M,N) + \max(M,N,NRHS)$.
For optimum performance $LWORK \geq \min(M,N) + \max(M,N,NRHS)*NB$, where NB is the optimum block size.

INFO (output) INTEGER
= 0: successful exit
< 0: if INFO = −i, the ith argument had an illegal value

SGELSS/CGELSS

```
SUBROUTINE SGELSS( M, N, NRHS, A, LDA, B, LDB, S, RCOND, RANK,
$                  WORK, LWORK, INFO )
INTEGER           INFO, LDA, LDB, LWORK, M, N, NRHS, RANK
REAL              RCOND
REAL              A( LDA, * ), B( LDB, * ), S( * ), WORK( * )

SUBROUTINE CGELSS( M, N, NRHS, A, LDA, B, LDB, S, RCOND, RANK,
$                  WORK, LWORK, RWORK, INFO )
INTEGER           INFO, LDA, LDB, LWORK, M, N, NRHS, RANK
REAL              RCOND
REAL              RWORK( * ), S( * )
COMPLEX           A( LDA, * ), B( LDB, * ), WORK( * )
```

Purpose

SGELSS/CGELSS computes the minimum norm solution to a real/complex linear least squares problem:

$$\text{minimize } \| b - A*x \|_2.$$

using the singular value decomposition (SVD) of A. A is an m-by-n matrix which may be rank-deficient.

Several right hand side vectors b and solution vectors x can be handled in a single call; they are stored as the columns of the m-by-nrhs right hand side matrix B and the n-by-nrhs solution matrix X.

The effective rank of A is determined by treating as zero those singular values which are less than RCOND times the largest singular value.

Arguments

M (input) INTEGER
The number of rows of the matrix A. $M \geq 0$.

N (input) INTEGER
The number of columns of the matrix A. $N \geq 0$.

NRHS (input) INTEGER
The number of right hand sides, i.e., the number of columns of the matrices B and X. $NRHS \geq 0$.

A (input/output) REAL/COMPLEX array, dimension (LDA,N)
On entry, the m-by-n matrix A.
On exit, the first min(m,n) rows of A are overwritten with its right singular vectors, stored rowwise.

SGELSX/CGELSX

```
SUBROUTINE SGELSX( M, N, NRHS, A, LDA, B, LDB, JPVT, RCOND, RANK,
$                  WORK, INFO )
INTEGER          INFO, LDA, LDB, M, N, NRHS, RANK
REAL             RCOND
INTEGER          JPVT( * )
REAL             A( LDA, * ), B( LDB, * ), WORK( * )

SUBROUTINE CGELSX( M, N, NRHS, A, LDA, B, LDB, JPVT, RCOND, RANK,
$                  WORK, RWORK, INFO )
INTEGER          INFO, LDA, LDB, M, N, NRHS, RANK
REAL             RCOND
INTEGER          JPVT( * )
REAL             RWORK( * )
COMPLEX          A( LDA, * ), B( LDB, * ), WORK( * )
```

Purpose

SGELSX/CGELSX computes the minimum norm solution to a real/complex linear least squares problem:

$$\text{minimize } \| b - A*x \|_2.$$

using a complete orthogonal factorization of A. A is an m-by-n matrix which may be rank-deficient.

Several right hand side vectors b and solution vectors x can be handled in a single call; they are stored as the columns of the m-by-nrhs right hand side matrix B and the n-by-nrhs solution matrix X.

The routine first computes a QR factorization with column pivoting:

$$A*P = Q*\begin{bmatrix} R_{11} & R_{12} \\ 0 & R_{22} \end{bmatrix}$$

with R_{11} defined as the largest leading submatrix whose estimated condition number is less than 1/RCOND. The order of R_{11}, RANK, is the effective rank of A.

Then, R_{22} is considered to be negligible, and R_{12} is annihilated by orthogonal/unitary transformations from the right, arriving at the complete orthogonal factorization:

$$A*P = Q*\begin{bmatrix} T_{11} & 0 \\ 0 & 0 \end{bmatrix}*Z$$

The minimum norm solution is then

$$x = P*Z^H*\begin{bmatrix} T_{11}^{-1}*Q_1^H*b \\ 0 \end{bmatrix}$$

where Q_1 consists of the first RANK columns of Q.

LDA (input) INTEGER
The leading dimension of the array A. LDA $\geq$ max(1,M).

B (input/output) REAL/COMPLEX array, dimension (LDB,NRHS)
On entry, the m-by-nrhs right hand side matrix B.
On exit, B is overwritten by the n-by-nrhs solution matrix X.
If $m \geq n$ and RANK = n, the residual sum-of-squares for the solution in the ith column is given by the sum of squares of elements n+1:m in that column.

LDB (input) INTEGER
The leading dimension of the array B. LDB $\geq$ max(1,M,N).

S (output) REAL array, dimension (min(M,N))
The singular values of A in decreasing order. The condition number of A in the 2-norm is $\kappa_2(A) = S(1)/S(\min(n,n))$.

RCOND (input) REAL
RCOND is used to determine the effective rank of A. Singular values S(i) which are less than or equal to RCOND*S(1), are treated as zero. If RCOND < 0, machine precision is used instead.

RANK (output) INTEGER
The effective rank of A, i.e., the number of singular values which are greater than RCOND*S(1).

WORK (workspace) REAL/COMPLEX array, dimension (LWORK)
On exit, if INFO = 0, WORK(1) returns the optimal LWORK.

LWORK (input) INTEGER
The dimension of the array WORK. LWORK $\geq$ 1, and also:
SGELSS
LWORK $\geq$ 3*N+max(2*N,NRHS,M) if $M \geq N$;
LWORK $\geq$ 3*M+max(2*M,NRHS,N) if $M < N$.
CGELSS
LWORK $\geq$ 2*N+max(NRHS,M) if $M \geq N$;
LWORK $\geq$ 2*M+max(NRHS,N) if $M < N$.
For good performance, LWORK should generally be larger.

RWORK *CGELSS only* (workspace) REAL array, dimension (max(5*min(M,N)−4,1))

INFO (output) INTEGER
= 0: successful exit
< 0: if INFO = −i, the ith argument had an illegal value.
> 0: the algorithm for computing the SVD failed to converge; if INFO
      = i, i off-diagonal elements of an intermediate bidiagonal form did not converge to zero.

Arguments

M   (input) INTEGER
         The number of rows of the matrix A. M ≥ 0.

N   (input) INTEGER
         The number of columns of the matrix A. N ≥ 0.

NRHS   (input) INTEGER
         The number of right hand sides, i.e. the number of columns of the matrices B and X. NRHS ≥ 0.

A   (input/output) REAL/COMPLEX array, dimension (LDA,N)
         On entry, the m-by-n matrix A.
         On exit, A has been overwritten by details of its complete orthogonal factorization.

LDA   (input) INTEGER
         The leading dimension of the array A. LDA ≥ max(1,M).

B   (input/output) REAL/COMPLEX array, dimension (LDB,NRHS)
         On entry, the m-by-nrhs right hand side matrix B.
         On exit, the n-by-nrhs solution matrix X.
         If $m \geq n$ and RANK = n, the residual sum-of-squares for the solution in the ith column is given by the sum of squares of elements n+1:m in that column.

LDB   (input) INTEGER
         The leading dimension of the array B. LDB ≥ max(1,M,N).

JPVT   (input/output) INTEGER array, dimension (N)
         On entry, if JPVT(i) ≠ 0, the ith column of A is an initial column, otherwise it is a free column. Before the QR factorization of A, all initial columns are permuted to the leading positions; only the remaining free columns are moved as a result of column pivoting during the factorization.
         On exit, if JPVT(i) = k, then the ith column of A*P was the kth column of A.

RCOND   (input) REAL
         RCOND is used to determine the effective rank of A, which is defined as the order of the largest leading triangular submatrix R_{11} in the QR factorization with pivoting of A, whose estimated condition number < 1/RCOND.

RANK   (output) INTEGER
         The effective rank of A, i.e., the order of the submatrix T_{11} in the complete orthogonal factorization of A.

WORK   (workspace) REAL/COMPLEX array, dimension
         SGELSX
         (max(min(M,N)+3*N, 2*min(M,N)+NRHS))
         CGELSX
         (min(M,N) + max(N, 2*min(M,N), min(M,N)+NRHS))

RWORK   *CGELSX only*   (workspace) REAL array, dimension (2*N)

INFO   (output) INTEGER
         = 0:   successful exit
         < 0:   if INFO = −i, the ith argument had an illegal value

---

SGEQLF/CGEQLF

```
SUBROUTINE SGEQLF( M, N, A, LDA, TAU, WORK, LWORK, INFO )
INTEGER         INFO, LDA, LWORK, M, N
REAL            A( LDA, * ), TAU( * ), WORK( LWORK )

SUBROUTINE CGEQLF( M, N, A, LDA, TAU, WORK, LWORK, INFO )
INTEGER         INFO, LDA, LWORK, M, N
COMPLEX         A( LDA, * ), TAU( * ), WORK( LWORK )
```

Purpose

SGEQLF/CGEQLF computes a QL factorization of a real/complex m-by-n matrix A: A = Q*L.

Arguments

M   (input) INTEGER
         The number of rows of the matrix A. M ≥ 0.

N   (input) INTEGER
         The number of columns of the matrix A. N ≥ 0.

A   (input/output) REAL/COMPLEX array, dimension (LDA,N)
         On entry, the m-by-n matrix A.
         On exit, if $m \geq n$, the lower triangle of the subarray A(m−n+1:m,1:n) contains the n-by-n lower triangular matrix L; if $m < n$, the elements on and below the $(n-m)^{th}$ superdiagonal contain the m-by-n lower trapezoidal matrix L; the remaining elements, with the array TAU, represent the orthogonal/unitary matrix Q as a product of min(m,n) elementary reflectors.

LDA   (input) INTEGER
         The leading dimension of the array A. LDA ≥ max(1,M).

TAU   (output) REAL/COMPLEX array, dimension (min(M,N))
         The scalar factors of the elementary reflectors.

WORK   (workspace) REAL/COMPLEX array, dimension (LWORK)
         On exit, if INFO = 0, WORK(1) returns the optimal LWORK.

LWORK   (input) INTEGER
         The dimension of the array WORK. LWORK ≥ max(1,N).
         For optimum performance LWORK ≥ N*NB, where NB is the optimal block size.

SGEQLF/CGEQLF

INFO (output) INTEGER
= 0: successful exit
< 0: if INFO = −i, the ith argument had an illegal value

SGEQPF/CGEQPF

```
SUBROUTINE SGEQPF( M, N, A, LDA, JPVT, TAU, WORK, INFO )
INTEGER          INFO, LDA, M, N
INTEGER          JPVT( * )
REAL             A( LDA, * ), TAU( * ), WORK( * )
SUBROUTINE CGEQPF( M, N, A, LDA, JPVT, TAU, WORK, RWORK, INFO )
INTEGER          INFO, LDA, M, N
INTEGER          JPVT( * )
REAL             RWORK( * )
COMPLEX          A( LDA, * ), TAU( * ), WORK( * )
```

Purpose

SGEQPF/CGEQPF computes a QR factorization with column pivoting of a real/complex m-by-n matrix A: A*P = Q*R.

Arguments

M   (input) INTEGER
The number of rows of the matrix A. M ≥ 0.

N   (input) INTEGER
The number of columns of the matrix A. N ≥ 0.

A   (input/output) REAL/COMPLEX array, dimension (LDA,N)
On entry, the m-by-n matrix A.
On exit, the elements on and above the diagonal of the array contain the min(m,n)-by-n upper trapezoidal matrix R (R is upper triangular if m ≥ n); the elements below the diagonal, with the array TAU, represent the orthogonal/unitary matrix Q as a product of min(m,n) elementary reflectors.

LDA   (input) INTEGER
The leading dimension of the array A. LDA ≥ max(1,M).

JPVT   (input/output) INTEGER array, dimension (N)
On entry: if JPVT(i) ≠ 0, the ith column of A is permuted to the front of A*P (a leading column); if JPVT(i) = 0, the ith column of A is a free column. On exit: if JPVT(i) = k, then the ith column of A*P was the kth column of A.

TAU   (output) REAL/COMPLEX array, dimension (min(M,N))
The scalar factors of the elementary reflectors.

WORK   SGEQPF (workspace) REAL array, dimension (3*N)
    CGEQPF (workspace) COMPLEX array, dimension (N)

RWORK   CGEQPF only (workspace) REAL array, dimension (2*N)

INFO   (output) INTEGER
= 0: successful exit
< 0: if INFO = −i, the ith argument had an illegal value

SGEQRF/CGEQRF

```
SUBROUTINE SGEQRF( M, N, A, LDA, TAU, WORK, LWORK, INFO )
INTEGER          INFO, LDA, LWORK, M, N
REAL             A( LDA, * ), TAU( * ), WORK( LWORK )
SUBROUTINE CGEQRF( M, N, A, LDA, TAU, WORK, LWORK, INFO )
INTEGER          INFO, LDA, LWORK, M, N
COMPLEX          A( LDA, * ), TAU( * ), WORK( LWORK )
```

Purpose

SGEQRF/CGEQRF computes a QR factorization of a real/complex m-by-n matrix A: A = Q*R.

Arguments

M   (input) INTEGER
The number of rows of the matrix A. M ≥ 0.

N   (input) INTEGER
The number of columns of the matrix A. N ≥ 0.

A   (input/output) REAL/COMPLEX array, dimension (LDA,N)
On entry, the m-by-n matrix A.
On exit, the elements on and above the diagonal of the array contain the min(m,n)-by-n upper trapezoidal matrix R (R is upper triangular if m ≥ n); the elements below the diagonal, with the array TAU, represent the orthogonal/unitary matrix Q as a product of min(m,n) elementary reflectors.

LDA   (input) INTEGER
The leading dimension of the array A. LDA ≥ max(1,M).

TAU   (output) REAL/COMPLEX array, dimension (min(M,N))
The scalar factors of the elementary reflectors.

WORK   (workspace) REAL/COMPLEX array, dimension (LWORK)
On exit, if INFO = 0, WORK(1) returns the optimal LWORK.

LWORK   (input) INTEGER
The dimension of the array WORK. LWORK ≥ max(1,N).
For optimum performance LWORK ≥ N*NB, where NB is the optimal block size.

INFO (output) INTEGER
= 0: successful exit
< 0: if INFO = −i, the ith argument had an illegal value

SGERFS/CGERFS

```
SUBROUTINE SGERFS( TRANS, N, NRHS, A, LDA, AF, LDAF, IPIV, B, LDB,
$                   X, LDX, FERR, BERR, WORK, IWORK, INFO )
      CHARACTER      TRANS
      INTEGER        INFO, LDA, LDAF, LDB, LDX, N, NRHS
      INTEGER        IPIV( * ), IWORK( * )
      REAL           A( LDA, * ), AF( LDAF, * ), B( LDB, * ),
$                    BERR( * ), FERR( * ), WORK( * ), X( LDX, * )

SUBROUTINE CGERFS( TRANS, N, NRHS, A, LDA, AF, LDAF, IPIV, B, LDB,
$                   X, LDX, FERR, BERR, WORK, RWORK, INFO )
      CHARACTER      TRANS
      INTEGER        INFO, LDA, LDAF, LDB, LDX, N, NRHS
      INTEGER        IPIV( * )
      REAL           BERR( * ), FERR( * ), RWORK( * )
      COMPLEX        A( LDA, * ), AF( LDAF, * ), B( LDB, * ),
$                    WORK( * ), X( LDX, * )
```

Purpose

SGERFS/CGERFS improves the computed solution to a system of linear equations, and provides error bounds and backward error estimates for the solution.

Arguments

TRANS (input) CHARACTER*1
Specifies the form of the system of equations:
= 'N': A*X = B (No transpose)
= 'T': A^T*X = B (Transpose)
= 'C': A^H*X = B (Conjugate transpose)

N (input) INTEGER
The order of the matrix A. N $\geq$ 0.

NRHS (input) INTEGER
The number of right hand sides, i.e., the number of columns of the matrices B and X. NRHS $\geq$ 0.

A (input) REAL/COMPLEX array, dimension (LDA,N)
The original n-by-n matrix A.

LDA (input) INTEGER
The leading dimension of the array A. LDA $\geq$ max(1,N).

AF (input) REAL/COMPLEX array, dimension (LDAF,N)
The factors L and U from the factorization A = P*L*U as computed by SGETRF/CGETRF.

LDAF (input) INTEGER
The leading dimension of the array AF. LDAF $\geq$ max(1,N).

IPIV (input) INTEGER array, dimension (N)
The pivot indices from SGETRF/CGETRF; for $1 \leq i \leq N$, row i of the matrix was interchanged with row IPIV(i).

B (input) REAL/COMPLEX array, dimension (LDB,NRHS)
The right hand side matrix B.

LDB (input) INTEGER
The leading dimension of the array B. LDB $\geq$ max(1,N).

X (input/output) REAL/COMPLEX array, dimension (LDX,NRHS)
On entry, the solution matrix X, as computed by SGETRS/CGETRS. On exit, the improved solution matrix X.

LDX (input) INTEGER
The leading dimension of the array X. LDX $\geq$ max(1,N).

FERR (output) REAL array, dimension (NRHS)
The estimated forward error bound for each solution vector X(j) (the jth column of the solution matrix X). If XTRUE is the true solution corresponding to X(j), FERR(j) bounds the magnitude of the largest element in (X(j) − XTRUE) divided by the magnitude of the largest element in X(j). The quality of the error bound depends on the quality of the estimate of $\|A^{-1}\|$ computed in the code; if the estimate of $\|A^{-1}\|$ is accurate, the error bound is guaranteed.

BERR (output) REAL array, dimension (NRHS)
The componentwise relative backward error of each solution vector X(j) (i.e., the smallest relative change in any element of A or B that makes X(j) an exact solution).

WORK SGERFS (workspace) REAL array, dimension (3*N)
CGERFS (workspace) COMPLEX array, dimension (2*N)

IWORK SGERFS only (workspace) INTEGER array, dimension (N)

RWORK CGERFS only (workspace) REAL array, dimension (N)

INFO (output) INTEGER
= 0: successful exit
< 0: if INFO = −i, the ith argument had an illegal value

SGERQF/CGERQF

```
SUBROUTINE SGERQF( M, N, A, LDA, TAU, WORK, LWORK, INFO )
INTEGER           INFO, LDA, LWORK, M, N
REAL              A( LDA, * ), TAU( * ), WORK( LWORK )

SUBROUTINE CGERQF( M, N, A, LDA, TAU, WORK, LWORK, INFO )
INTEGER           INFO, LDA, LWORK, M, N
COMPLEX           A( LDA, * ), TAU( * ), WORK( LWORK )
```

Purpose

SGERQF/CGERQF computes an RQ factorization of a real/complex m-by-n matrix A: $A = R*Q$.

Arguments

M (input) INTEGER
The number of rows of the matrix A. $M \geq 0$.

N (input) INTEGER
The number of columns of the matrix A. $N \geq 0$.

A (input/output) REAL/COMPLEX array, dimension (LDA,N)
On entry, the m-by-n matrix A.
On exit, if $m \leq n$, the upper triangle of the subarray $A(1:m, n-m+1:n)$ contains the m-by-m upper triangular matrix R; if $m > n$, the elements on and above the $(m-n)^{th}$ subdiagonal contain the m-by-n upper trapezoidal matrix R; the remaining elements, with the array TAU, represent the orthogonal/unitary matrix Q as a product of $\min(m,n)$ elementary reflectors.

LDA (input) INTEGER
The leading dimension of the array A. $LDA \geq \max(1, M)$.

TAU (output) REAL/COMPLEX array, dimension $(\min(M,N))$
The scalar factors of the elementary reflectors.

WORK (workspace) REAL/COMPLEX array, dimension (LWORK)
On exit, if $INFO = 0$, WORK(1) returns the optimal LWORK.

LWORK (input) INTEGER
The dimension of the array WORK. $LWORK \geq \max(1, M)$.
For optimum performance $LWORK \geq M*NB$, where NB is the optimal block size.

INFO (output) INTEGER
= 0: successful exit
< 0: if $INFO = -i$, the ith argument had an illegal value

SGESV/CGESV

```
SUBROUTINE SGESV( N, NRHS, A, LDA, IPIV, B, LDB, INFO )
INTEGER          INFO, LDA, LDB, N, NRHS
INTEGER          IPIV( * )
REAL             A( LDA, * ), B( LDB, * )

SUBROUTINE CGESV( N, NRHS, A, LDA, IPIV, B, LDB, INFO )
INTEGER          INFO, LDA, LDB, N, NRHS
INTEGER          IPIV( * )
COMPLEX          A( LDA, * ), B( LDB, * )
```

Purpose

SGESV/CGESV computes the solution to a real/complex system of linear equations $A*X = B$, where A is an n-by-n matrix and X and B are n-by-nrhs matrices.

The LU decomposition with partial pivoting and row interchanges is used to factor A as $A = P*L*U$, where P is a permutation matrix, L is unit lower triangular, and U is upper triangular. The factored form of A is then used to solve the system of equations $A*X = B$.

Arguments

N (input) INTEGER
The number of linear equations, i.e., the order of the matrix A. $N \geq 0$.

NRHS (input) INTEGER
The number of right hand sides, i.e., the number of columns of the matrix B. $NRHS \geq 0$.

A (input/output) REAL/COMPLEX array, dimension (LDA,N)
On entry, the n-by-n coefficient matrix A.
On exit, the factors L and U from the factorization $A = P*L*U$; the unit diagonal elements of L are not stored.

LDA (input) INTEGER
The leading dimension of the array A. $LDA \geq \max(1, N)$.

IPIV (output) INTEGER array, dimension (N)
The pivot indices that define the permutation matrix P; row i of the matrix was interchanged with row IPIV(i).

B (input/output) REAL/COMPLEX array, dimension (LDB,NRHS)
On entry, the n-by-nrhs right hand side matrix B.
On exit, if $INFO = 0$, the n-by-nrhs solution matrix X.

LDB (input) INTEGER
The leading dimension of the array B. $LDB \geq \max(1, N)$.

INFO (output) INTEGER
= 0: successful exit
< 0: if $INFO = -i$, the ith argument had an illegal value

> 0: if INFO = i, U(i,i) is exactly zero. The factorization has been completed, but the factor U is exactly singular, so the solution could not be computed.

SGESVD/CGESVD

```
SUBROUTINE SGESVD( JOBU, JOBVT, M, N, A, LDA, S, U, LDU, VT, LDVT,
$                  WORK, LWORK, INFO )
CHARACTER          JOBU, JOBVT
INTEGER            INFO, LDA, LDU, LDVT, LWORK, M, N
REAL               A( LDA, * ), S( * ), U( LDU, * ),
$                  VT( LDVT, * ), WORK( * )

SUBROUTINE CGESVD( JOBU, JOBVT, M, N, A, LDA, S, U, LDU, VT, LDVT,
$                  WORK, LWORK, RWORK, INFO )
CHARACTER          JOBU, JOBVT
INTEGER            INFO, LDA, LDU, LDVT, LWORK, M, N
REAL               RWORK( * ), S( * )
COMPLEX            A( LDA, * ), U( LDU, * ), VT( LDVT, * ),
$                  WORK( * )
```

Purpose

SGESVD/CGESVD computes the singular value decomposition (SVD) of a real/complex m-by-n matrix A, optionally computing the left and/or right singular vectors. The SVD is written

$$A = U*\Sigma*V^H$$

where Σ is an m-by-n matrix which is zero except for its min(m,n) diagonal elements, U is an m-by-m orthogonal/unitary matrix, and V is an n-by-n orthogonal/unitary matrix. The diagonal elements of Σ are the singular values of A; they are real and non-negative, and are returned in descending order. The first min(m,n) columns of U and V are the left and right singular vectors of A.

Note that the routine returns V^H, not V.

Arguments

JOBU   (input) CHARACTER*1
       Specifies options for computing all or part of the matrix U:
       = 'A': all m columns of U are returned in the array U;
       = 'S': the first min(m,n) columns of U (the left singular vectors) are returned in the array U;
       = 'O': the first min(m,n) columns of U (the left singular vectors) are overwritten on the array A;
       = 'N': no columns of U (no left singular vectors) are computed.

JOBVT (input) CHARACTER*1
       Specifies options for computing all or part of the matrix V^H:
       = 'A': all n rows of V^H are returned in the array VT;
       = 'S': the first min(m,n) rows of V^H (the right singular vectors) are returned in the array VT;
       = 'O': the first min(m,n) rows of V^H (the right singular vectors) are overwritten on the array A;
       = 'N': no rows of V^H (no right singular vectors) are computed.
       JOBVT and JOBU cannot both be 'O'.

M   (input) INTEGER
       The number of rows of the matrix A. M $\geq$ 0.

N   (input) INTEGER
       The number of columns of the matrix A. N $\geq$ 0.

A   (input/output) REAL/COMPLEX array, dimension (LDA,N)
       On entry, the m-by-n matrix A.
       On exit,
       if JOBU = 'O', A is overwritten with the first min(m,n) columns of U (the left singular vectors, stored columnwise);
       if JOBVT = 'O', A is overwritten with the first min(m,n) rows of V^H (the right singular vectors, stored rowwise);
       if JOBU $\neq$ 'O' and JOBVT $\neq$ 'O', the contents of A are destroyed.

LDA   (input) INTEGER
       The leading dimension of the array A. LDA $\geq$ max(1,M).

S   (output) REAL array, dimension (min(M,N))
       The singular values of A, sorted so that S(i) $\geq$ S(i+1).

U   (output) REAL/COMPLEX array, dimension (LDU,M) if JOBU = 'A' or (LDU,min(M,N)) if JOBU = 'S'
       If JOBU = 'A', U contains the m-by-m orthogonal/unitary matrix U;
       if JOBU = 'S', U contains the first min(m,n) columns of U (the left singular vectors, stored columnwise);
       if JOBU = 'N' or 'O', U is not referenced.

LDU   (input) INTEGER
       The leading dimension of the array U. LDU $\geq$ 1; if JOBU = 'A' or 'S', LDU $\geq$ M.

VT   (output) REAL/COMPLEX array, dimension (LDVT,N)
       If JOBVT = 'A', VT contains the n-by-n orthogonal/unitary matrix V^H;
       if JOBVT = 'S', VT contains the first min(m,n) rows of V^H (the right singular vectors, stored rowwise);
       if JOBVT = 'N' or 'O', VT is not referenced.

LDVT   (input) INTEGER
       The leading dimension of the array VT. LDVT $\geq$ 1; if JOBVT = 'A', LDVT $\geq$ N; if JOBVT = 'S', LDVT $\geq$ min(M,N).

WORK   (workspace) REAL/COMPLEX array, dimension (LWORK)
       On exit, if INFO = 0, WORK(1) returns the optimal LWORK.

SGESVX/CGESVX

LWORK   (input) INTEGER
         The dimension of the array WORK. LWORK $\geq$ 1.
         LWORK $\geq$ max(3*min(M,N)+max(M,N),5*min(M,N)−4) (SGESVD)
         LWORK $\geq$ 2*min(M,N)+max(M,N) (CGESVD).
         For good performance, LWORK should generally be larger.

RWORK   CGESVD only (workspace) REAL array, dimension (5*max(M,N))

INFO   (output) INTEGER
         = 0: successful exit
         < 0: if INFO = −i, the ith argument had an illegal value.
         > 0: if INFO = i, the algorithm failed to converge; i off-diagonal el-
              ements of an intermediate bidiagonal form did not converge to
              zero.

SGESVX/CGESVX

```
SUBROUTINE SGESVX( FACT, TRANS, N, NRHS, A, LDA, AF, LDAF, IPIV,
$                  EQUED, R, C, B, LDB, X, LDX, RCOND, FERR, BERR,
$                  WORK, IWORK, INFO )
     CHARACTER     EQUED, FACT, TRANS
     INTEGER       INFO, LDA, LDAF, LDB, LDX, N, NRHS
     REAL          RCOND
     INTEGER       IPIV( * ), IWORK( * )
     REAL          A( LDA, * ), AF( LDAF, * ), B( LDB, * ),
$                  BERR( * ), C( * ), FERR( * ), R( * ),
$                  WORK( * ), X( LDX, * )

SUBROUTINE CGESVX( FACT, TRANS, N, NRHS, A, LDA, AF, LDAF, IPIV,
$                  EQUED, R, C, B, LDB, X, LDX, RCOND, FERR, BERR,
$                  WORK, RWORK, INFO )
     CHARACTER     EQUED, FACT, TRANS
     INTEGER       INFO, LDA, LDAF, LDB, LDX, N, NRHS
     REAL          RCOND
     INTEGER       IPIV( * )
     REAL          BERR( * ), C( * ), FERR( * ), R( * ),
$                  RWORK( * )
     COMPLEX       A( LDA, * ), AF( LDAF, * ), B( LDB, * ),
$                  WORK( * ), X( LDX, * )
```

Purpose

SGESVX/CGESVX uses the LU factorization to compute the solution to a
real/complex system of linear equations $A*X = B$, $A^T*X = B$, or $A^H*X = B$,
where A is an n-by-n matrix and X and B are n-by-nrhs matrices.

Error bounds on the solution and a condition estimate are also provided.

Description

The following steps are performed:

1. If FACT = 'E', real scaling factors are computed to equilibrate the system:

   TRANS = 'N': diag(R)*A*diag(C)*diag(C)$^{-1}$*X = diag(R)*B
   TRANS = 'T': (diag(R)*A*diag(C))^T*diag(R)$^{-1}$*X = diag(C)*B
   TRANS = 'C': (diag(R)*A*diag(C))^H*diag(R)$^{-1}$*X = diag(C)*B

   Whether or not the system will be equilibrated depends on the scaling of the
   matrix A, but if equilibration is used, A is overwritten by diag(R)*A*diag(C)
   and B by diag(R)*B (if TRANS='N') or diag(C)*B (if TRANS = 'T' or 'C').

2. If FACT = 'N' or 'E', the LU decomposition is used to factor the matrix A
   (after equilibration if FACT = 'E') as A = P*L*U, where P is a permutation
   matrix, L is a unit lower triangular matrix, and U is upper triangular.

3. The factored form of A is used to estimate the condition number of the matrix
   A. If the reciprocal of the condition number is less than machine precision, steps
   4–6 are skipped.

4. The system of equations is solved for X using the factored form of A.

5. Iterative refinement is applied to improve the computed solution vectors and
   calculate error bounds and backward error estimates for them.

6. If FACT = 'E' and equilibration was used, the vectors X are premultiplied by
   diag(C) (if TRANS = 'N') or diag(R) (if TRANS = 'T' or 'C') so that they
   solve the original system before equilibration.

Arguments

FACT   (input) CHARACTER*1
         Specifies whether or not the factored form of the matrix A is supplied
         on entry, and if not, whether the matrix A should be equilibrated before
         it is factored.
         = 'F':   On entry, AF and IPIV contain the factored form of A. A, AF,
                  and IPIV will not be modified.
         = 'N':   The matrix A will be copied to AF and factored.
         = 'E':   The matrix A will be equilibrated if necessary, then copied to
                  AF and factored.

TRANS   (input) CHARACTER*1
         Specifies the form of the system of equations:
         = 'N':   A*X = B (No transpose)
         = 'T': $A^T*X = B$ (Transpose)
         = 'C': $A^H*X = B$ (Conjugate transpose)

N   (input) INTEGER
         The number of linear equations, i.e., the order of the matrix A. N $\geq$ 0.

NRHS   (input) INTEGER
         The number of right hand sides, i.e., the number of columns of the

matrices B and X. NRHS $\geq$ 0.

A   (input/output) REAL/COMPLEX array, dimension (LDA,N)
On entry, the n-by-n matrix A. A is not modified if FACT = 'F' or 'N', or if FACT = 'E' and EQUED = 'N' on exit.
On exit, if EQUED $\neq$ 'N', A is scaled as follows:
EQUED = 'R': A := diag(R)*A;
EQUED = 'C': A := A*diag(C);
EQUED = 'B': A := diag(R)*A*diag(C).

LDA   (input) INTEGER
The leading dimension of the array A. LDA $\geq$ max(1,N).

AF   (input or output) REAL/COMPLEX array, dimension (LDAF,N)
If FACT = 'F', then AF is an input argument and on entry contains the factors L and U from the factorization A = P*L*U as computed by SGETRF/CGETRF.
If FACT = 'N', then AF is an output argument and on exit returns the factors L and U from the factorization A = P*L*U of the original matrix A.
If FACT = 'E', then AF is an output argument and on exit returns the factors L and U from the factorization A = P*L*U of the equilibrated matrix A (see the description of A for the form of the equilibrated matrix).

LDAF   (input) INTEGER
The leading dimension of the array AF. LDAF $\geq$ max(1,N).

IPIV   (input or output) INTEGER array, dimension (N)
If FACT = 'F', then IPIV is an input argument and on entry contains the pivot indices from the factorization A = P*L*U as computed by SGETRF/CGETRF; row i of the matrix was interchanged with row IPIV(i).
If FACT = 'N', then IPIV is an output argument and on exit contains the pivot indices from the factorization A = P*L*U of the original matrix A.
If FACT = 'E', then IPIV is an output argument and on exit contains the pivot indices from the factorization A = P*L*U of the equilibrated matrix A.

EQUED   (output) CHARACTER*1
Specifies the form of equilibration that was done.
= 'N': No equilibration (always true if FACT = 'F' or 'N').
= 'R': Row equilibration, i.e., A has been premultiplied by diag(R).
= 'C': Column equilibration, i.e., A has been postmultiplied by diag(C).
= 'B': Both row and column equilibration, i.e., A has been replaced by diag(R)*A*diag(C).

R   (output) REAL array, dimension (N)
The row scale factors for A.
If EQUED = 'R' or 'B', A is multiplied on the left by diag(R).
R is not assigned if FACT = 'F' or 'N'.

C   (output) REAL array, dimension (N)
The column scale factors for A.
If EQUED = 'C' or 'B', A is multiplied on the right by diag(C).
C is not assigned if FACT = 'F' or 'N'.

B   (input/output) REAL/COMPLEX array, dimension (LDB,NRHS)
On entry, the n-by-nrhs right hand side matrix B.
On exit, if EQUED = 'N', B is not modified; if TRANS = 'N' and EQUED = 'R' or 'B', B is overwritten by diag(R)*B; if TRANS = 'T' or 'C' and EQUED = 'C' or 'B', B is overwritten by diag(C)*B.

LDB   (input) INTEGER
The leading dimension of the array B. LDB $\geq$ max(1,N).

X   (output) REAL/COMPLEX array, dimension (LDX,NRHS)
If INFO = 0, the n-by-nrhs solution matrix X to the original system of equations. Note that A and B are modified on exit if EQUED $\neq$ 'N', and the solution to the equilibrated system is diag(C)$^{-1}$*X if TRANS = 'N' and EQUED = 'C' or 'B', or diag(R)$^{-1}$*X if TRANS = 'T' or 'C' and EQUED = 'R' or 'B'.

LDX   (input) INTEGER
The leading dimension of the array X. LDX $\geq$ max(1,N).

RCOND   (output) REAL
The estimate of the reciprocal condition number of the matrix A. If RCOND is less than the machine precision (in particular, if RCOND = 0), the matrix is singular to working precision. This condition is indicated by a return code of INFO > 0, and the solution and error bounds are not computed.

FERR   (output) REAL array, dimension (NRHS)
The estimated forward error bound for each solution vector X(j) (the jth column of the solution matrix X). If XTRUE is the true solution corresponding to X(j), FERR(j) bounds the magnitude of the largest element in (X(j) − XTRUE) divided by the magnitude of the largest element in X(j). The quality of the error bound depends on the quality of the estimate of $||A^{-1}||$ computed in the code; if the estimate of $||A^{-1}||$ is accurate, the error bound is guaranteed.

BERR   (output) REAL array, dimension (NRHS)
The componentwise relative backward error of each solution vector X(j) (i.e., the smallest relative change in any element of A or B that makes X(j) an exact solution).

WORK   SGESVX (workspace) REAL array, dimension (3*N)
CGESVX (workspace) COMPLEX array, dimension (2*N)

IWORK   SGESVX *only* (workspace) INTEGER array, dimension (N)

RWORK   CGESVX *only* (workspace) REAL array, dimension (N)

INFO   (output) INTEGER
= 0: successful exit
< 0: if INFO = −i, the ith argument had an illegal value

> 0: if INFO = i, and i is

≤ N: U(i,i) is exactly zero. The factorization has been completed, but the factor U is exactly singular, so the solution and error bounds could not be computed.

= N+1: RCOND is less than machine precision. The factorization has been completed, but the matrix is singular to working precision, and the solution and error bounds have not been computed.

SGETRF/CGETRF

```
SUBROUTINE SGETRF( M, N, A, LDA, IPIV, INFO )
INTEGER       INFO, LDA, M, N
INTEGER       IPIV( * )
REAL          A( LDA, * )

SUBROUTINE CGETRF( M, N, A, LDA, IPIV, INFO )
INTEGER       INFO, LDA, M, N
INTEGER       IPIV( * )
COMPLEX       A( LDA, * )
```

Purpose

SGETRF/CGETRF computes an LU factorization of a general m-by-n matrix A using partial pivoting with row interchanges.

The factorization has the form $A = P*L*U$ where P is a permutation matrix, L is lower triangular with unit diagonal elements (lower trapezoidal if m > n), and U is upper triangular (upper trapezoidal if m < n).

Arguments

M   (input) INTEGER
    The number of rows of the matrix A. M ≥ 0.

N   (input) INTEGER
    The number of columns of the matrix A. N ≥ 0.

A   (input/output) REAL/COMPLEX array, dimension (LDA,N)
    On entry, the m-by-n matrix to be factored.
    On exit, the factors L and U from the factorization $A = P*L*U$; the unit diagonal elements of L are not stored.

LDA (input) INTEGER
    The leading dimension of the array A. LDA ≥ max(1,M).

IPIV (output) INTEGER array, dimension (min(M,N))
    The pivot indices; for $1 \leq i \leq \min(m,n)$, row i of the matrix was interchanged with row IPIV(i).

INFO (output) INTEGER

= 0: successful exit

< 0: if INFO = -i, the ith argument had an illegal value

> 0: if INFO = i, U(i,i) is exactly zero. The factorization has been completed, but the factor U is exactly singular, and division by zero will occur if it is used to solve a system of equations.

SGETRI/CGETRI

```
SUBROUTINE SGETRI( N, A, LDA, IPIV, WORK, LWORK, INFO )
INTEGER       INFO, LDA, LWORK, N
INTEGER       IPIV( * )
REAL          A( LDA, * ), WORK( LWORK )

SUBROUTINE CGETRI( N, A, LDA, IPIV, WORK, LWORK, INFO )
INTEGER       INFO, LDA, LWORK, N
INTEGER       IPIV( * )
COMPLEX       A( LDA, * ), WORK( LWORK )
```

Purpose

SGETRI/CGETRI computes the inverse of a matrix using the LU factorization computed by SGETRF/CGETRF.

This method inverts U and then computes A^{-1} by solving the system $A^{-1}*L = U^{-1}$ for A^{-1}.

Arguments

N   (input) INTEGER
    The order of the matrix A. N ≥ 0.

A   (input/output) REAL/COMPLEX array, dimension (LDA,N)
    On entry, the factors L and U from the factorization $A = P*L*U$ as computed by SGETRF/CGETRF.
    On exit, if INFO = 0, the inverse of the original matrix A.

LDA (input) INTEGER
    The leading dimension of the array A. LDA ≥ max(1,N).

IPIV (input) INTEGER array, dimension (N)
    The pivot indices from SGETRF/CGETRF; for $1 \leq i \leq N$, row i of the matrix was interchanged with row IPIV(i).

WORK (workspace) REAL/COMPLEX array, dimension (LWORK)
    On exit, if INFO = 0, WORK(1) returns the optimal LWORK.

LWORK (input) INTEGER
    The dimension of the array WORK. LWORK ≥ max(1,N). For optimal performance LWORK ≥ N*NB, where NB is the optimal block size returned by ILAENV.

INFO (output) INTEGER
= 0: successful exit
< 0: if INFO = -i, the ith argument had an illegal value
> 0: if INFO = i, U(i,i) is exactly zero; the matrix is singular and its inverse could not be computed.

SGETRS/CGETRS

```
SUBROUTINE SGETRS( TRANS, N, NRHS, A, LDA, IPIV, B, LDB, INFO )
CHARACTER      TRANS
INTEGER        INFO, LDA, LDB, N, NRHS
INTEGER        IPIV( * )
REAL           A( LDA, * ), B( LDB, * )

SUBROUTINE CGETRS( TRANS, N, NRHS, A, LDA, IPIV, B, LDB, INFO )
CHARACTER      TRANS
INTEGER        INFO, LDA, LDB, N, NRHS
INTEGER        IPIV( * )
COMPLEX        A( LDA, * ), B( LDB, * )
```

Purpose

SGETRS/CGETRS solves a system of linear equations $A*X = B$, $A^T*X = B$, or $A^H*X = B$, with a general n-by-n matrix A using the LU factorization computed by SGETRF/CGETRF.

Arguments

TRANS (input) CHARACTER*1
Specifies the form of the system of equations:
= 'N': $A*X = B$ (No transpose)
= 'T': $A^T*X = B$ (Transpose)
= 'C': $A^H*X = B$ (Conjugate transpose)

N (input) INTEGER
The order of the matrix A. $N \geq 0$.

NRHS (input) INTEGER
The number of right hand sides, i.e., the number of columns of the matrix B. $NRHS \geq 0$.

A (input) REAL/COMPLEX array, dimension (LDA,N)
The factors L and U from the factorization $A = P*L*U$ as computed by SGETRF/CGETRF.

LDA (input) INTEGER
The leading dimension of the array A. $LDA \geq max(1,N)$.

IPIV (input) INTEGER array, dimension (N)
The pivot indices from SGETRF/CGETRF; for $1 \leq i \leq N$, row i of the matrix was interchanged with row IPIV(i).

B (input/output) REAL/COMPLEX array, dimension (LDB,NRHS)
On entry, the right hand side matrix B.
On exit, the solution matrix X.

LDB (input) INTEGER
The leading dimension of the array B. $LDB \geq max(1,N)$.

INFO (output) INTEGER
= 0: successful exit
< 0: if INFO = -i, the ith argument had an illegal value

SGTCON/CGTCON

```
SUBROUTINE SGTCON( NORM, N, DL, D, DU, DU2, IPIV, ANORM, RCOND,
$                  WORK, IWORK, INFO )
CHARACTER      NORM
INTEGER        INFO, N
REAL           ANORM, RCOND
INTEGER        IPIV( * ), IWORK( * )
REAL           D( * ), DL( * ), DU( * ), DU2( * ), WORK( * )

SUBROUTINE CGTCON( NORM, N, DL, D, DU, DU2, IPIV, ANORM, RCOND,
$                  WORK, INFO )
CHARACTER      NORM
INTEGER        INFO, N
REAL           ANORM, RCOND
INTEGER        IPIV( * )
COMPLEX        D( * ), DL( * ), DU( * ), DU2( * ), WORK( * )
```

Purpose

SGTCON/CGTCON estimates the reciprocal of the condition number of a real/complex tridiagonal matrix A using the LU factorization as computed by SGTTRF/CGTTRF.

An estimate is obtained for $\|A^{-1}\|$, and the reciprocal of the condition number is computed as $RCOND = 1/(\|A\| * \|A^{-1}\|)$.

Arguments

NORM (input) CHARACTER*1
Specifies whether the 1-norm condition number or the infinity-norm condition number is required:
= '1' or 'O': 1-norm;
= 'I': Infinity-norm.

N (input) INTEGER
The order of the matrix A. $N \geq 0$.

DL   (input) REAL/COMPLEX array, dimension (N−1)
The (n−1) multipliers that define the matrix L from the LU factorization of A as computed by SGTTRF/CGTTRF.

D   (input) REAL/COMPLEX array, dimension (N)
The n diagonal elements of the upper triangular matrix U from the LU factorization of A.

DU   (input) REAL/COMPLEX array, dimension (N−1)
The (n−1) elements of the first superdiagonal of U.

DU2   (input) REAL/COMPLEX array, dimension (N−2)
The (n−2) elements of the second superdiagonal of U.

IPIV   (input) INTEGER array, dimension (N)
The pivot indices; for $1 \le i \le n$, row i of the matrix was interchanged with row IPIV(i). IPIV(i) will always be either i or $i+1$; IPIV(i) $= i$ indicates a row interchange was not required.

ANORM   (input) REAL
The 1-norm of the original matrix A.

RCOND   (output) REAL
The reciprocal of the condition number of the matrix A, computed as $\text{RCOND} = 1/(\|A\| . \|A^{-1}\|)$.

WORK   (workspace) REAL/COMPLEX array, dimension (N)

IWORK   *SGTCON only* (workspace) INTEGER array, dimension (N)

INFO   (output) INTEGER
= 0: successful exit
< 0: if INFO = −i, the ith argument had an illegal value

SGTRFS/CGTRFS

```
SUBROUTINE SGTRFS( TRANS, N, NRHS, DL, D, DU, DLF, DF, DUF, DU2,
$                   IPIV, B, LDB, X, LDX, FERR, BERR, WORK, IWORK,
$                   INFO )
   CHARACTER      TRANS
   INTEGER        INFO, LDB, LDX, N, NRHS
   INTEGER        IPIV( * ), IWORK( * )
   REAL           B( LDB, * ), BERR( * ), D( * ), DF( * ),
$                 DL( * ), DLF( * ), DU( * ), DU2( * ), DUF( * ),
$                 FERR( * ), WORK( * ), X( LDX, * )
```

```
SUBROUTINE CGTRFS( TRANS, N, NRHS, DL, D, DU, DLF, DF, DUF, DU2,
$                   IPIV, B, LDB, X, LDX, FERR, BERR, WORK, RWORK,
$                   INFO )
   CHARACTER      TRANS
   INTEGER        INFO, LDB, LDX, N, NRHS
   INTEGER        IPIV( * )
   REAL           BERR( * ), FERR( * ), RWORK( * )
   COMPLEX        B( LDB, * ), D( * ), DF( * ), DL( * ),
$                 DLF( * ), DU( * ), DU2( * ), DUF( * ),
$                 WORK( * ), X( LDX, * )
```

Purpose

SGTRFS/CGTRFS improves the computed solution to a system of linear equations when the coefficient matrix is tridiagonal, and provides error bounds and backward error estimates for the solution.

Arguments

TRANS   (input) CHARACTER*1
Specifies the form of the system of equations:
= 'N': $A*X = B$ (No transpose)
= 'T': $A^T*X = B$ (Transpose)
= 'C': $A^H*X = B$ (Conjugate transpose)

N   (input) INTEGER
The order of the matrix A. N $\ge$ 0.

NRHS   (input) INTEGER
The number of right hand sides, i.e., the number of columns of the matrix B. NRHS $\ge$ 0.

DL   (input) REAL/COMPLEX array, dimension (N−1)
The (n−1) subdiagonal elements of A.

D   (input) REAL/COMPLEX array, dimension (N)
The diagonal elements of A.

DU   (input) REAL/COMPLEX array, dimension (N−1)
The (n−1) superdiagonal elements of A.

DLF   (input) REAL/COMPLEX array, dimension (N−1)
The (n−1) multipliers that define the matrix L from the LU factorization of A as computed by SGTTRF/CGTTRF.

DF   (input) REAL/COMPLEX array, dimension (N)
The n diagonal elements of the upper triangular matrix U from the LU factorization of A.

DUF   (input) REAL/COMPLEX array, dimension (N−1)
The (n−1) elements of the first superdiagonal of U.

DU2   (input) REAL/COMPLEX array, dimension (N−2)
The (n−2) elements of the second superdiagonal of U.

Purpose

SGTSV/CGTSV solves the equation $A*X = B$, where A is an n-by-n tridiagonal matrix, by Gaussian elimination with partial pivoting.

Note that the equation $A^H*X = B$ may be solved by interchanging the order of the arguments DU and DL.

Arguments

N   (input) INTEGER
        The order of the matrix A. $N \geq 0$.

NRHS   (input) INTEGER
        The number of right hand sides, i.e., the number of columns of the matrix B. $NRHS \geq 0$.

DL   (input/output) REAL/COMPLEX array, dimension (N−1)
        On entry, DL must contain the (n−1) subdiagonal elements of A.
        On exit, DL is overwritten by the (n−2) elements of the second superdiagonal of the upper triangular matrix U from the LU factorization of A, in DL(1),···, DL(n−2).

D   (input/output) REAL/COMPLEX array, dimension (N)
        On entry, D must contain the n diagonal elements of A.
        On exit, D is overwritten by the n diagonal elements of U.

DU   (input/output) REAL/COMPLEX array, dimension (N−1)
        On entry, DU must contain the (n−1) superdiagonal elements of A.
        On exit, DU is overwritten by the (n−1) elements of the first superdiagonal of U.

B   (input/output) REAL/COMPLEX array, dimension (LDB,N)
        On entry, the n-by-nrhs right hand side matrix B.
        On exit, if INFO = 0, the n-by-nrhs solution matrix X.

LDB   (input) INTEGER
        The leading dimension of the array B. $LDB \geq \max(1,N)$.

INFO   (output) INTEGER
        = 0: successful exit
        < 0: if INFO = −i, the ith argument had an illegal value
        > 0: if INFO = i, U(i,i) is exactly zero, and the solution has not been computed. The factorization has not been completed unless i = N.

IPIV   (input) INTEGER array, dimension (N)
        The pivot indices; for $1 \leq i \leq n$, row i of the matrix was interchanged with row IPIV(i). IPIV(i) will always be either i or i+1; IPIV(i) = i indicates a row interchange was not required.

B   (input) REAL/COMPLEX array, dimension (LDB,NRHS)
        The right hand side matrix B.

LDB   (input) INTEGER
        The leading dimension of the array B. $LDB \geq \max(1,N)$.

X   (input/output) REAL/COMPLEX array, dimension (LDX,NRHS)
        On entry, the solution matrix X, as computed by SGTTRS/CGTTRS.
        On exit, the improved solution matrix X.

LDX   (input) INTEGER
        The leading dimension of the array X. $LDX \geq \max(1,N)$.

FERR   (output) REAL array, dimension (NRHS)
        The estimated forward error bound for each solution vector X(j) (the jth column of the solution matrix X). If XTRUE is the true solution corresponding to X(j), FERR(j) bounds the magnitude of the largest element in (X(j) − XTRUE) divided by the magnitude of the largest element in X(j). The quality of the error bound depends on the quality of the estimate of $\|A^{-1}\|$ computed in the code; if the estimate of $\|A^{-1}\|$ is accurate, the error bound is guaranteed.

BERR   (output) REAL array, dimension (NRHS)
        The componentwise relative backward error of each solution vector X(j) (i.e., the smallest relative change in any element of A or B that makes X(j) an exact solution).

WORK   SGTRFS (workspace) REAL array, dimension (3*N)
        CGTRFS (workspace) COMPLEX array, dimension (2*N)

IWORK   SGTRFS only (workspace) INTEGER array, dimension (N)

RWORK   CGTRFS only (workspace) INTEGER array, dimension (N)

INFO   (output) INTEGER
        = 0: successful exit
        < 0: if INFO = −i, the ith argument had an illegal value

SGTSV/CGTSV

```
SUBROUTINE SGTSV( N, NRHS, DL, D, DU, B, LDB, INFO )
INTEGER    INFO, LDB, N, NRHS
REAL       B( LDB, * ), D( * ), DL( * ), DU( * )

SUBROUTINE CGTSV( N, NRHS, DL, D, DU, B, LDB, INFO )
INTEGER    INFO, LDB, N, NRHS
COMPLEX    B( LDB, * ), D( * ), DL( * ), DU( * )
```

SGTSVX/CGTSVX

```
SUBROUTINE SGTSVX( FACT, TRANS, N, NRHS, DL, D, DU, DLF, DF, DUF,
$                  DU2, IPIV, B, LDB, X, LDX, RCOND, FERR, BERR,
$                  WORK, IWORK, INFO )
        CHARACTER      FACT, TRANS
        INTEGER        INFO, LDB, LDX, N, NRHS
        REAL           RCOND
        INTEGER        IPIV( * ), IWORK( * )
        REAL           B( LDB, * ), BERR( * ), D( * ), DF( * ),
$                      DL( * ), DLF( * ), DU( * ), DU2( * ), DUF( * ),
$                      FERR( * ), WORK( * ), X( LDX, * )

SUBROUTINE CGTSVX( FACT, TRANS, N, NRHS, DL, D, DU, DLF, DF, DUF,
$                  DU2, IPIV, B, LDB, X, LDX, RCOND, FERR, BERR,
$                  WORK, RWORK, INFO )
        CHARACTER      FACT, TRANS
        INTEGER        INFO, LDB, LDX, N, NRHS
        REAL           RCOND
        INTEGER        IPIV( * )
        REAL           BERR( * ), FERR( * ), RWORK( * )
        COMPLEX        B( LDB, * ), D( * ), DF( * ), DL( * ),
$                      DLF( * ), DU( * ), DU2( * ), DUF( * ),
$                      WORK( * ), X( LDX, * )
```

Purpose

SGTSVX/CGTSVX uses the LU factorization to compute the solution to a real/complex system of linear equations $A*X = B$, $A^T*X = B$, or $A^H*X = B$, where A is a tridiagonal matrix of order n and X and B are n-by-nrhs matrices.

Error bounds on the solution and a condition estimate are also provided.

Description

The following steps are performed:

1. If FACT = 'N', the LU decomposition is used to factor the matrix A as $A = L*U$, where L is a product of permutation and unit lower bidiagonal matrices and U is upper triangular with nonzeros in only the main diagonal and first two superdiagonals.

2. The factored form of A is used to estimate the condition number of the matrix A. If the reciprocal of the condition number is less than machine precision, steps 3 and 4 are skipped.

3. The system of equations is solved for X using the factored form of A.

4. Iterative refinement is applied to improve the computed solution vectors and calculate error bounds and backward error estimates for them.

Arguments

FACT   (input) CHARACTER*1
        Specifies whether or not the factored form of the matrix A is supplied on entry.
        = 'F':   On entry, DLF, DF, DUF, DU2, and IPIV contain the factored form of A; DL, D, DU, DLF, DF, DU2 and IPIV will not be modified.
        = 'N':   The matrix will be copied to DLF, DF, and DUF and factored.

TRANS   (input) CHARACTER*1
        Specifies the form of the system of equations:
        = 'N': $A*X = B$ (No transpose)
        = 'T': $A^T*X = B$ (Transpose)
        = 'C': $A^H*X = B$ (Conjugate transpose)

N   (input) INTEGER
        The number of linear equations, i.e., the order of the matrix A. $N \geq 0$.

NRHS   (input) INTEGER
        The number of right hand sides, i.e., the number of columns of the matrix B. $NRHS \geq 0$.

DL   (input) REAL/COMPLEX array, dimension (N−1)
        The (n−1) subdiagonal elements of A.

D   (input) REAL/COMPLEX array, dimension (N)
        The n diagonal elements of A.

DU   (input) REAL/COMPLEX array, dimension (N−1)
        The (n−1) superdiagonal elements of A.

DLF   (input or output) REAL/COMPLEX array, dimension (N−1)
        If FACT = 'F', then DLF is an input argument and on entry contains the (n−1) multipliers that define the matrix L from the LU factorization of A as computed by SGTTRF/CGTTRF.
        If FACT = 'N', then DLF is an output argument and on exit contains the (n−1) multipliers that define the matrix L from the LU factorization of A.

DF   (input or output) REAL/COMPLEX array, dimension (N)
        If FACT = 'F', then DF is an input argument and on entry contains the n diagonal elements of the upper triangular matrix U from the LU factorization of A.
        If FACT = 'N', then DF is an output argument and on exit contains the n diagonal elements of the upper triangular matrix U from the LU factorization of A.

DUF   (input or output) REAL/COMPLEX array, dimension (N−1)
        If FACT = 'F', then DUF is an input argument and on entry contains the (n−1) elements of the first superdiagonal of U.
        If FACT = 'N', then DUF is an output argument and on exit contains the (n−1) elements of the first superdiagonal of U.

INFO (output) INTEGER
= 0: successful exit
< 0: if INFO = −i, the ith argument had an illegal value
> 0: if INFO = i, and i is
≤ N: if INFO = i, U(i,i) is exactly zero. The factorization has not been completed unless i = N, but the factor U is exactly singular, so the solution and error bounds could not be computed.
= N+1: RCOND is less than machine precision. The factorization has been completed, but the matrix is singular to working precision, and the solution and error bounds have not been computed.

SGTTRF/CGTTRF

```
SUBROUTINE SGTTRF( N, DL, D, DU, DU2, IPIV, INFO )
INTEGER    INFO, N
INTEGER    IPIV( * )
REAL       D( * ), DL( * ), DU( * ), DU2( * )

SUBROUTINE CGTTRF( N, DL, D, DU, DU2, IPIV, INFO )
INTEGER    INFO, N
INTEGER    IPIV( * )
COMPLEX    D( * ), DL( * ), DU( * ), DU2( * )
```

Purpose

SGTTRF/CGTTRF computes an LU factorization of a real/complex tridiagonal matrix A using partial pivoting and row interchanges.

The factorization has the form A = L*U where L is a product of permutation and unit lower bidiagonal matrices and U is upper triangular with nonzeros in only the main diagonal and first two superdiagonals.

Arguments

N (input) INTEGER
The order of the matrix A. N ≥ 0.

DL (input/output) REAL/COMPLEX array, dimension (N−1)
On entry, DL must contain the (n−1) subdiagonal elements of A.
On exit, DL is overwritten by the (n−1) multipliers that define the matrix L from the LU factorization of A.

D (input/output) REAL/COMPLEX array, dimension (N)
On entry, D must contain the diagonal elements of A.
On exit, D is overwritten by the n diagonal elements of the upper triangular matrix U from the LU factorization of A.

DU2 (input or output) REAL/COMPLEX array, dimension (N−2)
If FACT = 'F', then DU2 is an input argument and on entry contains the (n−2) elements of the second superdiagonal of U.
If FACT = 'N', then DU2 is an output argument and on exit contains the (n−2) elements of the second superdiagonal of U.

IPIV (input) INTEGER array, dimension (N)
If FACT = 'F', then IPIV is an input argument and on entry contains the pivot indices from the LU factorization of A as computed by SGTTRF/CGTTRF.
If FACT = 'N', then IPIV is an output argument and on exit contains the pivot indices from the LU factorization of A; row i of the matrix was interchanged with row IPIV(i). IPIV(i) will always be either i or i+1; IPIV(i) = i indicates a row interchange was not required.

B (input) REAL/COMPLEX array, dimension (LDB,NRHS)
The n-by-nrhs right hand side matrix B.

LDB (input) INTEGER
The leading dimension of the array B. LDB ≥ max(1,N).

X (output) REAL/COMPLEX array, dimension (LDX,NRHS)
If INFO = 0, the n-by-nrhs solution matrix X.

LDX (input) INTEGER
The leading dimension of the array X. LDX ≥ max(1,N).

RCOND (output) REAL
The estimate of the reciprocal condition number of the matrix A. If RCOND < the machine precision (in particular, if RCOND = 0), the matrix is singular to working precision. This condition is indicated by a return code of INFO > 0, and the solution and error bounds are not computed.

FERR (output) REAL array, dimension (NRHS)
The estimated forward error bound for each solution vector X(j) (the jth column of the solution matrix X). If XTRUE is the true solution corresponding to X(j), FERR(j) bounds the magnitude of the largest element in (X(j) − XTRUE) divided by the magnitude of the largest element in X(j). The quality of the error bound depends on the quality of the estimate of $\|A^{-1}\|$ computed in the code; if the estimate of $\|A^{-1}\|$ is accurate, the error bound is guaranteed.

BERR (output) REAL array, dimension (NRHS)
The componentwise relative backward error of each solution vector X(j) (i.e., the smallest relative change in any element of A or B that makes X(j) an exact solution).

WORK SGTSVX (workspace) REAL array, dimension (3*N)
CGTSVX (workspace) COMPLEX array, dimension (2*N)

IWORK SGTSVX only (workspace) INTEGER array, dimension (N)

RWORK CGTSVX only (workspace) REAL array, dimension (N)

DU (input/output) REAL/COMPLEX array, dimension (N−1)
On entry, DU must contain the (n−1) superdiagonal elements of A.
On exit, DU is overwritten by the (n−1) elements of the first superdiagonal of U.

DU2 (output) REAL/COMPLEX array, dimension (N−2)
On exit, DU2 is overwritten by the (n−2) elements of the second superdiagonal of U.

IPIV (output) INTEGER array, dimension (N)
The pivot indices; for $1 \leq i \leq N$, row i of the matrix was interchanged with row IPIV(i). IPIV(i) will always be either i or i+1; IPIV(i) = i indicates a row interchange was not required.

INFO (output) INTEGER
= 0: successful exit
< 0: if INFO = −i, the ith argument had an illegal value
> 0: if INFO = i, U(i,i) is exactly zero. The factorization has been completed, but the factor U is exactly singular, and division by zero will occur if it is used to solve a system of equations.

SGTTRS/CGTTRS

```
SUBROUTINE SGTTRS( TRANS, N, NRHS, DL, D, DU, DU2, IPIV, B, LDB,
$                  INFO )
    CHARACTER    TRANS
    INTEGER      INFO, LDB, N, NRHS
    INTEGER      IPIV( * )
    REAL         B( LDB, * ), D( * ), DL( * ), DU( * ), DU2( * )

SUBROUTINE CGTTRS( TRANS, N, NRHS, DL, D, DU, DU2, IPIV, B, LDB,
$                  INFO )
    CHARACTER    TRANS
    INTEGER      INFO, LDB, N, NRHS
    INTEGER      IPIV( * )
    COMPLEX      B( LDB, * ), D( * ), DL( * ), DU( * ), DU2( * )
```

Purpose

SGTTRS/CGTTRS solves one of the systems of equations $A*X = B$, $A^T*X = B$, or $A^H*X = B$, with a tridiagonal matrix A using the LU factorization computed by SGTTRF/CGTTRF.

Arguments

TRANS (input) CHARACTER*1
Specifies the form of the system of equations:
= 'N': $A*X = B$ (No transpose)
= 'T': $A^T*X = B$ (Transpose)
= 'C': $A^H*X = B$ (Conjugate transpose)

N (input) INTEGER
The order of the matrix A. N ≥ 0.

NRHS (input) INTEGER
The number of right hand sides, i.e., the number of columns of the matrix B. NRHS ≥ 0.

DL (input) REAL/COMPLEX array, dimension (N−1)
The (n−1) multipliers that define the matrix L from the LU factorization of A.

D (input) REAL/COMPLEX array, dimension (N)
The n diagonal elements of the upper triangular matrix U from the LU factorization of A.

DU (input) REAL/COMPLEX array, dimension (N−1)
The (n−1) elements of the first superdiagonal of U.

DU2 (input) REAL/COMPLEX array, dimension (N−2)
The (n−2) elements of the second superdiagonal of U.

IPIV (input) INTEGER array, dimension (N)
The pivot indices; for $1 \leq i \leq N$, row i of the matrix was interchanged with row IPIV(i). IPIV(i) will always be either i or i+1; IPIV(i) = i indicates a row interchange was not required.

B (input/output) REAL/COMPLEX array, dimension (LDB,NRHS)
On entry, the right hand side matrix B.
On exit, B is overwritten by the solution matrix X.

LDB (input) INTEGER
The leading dimension of the array B. LDB ≥ max(1,N).

INFO (output) INTEGER
= 0: successful exit
< 0: if INFO = −i, the ith argument had an illegal value

SHSEIN/CHSEIN

```
SUBROUTINE SHSEIN( JOB, EIGSRC, INITV, SELECT, N, H, LDH, WR, WI,
$                  VL, LDVL, VR, LDVR, MM, M, WORK, IFAILL,
$                  IFAILR, INFO )
    CHARACTER    EIGSRC, INITV, JOB
    INTEGER      INFO, LDH, LDVL, LDVR, M, MM, N
    LOGICAL      SELECT( * )
    INTEGER      IFAILL( * ), IFAILR( * )
    REAL         H( LDH, * ), VL( LDVL, * ), VR( LDVR, * ),
$                WI( * ), WORK( * ), WR( * )
```

```
SUBROUTINE CHSEIN( JOB, EIGSRC, INITV, SELECT, N, H, LDH, W, VL,
$                  LDVL, VR, LDVR, MM, M, WORK, RWORK, IFAILL,
$                  IFAILR, INFO )
   CHARACTER      EIGSRC, INITV, JOB
   INTEGER        INFO, LDH, LDVL, LDVR, N, MM, M
   LOGICAL        SELECT( * )
   INTEGER        IFAILL( * ), IFAILR( * )
   REAL           RWORK( * )
   COMPLEX        H( LDH, * ), VL( LDVL, * ), VR( LDVR, * ),
$                  W( * ), WORK( * )
```

Purpose

SHSEIN/CHSEIN uses inverse iteration to find specified right and/or left eigenvectors of a real/complex upper Hessenberg matrix H.

The right eigenvector x and the left eigenvector y of the matrix H corresponding to an eigenvalue w are defined by:

$$H*x = w*x, \quad y^H*H = w*y^H .$$

Arguments

JOB   (input) CHARACTER*1
       = 'R': compute right eigenvectors only;
       = 'L': compute left eigenvectors only;
       = 'B': compute both right and left eigenvectors.

EIGSRC (input) CHARACTER*1
       Specifies the source of eigenvalues supplied in (WR,WI)/(W):
       = 'Q': the eigenvalues were found using SHSEQR/CHSEQR; thus, if H has zero subdiagonal elements, and so is block-triangular, then the jth eigenvalue can be assumed to be an eigenvalue of the block containing the jth row/column. This property allows SHSEIN/CHSEIN to perform inverse iteration on just one diagonal block.
       = 'N': no assumptions are made on the correspondence between eigenvalues and diagonal blocks. In this case, SHSEIN/CHSEIN must always perform inverse iteration using the whole matrix H.

INITV (input) CHARACTER*1
       = 'N': no initial vectors are supplied;
       = 'U': user-supplied initial vectors are stored in the arrays VL and/or VR.

SELECT SHSEIN (input/output) LOGICAL array, dimension(N)
       CHSEIN (input) LOGICAL array, dimension (N)
       SHSEIN
       Specifies the eigenvectors to be computed. To select the real eigenvector corresponding to a real eigenvalue WR(j), SELECT(j) must be set to .TRUE.. To select the complex eigenvector corresponding to a complex eigenvalue (WR(j),WI(j)), with complex conjugate (WR(j+1),WI(j+1)), either SELECT(j) or SELECT(j+1) or both must be set to .TRUE.; then on exit SELECT(j) is .TRUE. and SELECT(j+1) is .FALSE..
       CHSEIN
       Specifies the eigenvectors to be computed. To select the eigenvector corresponding to the eigenvalue W(j), SELECT(j) must be set to .TRUE..

N   (input) INTEGER
       The order of the matrix H. N ≥ 0.

H   (input) REAL/COMPLEX array, dimension (LDH,N)
       The upper Hessenberg matrix H.

LDH   (input) INTEGER
       The leading dimension of the array H. LDH ≥ max(1,N).

WR   SHSEIN only (input/output) REAL array, dimension (N)
WI   SHSEIN only (input) REAL array, dimension (N)
       On entry, the real and imaginary parts of the eigenvalues of H; a complex conjugate pair of eigenvalues must be stored in consecutive elements of WR and WI.
       On exit, WR may have been altered since close eigenvalues are perturbed slightly in searching for independent eigenvectors.

W   CHSEIN only (input/output) COMPLEX array, dimension (N)
       On entry, the eigenvalues of H.
       On exit, the real parts of W may have been altered since close eigenvalues are perturbed slightly in searching for independent eigenvectors.

VL   (input/output) REAL/COMPLEX array, dimension (LDVL,MM)
       On entry, if INITV = 'U' and JOB = 'L' or 'B', VL must contain starting vectors for the inverse iteration for the left eigenvectors; the starting vector for each eigenvector must be in the same column(s) in which the eigenvector will be stored.
       On exit, if JOB = 'L' or 'B', the left eigenvectors specified by SELECT will be stored one after another in the columns of VL, in the same order as their eigenvalues. If JOB = 'R', VL is not referenced.
       SHSEIN only
       A complex eigenvector corresponding to a complex eigenvalue is stored in two consecutive columns, the first holding the real part and the second the imaginary part.

LDVL   (input) INTEGER
       The leading dimension of the array VL.
       LDVL ≥ max(1,N) if JOB = 'L' or 'B'; LDVL ≥ 1 otherwise.

VR   (input/output) REAL/COMPLEX array, dimension (LDVR,MM)
       On entry, if INITV = 'U' and JOB = 'R' or 'B', VR must contain starting vectors for the inverse iteration for the right eigenvectors; the starting vector for each eigenvector must be in the same column(s) in which the eigenvector will be stored.
       On exit, if JOB = 'R' or 'B', the right eigenvectors specified by SELECT will be stored one after another in the columns of VR, in the same order as their eigenvalues. If JOB = 'L', VR is not referenced.
```
```

SHSEIN

A complex eigenvector corresponding to a complex eigenvalue is stored in two consecutive columns, the first holding the real part and the second the imaginary part.

LDVR   (input) INTEGER
The leading dimension of the array VR.
LDVR $\geq$ max(1,N) if JOB = 'R' or 'B'; LDVR $\geq$ 1 otherwise.

MM   (input) INTEGER
The number of columns in the arrays VL and/or VR. MM $\geq$ M.

M   (output) INTEGER
The number of columns in the arrays VL and/or VR actually used to store the eigenvectors.
SHSEIN
Each selected real eigenvector occupies one column and each selected complex eigenvector occupies two columns.
CHSEIN
Each selected eigenvector occupies one column.

WORK   *SHSEIN* (workspace) REAL array, dimension ((N+2)*N)
        CHSEIN (workspace) COMPLEX array, dimension (N*N)

RWORK   *CHSEIN only* (workspace) REAL array, dimension (N)

IFAILL (output) INTEGER array, dimension (MM)
If JOB = 'L' or 'B', IFAILL(i) = j > 0 if the left eigenvector in the ith column of VL (corresponding to the jth eigenvalue) failed to converge.
IFAILL(i) = 0 if the eigenvector converged satisfactorily.
If JOB = 'R', IFAILL is not referenced.
SHSEIN only
If the ith and $(i+1)^{st}$ columns of VL hold a complex eigenvector, then IFAILL(i) and IFAILL(i+1) are set to the same value.

IFAILR (output) INTEGER array, dimension (MM)
If JOB = 'R' or 'B', IFAILR(i) = j > 0 if the right eigenvector in the ith column of VR (corresponding to the jth eigenvalue) failed to converge.
IFAILR(i) = 0 if the eigenvector converged satisfactorily.
If JOB = 'L', IFAILR is not referenced.
SHSEIN only
If the ith and $(i+1)^{st}$ columns of VR hold a complex eigenvector, then IFAILR(i) and IFAILR(i+1) are set to the same value.

INFO   (output) INTEGER
= 0: successful exit
< 0: if INFO = $-i$, the ith argument had an illegal value
> 0: if INFO = i, INFO is the number of eigenvectors which failed to converge; see IFAILL and IFAILR for further details.

SHSEQR/CHSEQR

```
SUBROUTINE SHSEQR( JOB, COMPZ, N, ILO, IHI, H, LDH, WR, WI, Z,
$                  LDZ, WORK, LWORK, INFO )
CHARACTER          COMPZ, JOB
INTEGER            IHI, ILO, INFO, LDH, LDZ, LWORK, N
REAL               H( LDH, * ), WI( * ), WORK( * ), WR( * ),
$                  Z( LDZ, * )

SUBROUTINE CHSEQR( JOB, COMPZ, N, ILO, IHI, H, LDH, W, Z, LDZ,
$                  WORK, LWORK, INFO )
CHARACTER          COMPZ, JOB
INTEGER            IHI, ILO, INFO, LDH, LDZ, LWORK, N
COMPLEX            H( LDH, * ), W( * ), WORK( * ), Z( LDZ, * )
```

Purpose

SHSEQR/CHSEQR computes the eigenvalues of a real/complex upper Hessenberg matrix H and, optionally, the matrices T and Z from the Schur decomposition $H = Z*T*Z^H$, where T is an upper quasi-triangular/triangular matrix (the Schur form), and Z is the orthogonal/unitary matrix of Schur vectors.

Optionally Z may be postmultiplied into an input orthogonal/unitary matrix Q, so that this routine can give the Schur factorization of a matrix A which has been reduced to the Hessenberg form H by the orthogonal/unitary matrix Q: $A = Q*H*Q^H = (Q*Z)*T*(Q*Z)^H$.

Arguments

JOB   (input) CHARACTER*1
= 'E':   compute eigenvalues only;
= 'S':   compute eigenvalues and the Schur form T.

COMPZ   (input) CHARACTER*1
= 'N':   no Schur vectors are computed;
= 'I':   Z is initialized to the unit matrix and the matrix Z of Schur vectors of H is returned;
= 'V':   Z must contain an orthogonal/unitary matrix Q on entry, and the product Q*Z is returned.

N   (input) INTEGER
The order of the matrix H. N $\geq$ 0.

ILO, IHI (input) INTEGER
It is assumed that H is already upper triangular in rows and columns 1 to ILO-1 and IHI+1 to N. ILO and IHI are normally set by a previous call to SGEBAL/CGEBAL, and then passed to SGEHRD/CGEHRD when the matrix output by SGEBAL/CGEBAL is reduced to Hessenberg form. Otherwise ILO and IHI should be set to 1 and N respectively.
min(ILO,N) $\leq$ IHI $\leq$ N; ILO $\geq$ 1.

H   (input/output) REAL/COMPLEX array, dimension (LDH,N)
On entry, the upper Hessenberg matrix H.

SOPGTR/CUPGTR

```
SUBROUTINE SOPGTR( UPLO, N, AP, TAU, Q, LDQ, WORK, INFO )
    CHARACTER     UPLO
    INTEGER       INFO, LDQ, N
    REAL          AP( * ), Q( LDQ, * ), TAU( * ), WORK( * )

SUBROUTINE CUPGTR( UPLO, N, AP, TAU, Q, LDQ, WORK, INFO )
    CHARACTER     UPLO
    INTEGER       INFO, LDQ, N
    COMPLEX       AP( * ), Q( LDQ, * ), TAU( * ), WORK( * )
```

Purpose

SOPGTR/CUPGTR generates a real/complex orthogonal/unitary matrix Q which is defined as the product of $n-1$ elementary reflectors H_i of order n, as returned by SSPTRD/CHPTRD using packed storage:

if UPLO = 'U', $Q = H_{n-1} \cdots H_2 H_1$,

if UPLO = 'L', $Q = H_1 H_2 \cdots H_{n-1}$.

Arguments

UPLO   (input) CHARACTER*1
     = 'U': Upper triangular packed storage used in previous call to SSPTRD/CHPTRD;
     = 'L': Lower triangular packed storage used in previous call to SSPTRD/CHPTRD.

N   (input) INTEGER
    The order of the matrix Q. $N \geq 0$.

AP   (input) REAL/COMPLEX array, dimension $(N*(N+1)/2)$
    The vectors which define the elementary reflectors, as returned by SSPTRD/CHPTRD.

TAU (input) REAL/COMPLEX array, dimension (N−1)
    TAU(i) must contain the scalar factor of the elementary reflector H_i, as returned by SSPTRD/CHPTRD.

Q   (output) REAL/COMPLEX array, dimension (LDQ,N)
    The n-by-n orthogonal/unitary matrix Q.

LDQ (input) INTEGER
    The leading dimension of the array Q. $LDQ \geq \max(1,N)$.

WORK (workspace) REAL/COMPLEX array, dimension (N−1)

INFO (output) INTEGER
    = 0: successful exit
    < 0: if INFO = −i, the ith argument had an illegal value

---

On exit, if JOB = 'S', H contains the upper quasi-triangular/triangular matrix T from the Schur decomposition (the Schur form). If JOB = 'E', the contents of H are unspecified on exit.

SHSEQR only
2-by-2 diagonal blocks (corresponding to complex conjugate pairs of eigenvalues) are returned in standard form, with H(i,i) = H(i+1,i+1) and H(i+1,i)*H(i,i+1) < 0.

LDH (input) INTEGER
    The leading dimension of the array H. $LDH \geq \max(1,N)$.

WR, WI *SHSEQR only* (output) REAL array, dimension (N)
    The real and imaginary parts, respectively, of the computed eigenvalues. If two eigenvalues are computed as a complex conjugate pair, they are stored in consecutive elements of WR and WI, say the ith and $(i+1)^{st}$, with WI(i) > 0 and WI(i+1) < 0. If JOB = 'S', the eigenvalues are stored in the same order as on the diagonal of the Schur form returned in H, with WR(i) = H(i,i) and, if H(i:i+1,i:i+1) is a 2-by-2 diagonal block, $WI(i) = \sqrt{(H(i+1,i)*H(i,i+1))}$ and WI(i+1) = −WI(i).

W   *CHSEQR only* (output) COMPLEX array, dimension (N)
    The computed eigenvalues. If JOB = 'S', the eigenvalues are stored in the same order as on the diagonal of the Schur form returned in H, with W(i) = H(i,i).

Z   (input/output) REAL/COMPLEX array, dimension (LDZ,N)
    If COMPZ = 'N': Z is not referenced.
    If COMPZ = 'I': on entry, Z need not be set, and on exit, Z contains the orthogonal/unitary matrix Z of the Schur vectors of H.
    If COMPZ = 'V': on entry, Z must contain an n-by-n matrix Q, which is assumed to be equal to the unit matrix except for the submatrix Z(ilo:ihi,ilo:ihi); on exit Z contains Q*Z. Normally Q is the orthogonal/unitary matrix generated by SORGHR/CUNGHR after the call to SGEHRD/CGEHRD which formed the Hessenberg matrix H.

LDZ (input) INTEGER
    The leading dimension of the array Z. $LDZ \geq \max(1,N)$.

WORK (workspace) REAL/COMPLEX array, dimension (N)

LWORK (input) INTEGER
    This argument is currently redundant.

INFO (output) INTEGER
    = 0: successful exit
    < 0: if INFO = −i, the ith argument had an illegal value
    > 0: if INFO = i, SHSEQR/CHSEQR failed to compute all the eigenvalues in a total of 30*(IHI−ILO+1) iterations; elements 1:ilo−1 and i+1:n of WR and WI (*SHSEQR*) or of W (*CHSEQR*) contain those eigenvalues which have been successfully computed.

SOPMTR/CUPMTR

```
SUBROUTINE SOPMTR( SIDE, UPLO, TRANS, M, N, AP, TAU, C, LDC, WORK,
$                  INFO )
     CHARACTER      SIDE, TRANS, UPLO
     INTEGER        INFO, LDC, M, N
     REAL           AP( * ), C( LDC, * ), TAU( * ), WORK( * )

SUBROUTINE CUPMTR( SIDE, UPLO, TRANS, M, N, AP, TAU, C, LDC, WORK,
$                  INFO )
     CHARACTER      SIDE, TRANS, UPLO
     INTEGER        INFO, LDC, M, N
     COMPLEX        AP( * ), C( LDC, * ), TAU( * ), WORK( * )
```

Purpose

SOPMTR/CUPMTR overwrites the general real/complex m-by-n matrix C with

	SIDE = 'L'	SIDE = 'R'	
TRANS = 'N':	$Q*C$	$C*Q$	
TRANS = 'T':	Q^T*C	$C*Q^T$	(*SOPMTR only*)
TRANS = 'C':	Q^H*C	$C*Q^H$	(*CUPMTR only*)

where Q is a real/complex orthogonal/unitary matrix of order NQ, with NQ = M if SIDE = 'L', and NQ = N if SIDE = 'R'. Q is defined as the product of nq−1 elementary reflectors H_i, of order nq, as returned by SSPTRD/CHPTRD using packed storage:

if UPLO = 'U', $Q = H_{nq-1} \cdots H_2 H_1$;

if UPLO = 'L', $Q = H_1 H_2 \cdots H_{nq-1}$.

Arguments

SIDE   (input) CHARACTER*1
 = 'L': apply Q or Q^H from the Left;
 = 'R': apply Q or Q^H from the Right.

UPLO   (input) CHARACTER*1
 = 'U': Upper triangular packed storage used in previous call to SSPTRD/CHPTRD;
 = 'L': Lower triangular packed storage used in previous call to SSPTRD/CHPTRD.

TRANS   (input) CHARACTER*1
 Specifies whether the matrix Q, Q^T, or Q^H is applied to C.
 = 'N': No transpose, apply Q
 = 'T': Transpose, apply Q^T (*SOPMTR only*)
 = 'C': Conjugate transpose, apply Q^H (*CUPMTR only*)

M   (input) INTEGER
 The number of rows of the matrix C. M ≥ 0.

N   (input) INTEGER
 The number of columns of the matrix C. N ≥ 0.

AP   (input) REAL/COMPLEX array, dimension (M*(M+1)/2) if SIDE = 'L', or (N*(N+1)/2) if SIDE = 'R'.
 The vectors which define the elementary reflectors, as returned by SSPTRD/CHPTRD. AP is modified by the routine but restored on exit.

TAU   (input) REAL/COMPLEX array, dimension (M−1) if SIDE = 'L' or (N−1) if SIDE = 'R'
 TAU(i) must contain the scalar factor of the elementary reflector H_i, as returned by SSPTRD/CHPTRD.

C   (input/output) REAL/COMPLEX array, dimension (LDC,N)
 On entry, the m-by-n matrix C.
 On exit, C is overwritten by $Q*C$ or Q^H*C or $C*Q^H$ or $C*Q$.

LDC   (input) INTEGER
 The leading dimension of the array C. LDC ≥ max(1,M).

WORK   (workspace) REAL/COMPLEX array, dimension
 (N) if SIDE = 'L',
 (M) if SIDE = 'R'

INFO   (output) INTEGER
 = 0:   successful exit
 < 0:   if INFO = −i, the ith argument had an illegal value

SORGBR/CUNGBR

```
SUBROUTINE SORGBR( VECT, M, N, K, A, LDA, TAU, WORK, LWORK, INFO )
     CHARACTER      VECT
     INTEGER        INFO, K, LDA, LWORK, M, N
     REAL           A( LDA, * ), TAU( * ), WORK( LWORK )

SUBROUTINE CUNGBR( VECT, M, N, K, A, LDA, TAU, WORK, LWORK, INFO )
     CHARACTER      VECT
     INTEGER        INFO, K, LDA, LWORK, M, N
     COMPLEX        A( LDA, * ), TAU( * ), WORK( LWORK )
```

Purpose

SORGBR/CUNGBR generates one of the orthogonal/unitary matrices Q or P^H determined by SGEBRD/CGEBRD when reducing a real/complex matrix A to bidiagonal form: $A = Q*B*P^H$. Q and P^H are defined as products of elementary reflectors H_i or G_i respectively.

If VECT = 'Q', A is assumed to have been an m-by-k matrix, and Q is of order M: if M ≥ K, $Q = H_1 H_2 \cdots H_k$ and SORGBR/CUNGBR returns the first N columns of Q, where $M \geq N \geq K$; if $M < K$, $Q = H_1H_2 \cdots H_{m-1}$ and SORGBR/CUNGBR returns Q as an m-by-m matrix.

If VECT = 'P', A is assumed to have been a k-by-n matrix, and P^H is of order n: if $K < N$, $P^H = G_k \cdots G_2G_1$ and SORGBR/CUNGBR returns the first M rows of P^H, where $N \geq M \geq K$; if $K \geq N$, $P^H = G_{n-1} \cdots G_2G_1$ and SORGBR/CUNGBR returns P^H as an n-by-n matrix.

Arguments

VECT   (input) CHARACTER*1
Specifies whether the matrix Q or the matrix P^H is required, as defined in the transformation applied by SGEBRD/CGEBRD:
= 'Q': generate Q;
= 'P': generate P^H.

M   (input) INTEGER
The number of rows of the matrix Q or P^H to be returned. $M \geq 0$.

N   (input) INTEGER
The number of columns of the matrix Q or P^H to be returned. $N \geq 0$.
If VECT = 'Q', $M \geq N \geq \min(M,K)$;
if VECT = 'P', $N \geq M \geq \min(N,K)$.

K   (input) INTEGER
$K \geq 0$.
If VECT = 'Q', the number of columns in the original m-by-k matrix reduced by SGEBRD/CGEBRD.
If VECT = 'P', the number of rows in the original k-by-n matrix reduced by SGEBRD/CGEBRD.

A   (input/output) REAL/COMPLEX array, dimension (LDA,N)
On entry, the vectors which define the elementary reflectors, as returned by SGEBRD/CGEBRD.
On exit, the m-by-n matrix Q or P^H.

LDA   (input) INTEGER
The leading dimension of the array A. LDA $\geq \max(1,M)$.

TAU   (input) REAL/COMPLEX array, dimension
(min(M,K)) if VECT = 'Q', or (min(N,K)) if VECT = 'P'
TAU(i) must contain the scalar factor of the elementary reflector H_i or G_i, which determines Q or P^H, as returned by SGEBRD/CGEBRD in its array argument TAUQ or TAUP.

WORK   (workspace) REAL/COMPLEX array, dimension (LWORK)
On exit, if INFO = 0, WORK(1) returns the optimal LWORK.

LWORK   (input) INTEGER
The dimension of the array WORK. LWORK $\geq \max(1,\min(M,N))$.
For optimum performance LWORK $\geq \min(M,N)*$NB, where NB is the optimal block size.

INFO   (output) INTEGER
= 0: successful exit

< 0:   if INFO = −i, the ith argument had an illegal value

SORGHR/CUNGHR.

```
SUBROUTINE SORGHR( N, ILO, IHI, A, LDA, TAU, WORK, LWORK, INFO )
INTEGER       IHI, ILO, INFO, LDA, LWORK, N
REAL          A( LDA, * ), TAU( * ), WORK( LWORK )

SUBROUTINE CUNGHR( N, ILO, IHI, A, LDA, TAU, WORK, LWORK, INFO )
INTEGER       IHI, ILO, INFO, LDA, LWORK, N
COMPLEX       A( LDA, * ), TAU( * ), WORK( LWORK )
```

Purpose

SORGHR/CUNGHR generates a real/complex orthogonal/unitary matrix Q which is defined as the product of IHI–ILO elementary reflectors H_i of order n, as returned by SGEHRD/CGEHRD:

$$Q = H_{ilo}H_{ilo+1} \cdots H_{ihi-1}.$$

Arguments

N   (input) INTEGER
The order of the matrix Q. $N \geq 0$.

ILO, IHI (input) INTEGER
ILO and IHI must have the same values as in the previous call of SGEHRD/CGEHRD. Q is equal to the unit matrix except in the submatrix Q(ilo+1:ihi,ilo+1:ihi). If $N > 0$, $1 \leq \text{ILO} \leq \text{IHI} \leq N$; otherwise ILO = 1 and IHI = N.

A   (input/output) REAL/COMPLEX array, dimension (LDA,N)
On entry, the vectors which define the elementary reflectors, as returned by SGEHRD/CGEHRD.
On exit, the n-by-n orthogonal/unitary matrix Q.

LDA   (input) INTEGER
The leading dimension of the array A. LDA $\geq \max(1,N)$.

TAU   (input) REAL/COMPLEX array, dimension (N−1)
TAU(i) must contain the scalar factor of the elementary reflector H_i, as returned by SGEHRD/CGEHRD.

WORK   (workspace) REAL/COMPLEX array, dimension (LWORK)
On exit, if INFO = 0, WORK(1) returns the optimal LWORK.

LWORK   (input) INTEGER
The dimension of the array WORK. LWORK $\geq \max(1,\text{IHI−ILO})$.
For optimum performance LWORK $\geq (\text{IHI−ILO})*$NB, where NB is the optimal block size.

INFO　　(output) INTEGER
　　　　= 0:　successful exit
　　　　< 0:　if INFO = −i, the ith argument had an illegal value

SORGLQ/CUNGLQ

```
SUBROUTINE SORGLQ( M, N, K, A, LDA, TAU, WORK, LWORK, INFO )
INTEGER          INFO, K, LDA, LWORK, M, N
REAL             A( LDA, * ), TAU( * ), WORK( LWORK )

SUBROUTINE CUNGLQ( M, N, K, A, LDA, TAU, WORK, LWORK, INFO )
INTEGER          INFO, K, LDA, LWORK, M, N
COMPLEX          A( LDA, * ), TAU( * ), WORK( LWORK )
```

Purpose

SORGLQ/CUNGLQ generates an m-by-n real/complex matrix Q with orthonormal rows, which is defined as the first m rows of a product of k elementary reflectors H_i of order n

$Q = H_k \cdots H_2 H_1$ (SORGLQ)

$Q = H_k{}^H \cdots H_2{}^H H_1{}^H$ (CUNGLQ)

as returned by SGELQF/CGELQF.

Arguments

M　　(input) INTEGER
　　　The number of rows of the matrix Q. M ≥ 0.

N　　(input) INTEGER
　　　The number of columns of the matrix Q. N ≥ M.

K　　(input) INTEGER
　　　The number of elementary reflectors whose product defines the matrix Q. M ≥ K ≥ 0.

A　　(input/output) REAL/COMPLEX array, dimension (LDA,N)
　　　On entry, the ith row must contain the vector which defines the elementary reflector H_i, for i = 1,2,...,k, as returned by SGELQF/CGELQF in the first k rows of its array argument A. On exit, the m-by-n matrix Q.

LDA　(input) INTEGER
　　　The first dimension of the array A. LDA ≥ max(1,M).

TAU　(input) REAL/COMPLEX array, dimension (K)
　　　TAU(i) must contain the scalar factor of the elementary reflector H_i, as returned by SGELQF/CGELQF.

WORK　　(workspace) REAL/COMPLEX array, dimension (LWORK)
　　　　On exit, if INFO = 0, WORK(1) returns the optimal LWORK.

LWORK　(input) INTEGER
　　　　The dimension of the array WORK. LWORK ≥ max(1,M).
　　　　For optimum performance LWORK ≥ M*NB, where NB is the optimal block size.

INFO　　(output) INTEGER
　　　　= 0:　successful exit
　　　　< 0:　if INFO = −i, the ith argument has an illegal value

SORGQL/CUNGQL

```
SUBROUTINE SORGQL( M, N, K, A, LDA, TAU, WORK, LWORK, INFO )
INTEGER          INFO, K, LDA, LWORK, M, N
REAL             A( LDA, * ), TAU( * ), WORK( LWORK )

SUBROUTINE CUNGQL( M, N, K, A, LDA, TAU, WORK, LWORK, INFO )
INTEGER          INFO, K, LDA, LWORK, M, N
COMPLEX          A( LDA, * ), TAU( * ), WORK( LWORK )
```

Purpose

SORGQL/CUNGQL generates an m-by-n real/complex matrix Q with orthonormal columns, which is defined as the last n columns of a product of k elementary reflectors H_i of order m

$Q = H_k \cdots H_2 H_1$

as returned by SGEQLF/CGEQLF.

Arguments

M　　(input) INTEGER
　　　The number of rows of the matrix Q. M ≥ 0.

N　　(input) INTEGER
　　　The number of columns of the matrix Q. M ≥ N ≥ 0.

K　　(input) INTEGER
　　　The number of elementary reflectors whose product defines the matrix Q. N ≥ K ≥ 0.

A　　(input/output) REAL/COMPLEX array, dimension (LDA,N)
　　　On entry, the (n−k+i)th column must contain the vector which defines the elementary reflector H_i, for i = 1,2,...,k, as returned by SGEQLF/CGEQLF in the last k columns of its array argument A. On exit, the m-by-n matrix Q.

the elementary reflector H_i, for $i = 1, 2, \ldots, k$, as returned by SGEQRF/CGEQRF in the first k columns of its array argument A. On exit, the m-by-n matrix Q.

LDA   (input) INTEGER
The first dimension of the array A. LDA ≥ max(1,M).

TAU   (input) REAL/COMPLEX array, dimension (K)
TAU(i) must contain the scalar factor of the elementary reflector H_i, as returned by SGEQRF/CGEQRF.

WORK   (workspace) REAL/COMPLEX array, dimension (LWORK)
On exit, if INFO = 0, WORK(1) returns the optimal LWORK.

LWORK   (input) INTEGER
The dimension of the array WORK. LWORK ≥ max(1,N). For optimum performance LWORK ≥ N*NB, where NB is the optimal block size.

INFO   (output) INTEGER
= 0:   successful exit;
< 0:   if INFO = -i, the ith argument has an illegal value

SORGRQ/CUNGRQ

```
SUBROUTINE SORGRQ( M, N, K, A, LDA, TAU, WORK, LWORK, INFO )
INTEGER          INFO, K, LDA, LWORK, M, N
REAL             A( LDA, * ), TAU( * ), WORK( LWORK )

SUBROUTINE CUNGRQ( M, N, K, A, LDA, TAU, WORK, LWORK, INFO )
INTEGER          INFO, K, LDA, LWORK, M, N
COMPLEX          A( LDA, * ), TAU( * ), WORK( LWORK )
```

Purpose

SORGRQ/CUNGRQ generates an m-by-n real/complex matrix Q with orthonormal rows, which is defined as the last m rows of a product of k elementary reflectors H_i of order n

$Q = H_1 H_2 \cdots H_k$ (SORGRQ)

$Q = H_1^H H_2^H \cdots H_k^H$ (CUNGRQ)

as returned by SGERQF/CGERQF.

Arguments

M   (input) INTEGER
The number of rows of the matrix Q. M ≥ 0.

N   (input) INTEGER
The number of columns of the matrix Q. N ≥ M.

LDA   (input) INTEGER
The first dimension of the array A. LDA ≥ max(1,M).

TAU   (input) REAL/COMPLEX array, dimension (K)
TAU(i) must contain the scalar factor of the elementary reflector H_i, as returned by SGEQLF/CGEQLF.

WORK   (workspace) REAL/COMPLEX array, dimension (LWORK)
On exit, if INFO = 0, WORK(1) returns the optimal LWORK.

LWORK   (input) INTEGER
The dimension of the array WORK. LWORK ≥ max(1,N). For optimum performance LWORK ≥ N*NB, where NB is the optimal block size.

INFO   (output) INTEGER
= 0:   successful exit
< 0:   if INFO = -i, the ith argument has an illegal value

SORGQR/CUNGQR

```
SUBROUTINE SORGQR( M, N, K, A, LDA, TAU, WORK, LWORK, INFO )
INTEGER          INFO, K, LDA, LWORK, M, N
REAL             A( LDA, * ), TAU( * ), WORK( LWORK )

SUBROUTINE CUNGQR( M, N, K, A, LDA, TAU, WORK, LWORK, INFO )
INTEGER          INFO, K, LDA, LWORK, M, N
COMPLEX          A( LDA, * ), TAU( * ), WORK( LWORK )
```

Purpose

SORGQR/CUNGQR generates an m-by-n real/complex matrix Q with orthonormal columns, which is defined as the first n columns of a product of k elementary reflectors H_i of order m

$Q = H_1 H_2 \cdots H_k$

as returned by SGEQRF/CGEQRF.

Arguments

M   (input) INTEGER
The number of rows of the matrix Q. M ≥ 0.

N   (input) INTEGER
The number of columns of the matrix Q. M ≥ N ≥ 0.

K   (input) INTEGER
The number of elementary reflectors whose product defines the matrix Q. N ≥ K ≥ 0.

A   (input/output) REAL/COMPLEX array, dimension (LDA,N)
On entry, the ith column must contain the vector which defines

K (input) INTEGER
The number of elementary reflectors whose product defines the matrix Q. $M \geq K \geq 0$.

A (input/output) REAL/COMPLEX array, dimension (LDA,N)
On entry, the $(m-k+i)^{th}$ row must contain the vector which defines the elementary reflector H_i, for $i = 1,2,\ldots,k$, as returned by SGERQF/CGERQF in the last k rows of its array argument A.
On exit, the m-by-n matrix Q.

LDA (input) INTEGER
The leading dimension of the array A. $LDA \geq max(1,M)$.

TAU (input) REAL/COMPLEX array, dimension (K)
TAU(i) must contain the scalar factor of the elementary reflector H_i, as returned by SGERQF/CGERQF.

WORK (workspace) REAL/COMPLEX array, dimension (LWORK)
On exit, if INFO = 0, WORK(1) returns the optimal LWORK.

LWORK (input) INTEGER
The dimension of the array WORK. $LWORK \geq max(1,M)$. For optimum performance $LWORK \geq M*NB$, where NB is the optimal block size.

INFO (output) INTEGER
= 0:   successful exit
< 0:   if INFO = -i, the ith argument has an illegal value

SORGTR/CUNGTR

```
SUBROUTINE SORGTR( UPLO, N, A, LDA, TAU, WORK, LWORK, INFO )
    CHARACTER        UPLO
    INTEGER          INFO, LDA, LWORK, N
    REAL             A( LDA, * ), TAU( * ), WORK( LWORK )

SUBROUTINE CUNGTR( UPLO, N, A, LDA, TAU, WORK, LWORK, INFO )
    CHARACTER        UPLO
    INTEGER          INFO, LDA, LWORK, N
    COMPLEX          A( LDA, * ), TAU( * ), WORK( LWORK )
```

Purpose

SORGTR/CUNGTR generates a real/complex orthogonal/unitary matrix Q which is defined as the product of n−1 elementary H_i reflectors of order n, as returned by SSYTRD/CHETRD:

if UPLO = 'U', $Q = H_{n-1} \cdots H_2 H_1$,

if UPLO = 'L', $Q = H_1 H_2 \cdots H_{n-1}$.

Arguments

UPLO (input) CHARACTER*1
= 'U':   Upper triangle of A contains elementary reflectors from SSYTRD/CHETRD;
= 'L':   Lower triangle of A contains elementary reflectors from SSYTRD/CHETRD.

N (input) INTEGER
The order of the matrix Q. $N \geq 0$.

A (input/output) REAL/COMPLEX array, dimension (LDA,N)
On entry, the vectors which define the elementary reflectors, as returned by SSYTRD/CHETRD.
On exit, the n-by-n orthogonal/unitary matrix Q.

LDA (input) INTEGER
The leading dimension of the array A. $LDA \geq max(1,N)$.

TAU (input) REAL/COMPLEX array, dimension (N−1)
TAU(i) must contain the scalar factor of the elementary reflector H_i, as returned by SSYTRD/CHETRD.

WORK (workspace) REAL/COMPLEX array, dimension (LWORK)
On exit, if INFO = 0, WORK(1) returns the optimal LWORK.

LWORK (input) INTEGER
The dimension of the array WORK. $LWORK \geq max(1,N-1)$. For optimum performance $LWORK \geq (N-1)*NB$, where NB is the optimal block size.

INFO (output) INTEGER
= 0:   successful exit
< 0:   if INFO = -i, the ith argument had an illegal value

SORMBR/CUNMBR

```
SUBROUTINE SORMBR( VECT, SIDE, TRANS, M, N, K, A, LDA, TAU, C,
$                   LDC, WORK, LWORK, INFO )
    CHARACTER        SIDE, TRANS, VECT
    INTEGER          INFO, K, LDA, LDC, LWORK, M, N
    REAL             A( LDA, * ), C( LDC, * ), TAU( * ),
$                   WORK( LWORK )

SUBROUTINE CUNMBR( VECT, SIDE, TRANS, M, N, K, A, LDA, TAU, C,
$                   LDC, WORK, LWORK, INFO )
    CHARACTER        SIDE, TRANS, VECT
    INTEGER          INFO, K, LDA, LDC, LWORK, M, N
    COMPLEX          A( LDA, * ), C( LDC, * ), TAU( * ),
$                   WORK( LWORK )
```

Purpose

If VECT = 'Q', SORMBR/CUNMBR overwrites the general real/complex m-by-n matrix C with

	SIDE = 'L'	SIDE = 'R'	
TRANS = 'N':	$Q*C$	$C*Q$	
TRANS = 'T':	Q^T*C	$C*Q^T$	(*SORMBR only*)
TRANS = 'C':	Q^H*C	$C*Q^H$	(*CUNMBR only*)

If VECT = 'P', SORMBR/CUNMBR overwrites the general real/complex m-by-n matrix C with

	SIDE = 'L'	SIDE = 'R'	
TRANS = 'N':	$P*C$	$C*P$	
TRANS = 'T':	P^T*C	$C*P^T$	(*SORMBR only*)
TRANS = 'C':	P^H*C	$C*P^H$	(*CUNMBR only*)

Here Q and P^H are the orthogonal/unitary matrices determined by SGEBRD/CGEBRD when reducing a real/complex matrix A to bidiagonal form: $A = Q*B*P^H$. Q and P^H are defined as products of elementary reflectors H_i and G_i, respectively.

Let NQ = M if SIDE = 'L' and NQ = N if SIDE = 'R'. Thus NQ is the order of the orthogonal/unitary matrix Q or P^H that is applied.

If VECT = 'Q', A is assumed to have been an nq-by-k matrix: if NQ ≥ K, $Q = H_1 H_2 \cdots H_k$; if NQ < K, $Q = H_1 H_2 \cdots H_{nq-1}$.

If VECT = 'P', A is assumed to have been a k-by-nq matrix: if K ≥ NQ, $P = G_1 G_2 \cdots G_k$; if K < NQ, $P = G_1 G_2 \cdots G_{nq-1}$.

Arguments

VECT (input) CHARACTER*1
= 'Q': apply Q or Q^H;
= 'P': apply P or P^H.

SIDE (input) CHARACTER*1
= 'L': apply Q, Q^H, P or P^H from the Left;
= 'R': apply Q, Q^H, P or P^H from the Right.

TRANS (input) CHARACTER*1
= 'N': No transpose, apply Q or P
= 'T': Transpose, apply Q^T or P^T (*SORMBR only*)
= 'C': Conjugate transpose, apply Q^H or P^H (*CUNMBR only*)

M (input) INTEGER
The number of rows of the matrix C. M ≥ 0.

N (input) INTEGER
The number of columns of the matrix C. N ≥ 0.

K (input) INTEGER
If VECT = 'Q', the number of columns in the original matrix reduced

by SGEBRD/CGEBRD. If VECT = 'P', the number of rows in the original matrix reduced by SGEBRD/CGEBRD. K ≥ 0.

A (input) REAL/COMPLEX array, dimension
(LDA,min(NQ,K)) if VECT = 'Q', or (LDA,NQ) if VECT = 'P'
The vectors which define the elementary reflectors H_i and G_i, whose products determine the matrices Q and P, as returned by SGEBRD/CGEBRD. A is modified by the routine but restored on exit.

LDA (input) INTEGER
The leading dimension of the array A. If VECT = 'Q', LDA ≥ max(1,NQ); if VECT = 'P', LDA ≥ max(1,min(NQ,K)).

TAU (input) REAL/COMPLEX array, dimension (min(NQ,K))
TAU(i) must contain the scalar factor of the elementary reflector H_i or G_i which determines Q or P, as returned by SGEBRD/CGEBRD in the array argument TAUQ or TAUP.

C (input/output) REAL/COMPLEX array, dimension (LDC,N)
On entry, the m-by-n matrix C.
On exit, C is overwritten by $Q*C$ or Q^H*C or $C*Q^H$ or $C*Q$ or $P*C$ or P^H*C or $C*P$ or $C*P^H$.

LDC (input) INTEGER
The leading dimension of the array C. LDC ≥ max(1,M).

WORK (workspace) REAL/COMPLEX array, dimension (LWORK)
On exit, if INFO = 0, WORK(1) returns the optimal LWORK.

LWORK (input) INTEGER
The dimension of the array WORK.
If SIDE = 'L', LWORK ≥ max(1,N);
if SIDE = 'R', LWORK ≥ max(1,M).
For optimum performance LWORK ≥ N*NB if SIDE = 'L', and ≥ M*NB if SIDE = 'R', where NB is the optimal block size.

INFO (output) INTEGER
= 0: successful exit
< 0: if INFO = -i, the ith argument had an illegal value

SORMHR/CUNMHR

```
SUBROUTINE SORMHR( SIDE, TRANS, M, N, ILO, IHI, A, LDA, TAU, C,
$                   LDC, WORK, LWORK, INFO )
    CHARACTER        SIDE, TRANS
    INTEGER          IHI, ILO, INFO, LDA, LDC, LWORK, M, N
    REAL             A( LDA, * ), C( LDC, * ), TAU( * ),
$                    WORK( LWORK )
```

```
SUBROUTINE CUNMHR( SIDE, TRANS, M, N, ILO, IHI, A, LDA, TAU, C,
$                  LDC, WORK, LWORK, INFO )
   CHARACTER     SIDE, TRANS
   INTEGER       IHI, ILO, INFO, LDA, LDC, LWORK, M, N
   COMPLEX       A( LDA, * ), C( LDC, * ), TAU( * ),
$                WORK( LWORK )
```

Purpose

SORMHR/CUNMHR overwrites the general real/complex m-by-n matrix C with

	SIDE = 'L'	SIDE = 'R'	
TRANS = 'N':	$Q*C$	$C*Q$	
TRANS = 'T':	Q^T*C	$C*Q^T$	(SORMHR only)
TRANS = 'C':	Q^H*C	$C*Q^H$	(CUNMHR only)

where Q is a real/complex orthogonal/unitary matrix of order NQ, with NQ = M if SIDE = 'L' and NQ = N if SIDE = 'R'. Q is defined as the product of IHI–ILO elementary reflectors H_i, as returned by SGEHRD/CGEHRD:

$Q = H_{ilo}H_{ilo+1} \cdots H_{ihi-1}$.

Arguments

SIDE   (input) CHARACTER*1
      = 'L': apply Q or Q^H from the Left;
      = 'R': apply Q or Q^H from the Right.

TRANS (input) CHARACTER*1
      Specifies whether the matrix Q, Q^T, or Q^H is applied to C.
      = 'N': No transpose, apply Q
      = 'T': Transpose, apply Q^T (SORMHR only)
      = 'C': Conjugate transpose, apply Q^H (CUNMHR only)

M   (input) INTEGER
      The number of rows of the matrix C. M ≥ 0.

N   (input) INTEGER
      The number of columns of the matrix C. N ≥ 0.

ILO, IHI (input) INTEGER
      ILO and IHI must have the same values as in the previous call of SGEHRD/CGEHRD. Q is equal to the unit matrix except in the submatrix Q(ilo+1:ihi,ilo+1:ihi).
      If SIDE = 'L', 1 ≤ ILO and min(M,ILO) ≤ IHI ≤ M;
      if SIDE = 'R', 1 ≤ ILO and min(N,ILO) ≤ IHI ≤ N.

A   (input) REAL/COMPLEX array, dimension
      (LDA,M) if SIDE = 'L', or (LDA,N) if SIDE = 'R'
      The vectors which define the elementary reflectors, as returned by SGEHRD/CGEHRD. A is modified by the routine but restored on exit.

LDA   (input) INTEGER
      The leading dimension of the array A. LDA ≥ max(1,M) if SIDE = 'L';
      LDA ≥ max(1,N) if SIDE = 'R'.

TAU   (input) REAL/COMPLEX array, dimension
      (M–1) if SIDE = 'L', or (N–1) if SIDE = 'R'
      TAU(i) must contain the scalar factor of the elementary reflector H_i, as returned by SGEHRD/CGEHRD.

C   (input/output) REAL/COMPLEX array, dimension (LDC,N)
      On entry, the m-by-n matrix C.
      On exit, C is overwritten by Q*C or Q^H*C or $C*Q^H$ or C*Q.

LDC   (input) INTEGER
      The leading dimension of the array C. LDC ≥ max(1,M).

WORK (workspace) REAL/COMPLEX array, dimension (LWORK)
      On exit, if INFO = 0, WORK(1) returns the optimal LWORK.

LWORK (input) INTEGER
      The dimension of the array WORK. If SIDE = 'L', LWORK ≥ max(1,N); if SIDE = 'R', LWORK ≥ max(1,M). For optimum performance LWORK ≥ N*NB if SIDE = 'L' and ≥ M*NB if SIDE = 'R', where NB is the optimal block size.

INFO (output) INTEGER
      = 0: successful exit
      < 0: if INFO = –i, the ith argument had an illegal value

SORMLQ/CUNMLQ

```
SUBROUTINE SORMLQ( SIDE, TRANS, M, N, K, A, LDA, TAU, C, LDC,
$                  WORK, LWORK, INFO )
   CHARACTER     SIDE, TRANS
   INTEGER       INFO, K, LDA, LDC, LWORK, M, N
   REAL          A( LDA, * ), C( LDC, * ), TAU( * ),
$                WORK( LWORK )

SUBROUTINE CUNMLQ( SIDE, TRANS, M, N, K, A, LDA, TAU, C, LDC,
$                  WORK, LWORK, INFO )
   CHARACTER     SIDE, TRANS
   INTEGER       INFO, K, LDA, LDC, LWORK, M, N
   COMPLEX       A( LDA, * ), C( LDC, * ), TAU( * ),
$                WORK( LWORK )
```

Purpose

SORMLQ/CUNMLQ overwrites the general real/complex m-by-n matrix C with

	SIDE = 'L'	SIDE = 'R'	
TRANS = 'N':	$Q*C$	$C*Q$	
TRANS = 'T':	Q^T*C	$C*Q^T$	(SORMLQ only)
TRANS = 'C':	Q^H*C	$C*Q^H$	(CUNMLQ only)

where Q is a real/complex orthogonal/unitary matrix defined as the product of k elementary reflectors H_i

$$Q = H_k \cdots H_2 H_1 \quad (SORMLQ)$$

$$Q = H_k^H \cdots H_2^H H_1^H \quad (CUNMLQ)$$

as returned by SGELQF/CGELQF. Q is of order m if SIDE = 'L' and of order n if SIDE = 'R'.

Arguments

SIDE   (input) CHARACTER*1
        = 'L':   apply Q or Q^H from the Left;
        = 'R':   apply Q or Q^H from the Right.

TRANS   (input) CHARACTER*1
        = 'N':   No transpose, apply Q
        = 'T':   Transpose, apply Q^T (SORMLQ only)
        = 'C':   Conjugate transpose, apply Q^H (CUNMLQ only)

M   (input) INTEGER
        The number of rows of the matrix C. M ≥ 0.

N   (input) INTEGER
        The number of columns of the matrix C. N ≥ 0.

K   (input) INTEGER
        The number of elementary reflectors whose product defines the matrix Q. If SIDE = 'L', M ≥ K ≥ 0; if SIDE = 'R', N ≥ K ≥ 0.

A   (input) REAL/COMPLEX array, dimension
        (LDA,M) if SIDE = 'L', or (LDA,N) if SIDE = 'R'.
        The ith row must contain the vector which defines the elementary reflector H_i, for i = 1,2,...,k, as returned by SGELQF/CGELQF in the first k rows of its array argument A. A is modified by the routine but restored on exit.

LDA   (input) INTEGER
        The leading dimension of the array A. LDA ≥ max(1,K).

TAU   (input) REAL/COMPLEX array, dimension (K)
        TAU(i) must contain the scalar factor of the elementary reflector H_i, as returned by SGELQF/CGELQF.

C   (input/output) REAL/COMPLEX array, dimension (LDC,N)
        On entry, the m-by-n matrix C.
        On exit, C is overwritten by Q*C or Q^H*C or $C*Q^H$ or C*Q.

LDC   (input) INTEGER
        The leading dimension of the array C. LDC ≥ max(1,M).

WORK   (workspace) REAL/COMPLEX array, dimension (LWORK)
        On exit, if INFO = 0, WORK(1) returns the optimal LWORK.

LWORK   (input) INTEGER
        The dimension of the array WORK. If SIDE = 'L', LWORK ≥ max(1,N); if SIDE = 'R', LWORK ≥ max(1,M). For optimum performance LWORK ≥ N*NB if SIDE = 'L', and LWORK ≥ M*NB if SIDE = 'R', where NB is the optimal block size.

INFO   (output) INTEGER
        = 0:   successful exit
        < 0:   if INFO = -i, the ith argument had an illegal value

SORMQL/CUNMQL

```
SUBROUTINE SORMQL( SIDE, TRANS, M, N, K, A, LDA, TAU, C, LDC,
    $                  WORK, LWORK, INFO )
    CHARACTER         SIDE, TRANS
    INTEGER           INFO, K, LDA, LDC, LWORK, M, N
    REAL              A( LDA, * ), C( LDC, * ), TAU( * ),
    $                  WORK( LWORK )

SUBROUTINE CUNMQL( SIDE, TRANS, M, N, K, A, LDA, TAU, C, LDC,
    $                  WORK, LWORK, INFO )
    CHARACTER         SIDE, TRANS
    INTEGER           INFO, K, LDA, LDC, LWORK, M, N
    COMPLEX           A( LDA, * ), C( LDC, * ), TAU( * ),
    $                  WORK( LWORK )
```

Purpose

SORMQL/CUNMQL overwrites the general real/complex m-by-n matrix C with

	SIDE = 'L'	SIDE = 'R'
TRANS = 'N':	Q*C	C*Q
TRANS = 'T':	Q^T*C	$C*Q^T$
TRANS = 'C':	Q^H*C	$C*Q^H$

where Q is a real/complex orthogonal/unitary matrix defined as the product of k elementary reflectors H_i

$$Q = H_k \cdots H_2 H_1$$

as returned by SGEQLF/CGEQLF. Q is of order m if SIDE = 'L' and of order n if SIDE = 'R'.

Arguments

SIDE   (input) CHARACTER*1
        = 'L':   apply Q or Q^H from the Left;
        = 'R':   apply Q or Q^H from the Right.

TRANS (input) CHARACTER*1
= 'N': No transpose, apply Q
= 'T': Transpose, apply Q^T (*SORMQL only*)
= 'C': Conjugate transpose, apply Q^H (*CUNMQL only*)

M (input) INTEGER
The number of rows of the matrix C. M ≥ 0.

N (input) INTEGER
The number of columns of the matrix C. N ≥ 0.

K (input) INTEGER
The number of elementary reflectors whose product defines the matrix Q. If SIDE = 'L', M ≥ K ≥ 0; if SIDE = 'R', N ≥ K ≥ 0.

A (input) REAL/COMPLEX array, dimension (LDA,K)
The ith column must contain the vector which defines the elementary reflector H_i, for i = 1,2,...,k, as returned by SGEQLF/CGEQLF in the last k columns of its array argument A. A is modified by the routine but restored on exit.

LDA (input) INTEGER
The leading dimension of the array A. If SIDE = 'L', LDA ≥ max(1,M); if SIDE = 'R', LDA ≥ max(1,N).

TAU (input) REAL/COMPLEX array, dimension (K)
TAU(i) must contain the scalar factor of the elementary reflector H_i, as returned by SGEQLF/CGEQLF.

C (input/output) REAL/COMPLEX array, dimension (LDC,N)
On entry, the m-by-n matrix C.
On exit, C is overwritten by Q*C or Q^H*C or $C*Q^H$ or C*Q.

LDC (input) INTEGER
The leading dimension of the array C. LDC ≥ max(1,M).

WORK (workspace) REAL/COMPLEX array, dimension (LWORK)
On exit, if INFO = 0, WORK(1) returns the optimal LWORK.

LWORK (input) INTEGER
The dimension of the array WORK. If SIDE = 'L', LWORK ≥ max(1,N); if SIDE = 'R', LWORK ≥ max(1,M). For optimum performance LWORK ≥ N*NB if SIDE = 'L' and LWORK ≥ M*NB if SIDE = 'R', where NB is the optimal block size.

INFO (output) INTEGER
= 0: successful exit
< 0: if INFO = -i, the ith argument had an illegal value

SORMQR/CUNMQR

```
SUBROUTINE SORMQR( SIDE, TRANS, M, N, K, A, LDA, TAU, C, LDC,
$                  WORK, LWORK, INFO )
    CHARACTER      SIDE, TRANS
    INTEGER        INFO, K, LDA, LDC, LWORK, M, N
    REAL           A( LDA, * ), C( LDC, * ), TAU( * ),
$                  WORK( LWORK )

SUBROUTINE CUNMQR( SIDE, TRANS, M, N, K, A, LDA, TAU, C, LDC,
$                  WORK, LWORK, INFO )
    CHARACTER      SIDE, TRANS
    INTEGER        INFO, K, LDA, LDC, LWORK, M, N
    COMPLEX        A( LDA, * ), C( LDC, * ), TAU( * ),
$                  WORK( LWORK )
```

Purpose

SORMQR/CUNMQR overwrites the general real/complex m-by-n matrix C with

	SIDE = 'L'	SIDE = 'R'
TRANS = 'N':	Q*C	C*Q
TRANS = 'T':	Q^T*C	$C*Q^T$	(*SORMQR only*)
TRANS = 'C':	Q^H*C	$C*Q^H$	(*CUNMQR only*)

where Q is a real/complex orthogonal/unitary matrix defined as the product of k elementary reflectors H_i

$$Q = H_1 H_2 \cdots H_k$$

as returned by SGEQRF/CGEQRF. Q is of order m if SIDE = 'L' and of order n if SIDE = 'R'.

Arguments

SIDE (input) CHARACTER*1
= 'L': apply Q or Q^H from the Left;
= 'R': apply Q or Q^H from the Right.

TRANS (input) CHARACTER*1
= 'N': No transpose, apply Q
= 'T': Transpose, apply Q^T (*SORMQR only*)
= 'C': Conjugate transpose, apply Q^H (*CUNMQR only*)

M (input) INTEGER
The number of rows of the matrix C. M ≥ 0.

N (input) INTEGER
The number of columns of the matrix C. N ≥ 0.

K (input) INTEGER
The number of elementary reflectors whose product defines the matrix Q. If SIDE = 'L', M ≥ K ≥ 0; if SIDE = 'R', N ≥ K ≥ 0.

A (input) REAL/COMPLEX array, dimension (LDA,K)
The ith column must contain the vector which defines the elementary reflector H_i, for $i = 1,2,\dots,k$, as returned by SGEQRF/CGEQRF in the first k columns of its array argument A. A is modified by the routine but restored on exit.

LDA (input) INTEGER
The leading dimension of the array A. If SIDE = 'L', LDA $\geq$ max(1,M); if SIDE = 'R', LDA $\geq$ max(1,N).

TAU (input) REAL/COMPLEX array, dimension (K)
TAU(i) must contain the scalar factor of the elementary reflector H_i, as returned by SGEQRF/CGEQRF.

C (input/output) REAL/COMPLEX array, dimension (LDC,N)
On entry, the m-by-n matrix C.
On exit, C is overwritten by $Q*C$ or Q^H*C or $C*Q^H$ or $C*Q$.

LDC (input) INTEGER
The leading dimension of the array C. LDC $\geq$ max(1,M).

WORK (workspace) REAL/COMPLEX array, dimension (LWORK)
On exit, if INFO = 0, WORK(1) returns the optimal LWORK.

LWORK (input) INTEGER
The dimension of the array WORK. If SIDE = 'L', LWORK $\geq$ max(1,N); if SIDE = 'R', LWORK $\geq$ max(1,M). For optimum performance LWORK $\geq$ N*NB if SIDE = 'L' and $\geq$ M*NB if SIDE = 'R', where NB is the optimal block size.

INFO (output) INTEGER
= 0: successful exit
< 0: if INFO = $-i$, the ith argument had an illegal value

SORMRQ/CUNMRQ

```
SUBROUTINE SORMRQ( SIDE, TRANS, M, N, K, A, LDA, TAU, C, LDC,
$                  WORK, LWORK, INFO )
    CHARACTER     SIDE, TRANS
    INTEGER       INFO, K, LDA, LDC, LWORK, M, N
    REAL          A( LDA, * ), C( LDC, * ), TAU( * ),
$                 WORK( LWORK )

SUBROUTINE CUNMRQ( SIDE, TRANS, M, N, K, A, LDA, TAU, C, LDC,
$                  WORK, LWORK, INFO )
    CHARACTER     SIDE, TRANS
    INTEGER       INFO, K, LDA, LDC, LWORK, M, N
    COMPLEX       A( LDA, * ), C( LDC, * ), TAU( * ),
$                 WORK( LWORK )
```

Purpose

SORMRQ/CUNMRQ overwrites the general real/complex m-by-n matrix C with

	SIDE = 'L'	SIDE = 'R'	
TRANS = 'N':	$Q*C$	$C*Q$	(SORMRQ only)
TRANS = 'T':	Q^T*C	$C*Q^T$	
TRANS = 'C':	Q^H*C	$C*Q^H$	(CUNMRQ only)

where Q is a real/complex orthogonal/unitary matrix defined as the product of k elementary reflectors H_i

$$Q = H_1 H_2 \cdots H_k \quad (SORMRQ)$$

$$Q = H_1^H H_2^H \cdots H_k^H \quad (CUNMRQ)$$

as returned by SGERQF/CGERQF. Q is of order m if SIDE = 'L' and of order n if SIDE = 'R'.

Arguments

SIDE (input) CHARACTER*1
= 'L': apply Q or Q^H from the Left;
= 'R': apply Q or Q^H from the Right.

TRANS (input) CHARACTER*1
= 'N': No transpose, apply Q
= 'T': Transpose, apply Q^T (SORMRQ only)
= 'C': Conjugate transpose, apply Q^H (CUNMRQ only)

M (input) INTEGER
The number of rows of the matrix C. M $\geq$ 0.

N (input) INTEGER
The number of columns of the matrix C. N $\geq$ 0.

K (input) INTEGER
The number of elementary reflectors whose product defines the matrix Q. If SIDE = 'L', M $\geq$ K $\geq$ 0; if SIDE = 'R', N $\geq$ K $\geq$ 0.

A (input) REAL/COMPLEX array, dimension (LDA,M) if SIDE = 'L', or (LDA,N) if SIDE = 'R'
The ith row must contain the vector which defines the elementary reflector H_i, for $i = 1,2,\dots,k$, as returned by SGERQF/CGERQF in the last k rows of its array argument A. A is modified by the routine but restored on exit.

LDA (input) INTEGER
The leading dimension of the array A. LDA $\geq$ max(1,K).

TAU (input) REAL/COMPLEX array, dimension (K)
TAU(i) must contain the scalar factor of the elementary reflector H_i, as returned by SGERQF/CGERQF.

C   (input/output) REAL/COMPLEX array, dimension (LDC,N)
On entry, the m-by-n matrix C.
On exit, C is overwritten by $Q*C$ or Q^H*C or $C*Q^H$ or $C*Q$.

LDC   (input) INTEGER
The leading dimension of the array C. LDC $\geq$ max(1,M).

WORK (workspace) REAL/COMPLEX array, dimension (LWORK)
On exit, if INFO = 0, WORK(1) returns the optimal LWORK.

LWORK (input) INTEGER
The dimension of the array WORK. If SIDE = 'L', LWORK $\geq$ max(1,N); if SIDE = 'R', LWORK $\geq$ max(1,M). For optimum performance LWORK $\geq$ N*NB if SIDE = 'L', and LWORK $\geq$ M*NB if SIDE = 'R', where NB is the optimal block size.

INFO   (output) INTEGER
= 0: successful exit
< 0: if INFO = $-i$, the ith argument had an illegal value

SORMTR/CUNMTR

```
SUBROUTINE SORMTR( SIDE, UPLO, TRANS, M, N, A, LDA, TAU, C, LDC,
$                  WORK, LWORK, INFO )
CHARACTER         SIDE, TRANS, UPLO
INTEGER           INFO, LDA, LDC, LWORK, M, N
REAL              A( LDA, * ), C( LDC, * ), TAU( * ),
$                  WORK( LWORK )

SUBROUTINE CUNMTR( SIDE, UPLO, TRANS, M, N, A, LDA, TAU, C, LDC,
$                  WORK, LWORK, INFO )
CHARACTER         SIDE, TRANS, UPLO
INTEGER           INFO, LDA, LDC, LWORK, M, N
COMPLEX           A( LDA, * ), C( LDC, * ), TAU( * ),
$                  WORK( LWORK )
```

Purpose

SORMTR/CUNMTR overwrites the general real/complex m-by-n matrix C with

	SIDE = 'L'	SIDE = 'R'	
TRANS = 'N':	$Q*C$	$C*Q$	
TRANS = 'T':	Q^T*C	$C*Q^T$	(*SORMTR only*)
TRANS = 'C':	Q^H*C	$C*Q^H$	(*CUNMTR only*)

where Q is a real/complex orthogonal/unitary matrix of order NQ, with NQ = M if SIDE = 'L' and NQ = N if SIDE = 'R'. Q is defined as the product of NQ−1 elementary reflectors H_i, as returned by SSYTRD/CHETRD:

if UPLO = 'U', $Q = H_{nq-1} \cdots H_2 H_1$;

if UPLO = 'L', $Q = H_1 H_2 \cdots H_{nq-1}$.

Arguments

SIDE   (input) CHARACTER*1
= 'L': apply Q or Q^H from the Left;
= 'R': apply Q or Q^H from the Right.

UPLO   (input) CHARACTER*1
= 'U': Upper triangle of A contains elementary reflectors from SSYTRD/CHETRD;
= 'L': Lower triangle of A contains elementary reflectors from SSYTRD/CHETRD.

TRANS (input) CHARACTER*1
= 'N': No transpose, apply Q
= 'T': Transpose, apply Q^T (*SORMTR only*)
= 'C': Conjugate transpose, apply Q^H (*CUNMTR only*)

M   (input) INTEGER
The number of rows of the matrix C. M $\geq$ 0.

N   (input) INTEGER
The number of columns of the matrix C. N $\geq$ 0.

A   (input) REAL/COMPLEX array, dimension (LDA,M) if SIDE = 'L', or (LDA,N) if SIDE = 'R'
The vectors which define the elementary reflectors, as returned by SSYTRD/CHETRD. A is modified by the routine but restored on exit.

LDA (input) INTEGER
The leading dimension of the array A. LDA $\geq$ max(1,M) if SIDE = 'L'; LDA $\geq$ max(1,N) if SIDE = 'R'.

TAU (input) REAL/COMPLEX array, dimension (M−1) if SIDE = 'L', or (N−1) if SIDE = 'R'
TAU(i) must contain the scalar factor of the elementary reflector H_i, as returned by SSYTRD/CHETRD.

C   (input/output) REAL/COMPLEX array, dimension (LDC,N)
On entry, the m-by-n matrix C.
On exit, C is overwritten by $Q*C$ or Q^H*C or $C*Q^H$ or $C*Q$.

LDC (input) INTEGER
The leading dimension of the array C. LDC $\geq$ max(1,M).

WORK (workspace) REAL/COMPLEX array, dimension (LWORK)
On exit, if INFO = 0, WORK(1) returns the optimal LWORK.

LWORK (input) INTEGER
The dimension of the array WORK. If SIDE = 'L', LWORK $\geq$ max(1,N); if SIDE = 'R', LWORK $\geq$ max(1,M). For optimum performance LWORK $\geq$ N*NB if SIDE = 'L' and $\geq$ M*NB if SIDE = 'R', where NB is the optimal block size.

INFO   (output) INTEGER

if UPLO ='U', AB(kd+1+i-jj) = U(ij) for max(1,j-kd)$\leq$i$\leq$j;
if UPLO ='L', AB(1+i-jj) = L(ij) for j$\leq$i$\leq$min(n,j+kd).

LDAB   (input) INTEGER
     The leading dimension of the array AB. LDAB $\geq$ KD+1.

ANORM   (input) REAL
     The 1-norm (or infinity-norm) of the symmetric/Hermitian band matrix A.

RCOND   (output) REAL
     The reciprocal of the condition number of the matrix A, computed as RCOND = $1/(\|A\| \cdot \|A^{-1}\|)$.

WORK   SPBCON (workspace) REAL array, dimension (3*N)
     CPBCON (workspace) COMPLEX array, dimension (2*N)

IWORK   SPBCON *only* (workspace) INTEGER array, dimension (N)

RWORK   CPBCON *only* (workspace) REAL array, dimension (N)

INFO   (output) INTEGER
     = 0:   successful exit
     < 0:   if INFO = -i, the ith argument had an illegal value

SPBEQU/CPBEQU

```
SUBROUTINE SPBEQU( UPLO, N, KD, AB, LDAB, S, SCOND, AMAX, INFO )
CHARACTER    UPLO
INTEGER      INFO, KD, LDAB, N
REAL         AMAX, SCOND
REAL         AB( LDAB, * ), S( * )

SUBROUTINE CPBEQU( UPLO, N, KD, AB, LDAB, S, SCOND, AMAX, INFO )
CHARACTER    UPLO
INTEGER      INFO, KD, LDAB, N
REAL         AMAX, SCOND
REAL         S( * )
COMPLEX      AB( LDAB, * )
```

Purpose

SPBEQU/CPBEQU computes row and column scalings intended to equilibrate a symmetric/Hermitian positive definite band matrix A and reduce its condition number (with respect to the two-norm). S contains the scale factors, S(i) = $1/\sqrt{A(i,i)}$, chosen so that the scaled matrix B with elements B(ij) = S(i)*A(i,j)*S(j) has ones on the diagonal. This choice of S puts the condition number of B within a factor N of the smallest possible condition number over all possible diagonal scalings.

= 0:   successful exit
< 0:   if INFO = -i, the ith argument had an illegal value

SPBCON/CPBCON

```
SUBROUTINE SPBCON( UPLO, N, KD, AB, LDAB, ANORM, RCOND, WORK,
$                  IWORK, INFO )
CHARACTER    UPLO
INTEGER      INFO, KD, LDAB, N
REAL         ANORM, RCOND
INTEGER      IWORK( * )
REAL         AB( LDAB, * ), WORK( * )

SUBROUTINE CPBCON( UPLO, N, KD, AB, LDAB, ANORM, RCOND, WORK,
$                  RWORK, INFO )
CHARACTER    UPLO
INTEGER      INFO, KD, LDAB, N
REAL         ANORM, RCOND
REAL         RWORK( * )
COMPLEX      AB( LDAB, * ), WORK( * )
```

Purpose

SPBCON/CPBCON estimates the reciprocal of the condition number (in the 1-norm) of a real/complex symmetric/Hermitian positive definite band matrix using the Cholesky factorization A = $U^H * U$ or A = $L * L^H$ computed by SPBTRF/CPBTRF.

An estimate is obtained for $\|A^{-1}\|$, and the reciprocal of the condition number is computed as RCOND = $1/(\|A\| \cdot \|A^{-1}\|)$.

Arguments

UPLO   (input) CHARACTER*1
     = 'U':   Upper triangular factor stored in AB;
     = 'L':   Lower triangular factor stored in AB.

N   (input) INTEGER
     The order of the matrix A. N $\geq$ 0.

KD   (input) INTEGER
     The number of superdiagonals of the matrix A if UPLO = 'U', or the number of subdiagonals if UPLO = 'L'. KD $\geq$ 0.

AB   (input) REAL/COMPLEX array, dimension (LDAB,N)
     The triangular factor U or L from the Cholesky factorization A = $U^H * U$ or A = $L * L^H$ of the band matrix A, stored in the first kd+1 rows of the array. The jth column of U or L is stored in jth column of the array AB as follows:

Arguments

UPLO   (input) CHARACTER*1
 = 'U': Upper triangle of A is stored;
 = 'L': Lower triangle of A is stored.

N   (input) INTEGER
 The order of the matrix A. $N \geq 0$.

KD   (input) INTEGER
 The number of superdiagonals of the matrix A if UPLO = 'U', or the number of subdiagonals if UPLO = 'L'. $KD \geq 0$.

AB   (input) REAL/COMPLEX array, dimension (LDAB,N)
 The upper or lower triangle of the symmetric/Hermitian band matrix A, stored in the first kd+1 rows of the array. The jth column of A is stored in the jth column of the array AB as follows:
 if UPLO = 'U', $AB(kd+1+i-j,j) = A(i,j)$ for $\max(1,j-kd) \leq i \leq j$;
 if UPLO = 'L', $AB(1+i-j,j) = A(i,j)$ for $j \leq i \leq \min(n,j+kd)$.

LDAB   (input) INTEGER
 The leading dimension of the array A. $LDAB \geq KD+1$.

S   (output) REAL array, dimension (N)
 If INFO = 0, S contains the scale factors for A.

SCOND   (output) REAL
 If INFO = 0, S contains the ratio of the smallest S(i) to the largest S(i). If $SCOND \geq 0.1$ and AMAX is neither too large nor too small, it is not worth scaling by S.

AMAX   (output) REAL
 Absolute value of largest matrix element. If AMAX is very close to overflow or very close to underflow, the matrix should be scaled.

INFO   (output) INTEGER
 = 0: successful exit
 < 0: if INFO = -i, the ith argument had an illegal value.
 > 0: if INFO = i, the ith diagonal element is nonpositive.

SPBRFS/CPBRFS

```
SUBROUTINE SPBRFS( UPLO, N, KD, NRHS, AB, LDAB, AFB, LDAFB, B,
$                  LDB, X, LDX, FERR, BERR, WORK, IWORK, INFO )
     CHARACTER          UPLO
     INTEGER            INFO, KD, LDAB, LDAFB, LDB, LDX, N, NRHS
     INTEGER            IWORK( * )
     REAL               AB( LDAB, * ), AFB( LDAFB, * ), B( LDB, * ),
$                       BERR( * ), FERR( * ), WORK( * ), X( LDX, * )
```

```
SUBROUTINE CPBRFS( UPLO, N, KD, NRHS, AB, LDAB, AFB, LDAFB, B,
$                  LDB, X, LDX, FERR, BERR, WORK, RWORK, INFO )
     CHARACTER          UPLO
     INTEGER            INFO, KD, LDAB, LDAFB, LDB, LDX, N, NRHS
     REAL               BERR( * ), FERR( * ), RWORK( * )
     COMPLEX            AB( LDAB, * ), AFB( LDAFB, * ), B( LDB, * ),
$                       WORK( * ), X( LDX, * )
```

Purpose

SPBRFS/CPBRFS improves the computed solution to a system of linear equations when the coefficient matrix is symmetric/Hermitian positive definite and banded, and provides error bounds and backward error estimates for the solution.

Arguments

UPLO   (input) CHARACTER*1
 = 'U': Upper triangle of A is stored;
 = 'L': Lower triangle of A is stored.

N   (input) INTEGER
 The order of the matrix A. $N \geq 0$.

KD   (input) INTEGER
 The number of superdiagonals of the matrix A if UPLO = 'U', or the number of subdiagonals if UPLO = 'L'. $KD \geq 0$.

NRHS   (input) INTEGER
 The number of right hand sides, i.e., the number of columns of the matrices B and X. $NRHS \geq 0$.

AB   (input) REAL array, dimension (LDAB,N)
 The upper or lower triangle of the symmetric/Hermitian band matrix A, stored in the first kd+1 rows of the array. The jth column of A is stored in the jth column of the array AB as follows:
 if UPLO = 'U', $AB(kd+1+i-j,j) = A(i,j)$ for $\max(1,j-kd) \leq i \leq j$;
 if UPLO = 'L', $AB(1+i-j,j) = A(i,j)$ for $j \leq i \leq \min(n,j+kd)$.

LDAB   (input) INTEGER
 The leading dimension of the array AB. $LDAB \geq KD+1$.

AFB   (input) REAL/COMPLEX array, dimension (LDAFB,N)
 The triangular factor U or L from the Cholesky factorization $A = U^H*U$ or $A = L*L^H$ of the band matrix A as computed by SPBTRF/CPBTRF, in the same storage format as A (see AB).

LDAFB   (input) INTEGER
 The leading dimension of the array AFB. $LDAFB \geq KD+1$.

B   (input) REAL/COMPLEX array, dimension (LDB,NRHS)
 The right hand side matrix B.

LDB   (input) INTEGER
 The leading dimension of the array B. $LDB \geq \max(1,N)$.

X — (input/output) REAL/COMPLEX array, dimension (LDX,NRHS)
On entry, the solution matrix X, as computed by SPBTRS/CPBTRS.
On exit, the improved solution matrix X.

LDX — (input) INTEGER
The leading dimension of the array X. LDX $\geq$ max(1,N).

FERR — (output) REAL array, dimension (NRHS)
The estimated forward error bound for each solution vector X(j) (the jth column of the solution matrix X). If XTRUE is the true solution corresponding to X(j), FERR(j) bounds the magnitude of the largest element in (X(j) − XTRUE) divided by the magnitude of the largest element in X(j). The quality of the error bound depends on the quality of the estimate of $\|A^{-1}\|$ computed in the code; if the estimate of $\|A^{-1}\|$ is accurate, the error bound is guaranteed.

BERR — (output) REAL array, dimension (NRHS)
The componentwise relative backward error of each solution vector X(j) (i.e., the smallest relative change in any element of A or B that makes X(j) an exact solution).

WORK — SPBRFS (workspace) REAL array, dimension (3*N)
CPBRFS (workspace) COMPLEX array, dimension (2*N)

IWORK — SPBRFS only (workspace) INTEGER array, dimension (N)

RWORK — CPBRFS only (workspace) REAL array, dimension (N)

INFO — (output) INTEGER
= 0: successful exit
< 0: if INFO = −i, the ith argument had an illegal value

SPBSV/CPBSV

```
SUBROUTINE SPBSV( UPLO, N, KD, NRHS, AB, LDAB, B, LDB, INFO )
CHARACTER        UPLO
INTEGER          INFO, KD, LDAB, LDB, N, NRHS
REAL             AB( LDAB, * ), B( LDB, * )

SUBROUTINE CPBSV( UPLO, N, KD, NRHS, AB, LDAB, B, LDB, INFO )
CHARACTER        UPLO
INTEGER          INFO, KD, LDAB, LDB, N, NRHS
COMPLEX          AB( LDAB, * ), B( LDB, * )
```

Purpose

SPBSV/CPBSV computes the solution to a real/complex system of linear equations A*X = B, where A is an n-by-n symmetric/Hermitian positive definite band matrix and X and B are n-by-nrhs matrices.

The Cholesky decomposition is used to factor A as $A = U^H*U$, if UPLO = 'U', or $A = L*L^H$, if UPLO = 'L', where U is an upper triangular band matrix and L is a lower triangular band matrix, with the same number of superdiagonals or subdiagonals as A. The factored form of A is then used to solve the system of equations A*X = B.

Arguments

UPLO — (input) CHARACTER*1
= 'U': Upper triangle of A is stored.
= 'L': Lower triangle of A is stored.

N — (input) INTEGER
The number of linear equations, i.e., the order of the matrix A. N $\geq$ 0.

KD — (input) INTEGER
The number of superdiagonals of the matrix A if UPLO = 'U', or the number of subdiagonals if UPLO = 'L'. KD $\geq$ 0.

NRHS — (input) INTEGER
The number of right hand sides, i.e., the number of columns of the matrix B. NRHS $\geq$ 0.

AB — (input/output) REAL/COMPLEX array, dimension (LDAB,N)
On entry, the upper or lower triangle of the symmetric/Hermitian band matrix A, stored in the first kd+1 rows of the array. The jth column of A is stored in the jth column of the array AB as follows:
if UPLO = 'U', $AB(kd+1+i-j,j) = A(i,j)$ for $\max(1,j-kd)\leq i\leq j$;
if UPLO = 'L', $AB(1+i-j,j) = A(i,j)$ for $j\leq i\leq\min(n,j+kd)$.
On exit, if INFO = 0, the triangular factor U or L from the Cholesky factorization $A = U^H*U$ or $A = L*L^H$, in the same storage format as A.

LDAB — (input) INTEGER
The leading dimension of the array AB. LDAB $\geq$ KD+1.

B — (input/output) REAL/COMPLEX array, dimension (LDB,NRHS)
On entry, the n-by-nrhs right hand side matrix B.
On exit, if INFO = 0, the n-by-nrhs solution matrix X.

LDB — (input) INTEGER
The leading dimension of the array B. LDB $\geq$ max(1,N).

INFO — (output) INTEGER
= 0: successful exit
< 0: if INFO = −i, the ith argument had an illegal value
> 0: if INFO = i, the leading minor of order i of A is not positive definite, so the factorization could not be completed, and the solution has not been computed.

SPBSVX/CPBSVX

```
SUBROUTINE SPBSVX( FACT, UPLO, N, KD, NRHS, AB, LDAB, AFB, LDAFB,
$                  EQUED, S, B, LDB, X, LDX, RCOND, FERR, BERR,
$                  WORK, IWORK, INFO )
CHARACTER         EQUED, FACT, UPLO
INTEGER           INFO, KD, LDAB, LDAFB, LDB, LDX, N, NRHS
REAL              RCOND
INTEGER           IWORK( * )
REAL              AB( LDAB, * ), AFB( LDAFB, * ), B( LDB, * ),
$                  BERR( * ), FERR( * ), S( * ), WORK( * ),
$                  X( LDX, * )

SUBROUTINE CPBSVX( FACT, UPLO, N, KD, NRHS, AB, LDAB, AFB, LDAFB,
$                  EQUED, S, B, LDB, X, LDX, RCOND, FERR, BERR,
$                  WORK, RWORK, INFO )
CHARACTER         EQUED, FACT, UPLO
INTEGER           INFO, KD, LDAB, LDAFB, LDB, LDX, N, NRHS
REAL              RCOND
REAL              BERR( * ), FERR( * ), RWORK( * ), S( * )
COMPLEX           AB( LDAB, * ), AFB( LDAFB, * ), B( LDB, * ),
$                  WORK( * ), X( LDX, * )
```

Purpose

SPBSVX/CPBSVX uses the Cholesky factorization $A = U^H * U$ or $A = L * L^H$, where
to compute the solution to a real/complex system of linear equations $A*X = B$, where
A is an n-by-n symmetric/Hermitian positive definite band matrix and X and B are
n-by-nrhs matrices.

Error bounds on the solution and a condition estimate are also provided.

Description

The following steps are performed:

1. If FACT = 'E', real scaling factors are computed to equilibrate the system:

   $$\text{diag}(S)*A*\text{diag}(S)*(\text{diag}(S))^{-1}*X = \text{diag}(S)*B$$

   Whether or not the system will be equilibrated depends on the scaling of the
   matrix A, but if equilibration is used, A is overwritten by $\text{diag}(S)*A*\text{diag}(S)$
   and B by $\text{diag}(S)*B$.

2. If FACT = 'N' or 'E', the Cholesky decomposition is used to factor the matrix
   A (after equilibration if FACT = 'E') as
   $A = U^H * U$, if UPLO = 'U', or
   $A = L * L^H$, if UPLO = 'L',
   where U is an upper triangular band matrix, L is a lower triangular band matrix.

3. The factored form of A is used to estimate the condition number of the matrix
   A. If the reciprocal of the condition number is less than machine precision, steps

4-6 are skipped.

4. The system of equations is solved for X using the factored form of A.

5. Iterative refinement is applied to improve the computed solution vectors and
   calculate error bounds and backward error estimates for them.

6. If FACT = 'E' and equilibration was used, the vectors X are premultiplied by
   diag(S) so that they solve the original system before equilibration.

Arguments

FACT   (input) CHARACTER*1
        Specifies whether or not the factored form of the matrix A is supplied
        on entry, and if not, whether the matrix A should be equilibrated before
        it is factored.
        = 'F':   On entry, AFB contains the factored form of A. AB and AFB
                 will not be modified.
        = 'N':   The matrix A will be copied to AFB and factored.
        = 'E':   The matrix A will be equilibrated if necessary, then copied to
                 AFB and factored.

UPLO   (input) CHARACTER*1
        = 'U':   Upper triangle of A is stored.
        = 'L':   Lower triangle of A is stored.

N   (input) INTEGER
        The number of linear equations, i.e., the order of the matrix A. $N \geq 0$.

KD   (input) INTEGER
        The number of superdiagonals of the matrix A if UPLO = 'U', or the
        number of subdiagonals if UPLO = 'L'. $KD \geq 0$.

NRHS   (input) INTEGER
        The number of right hand sides, i.e., the number of columns of the
        matrices B and X. $NRHS \geq 0$.

AB   (input/output) REAL/COMPLEX array, dimension (LDAB,N)
        On entry, the upper or lower triangle of the symmetric/Hermitian band
        matrix A, stored in the first kd+1 rows of the array. The jth column of
        A is stored in the jth column of the array AB as follows:
        if UPLO = 'U', $AB(kd+1+i-j,j) = A(i,j)$ for $\max(1,j-kd) \leq i \leq j$;
        if UPLO = 'L', $AB(1+i-j,j) = A(i,j)$ for $j \leq i \leq \min(n,j+kd)$.
        On exit, if EQUED = 'Y', A is replaced by $\text{diag}(S)*A*\text{diag}(S)$.

LDAB   (input) INTEGER
        The leading dimension of the array A. $LDAB \geq KD+1$.

AFB   (input or output) REAL/COMPLEX array, dimension (LDAFB,N)
        If FACT = 'F', then AFB is an input argument and on entry contains
        the triangular factor U or L from the Cholesky factorization $A = U^H * U$
        or $A = L*L^H$, in the same storage format as A (see AB).
        If FACT = 'N', then AFB is an output argument and on exit returns
        the triangular factor U or L from the Cholesky factorization $A = U^H * U$

or $A = L*L^H$ of the original matrix A.
If FACT = 'E', then AFB is an output argument and on exit returns the triangular factor U or L from the Cholesky factorization $A = U^H*U$ or $A = L*L^H$ of the equilibrated matrix A (see the description of A for the form of the equilibrated matrix).

LDAFB (input) INTEGER
The leading dimension of the array AFB. LDAFB ≥ KD+1.

EQUED (output) CHARACTER*1
Specifies the form of equilibration that was done.
= 'N': No equilibration (always true if FACT = 'F' or 'N').
= 'Y': Equilibration was done, i.e., A has been replaced by diag(S)*A*diag(S).

S (output) REAL array, dimension (N)
The scale factors for A. Not assigned if FACT = 'F' or 'N'.

B (input/output) REAL/COMPLEX array, dimension (LDB,NRHS)
On entry, the n-by-nrhs right hand side matrix B.
On exit, if EQUED = 'N', B is not modified; if EQUED = 'Y', B is overwritten by diag(S)*B.

LDB (input) INTEGER
The leading dimension of the array B. LDB ≥ max(1,N).

X (output) REAL/COMPLEX array, dimension (LDX,NRHS)
If INFO = 0, the n-by-nrhs solution matrix X to the original system of equations. Note that if EQUED = 'Y', A and B are modified on exit, and the solution to the equilibrated system is $(\text{diag}(S))^{-1}*X$.

LDX (input) INTEGER
The leading dimension of the array X. LDX ≥ max(1,N).

RCOND (output) REAL
The estimate of the reciprocal condition number of the matrix A. If RCOND is less than the machine precision (in particular, if RCOND = 0), the matrix is singular to working precision. This condition is indicated by a return code of INFO > 0, and the solution and error bounds are not computed.

FERR (output) REAL array, dimension (NRHS)
The estimated forward error bound for each solution vector X(j) (the jth column of the solution matrix X). If XTRUE is the true solution corresponding to X(j), FERR(j) bounds the magnitude of the largest element in (X(j) − XTRUE) divided by the magnitude of the largest element in X(j). The quality of the error bound depends on the quality of the estimate of $||A^{-1}||$ computed in the code; if the estimate of $||A^{-1}||$ is accurate, the error bound is guaranteed.

BERR (output) REAL array, dimension (NRHS)
The componentwise relative backward error of each solution vector X(j) (i.e., the smallest relative change in any element of A or B that makes X(j) an exact solution).

WORK SPBSVX (workspace) REAL array, dimension (3*N)
      CPBSVX (workspace) COMPLEX array, dimension (2*N)

IWORK SPBSVX only (workspace) INTEGER array, dimension (N)

RWORK CPBSVX only (workspace) REAL array, dimension (N)

INFO (output) INTEGER
= 0: successful exit
< 0: if INFO = −i, the ith argument had an illegal value
> 0: if INFO = i, and i is
  ≤ N: if INFO = i, the leading minor of order i of A is not positive definite, so the factorization could not be completed, and the solution and error bounds could not be computed.
  = N+1: RCOND is less than machine precision. The factorization has been completed, but the matrix is singular to working precision, and the solution and error bounds have not been computed.

SPBTRF/CPBTRF

```
SUBROUTINE SPBTRF( UPLO, N, KD, AB, LDAB, INFO )
CHARACTER      UPLO
INTEGER        INFO, KD, LDAB, N
REAL           AB( LDAB, * )

SUBROUTINE CPBTRF( UPLO, N, KD, AB, LDAB, INFO )
CHARACTER      UPLO
INTEGER        INFO, KD, LDAB, N
COMPLEX        AB( LDAB, * )
```

Purpose

SPBTRF/CPBTRF computes the Cholesky factorization of a real/complex symmetric/Hermitian positive definite band matrix A.

The factorization has the form $A = U^H*U$, if UPLO = 'U', or $A = L*L^H$, if UPLO = 'L', where U is an upper triangular matrix and L is lower triangular.

Arguments

UPLO (input) CHARACTER*1
= 'U': Upper triangle of A is stored;
= 'L': Lower triangle of A is stored.

N (input) INTEGER
The order of the matrix A. N ≥ 0.

KD (input) INTEGER
The number of superdiagonals of the matrix A if UPLO = 'U', or the number of subdiagonals if UPLO = 'L'. KD ≥ 0.

AB   (input/output) REAL/COMPLEX array, dimension (LDAB,N)
On entry, the upper or lower triangle of the symmetric/Hermitian band matrix A, stored in the first kd+1 rows of the array. The jth column of A is stored in the jth column of the array AB as follows:
if UPLO ='U', AB(kd+1+i-j,j) = A(i,j) for max(1,j-kd)$\leq$i$\leq$j;
if UPLO ='L', AB(1+i-j,j) = A(i,j) for j$\leq$i$\leq$min(n,j+kd).
On exit, if INFO = 0, the triangular factor U or L from the Cholesky factorization A = U^H*U or A = $L*L^H$ of the band matrix A, in the same storage format as A.

LDAB   (input) INTEGER
The leading dimension of the array AB. LDAB $\geq$ KD+1.

INFO   (output) INTEGER
= 0:   successful exit
< 0:   if INFO = $-i$, the ith argument had an illegal value
> 0:   if INFO = i, the leading minor of order i is not positive definite, and the factorization could not be completed.

SPBTRS/CPBTRS

```
SUBROUTINE SPBTRS( UPLO, N, KD, NRHS, AB, LDAB, B, LDB, INFO )
CHARACTER        UPLO
INTEGER          INFO, KD, LDAB, LDB, N, NRHS
REAL             AB( LDAB, * ), B( LDB, * )

SUBROUTINE CPBTRS( UPLO, N, KD, NRHS, AB, LDAB, B, LDB, INFO )
CHARACTER        UPLO
INTEGER          INFO, KD, LDAB, LDB, N, NRHS
COMPLEX          AB( LDAB, * ), B( LDB, * )
```

Purpose

SPBTRS/CPBTRS solves a system of linear equations A*X = B with a symmetric/Hermitian positive definite band matrix A using the Cholesky factorization A = U^H*U or A = $L*L^H$ computed by SPBTRF/CPBTRF.

Arguments

UPLO   (input) CHARACTER*1
= 'U': Upper triangular factor stored in AB;
= 'L': Lower triangular factor stored in AB.

N   (input) INTEGER
The order of the matrix A. N $\geq$ 0.

KD   (input) INTEGER
The number of superdiagonals of the matrix A if UPLO = 'U', or the number of subdiagonals if UPLO = 'L'. KD $\geq$ 0.

NRHS   (input) INTEGER
The number of right hand sides, i.e., the number of columns of the matrix B. NRHS $\geq$ 0.

AB   (input) REAL/COMPLEX array, dimension (LDAB,N)
The triangular factor U or L from the Cholesky factorization A = U^H*U or A = $L*L^H$ of the band matrix A, stored in the first kd+1 rows of the array. The jth column of U or L is stored in the jth column of the array AB as follows:
if UPLO ='U', AB(kd+1+i-j,j) = U(i,j) for max(1,j-kd)$\leq$i$\leq$j;
if UPLO ='L', AB(1+i-j,j) = L(i,j) for j$\leq$i$\leq$min(n,j+kd).

LDAB   (input) INTEGER
The leading dimension of the array AB. LDAB $\geq$ KD+1.

B   (input/output) REAL/COMPLEX array, dimension (LDB,NRHS)
On entry, the right hand side matrix B.
On exit, the solution matrix X.

LDB   (input) INTEGER
The leading dimension of the array B. LDB $\geq$ max(1,N).

INFO   (output) INTEGER
= 0:   successful exit
< 0:   if INFO = $-i$, the ith argument had an illegal value

SPOCON/CPOCON

```
SUBROUTINE SPOCON( UPLO, N, A, LDA, ANORM, RCOND, WORK, IWORK,
$                   INFO )
CHARACTER          UPLO
INTEGER            INFO, LDA, N
REAL               ANORM, RCOND
INTEGER            IWORK( * )
REAL               A( LDA, * ), WORK( * )

SUBROUTINE CPOCON( UPLO, N, A, LDA, ANORM, RCOND, WORK, RWORK,
$                   INFO )
CHARACTER          UPLO
INTEGER            INFO, LDA, N
REAL               ANORM, RCOND
REAL               RWORK( * )
COMPLEX            A( LDA, * ), WORK( * )
```

Purpose

SPOCON/CPOCON estimates the reciprocal of the condition number (in the 1-norm) of a real/complex symmetric/Hermitian positive definite matrix using the Cholesky factorization A = U^H*U or A = $L*L^H$ computed by SPOTRF/CPOTRF.

INFO (output) INTEGER
= 0: successful exit
< 0: if INFO = −i, the ith argument had an illegal value

SGERFS/CGERFS

```
SUBROUTINE SGERFS( TRANS, N, NRHS, A, LDA, AF, LDAF, IPIV, B, LDB,
$                   X, LDX, FERR, BERR, WORK, IWORK, INFO )
CHARACTER          TRANS
INTEGER            INFO, LDA, LDAF, LDB, LDX, N, NRHS
INTEGER            IPIV( * ), IWORK( * )
REAL               A( LDA, * ), AF( LDAF, * ), B( LDB, * ),
$                   BERR( * ), FERR( * ), WORK( * ), X( LDX, * )

SUBROUTINE CGERFS( TRANS, N, NRHS, A, LDA, AF, LDAF, IPIV, B, LDB,
$                   X, LDX, FERR, BERR, WORK, RWORK, INFO )
CHARACTER          TRANS
INTEGER            INFO, LDA, LDAF, LDB, LDX, N, NRHS
INTEGER            IPIV( * )
REAL               BERR( * ), FERR( * ), RWORK( * )
COMPLEX            A( LDA, * ), AF( LDAF, * ), B( LDB, * ),
$                   WORK( * ), X( LDX, * )
```

Purpose

SGERFS/CGERFS improves the computed solution to a system of linear equations, and provides error bounds and backward error estimates for the solution.

Arguments

TRANS (input) CHARACTER*1
Specifies the form of the system of equations:
= 'N': $A*X = B$ (No transpose)
= 'T': $A^T*X = B$ (Transpose)
= 'C': $A^H*X = B$ (Conjugate transpose)

N (input) INTEGER
The order of the matrix A. N ≥ 0.

NRHS (input) INTEGER
The number of right hand sides, i.e., the number of columns of the matrices B and X. NRHS ≥ 0.

A (input) REAL/COMPLEX array, dimension (LDA,N)
The original n-by-n matrix A.

LDA (input) INTEGER
The leading dimension of the array A. LDA ≥ max(1,N).

AF (input) REAL/COMPLEX array, dimension (LDAF,N)
The factors L and U from the factorization A = P*L*U as computed by SGETRF/CGETRF.

LDAF (input) INTEGER
The leading dimension of the array AF. LDAF ≥ max(1,N).

IPIV (input) INTEGER array, dimension (N)
The pivot indices from SGETRF/CGETRF; for 1≤i≤N, row i of the matrix was interchanged with row IPIV(i).

B (input) REAL/COMPLEX array, dimension (LDB,NRHS)
The right hand side matrix B.

LDB (input) INTEGER
The leading dimension of the array B. LDB ≥ max(1,N).

X (input/output) REAL/COMPLEX array, dimension (LDX,NRHS)
On entry, the solution matrix X, as computed by SGETRS/CGETRS.
On exit, the improved solution matrix X.

LDX (input) INTEGER
The leading dimension of the array X. LDX ≥ max(1,N).

FERR (output) REAL array, dimension (NRHS)
The estimated forward error bound for each solution vector X(j) (the jth column of the solution matrix X). If XTRUE is the true solution corresponding to X(j), FERR(j) bounds the magnitude of the largest element in (X(j) − XTRUE) divided by the magnitude of the largest element in X(j). The quality of the error bound depends on the quality of the estimate of $\|A^{-1}\|$ computed in the code; if the estimate of $\|A^{-1}\|$ is accurate, the error bound is guaranteed.

BERR (output) REAL array, dimension (NRHS)
The componentwise relative backward error of each solution vector X(j) (i.e., the smallest relative change in any element of A or B that makes X(j) an exact solution).

WORK SGERFS (workspace) REAL array, dimension (3*N)
CGERFS (workspace) COMPLEX array, dimension (2*N)

IWORK SGERFS only (workspace) INTEGER array, dimension (N)

RWORK CGERFS only (workspace) REAL array, dimension (N)

INFO (output) INTEGER
= 0: successful exit
< 0: if INFO = −i, the ith argument had an illegal value

SGEQRF/CGEQRF

SGERQF/CGERQF

```
SUBROUTINE SGERQF( M, N, A, LDA, TAU, WORK, LWORK, INFO )
INTEGER           INFO, LDA, LWORK, M, N
REAL              A( LDA, * ), TAU( * ), WORK( LWORK )

SUBROUTINE CGERQF( M, N, A, LDA, TAU, WORK, LWORK, INFO )
INTEGER           INFO, LDA, LWORK, M, N
COMPLEX           A( LDA, * ), TAU( * ), WORK( LWORK )
```

Purpose

SGERQF/CGERQF computes an RQ factorization of a real/complex m-by-n matrix A: A = R*Q.

Arguments

M (input) INTEGER
   The number of rows of the matrix A. $M \geq 0$.

N (input) INTEGER
   The number of columns of the matrix A. $N \geq 0$.

A (input/output) REAL/COMPLEX array, dimension (LDA,N)
   On entry, the m-by-n matrix A.
   On exit, if $m \leq n$, the upper triangle of the subarray A(1:m,n−m+1:n) contains the m-by-m upper triangular matrix R; if $m > n$, the elements on and above the $(m-n)^{th}$ subdiagonal contain the m-by-n upper trapezoidal matrix R; the remaining elements, with the array TAU, represent the orthogonal/unitary matrix Q as a product of min(m,n) elementary reflectors.

LDA (input) INTEGER
   The leading dimension of the array A. $LDA \geq \max(1,M)$.

TAU (output) REAL/COMPLEX array, dimension (min(M,N))
   The scalar factors of the elementary reflectors.

WORK (workspace) REAL/COMPLEX array, dimension (LWORK)
   On exit, if INFO = 0, WORK(1) returns the optimal LWORK.

LWORK (input) INTEGER
   The dimension of the array WORK. $LWORK \geq \max(1,M)$.
   For optimum performance $LWORK \geq M*NB$, where NB is the optimal block size.

INFO (output) INTEGER
   = 0: successful exit
   < 0: if INFO = −i, the ith argument had an illegal value

SGESV/CGESV

```
SUBROUTINE SGESV( N, NRHS, A, LDA, IPIV, B, LDB, INFO )
INTEGER          INFO, LDA, LDB, N, NRHS
INTEGER          IPIV( * )
REAL             A( LDA, * ), B( LDB, * )

SUBROUTINE CGESV( N, NRHS, A, LDA, IPIV, B, LDB, INFO )
INTEGER          INFO, LDA, LDB, N, NRHS
INTEGER          IPIV( * )
COMPLEX          A( LDA, * ), B( LDB, * )
```

Purpose

SGESV/CGESV computes the solution to a real/complex system of linear equations A*X = B, where A is an n-by-n matrix and X and B are n-by-nrhs matrices.

The LU decomposition with partial pivoting and row interchanges is used to factor A as A = P*L*U, where P is a permutation matrix, L is unit lower triangular, and U is upper triangular. The factored form of A is then used to solve the system of equations A*X = B.

Arguments

N (input) INTEGER
   The number of linear equations, i.e., the order of the matrix A. $N \geq 0$.

NRHS (input) INTEGER
   The number of right hand sides, i.e., the number of columns of the matrix B. $NRHS \geq 0$.

A (input/output) REAL/COMPLEX array, dimension (LDA,N)
   On entry, the n-by-n coefficient matrix A.
   On exit, the factors L and U from the factorization A = P*L*U; the unit diagonal elements of L are not stored.

LDA (input) INTEGER
   The leading dimension of the array A. $LDA \geq \max(1,N)$.

IPIV (output) INTEGER array, dimension (N)
   The pivot indices that define the permutation matrix P; row i of the matrix was interchanged with row IPIV(i).

B (input/output) REAL/COMPLEX array, dimension (LDB,NRHS)
   On entry, the n-by-nrhs right hand side matrix B.
   On exit, if INFO = 0, the n-by-nrhs solution matrix X.

LDB (input) INTEGER
   The leading dimension of the array B. $LDB \geq \max(1,N)$.

INFO (output) INTEGER
   = 0: successful exit
   < 0: if INFO = −i, the ith argument had an illegal value

> 0: if INFO = i, U(i,i) is exactly zero. The factorization has been completed, but the factor U is exactly singular, so the solution could not be computed.

SGESVD/CGESVD

```
SUBROUTINE SGESVD( JOBU, JOBVT, M, N, A, LDA, S, U, LDU, VT, LDVT,
$                  WORK, LWORK, INFO )
CHARACTER          JOBU, JOBVT
INTEGER            INFO, LDA, LDU, LDVT, LWORK, M, N
REAL               A( LDA, * ), S( * ), U( LDU, * ),
$                  VT( LDVT, * ), WORK( * )

SUBROUTINE CGESVD( JOBU, JOBVT, M, N, A, LDA, S, U, LDU, VT, LDVT,
$                  WORK, LWORK, RWORK, INFO )
CHARACTER          JOBU, JOBVT
INTEGER            INFO, LDA, LDU, LDVT, LWORK, M, N
REAL               RWORK( * ), S( * )
COMPLEX            A( LDA, * ), U( LDU, * ), VT( LDVT, * ),
$                  WORK( * )
```

Purpose

SGESVD/CGESVD computes the singular value decomposition (SVD) of a real/complex m-by-n matrix A, optionally computing the left and/or right singular vectors. The SVD is written

$$A = U*\Sigma*V^H$$

where Σ is an m-by-n matrix which is zero except for its min(m,n) diagonal elements, U is an m-by-m orthogonal/unitary matrix, and V is an n-by-n orthogonal/unitary matrix. The diagonal elements of Σ are the singular values of A; they are real and non-negative, and are returned in descending order. The first min(m,n) columns of U and V are the left and right singular vectors of A.

Note that the routine returns V^H, not V.

Arguments

JOBU   (input) CHARACTER*1
        Specifies options for computing all or part of the matrix U:
        = 'A': all m columns of U are returned in the array U;
        = 'S': the first min(m,n) columns of U (the left singular vectors) are returned in the array U;
        = 'O': the first min(m,n) columns of U (the left singular vectors) are overwritten on the array A;
        = 'N': no columns of U (no left singular vectors) are computed.

JOBVT   (input) CHARACTER*1
        Specifies options for computing all or part of the matrix V^H:
        = 'A': all n rows of V^H are returned in the array VT;
        = 'S': the first min(m,n) rows of V^H (the right singular vectors) are returned in the array VT;
        = 'O': the first min(m,n) rows of V^H (the right singular vectors) are overwritten on the array A;
        = 'N': no rows of V^H (no right singular vectors) are computed.
        JOBVT and JOBU cannot both be 'O'.

M   (input) INTEGER
        The number of rows of the matrix A. M ≥ 0.

N   (input) INTEGER
        The number of columns of the matrix A. N ≥ 0.

A   (input/output) REAL/COMPLEX array, dimension (LDA,N)
        On entry, the m-by-n matrix A.
        On exit,
        if JOBU = 'O', A is overwritten with the first min(m,n) columns of U (the left singular vectors, stored columnwise);
        if JOBVT = 'O', A is overwritten with the first min(m,n) rows of V^H (the right singular vectors, stored rowwise);
        if JOBU ≠ 'O' and JOBVT ≠ 'O', the contents of A are destroyed.

LDA   (input) INTEGER
        The leading dimension of the array A. LDA ≥ max(1,M).

S   (output) REAL array, dimension (min(M,N))
        The singular values of A, sorted so that S(i) ≥ S(i+1).

U   (output) REAL/COMPLEX array, dimension (LDU,M) if JOBU = 'A' or (LDU,min(M,N)) if JOBU = 'S'
        If JOBU = 'A', U contains the m-by-m orthogonal/unitary matrix U;
        if JOBU = 'S', U contains the first min(m,n) columns of U (the left singular vectors, stored columnwise);
        if JOBU = 'N' or 'O', U is not referenced.

LDU   (input) INTEGER
        The leading dimension of the array U. LDU ≥ 1; if JOBU = 'A' or 'S', LDU ≥ M.

VT   (output) REAL/COMPLEX array, dimension (LDVT,N)
        If JOBVT = 'A', VT contains the n-by-n orthogonal/unitary matrix V^H;
        if JOBVT = 'S', VT contains the first min(m,n) rows of V^H (the right singular vectors, stored rowwise);
        if JOBVT = 'N' or 'O', VT is not referenced.

LDVT   (input) INTEGER
        The leading dimension of the array VT. LDVT ≥ 1; if JOBVT = 'A', LDVT ≥ N; if JOBVT = 'S', LDVT ≥ min(M,N).

WORK   (workspace) REAL/COMPLEX array, dimension (LWORK)
        On exit, if INFO = 0, WORK(1) returns the optimal LWORK.

LWORK   (input) INTEGER
         The dimension of the array WORK. LWORK ≥ 1.
         LWORK ≥ max(3*min(M,N)+max(M,N),5*min(M,N)−4) (SGESVD)
         LWORK ≥ 2*min(M,N)+max(M,N) (CGESVD).
         For good performance, LWORK should generally be larger.

RWORK   CGESVD only (workspace) REAL array, dimension (5*max(M,N))

INFO   (output) INTEGER
         = 0: successful exit
         < 0: if INFO = −i, the ith argument had an illegal value.
         > 0: if INFO = i, the algorithm failed to converge; i off-diagonal el-
               ements of an intermediate bidiagonal form did not converge to
               zero.

SGESVX/CGESVX

Description

The following steps are performed:

1. If FACT = 'E', real scaling factors are computed to equilibrate the system:

   TRANS = 'N': diag(R)*A*diag(C)$^{-1}$*diag(C)*X = diag(R)*B
   TRANS = 'T': (diag(R)*A*diag(C))^T*diag(R)$^{-1}$*X = diag(C)*B
   TRANS = 'C': (diag(R)*A*diag(C))^H*diag(R)$^{-1}$*X = diag(C)*B

   Whether or not the system will be equilibrated depends on the scaling of the
   matrix A, but if equilibration is used, A is overwritten by diag(R)*A*diag(C)
   and B by diag(R)*B (if TRANS='N') or diag(C)*B (if TRANS = 'T' or 'C').

2. If FACT = 'N' or 'E', the LU decomposition is used to factor the matrix A
   (after equilibration if FACT = 'E') as A = P*L*U, where P is a permutation
   matrix, L is a unit lower triangular matrix, and U is upper triangular.

3. The factored form of A is used to estimate the condition number of the matrix
   A. If the reciprocal of the condition number is less than machine precision, steps
   4–6 are skipped.

4. The system of equations is solved for X using the factored form of A.

5. Iterative refinement is applied to improve the computed solution vectors and
   calculate error bounds and backward error estimates for them.

6. If FACT = 'E' and equilibration was used, the vectors X are premultiplied by
   diag(C) (if TRANS = 'N') or diag(R) (if TRANS = 'T' or 'C') so that they
   solve the original system before equilibration.

Arguments

FACT   (input) CHARACTER*1
         Specifies whether or not the factored form of the matrix A is supplied
         on entry, and if not, whether the matrix A should be equilibrated before
         it is factored.
         = 'F': On entry, AF and IPIV contain the factored form of A. A, AF,
                 and IPIV will not be modified.
         = 'N': The matrix A will be copied to AF and factored.
         = 'E': The matrix A will be equilibrated if necessary, then copied to
                 AF and factored.

TRANS   (input) CHARACTER*1
         Specifies the form of the system of equations:
         = 'N': A*X = B (No transpose)
         = 'T': A^T*X = B (Transpose)
         = 'C': A^H*X = B (Conjugate transpose)

N   (input) INTEGER
         The number of linear equations, i.e., the order of the matrix A. N ≥ 0.

NRHS   (input) INTEGER
         The number of right hand sides, i.e., the number of columns of the

---

SUBROUTINE SGESVX(FACT, TRANS, N, NRHS, A, LDA, AF, LDAF, IPIV,
    $ EQUED, R, C, B, LDB, X, LDX, RCOND, FERR, BERR,
    $ WORK, IWORK, INFO)
    CHARACTER   EQUED, FACT, TRANS
    INTEGER   INFO, LDA, LDAF, LDB, LDX, N, NRHS
    REAL   RCOND
    INTEGER   IPIV(*), IWORK(*)
    REAL   A(LDA, *), AF(LDAF, *), B(LDB, *),
    $ BERR(*), C(*), FERR(*), R(*),
    $ WORK(*), X(LDX, *)

SUBROUTINE CGESVX(FACT, TRANS, N, NRHS, A, LDA, AF, LDAF, IPIV,
    $ EQUED, R, C, B, LDB, X, LDX, RCOND, FERR, BERR,
    $ WORK, RWORK, INFO)
    CHARACTER   EQUED, FACT, TRANS
    INTEGER   INFO, LDA, LDAF, LDB, LDX, N, NRHS
    REAL   RCOND
    INTEGER   IPIV(*)
    REAL   BERR(*), C(*), FERR(*), R(*),
    $ RWORK(*)
    COMPLEX   A(LDA, *), AF(LDAF, *), B(LDB, *),
    $ WORK(*), X(LDX, *)

Purpose

SGESVX/CGESVX uses the LU factorization to compute the solution to a
real/complex system of linear equations A*X = B, A^T*X = B, or A^H*X = B,
where A is an n-by-n matrix and X and B are n-by-nrhs matrices.

Error bounds on the solution and a condition estimate are also provided.

matrices B and X. NRHS ≥ 0.

A   (input/output) REAL/COMPLEX array, dimension (LDA,N)
On entry, the n-by-n matrix A. A is not modified if FACT = 'F' or 'N', or if FACT = 'E' and EQUED = 'N' on exit.
On exit, if EQUED ≠ 'N', A is scaled as follows:
EQUED = 'R': A := diag(R)*A;
EQUED = 'C': A := A*diag(C);
EQUED = 'B': A := diag(R)*A*diag(C).

LDA   (input) INTEGER
The leading dimension of the array A. LDA ≥ max(1,N).

AF   (input or output) REAL/COMPLEX array, dimension (LDAF,N)
If FACT = 'F', then AF is an input argument and on entry contains the factors L and U from the factorization A = P*L*U as computed by SGETRF/CGETRF.
If FACT = 'N', then AF is an output argument and on exit returns the factors L and U from the factorization A = P*L*U of the original matrix A.
If FACT = 'E', then AF is an output argument and on exit returns the factors L and U from the factorization A = P*L*U of the equilibrated matrix A (see the description of A for the form of the equilibrated matrix).

LDAF   (input) INTEGER
The leading dimension of the array AF. LDAF ≥ max(1,N).

IPIV   (input or output) INTEGER array, dimension (N)
If FACT = 'F', then IPIV is an input argument and on entry contains the pivot indices from the factorization A = P*L*U as computed by SGETRF/CGETRF; row i of the matrix was interchanged with row IPIV(i).
If FACT = 'N', then IPIV is an output argument and on exit contains the pivot indices from the factorization A = P*L*U of the original matrix A.
If FACT = 'E', then IPIV is an output argument and on exit contains the pivot indices from the factorization A = P*L*U of the equilibrated matrix A.

EQUED   (output) CHARACTER*1
Specifies the form of equilibration that was done.
= 'N': No equilibration (always true if FACT = 'F' or 'N').
= 'R': Row equilibration, i.e., A has been premultiplied by diag(R).
= 'C': Column equilibration, i.e., A has been postmultiplied by diag(C).
= 'B': Both row and column equilibration, i.e., A has been replaced by diag(R)*A*diag(C).

R   (output) REAL array, dimension (N)
The row scale factors for A.
If EQUED = 'R' or 'B', A is multiplied on the left by diag(R).
R is not assigned if FACT = 'F' or 'N'.

C   (output) REAL array, dimension (N)
The column scale factors for A.
If EQUED = 'C' or 'B', A is multiplied on the right by diag(C).
C is not assigned if FACT = 'F' or 'N'.

B   (input/output) REAL/COMPLEX array, dimension (LDB,NRHS)
On entry, the n-by-nrhs right hand side matrix B.
On exit, if EQUED = 'N', B is not modified; if TRANS = 'N' and EQUED = 'R' or 'B', B is overwritten by diag(R)*B; if TRANS = 'T' or 'C' and EQUED = 'C' or 'B', B is overwritten by diag(C)*B.

LDB   (input) INTEGER
The leading dimension of the array B. LDB ≥ max(1,N).

X   (output) REAL/COMPLEX array, dimension (LDX,NRHS)
If INFO = 0, the n-by-nrhs solution matrix X to the original system of equations. Note that A and B are modified on exit if EQUED ≠ 'N', and the solution to the equilibrated system is $\text{diag}(C)^{-1}*X$ if TRANS = 'N' and EQUED = 'C' or 'B', or $\text{diag}(R)^{-1}*X$ if TRANS = 'T' or 'C' and EQUED = 'R' or 'B'.

LDX   (input) INTEGER
The leading dimension of the array X. LDX ≥ max(1,N).

RCOND   (output) REAL
The estimate of the reciprocal condition number of the matrix A. If RCOND is less than the machine precision (in particular, if RCOND = 0), the matrix is singular to working precision. This condition is indicated by a return code of INFO > 0, and the solution and error bounds are not computed.

FERR   (output) REAL array, dimension (NRHS)
The estimated forward error bound for each solution vector X(j) (the jth column of the solution matrix X). If XTRUE is the true solution corresponding to X(j), FERR(j) bounds the magnitude of the largest element in (X(j) − XTRUE) divided by the magnitude of the largest element in X(j). The quality of the error bound depends on the quality of the estimate of $||A^{-1}||$ computed in the code; if the estimate of $||A^{-1}||$ is accurate, the error bound is guaranteed.

BERR   (output) REAL array, dimension (NRHS)
The componentwise relative backward error of each solution vector X(j) (i.e., the smallest relative change in any element of A or B that makes X(j) an exact solution).

WORK   SGESVX (workspace) REAL array, dimension (3*N)
CGESVX (workspace) COMPLEX array, dimension (2*N)

IWORK   SGESVX only (workspace) INTEGER array, dimension (N)

RWORK   CGESVX only (workspace) REAL array, dimension (N)

INFO   (output) INTEGER
= 0: successful exit
< 0: if INFO = −i, the ith argument had an illegal value

> 0:   if INFO = i, and i is

     ≤ N: U(i,i) is exactly zero. The factorization has been com-
pleted, but the factor U is exactly singular, so the solution
and error bounds could not be computed.

     = N+1: RCOND is less than machine precision. The factoriza-
tion has been completed, but the matrix is singular to
working precision, and the solution and error bounds have
not been computed.

SGETRF/CGETRF

```
SUBROUTINE SGETRF( M, N, A, LDA, IPIV, INFO )
INTEGER            INFO, LDA, M, N
INTEGER            IPIV( * )
REAL               A( LDA, * )

SUBROUTINE CGETRF( M, N, A, LDA, IPIV, INFO )
INTEGER            INFO, LDA, M, N
INTEGER            IPIV( * )
COMPLEX            A( LDA, * )
```

Purpose

SGETRF/CGETRF computes an LU factorization of a general m-by-n matrix A
using partial pivoting with row interchanges.

The factorization has the form $A = P*L*U$ where P is a permutation matrix, L is
lower triangular with unit diagonal elements (lower trapezoidal if m > n), and U is
upper triangular (upper trapezoidal if m < n).

Arguments

M   (input) INTEGER
       The number of rows of the matrix A. M ≥ 0.

N   (input) INTEGER
       The number of columns of the matrix A. N ≥ 0.

A   (input/output) REAL/COMPLEX array, dimension (LDA,N)
       On entry, the m-by-n matrix to be factored.
       On exit, the factors L and U from the factorization $A = P*L*U$; the
       unit diagonal elements of L are not stored.

LDA   (input) INTEGER
       The leading dimension of the array A. LDA ≥ max(1,M).

IPIV   (output) INTEGER array, dimension (min(M,N))
       The pivot indices; for 1 ≤ i ≤ min(m,n), row i of the matrix was inter-
       changed with row IPIV(i).

INFO   (output) INTEGER

     = 0:   successful exit

     < 0:   if INFO = -i, the ith argument had an illegal value

     > 0:   if INFO = i, U(i,i) is exactly zero. The factorization has been
completed, but the factor U is exactly singular, and division by
zero will occur if it is used to solve a system of equations.

SGETRI/CGETRI

```
SUBROUTINE SGETRI( N, A, LDA, IPIV, WORK, LWORK, INFO )
INTEGER            INFO, LDA, LWORK, N
INTEGER            IPIV( * )
REAL               A( LDA, * ), WORK( LWORK )

SUBROUTINE CGETRI( N, A, LDA, IPIV, WORK, LWORK, INFO )
INTEGER            INFO, LDA, LWORK, N
INTEGER            IPIV( * )
COMPLEX            A( LDA, * ), WORK( LWORK )
```

Purpose

SGETRI/CGETRI computes the inverse of a matrix using the LU factorization
computed by SGETRF/CGETRF.

This method inverts U and then computes A^{-1} by solving the system $A^{-1}*L = U^{-1}$
for A^{-1}.

Arguments

N   (input) INTEGER
       The order of the matrix A. N ≥ 0.

A   (input/output) REAL/COMPLEX array, dimension (LDA,N)
       On entry, the factors L and U from the factorization $A = P*L*U$ as
       computed by SGETRF/CGETRF.
       On exit, if INFO = 0, the inverse of the original matrix A.

LDA   (input) INTEGER
       The leading dimension of the array A. LDA ≥ max(1,N).

IPIV   (input) INTEGER array, dimension (N)
       The pivot indices from SGETRF/CGETRF; for 1≤i≤N, row i of the
       matrix was interchanged with row IPIV(i).

WORK   (workspace) REAL/COMPLEX array, dimension (LWORK)
       On exit, if INFO = 0, WORK(1) returns the optimal LWORK.

LWORK   (input) INTEGER
       The dimension of the array WORK. LWORK ≥ max(1,N).
       For optimal performance LWORK ≥ N*NB, where NB is the optimal
       block size returned by ILAENV.

B   (input/output) REAL/COMPLEX array, dimension (LDB,NRHS)
            On entry, the right hand side matrix B.
            On exit, the solution matrix X.

LDB   (input) INTEGER
            The leading dimension of the array B. LDB $\geq$ max(1,N).

INFO   (output) INTEGER
            = 0:   successful exit
            < 0:   if INFO = $-i$, the ith argument had an illegal value

SGTCON/CGTCON

```
SUBROUTINE SGTCON( NORM, N, DL, D, DU, DU2, IPIV, ANORM, RCOND,
$                  WORK, IWORK, INFO )
CHARACTER         NORM
INTEGER           INFO, N
REAL              ANORM, RCOND
INTEGER           IPIV( * ), IWORK( * )
REAL              D( * ), DL( * ), DU( * ), DU2( * ), WORK( * )

SUBROUTINE CGTCON( NORM, N, DL, D, DU, DU2, IPIV, ANORM, RCOND,
$                  WORK, INFO )
CHARACTER         NORM
INTEGER           INFO, N
REAL              ANORM, RCOND
INTEGER           IPIV( * )
COMPLEX           D( * ), DL( * ), DU( * ), DU2( * ), WORK( * )
```

Purpose

SGTCON/CGTCON estimates the reciprocal of the condition number of a real/complex tridiagonal matrix A using the LU factorization as computed by SGTTRF/CGTTRF.

An estimate is obtained for $||A^{-1}||$, and the reciprocal of the condition number is computed as RCOND = $1/(||A|| * ||A^{-1}||)$.

Arguments

NORM   (input) CHARACTER*1
            Specifies whether the 1-norm condition number or the infinity-norm condition number is required:
            = '1' or 'O': 1-norm;
            = 'I': Infinity-norm.

N   (input) INTEGER
            The order of the matrix A. N $\geq$ 0.

INFO   (output) INTEGER
            = 0:   successful exit
            < 0:   if INFO = $-i$, the ith argument had an illegal value
            > 0:   if INFO = i, U(i,i) is exactly zero; the matrix is singular and its inverse could not be computed.

SGETRS/CGETRS

```
SUBROUTINE SGETRS( TRANS, N, NRHS, A, LDA, IPIV, B, LDB, INFO )
CHARACTER         TRANS
INTEGER           INFO, LDA, LDB, N, NRHS
INTEGER           IPIV( * )
REAL              A( LDA, * ), B( LDB, * )

SUBROUTINE CGETRS( TRANS, N, NRHS, A, LDA, IPIV, B, LDB, INFO )
CHARACTER         TRANS
INTEGER           INFO, LDA, LDB, N, NRHS
INTEGER           IPIV( * )
COMPLEX           A( LDA, * ), B( LDB, * )
```

Purpose

SGETRS/CGETRS solves a system of linear equations A*X = B, A^T*X = B, or A^H*X = B, with a general n-by-n matrix A using the LU factorization computed by SGETRF/CGETRF.

Arguments

TRANS   (input) CHARACTER*1
            Specifies the form of the system of equations:
            = 'N': A*X = B (No transpose)
            = 'T': A^T*X = B (Transpose)
            = 'C': A^H*X = B (Conjugate transpose)

N   (input) INTEGER
            The order of the matrix A. N $\geq$ 0.

NRHS   (input) INTEGER
            The number of right hand sides, i.e., the number of columns of the matrix B. NRHS $\geq$ 0.

A   (input) REAL/COMPLEX array, dimension (LDA,N)
            The factors L and U from the factorization A = P*L*U as computed by SGETRF/CGETRF.

LDA   (input) INTEGER
            The leading dimension of the array A. LDA $\geq$ max(1,N).

IPIV   (input) INTEGER array, dimension (N)
            The pivot indices from SGETRF/CGETRF; for 1$\leq$i$\leq$N, row i of the matrix was interchanged with row IPIV(i).

DL   (input) REAL/COMPLEX array, dimension (N−1)
The (n−1) multipliers that define the matrix L from the LU factorization of A as computed by SGTTRF/CGTTRF.

D   (input) REAL/COMPLEX array, dimension (N)
The n diagonal elements of the upper triangular matrix U from the LU factorization of A.

DU   (input) REAL/COMPLEX array, dimension (N−1)
The (n−1) elements of the first superdiagonal of U.

DU2   (input) REAL/COMPLEX array, dimension (N−2)
The (n−2) elements of the second superdiagonal of U.

IPIV   (input) INTEGER array, dimension (N)
The pivot indices; for $1 \leq i \leq n$, row i of the matrix was interchanged with row IPIV(i). IPIV(i) will always be either i or i+1; IPIV(i) = i indicates a row interchange was not required.

ANORM   (input) REAL
The 1-norm of the original matrix A.

RCOND   (output) REAL
The reciprocal of the condition number of the matrix A, computed as RCOND $= 1/(\|A\|\cdot\|A^{-1}\|)$.

WORK   (workspace) REAL/COMPLEX array, dimension (N)

IWORK   *SGTCON only* (workspace) INTEGER array, dimension (N)

INFO   (output) INTEGER
= 0:   successful exit
< 0:   if INFO = −i, the ith argument had an illegal value

---

SGTRFS/CGTRFS

```
SUBROUTINE SGTRFS( TRANS, N, NRHS, DL, D, DU, DLF, DF, DUF, DU2,
     $                   IPIV, B, LDB, X, LDX, FERR, BERR, WORK, IWORK,
     $                   INFO )
    CHARACTER          TRANS
    INTEGER            INFO, LDB, LDX, N, NRHS
    INTEGER            IPIV( * ), IWORK( * )
    REAL               B( LDB, * ), BERR( * ), D( * ), DF( * ),
     $                   DL( * ), DLF( * ), DU( * ), DU2( * ), DUF( * ),
     $                   FERR( * ), WORK( * ), X( LDX, * )
```

```
SUBROUTINE CGTSVX( TRANS, N, NRHS, DL, D, DU, DLF, DF, DUF, DU2,
     $                   IPIV, B, LDB, X, LDX, FERR, BERR, WORK, RWORK,
     $                   INFO )
    CHARACTER          TRANS
    INTEGER            INFO, LDB, LDX, N, NRHS
    INTEGER            IPIV( * )
    REAL               BERR( * ), FERR( * ), RWORK( * )
    COMPLEX            B( LDB, * ), D( * ), DF( * ), DL( * ),
     $                   DLF( * ), DU( * ), DU2( * ), DUF( * ),
     $                   WORK( * ), X( LDX, * )
```

Purpose

SGTRFS/CGTRFS improves the computed solution to a system of linear equations when the coefficient matrix is tridiagonal, and provides error bounds and backward error estimates for the solution.

Arguments

TRANS   (input) CHARACTER*1
Specifies the form of the system of equations:
= 'N': $A*X = B$ (No transpose)
= 'T': $A^T*X = B$ (Transpose)
= 'C': $A^H*X = B$ (Conjugate transpose)

N   (input) INTEGER
The order of the matrix A. $N \geq 0$.

NRHS   (input) INTEGER
The number of right hand sides, i.e., the number of columns of the matrix B. NRHS ≥ 0.

DL   (input) REAL/COMPLEX array, dimension (N−1)
The (n−1) subdiagonal elements of A.

D   (input) REAL/COMPLEX array, dimension (N)
The diagonal elements of A.

DU   (input) REAL/COMPLEX array, dimension (N−1)
The (n−1) superdiagonal elements of A.

DLF   (input) REAL/COMPLEX array, dimension (N−1)
The (n−1) multipliers that define the matrix L from the LU factorization of A as computed by SGTTRF/CGTTRF.

DF   (input) REAL/COMPLEX array, dimension (N)
The n diagonal elements of the upper triangular matrix U from the LU factorization of A.

DUF   (input) REAL/COMPLEX array, dimension (N−1)
The (n−1) elements of the first superdiagonal of U.

DU2   (input) REAL/COMPLEX array, dimension (N−2)
The (n−2) elements of the second superdiagonal of U.

IPIV (input) INTEGER array, dimension (N)
The pivot indices; for $1 \leq i \leq n$, row i of the matrix was interchanged with row IPIV(i). IPIV(i) will always be either i or $i+1$; IPIV(i) = i indicates a row interchange was not required.

B (input) REAL/COMPLEX array, dimension (LDB,NRHS)
The right hand side matrix B.

LDB (input) INTEGER
The leading dimension of the array B. LDB $\geq$ max(1,N).

X (input/output) REAL/COMPLEX array, dimension (LDX,NRHS)
On entry, the solution matrix X, as computed by SGTTRS/CGTTRS.
On exit, the improved solution matrix X.

LDX (input) INTEGER
The leading dimension of the array X. LDX $\geq$ max(1,N).

FERR (output) REAL array, dimension (NRHS)
The estimated forward error bound for each solution vector X(j) (the jth column of the solution matrix X). If XTRUE is the true solution corresponding to X(j), FERR(j) bounds the magnitude of the largest element in (X(j) − XTRUE) divided by the magnitude of the largest element in X(j). The quality of the error bound depends on the quality of the estimate of $\|A^{-1}\|$ computed in the code; if the estimate of $\|A^{-1}\|$ is accurate, the error bound is guaranteed.

BERR (output) REAL array, dimension (NRHS)
The componentwise relative backward error of each solution vector X(j) (i.e., the smallest relative change in any element of A or B that makes X(j) an exact solution).

WORK SGTRFS (workspace) REAL array, dimension (3*N)
CGTRFS (workspace) COMPLEX array, dimension (2*N)

IWORK SGTRFS only (workspace) INTEGER array, dimension (N)

RWORK CGTRFS only (workspace) INTEGER array, dimension (N)

INFO (output) INTEGER
= 0: successful exit
< 0: if INFO = −i, the ith argument had an illegal value

Purpose

SGTSV/CGTSV solves the equation A*X = B, where A is an n-by-n tridiagonal matrix, by Gaussian elimination with partial pivoting.

Note that the equation A^H*X = B may be solved by interchanging the order of the arguments DU and DL.

Arguments

N (input) INTEGER
The order of the matrix A. N $\geq$ 0.

NRHS (input) INTEGER
The number of right hand sides, i.e., the number of columns of the matrix B. NRHS $\geq$ 0.

DL (input/output) REAL/COMPLEX array, dimension (N−1)
On entry, DL must contain the (n−1) subdiagonal elements of A.
On exit, DL is overwritten by the (n−2) elements of the second superdiagonal of the upper triangular matrix U from the LU factorization of A, in DL(1),…, DL(n−2).

D (input/output) REAL/COMPLEX array, dimension (N)
On entry, D must contain the n diagonal elements of A.
On exit, D is overwritten by the n diagonal elements of U.

DU (input/output) REAL/COMPLEX array, dimension (N−1)
On entry, DU must contain the (n−1) superdiagonal elements of A.
On exit, DU is overwritten by the (n−1) elements of the first superdiagonal of U.

B (input/output) REAL/COMPLEX array, dimension (LDB,N)
On entry, the n-by-nrhs right hand side matrix B.
On exit, if INFO = 0, the n-by-nrhs solution matrix X.

LDB (input) INTEGER
The leading dimension of the array B. LDB $\geq$ max(1,N).

INFO (output) INTEGER
= 0: successful exit
< 0: if INFO = −i, the ith argument had an illegal value
> 0: if INFO = i, U(i,i) is exactly zero, and the solution has not been computed. The factorization has not been completed unless i = N.

SGTSV/CGTSV

```
SUBROUTINE SGTSV( N, NRHS, DL, D, DU, B, LDB, INFO )
INTEGER          INFO, LDB, N, NRHS
REAL             B( LDB, * ), D( * ), DL( * ), DU( * )

SUBROUTINE CGTSV( N, NRHS, DL, D, DU, B, LDB, INFO )
INTEGER          INFO, LDB, N, NRHS
COMPLEX          B( LDB, * ), D( * ), DL( * ), DU( * )
```

SGTSVX/CGTSVX

```
SUBROUTINE SGTSVX( FACT, TRANS, N, NRHS, DL, D, DU, DLF, DF, DUF,
$                  DU2, IPIV, B, LDB, X, LDX, RCOND, FERR, BERR,
$                  WORK, IWORK, INFO )
     CHARACTER        FACT, TRANS
     INTEGER          INFO, LDB, LDX, N, NRHS
     REAL             RCOND
     INTEGER          IPIV( * ), IWORK( * )
     REAL             B( LDB, * ), BERR( * ), D( * ), DF( * ),
$                     DL( * ), DLF( * ), DU( * ), DU2( * ), DUF( * ),
$                     FERR( * ), WORK( * ), X( LDX, * )

SUBROUTINE CGTSVX( FACT, TRANS, N, NRHS, DL, D, DU, DLF, DF, DUF,
$                  DU2, IPIV, B, LDB, X, LDX, RCOND, FERR, BERR,
$                  WORK, RWORK, INFO )
     CHARACTER        FACT, TRANS
     INTEGER          INFO, LDB, LDX, N, NRHS
     REAL             RCOND
     INTEGER          IPIV( * )
     REAL             BERR( * ), FERR( * ), RWORK( * )
     COMPLEX          B( LDB, * ), D( * ), DF( * ), DL( * ),
$                     DLF( * ), DU( * ), DU2( * ), DUF( * ),
$                     WORK( * ), X( LDX, * )
```

Purpose

SGTSVX/CGTSVX uses the LU factorization to compute the solution to a real/complex system of linear equations $A*X = B$, $A^T*X = B$, or $A^H*X = B$, where A is a tridiagonal matrix of order n and X and B are n-by-nrhs matrices.

Error bounds on the solution and a condition estimate are also provided.

Description

The following steps are performed:

1. If FACT = 'N', the LU decomposition is used to factor the matrix A as $A = L*U$, where L is a product of permutation and unit lower bidiagonal matrices and U is upper triangular with nonzeros in only the main diagonal and first two superdiagonals.

2. The factored form of A is used to estimate the condition number of the matrix A. If the reciprocal of the condition number is less than machine precision, steps 3 and 4 are skipped.

3. The system of equations is solved for X using the factored form of A.

4. Iterative refinement is applied to improve the computed solution vectors and calculate error bounds and backward error estimates for them.

Arguments

FACT   (input) CHARACTER*1
        Specifies whether or not the factored form of the matrix A is supplied on entry.
        = 'F':   On entry, DLF, DF, DUF, DU2, and IPIV contain the factored form of A; DL, D, DU, DLF, DF, DUF, DU2 and IPIV will not be modified.
        = 'N':   The matrix will be copied to DLF, DF, and DUF and factored.

TRANS   (input) CHARACTER*1
        Specifies the form of the system of equations:
        = 'N': $A*X = B$ (No transpose)
        = 'T': $A^T*X = B$ (Transpose)
        = 'C': $A^H*X = B$ (Conjugate transpose)

N   (input) INTEGER
        The number of linear equations, i.e., the order of the matrix A. $N \geq 0$.

NRHS   (input) INTEGER
        The number of right hand sides, i.e., the number of columns of the matrix B. $NRHS \geq 0$.

DL   (input) REAL/COMPLEX array, dimension (N–1)
        The (n–1) subdiagonal elements of A.

D   (input) REAL/COMPLEX array, dimension (N)
        The n diagonal elements of A.

DU   (input) REAL/COMPLEX array, dimension (N–1)
        The (n–1) superdiagonal elements of A.

DLF   (input or output) REAL/COMPLEX array, dimension (N–1)
        If FACT = 'F', then DLF is an input argument and on entry contains the (n–1) multipliers that define the matrix L from the LU factorization of A as computed by SGTTRF/CGTTRF.
        If FACT = 'N', then DLF is an output argument and on exit contains the (n–1) multipliers that define the matrix L from the LU factorization of A.

DF   (input or output) REAL/COMPLEX array, dimension (N)
        If FACT = 'F', then DF is an input argument and on entry contains the n diagonal elements of the upper triangular matrix U from the LU factorization of A.
        If FACT = 'N', then DF is an output argument and on exit contains the n diagonal elements of the upper triangular matrix U from the LU factorization of A.

DUF   (input or output) REAL/COMPLEX array, dimension (N–1)
        If FACT = 'F', then DUF is an input argument and on entry contains the (n–1) elements of the first superdiagonal of U.
        If FACT = 'N', then DUF is an output argument and on exit contains the (n–1) elements of the first superdiagonal of U.

INFO   (output) INTEGER
- = 0: successful exit
- < 0: if INFO = -i, the ith argument had an illegal value
- > 0: if INFO = i, and i is
  - ≤ N: if INFO = i, U(i,i) is exactly zero. The factorization has not been completed unless i = N, but the factor U is exactly singular, so the solution and error bounds could not be computed.
  - = N+1: RCOND is less than machine precision. The factorization has been completed, but the matrix is singular to working precision, and the solution and error bounds have not been computed.

SGTTRF/CGTTRF

```
SUBROUTINE SGTTRF( N, DL, D, DU, DU2, IPIV, INFO )
INTEGER       INFO, N
INTEGER       IPIV( * )
REAL          D( * ), DL( * ), DU( * ), DU2( * )
SUBROUTINE CGTTRF( N, DL, D, DU, DU2, IPIV, INFO )
INTEGER       INFO, N
INTEGER       IPIV( * )
COMPLEX       D( * ), DL( * ), DU( * ), DU2( * )
```

Purpose

SGTTRF/CGTTRF computes an LU factorization of a real/complex tridiagonal matrix A using partial pivoting and row interchanges.

The factorization has the form A = L*U where L is a product of permutation and unit lower bidiagonal matrices and U is upper triangular with nonzeros in only the main diagonal and first two superdiagonals.

Arguments

N   (input) INTEGER
The order of the matrix A. N ≥ 0.

DL   (input/output) REAL/COMPLEX array, dimension (N-1)
On entry, DL must contain the (n-1) subdiagonal elements of A.
On exit, DL is overwritten by the (n-1) multipliers that define the matrix L from the LU factorization of A.

D   (input/output) REAL/COMPLEX array, dimension (N)
On entry, D must contain the diagonal elements of A.
On exit, D is overwritten by the n diagonal elements of the upper triangular matrix U from the LU factorization of A.

DU2   (input or output) REAL/COMPLEX array, dimension (N-2)
If FACT = 'F', then DU2 is an input argument and on entry contains the (n-2) elements of the second superdiagonal of U.
If FACT = 'N', then DU2 is an output argument and on exit contains the (n-2) elements of the second superdiagonal of U.

IPIV   (input) INTEGER array, dimension (N)
If FACT = 'F', then IPIV is an input argument and on entry contains the pivot indices from the LU factorization of A as computed by SGTTRF/CGTTRF.
If FACT = 'N', then IPIV is an output argument and on exit contains the pivot indices from the LU factorization of A; row i of the matrix was interchanged with row IPIV(i). IPIV(i) will always be either i or i+1; IPIV(i) = i indicates a row interchange was not required.

B   (input) REAL/COMPLEX array, dimension (LDB,NRHS)
The n-by-nrhs right hand side matrix B.

LDB   (input) INTEGER
The leading dimension of the array B. LDB ≥ max(1,N).

X   (output) REAL/COMPLEX array, dimension (LDX,NRHS)
If INFO = 0, the n-by-nrhs solution matrix X.

LDX   (input) INTEGER
The leading dimension of the array X. LDX ≥ max(1,N).

RCOND   (output) REAL
The estimate of the reciprocal condition number of the matrix A. If RCOND < the machine precision (in particular, if RCOND = 0), the matrix is singular to working precision. This condition is indicated by a return code of INFO > 0, and the solution and error bounds are not computed.

FERR   (output) REAL array, dimension (NRHS)
The estimated forward error bound for each solution vector X(j) (the jth column of the solution matrix X). If XTRUE is the true solution corresponding to X(j), FERR(j) bounds the magnitude of the largest element in (X(j) − XTRUE) divided by the magnitude of the largest element in X(j). The quality of the error bound depends on the quality of the estimate of $\|A^{-1}\|$ computed in the code; if the estimate of $\|A^{-1}\|$ is accurate, the error bound is guaranteed.

BERR   (output) REAL array, dimension (NRHS)
The componentwise relative backward error of each solution vector X(j) (i.e., the smallest relative change in any element of A or B that makes X(j) an exact solution).

WORK   SGTSVX (workspace) REAL array, dimension (3*N)
CGTSVX (workspace) COMPLEX array, dimension (2*N)

IWORK   SGTSVX only (workspace) INTEGER array, dimension (N)
RWORK   CGTSVX only (workspace) REAL array, dimension (N)

DU   (input/output) REAL/COMPLEX array, dimension (N−1)
      On entry, DU must contain the (n−1) superdiagonal elements of A.
      On exit, DU is overwritten by the (n−1) elements of the first superdiagonal of U.

DU2   (output) REAL/COMPLEX array, dimension (N−2)
      On exit, DU2 is overwritten by the (n−2) elements of the second superdiagonal of U.

IPIV (output) INTEGER array, dimension (N)
      The pivot indices; for $1 \le i \le N$, row i of the matrix was interchanged with row IPIV(i). IPIV(i) will always be either i or i+1; IPIV(i) = i indicates a row interchange was not required.

INFO (output) INTEGER
      = 0: successful exit
      < 0: if INFO = −i, the ith argument had an illegal value
      > 0: if INFO = i, U(i,i) is exactly zero. The factorization has been completed, but the factor U is exactly singular, and division by zero will occur if it is used to solve a system of equations.

SGTTRS/CGTTRS

```
      SUBROUTINE SGTTRS( TRANS, N, NRHS, DL, D, DU, DU2, IPIV, B, LDB,
     $                   INFO )
      CHARACTER          TRANS
      INTEGER            INFO, LDB, N, NRHS
      INTEGER            IPIV( * )
      REAL               B( LDB, * ), D( * ), DL( * ), DU( * ), DU2( * )

      SUBROUTINE CGTTRS( TRANS, N, NRHS, DL, D, DU, DU2, IPIV, B, LDB,
     $                   INFO )
      CHARACTER          TRANS
      INTEGER            INFO, LDB, N, NRHS
      INTEGER            IPIV( * )
      COMPLEX            B( LDB, * ), D( * ), DL( * ), DU( * ), DU2( * )
```

Purpose

SGTTRS/CGTTRS solves one of the systems of equations $A*X = B$, $A^T*X = B$, or $A^H*X = B$, with a tridiagonal matrix A using the LU factorization computed by SGTTRF/CGTTRF.

Arguments

TRANS (input) CHARACTER*1
      Specifies the form of the system of equations:
      = 'N': $A*X = B$ (No transpose)
      = 'T': $A^T*X = B$ (Transpose)
      = 'C': $A^H*X = B$ (Conjugate transpose)

N   (input) INTEGER
      The order of the matrix A. $N \ge 0$.

NRHS (input) INTEGER
      The number of right hand sides, i.e., the number of columns of the matrix B. $NRHS \ge 0$.

DL   (input) REAL/COMPLEX array, dimension (N−1)
      The (n−1) multipliers that define the matrix L from the LU factorization of A.

D   (input) REAL/COMPLEX array, dimension (N)
      The n diagonal elements of the upper triangular matrix U from the LU factorization of A.

DU   (input) REAL/COMPLEX array, dimension (N−1)
      The (n−1) elements of the first superdiagonal of U.

DU2   (input) REAL/COMPLEX array, dimension (N−2)
      The (n−2) elements of the second superdiagonal of U.

IPIV (input) INTEGER array, dimension (N)
      The pivot indices; for $1 \le i \le N$, row i of the matrix was interchanged with row IPIV(i). IPIV(i) will always be either i or i+1; IPIV(i) = i indicates a row interchange was not required.

B   (input/output) REAL/COMPLEX array, dimension (LDB,NRHS)
      On entry, the right hand side matrix B.
      On exit, B is overwritten by the solution matrix X.

LDB   (input) INTEGER
      The leading dimension of the array B. $LDB \ge \max(1,N)$.

INFO (output) INTEGER
      = 0: successful exit
      < 0: if INFO = −i, the ith argument had an illegal value

SHSEIN/CHSEIN

```
      SUBROUTINE SHSEIN( JOB, EIGSRC, INITV, SELECT, N, H, LDH, WR, WI,
     $                   VL, LDVL, VR, LDVR, MM, M, WORK, IFAILL,
     $                   IFAILR, INFO )
      CHARACTER          EIGSRC, INITV, JOB
      INTEGER            INFO, LDH, LDVL, LDVR, N, MM, M
      LOGICAL            SELECT( * )
      INTEGER            IFAILL( * ), IFAILR( * )
      REAL               H( LDH, * ), VL( LDVL, * ), VR( LDVR, * ),
     $                   WI( * ), WORK( * ), WR( * )
```

```
SUBROUTINE CHSEIN( JOB, EIGSRC, INITV, SELECT, N, H, LDH, W, VL,
$                  LDVL, VR, LDVR, MM, M, WORK, RWORK, IFAILL,
$                  IFAILR, INFO )
CHARACTER      EIGSRC, INITV, JOB
INTEGER        INFO, LDH, LDVL, LDVR, M, MM, N
LOGICAL        SELECT( * )
INTEGER        IFAILL( * ), IFAILR( * )
REAL           RWORK( * )
COMPLEX        H( LDH, * ), VL( LDVL, * ), VR( LDVR, * ),
$              W( * ), WORK( * )
```

Purpose

SHSEIN/CHSEIN uses inverse iteration to find specified right and/or left eigenvectors of a real/complex upper Hessenberg matrix H.

The right eigenvector x and the left eigenvector y of the matrix H corresponding to an eigenvalue w are defined by:

$$H*x = w*x, \quad y^H*H = w*y^H.$$

Arguments

JOB   (input) CHARACTER*1
    = 'R': compute right eigenvectors only;
    = 'L': compute left eigenvectors only;
    = 'B': compute both right and left eigenvectors.

EIGSRC (input) CHARACTER*1
    Specifies the source of eigenvalues supplied in (WR,WI)/(W):
    = 'Q': the eigenvalues were found using SHSEQR/CHSEQR; thus, if H has zero subdiagonal elements, and so is block-triangular, then the jth eigenvalue can be assumed to be an eigenvalue of the block containing the jth row/column. This property allows SHSEIN/CHSEIN to perform inverse iteration on just one diagonal block.
    = 'N': no assumptions are made on the correspondence between eigenvalues and diagonal blocks. In this case, SHSEIN/CHSEIN must always perform inverse iteration using the whole matrix H.

INITV   (input) CHARACTER*1
    = 'N': no initial vectors are supplied;
    = 'U': user-supplied initial vectors are stored in the arrays VL and/or VR.

SELECT *SHSEIN* (input/output) LOGICAL array, dimension(N)
    CHSEIN (input) LOGICAL array, dimension (N)
    SHSEIN
    Specifies the eigenvectors to be computed. To select the real eigenvector corresponding to a real eigenvalue WR(j), SELECT(j) must be set to .TRUE.. To select the complex eigenvector corresponding to a complex eigenvalue (WR(j),WI(j)), with complex conjugate (WR(j+1),WI(j+1)), either SELECT(j) or SELECT(j+1) or both must be set to .TRUE.; then on exit SELECT(j) is .TRUE. and SELECT(j+1) is .FALSE..
    CHSEIN
    Specifies the eigenvectors to be computed. To select the eigenvector corresponding to the eigenvalue W(j), SELECT(j) must be set to .TRUE..

N   (input) INTEGER
    The order of the matrix H. N ≥ 0.

H   (input) REAL/COMPLEX array, dimension (LDH,N)
    The upper Hessenberg matrix H.

LDH   (input) INTEGER
    The leading dimension of the array H. LDH ≥ max(1,N).

WR   *SHSEIN only* (input/output) REAL array, dimension (N)
WI   *SHSEIN only* (input) REAL array, dimension (N)
    On entry, the real and imaginary parts of the eigenvalues of H; a complex conjugate pair of eigenvalues must be stored in consecutive elements of WR and WI.
    On exit, WR may have been altered since close eigenvalues are perturbed slightly in searching for independent eigenvectors.

W   *CHSEIN only* (input/output) COMPLEX array, dimension (N)
    On entry, the eigenvalues of H.
    On exit, the real parts of W may have been altered since close eigenvalues are perturbed slightly in searching for independent eigenvectors.

VL   (input/output) REAL/COMPLEX array, dimension (LDVL,MM)
    On entry, if INITV = 'U' and JOB = 'L' or 'B', VL must contain starting vector for the inverse iteration for the left eigenvectors; the starting vector for each eigenvector must be in the same column(s) in which the eigenvector will be stored.
    On exit, if JOB = 'L' or 'B', the left eigenvectors specified by SELECT will be stored one after another in the columns of VL, in the same order as their eigenvalues. If JOB = 'R', VL is not referenced.
    SHSEIN only
    A complex eigenvector corresponding to a complex eigenvalue is stored in two consecutive columns, the first holding the real part and the second the imaginary part.

LDVL   (input) INTEGER
    The leading dimension of the array VL.
    LDVL ≥ max(1,N) if JOB = 'L' or 'B'; LDVL ≥ 1 otherwise.

VR   (input/output) REAL/COMPLEX array, dimension (LDVR,MM)
    On entry, if INITV = 'U' and JOB = 'R' or 'B', VR must contain starting vectors for the inverse iteration for the right eigenvectors; the starting vector for each eigenvector must be in the same column(s) in which the eigenvector will be stored.
    On exit, if JOB = 'R' or 'B', the right eigenvectors specified by SELECT will be stored one after another in the columns of VR, in the same order as their eigenvalues. If JOB = 'L', VR is not referenced.

SHSEIN

A complex eigenvector corresponding to a complex eigenvalue is stored in two consecutive columns, the first holding the real part and the second the imaginary part.

LDVR   (input) INTEGER
The leading dimension of the array VR.
LDVR $\geq$ max(1,N) if JOB = 'R' or 'B'; LDVR $\geq$ 1 otherwise.

MM   (input) INTEGER
The number of columns in the arrays VL and/or VR. MM $\geq$ M.

M   (output) INTEGER
The number of columns in the arrays VL and/or VR actually used to store the eigenvectors.
SHSEIN
Each selected real eigenvector occupies one column and each selected complex eigenvector occupies two columns.
CHSEIN
Each selected eigenvector occupies one column.

WORK   *SHSEIN* (workspace) REAL array, dimension ((N+2)*N)
CHSEIN (workspace) COMPLEX array, dimension (N*N)

RWORK   *CHSEIN only* (workspace) REAL array, dimension (N)

IFAILL   (output) INTEGER array, dimension (MM)
If JOB = 'L' or 'B', IFAILL(i) = j > 0 if left eigenvector in the ith column of VL (corresponding to the jth eigenvalue) failed to converge.
IFAILL(i) = 0 if the eigenvector converged satisfactorily.
If JOB = 'R', IFAILL is not referenced.
SHSEIN only
If the ith and $(i+1)^{st}$ columns of VL hold a complex eigenvector, then IFAILL(i) and IFAILL(i+1) are set to the same value.

IFAILR   (output) INTEGER array, dimension (MM)
If JOB = 'R' or 'B', IFAILR(i) = j > 0 if right eigenvector in the ith column of VR (corresponding to the jth eigenvalue) failed to converge.
IFAILR(i) = 0 if the eigenvector converged satisfactorily.
If JOB = 'L', IFAILR is not referenced.
SHSEIN only
If the ith and $(i+1)^{st}$ columns of VR hold a complex eigenvector, then IFAILR(i) and IFAILR(i+1) are set to the same value.

INFO   (output) INTEGER
= 0:   successful exit
< 0:   if INFO = $-i$, the ith argument had an illegal value
> 0:   if INFO = i, INFO is the number of eigenvectors which failed to converge; see IFAILL and IFAILR for further details.

SHSEQR/CHSEQR

```
SUBROUTINE SHSEQR( JOB, COMPZ, N, ILO, IHI, H, LDH, WR, WI, Z,
$                  LDZ, WORK, LWORK, INFO )
    CHARACTER    COMPZ, JOB
    INTEGER      IHI, ILO, INFO, LDH, LDZ, LWORK, N
    REAL         H( LDH, * ), WI( * ), WORK( * ), WR( * ),
$                Z( LDZ, * )

SUBROUTINE CHSEQR( JOB, COMPZ, N, ILO, IHI, H, LDH, W, Z, LDZ,
$                  WORK, LWORK, INFO )
    CHARACTER    COMPZ, JOB
    INTEGER      IHI, ILO, INFO, LDH, LDZ, LWORK, N
    COMPLEX      H( LDH, * ), W( * ), WORK( * ), Z( LDZ, * )
```

Purpose

SHSEQR/CHSEQR computes the eigenvalues of a real/complex upper Hessenberg matrix H and, optionally, the matrices T and Z from the Schur decomposition $H = Z*T*Z^H$, where T is an upper quasi-triangular/triangular matrix (the Schur form), and Z is the orthogonal/unitary matrix of Schur vectors.

Optionally Z may be postmultiplied into an input orthogonal/unitary matrix Q, so that this routine can give the Schur factorization of a matrix A which has been reduced to the Hessenberg form H by the orthogonal/unitary matrix Q:
$A = Q*H*Q^H = (Q*Z)*T*(Q*Z)^H$.

Arguments

JOB   (input) CHARACTER*1
= 'E':   compute eigenvalues only;
= 'S':   compute eigenvalues and the Schur form T.

COMPZ   (input) CHARACTER*1
= 'N':   no Schur vectors are computed;
= 'I':   Z is initialized to the unit matrix and the matrix Z of Schur vectors of H is returned;
= 'V':   Z must contain an orthogonal/unitary matrix Q on entry, and the product Q*Z is returned.

N   (input) INTEGER
The order of the matrix H. N $\geq$ 0.

ILO, IHI   (input) INTEGER
It is assumed that H is already upper triangular in rows and columns 1 to ILO-1 and IHI+1 to N. ILO and IHI are normally set by a previous call to SGEBAL/CGEBAL, and then passed to SGEHRD/CGEHRD when the matrix output by SGEBAL/CGEBAL is reduced to Hessenberg form. Otherwise ILO and IHI should be set to 1 and N respectively. min(ILO,N) $\leq$ IHI $\leq$ N; ILO $\geq$ 1.

H   (input/output) REAL/COMPLEX array, dimension (LDH,N)
On entry, the upper Hessenberg matrix H.

SOPGTR/CUPGTR

```
SUBROUTINE SOPGTR( UPLO, N, AP, TAU, Q, LDQ, WORK, INFO )
CHARACTER      UPLO
INTEGER        INFO, LDQ, N
REAL           AP( * ), Q( LDQ, * ), TAU( * ), WORK( * )

SUBROUTINE CUPGTR( UPLO, N, AP, TAU, Q, LDQ, WORK, INFO )
CHARACTER      UPLO
INTEGER        INFO, LDQ, N
COMPLEX        AP( * ), Q( LDQ, * ), TAU( * ), WORK( * )
```

Purpose

SOPGTR/CUPGTR generates a real/complex orthogonal/unitary matrix Q which is defined as the product of $n-1$ elementary reflectors H_i of order n, as returned by SSPTRD/CHPTRD using packed storage:

if UPLO = 'U', $Q = H_{n-1} \cdots H_2 H_1$,

if UPLO = 'L', $Q = H_1 H_2 \cdots H_{n-1}$.

Arguments

UPLO (input) CHARACTER*1
= 'U': Upper triangular packed storage used in previous call to SSPTRD/CHPTRD;
= 'L': Lower triangular packed storage used in previous call to SSPTRD/CHPTRD.

N (input) INTEGER
The order of the matrix Q. $N \geq 0$.

AP (input) REAL/COMPLEX array, dimension ($N*(N+1)/2$)
The vectors which define the elementary reflectors, as returned by SSPTRD/CHPTRD.

TAU (input) REAL/COMPLEX array, dimension ($N-1$)
TAU(i) must contain the scalar factor of the elementary reflector H_i, as returned by SSPTRD/CHPTRD.

Q (output) REAL/COMPLEX array, dimension (LDQ,N)
The n-by-n orthogonal/unitary matrix Q.

LDQ (input) INTEGER
The leading dimension of the array Q. $LDQ \geq \max(1,N)$.

WORK (workspace) REAL/COMPLEX array, dimension ($N-1$)

INFO (output) INTEGER
= 0: successful exit
< 0: if INFO = $-i$, the ith argument had an illegal value

---

On exit, if JOB = 'S', H contains the upper quasi-triangular/triangular matrix T from the Schur decomposition (the Schur form).
If JOB = 'E', the contents of H are unspecified on exit.
SHSEQR only
2-by-2 diagonal blocks (corresponding to complex conjugate pairs of eigenvalues) are returned in standard form, with $H(i,i) = H(i+1,i+1)$ and $H(i+1,i)*H(i,i+1) < 0$.

LDH (input) INTEGER
The leading dimension of the array H. $LDH \geq \max(1,N)$.

WR, WI *SHSEQR only* (output) REAL array, dimension (N)
The real and imaginary parts, respectively, of the computed eigenvalues. If two eigenvalues are computed as a complex conjugate pair, they are stored in consecutive elements of WR and WI, say the ith and $(i+1)^{st}$, with $WI(i) > 0$ and $WI(i+1) < 0$. If JOB = 'S', the eigenvalues are stored in the same order as on the diagonal of the Schur form returned in H, with $WR(i) = H(i,i)$ and, if $H(i:i+1,i:i+1)$ is a 2-by-2 diagonal block, $WI(i) = \sqrt{(H(i+1,i)*H(i,i+1))}$ and $WI(i+1) = -WI(i)$.

W *CHSEQR only* (output) COMPLEX array, dimension (N)
The computed eigenvalues. If JOB = 'S', the eigenvalues are stored in the same order as on the diagonal of the Schur form returned in H, with $W(i) = H(i,i)$.

Z (input/output) REAL/COMPLEX array, dimension (LDZ,N)
If COMPZ = 'N': Z is not referenced.
If COMPZ = 'I': on entry, Z need not be set, and on exit, Z contains the orthogonal/unitary matrix Z of the Schur vectors of H.
If COMPZ = 'V': on entry, Z must contain an n-by-n matrix Q, which is assumed to be equal to the unit matrix except for the submatrix Z(ilo:ihi,ilo:ihi); on exit Z contains Q*Z. Normally Q is the orthogonal/unitary matrix generated by SORGHR/CUNGHR after the call to SGEHRD/CGEHRD which formed the Hessenberg matrix H.

LDZ (input) INTEGER
The leading dimension of the array Z. $LDZ \geq \max(1,N)$.

WORK (workspace) REAL/COMPLEX array, dimension (N)

LWORK (input) INTEGER
This argument is currently redundant.

INFO (output) INTEGER
= 0: successful exit
< 0: if INFO = $-i$, the ith argument had an illegal value
> 0: if INFO = i, SHSEQR/CHSEQR failed to compute all the eigenvalues in a total of 30*(IHI−ILO+1) iterations; elements 1:ilo−1 and i+1:n of WR and WI (*SHSEQR*) or of W (*CHSEQR*) contain those eigenvalues which have been successfully computed.

SOPMTR/CUPMTR

```
SUBROUTINE SOPMTR( SIDE, UPLO, TRANS, M, N, AP, TAU, C, LDC, WORK,
$                  INFO )
     CHARACTER      SIDE, TRANS, UPLO
     INTEGER        INFO, LDC, M, N
     REAL           AP( * ), C( LDC, * ), TAU( * ), WORK( * )

SUBROUTINE CUPMTR( SIDE, UPLO, TRANS, M, N, AP, TAU, C, LDC, WORK,
$                  INFO )
     CHARACTER      SIDE, TRANS, UPLO
     INTEGER        INFO, LDC, M, N
     COMPLEX        AP( * ), C( LDC, * ), TAU( * ), WORK( * )
```

Purpose

SOPMTR/CUPMTR overwrites the general real/complex m-by-n matrix C with

	SIDE = 'L'	SIDE = 'R'	
TRANS = 'N':	$Q*C$	$C*Q$	
TRANS = 'T':	Q^T*C	$C*Q^T$	(*SOPMTR only*)
TRANS = 'C':	Q^H*C	$C*Q^H$	(*CUPMTR only*)

where Q is a real/complex orthogonal/unitary matrix of order NQ, with NQ = M if SIDE = 'L' and NQ = N if SIDE = 'R'. Q is defined as the product of nq−1 elementary reflectors H_i, of order nq, as returned by SSPTRD/CHPTRD using packed storage:

if UPLO = 'U', $Q = H_{nq-1} \cdots H_2 H_1$;

if UPLO = 'L', $Q = H_1 H_2 \cdots H_{nq-1}$.

Arguments

SIDE   (input) CHARACTER*1
        = 'L': apply Q or Q^H from the Left;
        = 'R': apply Q or Q^H from the Right.

UPLO   (input) CHARACTER*1
        = 'U': Upper triangular packed storage used in previous call to SSPTRD/CHPTRD;
        = 'L': Lower triangular packed storage used in previous call to SSPTRD/CHPTRD.

TRANS   (input) CHARACTER*1
        Specifies whether the matrix Q, Q^T, or Q^H is applied to C.
        = 'N': No transpose, apply Q
        = 'T': Transpose, apply Q^T (*SOPMTR only*)
        = 'C': Conjugate transpose, apply Q^H (*CUPMTR only*)

M   (input) INTEGER
        The number of rows of the matrix C. M ≥ 0.

N   (input) INTEGER
        The number of columns of the matrix C. N ≥ 0.

AP   (input) REAL/COMPLEX array, dimension (M*(M+1)/2) if SIDE = 'L', or (N*(N+1)/2) if SIDE = 'R'.
        The vectors which define the elementary reflectors, as returned by SSPTRD/CHPTRD. AP is modified by the routine but restored on exit.

TAU   (input) REAL/COMPLEX array, dimension (M−1) if SIDE = 'L' or (N−1) if SIDE = 'R'
        TAU(i) must contain the scalar factor of the elementary reflector H_i, as returned by SSPTRD/CHPTRD.

C   (input/output) REAL/COMPLEX array, dimension (LDC,N)
        On entry, the m-by-n matrix C.
        On exit, C is overwritten by Q*C or Q^H*C or $C*Q^H$ or C*Q.

LDC   (input) INTEGER
        The leading dimension of the array C. LDC ≥ max(1,M).

WORK   (workspace) REAL/COMPLEX array, dimension
        (N) if SIDE = 'L',
        (M) if SIDE = 'R'

INFO   (output) INTEGER
        = 0: successful exit
        < 0: if INFO = −i, the ith argument had an illegal value

SORGBR/CUNGBR

```
SUBROUTINE SORGBR( VECT, M, N, K, A, LDA, TAU, WORK, LWORK, INFO )
     CHARACTER      VECT
     INTEGER        INFO, K, LDA, LWORK, M, N
     REAL           A( LDA, * ), TAU( * ), WORK( LWORK )

SUBROUTINE CUNGBR( VECT, M, N, K, A, LDA, TAU, WORK, LWORK, INFO )
     CHARACTER      VECT
     INTEGER        INFO, K, LDA, LWORK, M, N
     COMPLEX        A( LDA, * ), TAU( * ), WORK( LWORK )
```

Purpose

SORGBR/CUNGBR generates one of the orthogonal/unitary matrices Q or P^H determined by SGEBRD/CGEBRD when reducing a real/complex matrix A to bidiagonal form: $A = Q*B*P^H$. Q and P^H are defined as products of elementary reflectors H_i or G_i, respectively.

If VECT = 'Q', A is assumed to have been an m-by-k matrix, and Q is of order M:
if M ≥ K, $Q = H_1 H_2 \cdots H_k$ and SORGBR/CUNGBR returns the first N columns

of Q, where M ≥ N ≥ K; if M < K, $Q = H_1 H_2 \cdots H_{m-1}$ and SORGBR/CUNGBR returns Q as an m-by-m matrix.

If VECT = 'P', A is assumed to have been a k-by-n matrix, and P^H is of order n: if K < N, $P^H = G_k \cdots G_2 G_1$ and SORGBR/CUNGBR returns the first M rows of P^H, where N ≥ M ≥ K; if K ≥ N, $P^H = G_{n-1} \cdots G_2 G_1$ and SORGBR/CUNGBR returns P^H as an n-by-n matrix.

Arguments

VECT (input) CHARACTER*1
Specifies whether the matrix Q or the matrix P^H is required, as defined in the transformation applied by SGEBRD/CGEBRD:
= 'Q': generate Q;
= 'P': generate P^H.

M (input) INTEGER
The number of rows of the matrix Q or P^H to be returned. M ≥ 0.

N (input) INTEGER
The number of columns of the matrix Q or P^H to be returned. N ≥ 0.
If VECT = 'Q', M ≥ N ≥ min(M,K);
if VECT = 'P', N ≥ M ≥ min(N,K).

K (input) INTEGER
K ≥ 0.
If VECT = 'Q', the number of columns in the original m-by-k matrix reduced by SGEBRD/CGEBRD.
If VECT = 'P', the number of rows in the original k-by-n matrix reduced by SGEBRD/CGEBRD.

A (input/output) REAL/COMPLEX array, dimension (LDA,N)
On entry, the vectors which define the elementary reflectors, as returned by SGEBRD/CGEBRD.
On exit, the m-by-n matrix Q or P^H.

LDA (input) INTEGER
The leading dimension of the array A. LDA ≥ max(1,M).

TAU (input) REAL/COMPLEX array, dimension
(min(M,K)) if VECT = 'Q', or (min(N,K)) if VECT = 'P'
TAU(i) must contain the scalar factor of the elementary reflector H_i or G_i, which determines Q or P^H, as returned by SGEBRD/CGEBRD in its array argument TAUQ or TAUP.

WORK (workspace) REAL/COMPLEX array, dimension (LWORK)
On exit, if INFO = 0, WORK(1) returns the optimal LWORK.

LWORK (input) INTEGER
The dimension of the array WORK. LWORK ≥ max(1,min(M,N)).
For optimum performance LWORK ≥ min(M,N)*NB, where NB is the optimal block size.

INFO (output) INTEGER
= 0: successful exit

< 0: if INFO = −i, the i-th argument had an illegal value

SORGHR/CUNGHR

```
SUBROUTINE SORGHR( N, ILO, IHI, A, LDA, TAU, WORK, LWORK, INFO )
INTEGER          N, ILO, IHI, INFO, LDA, LWORK
REAL             A( LDA, * ), TAU( * ), WORK( LWORK )

SUBROUTINE CUNGHR( N, ILO, IHI, A, LDA, TAU, WORK, LWORK, INFO )
INTEGER          N, ILO, IHI, INFO, LDA, LWORK
COMPLEX          A( LDA, * ), TAU( * ), WORK( LWORK )
```

Purpose

SORGHR/CUNGHR generates a real/complex orthogonal/unitary matrix Q which is defined as the product of IHI−ILO elementary reflectors H_i of order n, as returned by SGEHRD/CGEHRD:

$$Q = H_{ilo} H_{ilo+1} \cdots H_{ihi-1}.$$

Arguments

N (input) INTEGER
The order of the matrix Q. N ≥ 0.

ILO, IHI (input) INTEGER
ILO and IHI must have the same values as in the previous call of SGEHRD/CGEHRD. Q is equal to the unit matrix except in the submatrix Q(ilo+1:ihi,ilo+1:ihi). If N > 0, 1 ≤ ILO ≤ IHI ≤ N; otherwise ILO = 1 and IHI = N.

A (input/output) REAL/COMPLEX array, dimension (LDA,N)
On entry, the vectors which define the elementary reflectors, as returned by SGEHRD/CGEHRD.
On exit, the n-by-n orthogonal/unitary matrix Q.

LDA (input) INTEGER
The leading dimension of the array A. LDA ≥ max(1,N).

TAU (input) REAL/COMPLEX array, dimension (N−1)
TAU(i) must contain the scalar factor of the elementary reflector H_i, as returned by SGEHRD/CGEHRD.

WORK (workspace) REAL/COMPLEX array, dimension (LWORK)
On exit, if INFO = 0, WORK(1) returns the optimal LWORK.

LWORK (input) INTEGER
The dimension of the array WORK. LWORK ≥ max(1,IHI−ILO).
For optimum performance LWORK ≥ (IHI−ILO)*NB, where NB is the optimal block size.

INFO   (output) INTEGER
      = 0: successful exit
      < 0: if INFO = -i, the ith argument had an illegal value

SORGLQ/CUNGLQ

```
SUBROUTINE SORGLQ( M, N, K, A, LDA, TAU, WORK, LWORK, INFO )
INTEGER          INFO, K, LDA, LWORK, M, N
REAL             A( LDA, * ), TAU( * ), WORK( LWORK )

SUBROUTINE CUNGLQ( M, N, K, A, LDA, TAU, WORK, LWORK, INFO )
INTEGER          INFO, K, LDA, LWORK, M, N
COMPLEX          A( LDA, * ), TAU( * ), WORK( LWORK )
```

Purpose

SORGLQ/CUNGLQ generates an m-by-n real/complex matrix Q with orthonormal rows, which is defined as the first m rows of a product of k elementary reflectors H_i of order n

$$Q = H_k \cdots H_2 H_1 \quad (SORGLQ)$$

$$Q = H_k^H \cdots H_2^H H_1^H \quad (CUNGLQ)$$

as returned by SGELQF/CGELQF.

Arguments

M   (input) INTEGER
    The number of rows of the matrix Q. $M \geq 0$.

N   (input) INTEGER
    The number of columns of the matrix Q. $N \geq M$.

K   (input) INTEGER
    The number of elementary reflectors whose product defines the matrix Q. $M \geq K \geq 0$.

A   (input/output) REAL/COMPLEX array, dimension (LDA,N)
    On entry, the ith row must contain the vector which defines the elementary reflector H_i, for i = 1,2,...,k, as returned by SGELQF/CGELQF in the first k rows of its array argument A. On exit, the m-by-n matrix Q.

LDA   (input) INTEGER
    The first dimension of the array A. $LDA \geq \max(1,M)$.

TAU   (input) REAL/COMPLEX array, dimension (K)
    TAU(i) must contain the scalar factor of the elementary reflector H_i, as returned by SGELQF/CGELQF.

WORK   (workspace) REAL/COMPLEX array, dimension (LWORK)
    On exit, if INFO = 0, WORK(1) returns the optimal LWORK.

LWORK   (input) INTEGER
    The dimension of the array WORK. $LWORK \geq \max(1,M)$.
    For optimum performance $LWORK \geq M*NB$, where NB is the optimal block size.

INFO   (output) INTEGER
    = 0: successful exit
    < 0: if INFO = -i, the ith argument has an illegal value

SORGQL/CUNGQL

```
SUBROUTINE SORGQL( M, N, K, A, LDA, TAU, WORK, LWORK, INFO )
INTEGER          INFO, K, LDA, LWORK, M, N
REAL             A( LDA, * ), TAU( * ), WORK( LWORK )

SUBROUTINE CUNGQL( M, N, K, A, LDA, TAU, WORK, LWORK, INFO )
INTEGER          INFO, K, LDA, LWORK, M, N
COMPLEX          A( LDA, * ), TAU( * ), WORK( LWORK )
```

Purpose

SORGQL/CUNGQL generates an m-by-n real/complex matrix Q with orthonormal columns, which is defined as the last n columns of a product of k elementary reflectors H_i of order m

$$Q = H_k \cdots H_2 H_1$$

as returned by SGEQLF/CGEQLF.

Arguments

M   (input) INTEGER
    The number of rows of the matrix Q. $M \geq 0$.

N   (input) INTEGER
    The number of columns of the matrix Q. $M \geq N \geq 0$.

K   (input) INTEGER
    The number of elementary reflectors whose product defines the matrix Q. $N \geq K \geq 0$.

A   (input/output) REAL/COMPLEX array, dimension (LDA,N)
    On entry, the $(n-k+i)^{th}$ column must contain the vector which defines the elementary reflector H_i, for i = 1,2,...,k, as returned by SGEQLF/CGEQLF in the last k columns of its array argument A. On exit, the m-by-n matrix Q.

LDA
(input) INTEGER
The first dimension of the array A. LDA $\geq$ max(1,M).

TAU
(input) REAL/COMPLEX array, dimension (K)
TAU(i) must contain the scalar factor of the elementary reflector H_i, as returned by SGEQLF/CGEQLF.

WORK
(workspace) REAL/COMPLEX array, dimension (LWORK)
On exit, if INFO = 0, WORK(1) returns the optimal LWORK.

LWORK
(input) INTEGER
The dimension of the array WORK. LWORK $\geq$ max(1,N). For optimum performance LWORK $\geq$ N*NB, where NB is the optimal block size.

INFO
(output) INTEGER
= 0: successful exit
< 0: if INFO = $-i$, the ith argument has an illegal value

SORGQR/CUNGQR

```
SUBROUTINE SORGQR( M, N, K, A, LDA, TAU, WORK, LWORK, INFO )
INTEGER    INFO, K, LDA, LWORK, M, N
REAL       A( LDA, * ), TAU( * ), WORK( LWORK )

SUBROUTINE CUNGQR( M, N, K, A, LDA, TAU, WORK, LWORK, INFO )
INTEGER    INFO, K, LDA, LWORK, M, N
COMPLEX    A( LDA, * ), TAU( * ), WORK( LWORK )
```

Purpose

SORGQR/CUNGQR generates an m-by-n real/complex matrix Q with orthonormal columns, which is defined as the first n columns of a product of k elementary reflectors H_i of order m

$$Q = H_1 H_2 \cdots H_k$$

as returned by SGEQRF/CGEQRF.

Arguments

M
(input) INTEGER
The number of rows of the matrix Q. M $\geq$ 0.

N
(input) INTEGER
The number of columns of the matrix Q. M $\geq$ N $\geq$ 0.

K
(input) INTEGER
The number of elementary reflectors whose product defines the matrix Q. N $\geq$ K $\geq$ 0.

A
(input/output) REAL/COMPLEX array, dimension (LDA,N)
On entry, the ith column must contain the vector which defines the elementary reflector H_i, for i = 1,2,...,k, as returned by SGEQRF/CGEQRF in the first k columns of its array argument A. On exit, the m-by-n matrix Q.

LDA
(input) INTEGER
The first dimension of the array A. LDA $\geq$ max(1,M).

TAU
(input) REAL/COMPLEX array, dimension (K)
TAU(i) must contain the scalar factor of the elementary reflector H_i, as returned by SGEQRF/CGEQRF.

WORK
(workspace) REAL/COMPLEX array, dimension (LWORK)
On exit, if INFO = 0, WORK(1) returns the optimal LWORK.

LWORK
(input) INTEGER
The dimension of the array WORK. LWORK $\geq$ max(1,N). For optimum performance LWORK $\geq$ N*NB, where NB is the optimal block size.

INFO
(output) INTEGER
= 0: successful exit;
< 0: if INFO = $-i$, the ith argument has an illegal value

SORGRQ/CUNGRQ

```
SUBROUTINE SORGRQ( M, N, K, A, LDA, TAU, WORK, LWORK, INFO )
INTEGER    INFO, K, LDA, LWORK, M, N
REAL       A( LDA, * ), TAU( * ), WORK( LWORK )

SUBROUTINE CUNGRQ( M, N, K, A, LDA, TAU, WORK, LWORK, INFO )
INTEGER    INFO, K, LDA, LWORK, M, N
COMPLEX    A( LDA, * ), TAU( * ), WORK( LWORK )
```

Purpose

SORGRQ/CUNGRQ generates an m-by-n real/complex matrix Q with orthonormal rows, which is defined as the last m rows of a product of k elementary reflectors H_i of order n

$$Q = H_1 H_2 \cdots H_k \quad (SORGRQ)$$

$$Q = H_1^H H_2^H \cdots H_k^H \quad (CUNGRQ)$$

as returned by SGERQF/CGERQF.

Arguments

M
(input) INTEGER
The number of rows of the matrix Q. M $\geq$ 0.

N
(input) INTEGER
The number of columns of the matrix Q. N $\geq$ M.

SORGRQ/CUNGRQ

K (input) INTEGER
The number of elementary reflectors whose product defines the matrix Q. $M \geq K \geq 0$.

A (input/output) REAL/COMPLEX array, dimension (LDA,N)
On entry, the $(m-k+i)^{th}$ row must contain the vector which defines the elementary reflector H_i, for $i = 1,2,\ldots k$, as returned by SGERQF/CGERQF in the last k rows of its array argument A.
On exit, the m-by-n matrix Q.

LDA (input) INTEGER
The leading dimension of the array A. $LDA \geq \max(1,M)$.

TAU (input) REAL/COMPLEX array, dimension (K)
TAU(i) must contain the scalar factor of the elementary reflector H_i, as returned by SGERQF/CGERQF.

WORK (workspace) REAL/COMPLEX array, dimension (LWORK)
On exit, if INFO = 0, WORK(1) returns the optimal LWORK.

LWORK (input) INTEGER
The dimension of the array WORK. $LWORK \geq \max(1,M)$. For optimum performance $LWORK \geq M*NB$, where NB is the optimal block size.

INFO (output) INTEGER
= 0:   successful exit
< 0:   if INFO = $-i$, the ith argument has an illegal value

SORGTR/CUNGTR

```
SUBROUTINE SORGTR( UPLO, N, A, LDA, TAU, WORK, LWORK, INFO )
CHARACTER     UPLO
INTEGER       INFO, LDA, LWORK, N
REAL          A( LDA, * ), TAU( * ), WORK( LWORK )

SUBROUTINE CUNGTR( UPLO, N, A, LDA, TAU, WORK, LWORK, INFO )
CHARACTER     UPLO
INTEGER       INFO, LDA, LWORK, N
COMPLEX       A( LDA, * ), TAU( * ), WORK( LWORK )
```

Purpose

SORGTR/CUNGTR generates a real/complex orthogonal/unitary matrix Q which is defined as the product of n−1 elementary H_i reflectors of order n, as returned by SSYTRD/CHETRD:

if UPLO = 'U', $Q = H_{n-1} \cdots H_2 H_1$,

if UPLO = 'L', $Q = H_1 H_2 \cdots H_{n-1}$.

Arguments

UPLO (input) CHARACTER*1
= 'U':   Upper triangle of A contains elementary reflectors from SSYTRD/CHETRD;
= 'L':   Lower triangle of A contains elementary reflectors from SSYTRD/CHETRD.

N (input) INTEGER
The order of the matrix Q. $N \geq 0$.

A (input/output) REAL/COMPLEX array, dimension (LDA,N)
On entry, the vectors which define the elementary reflectors, as returned by SSYTRD/CHETRD.
On exit, the n-by-n orthogonal/unitary matrix Q.

LDA (input) INTEGER
The leading dimension of the array A. $LDA \geq \max(1,N)$.

TAU (input) REAL/COMPLEX array, dimension (N−1)
TAU(i) must contain the scalar factor of the elementary reflector H_i, as returned by SSYTRD/CHETRD.

WORK (workspace) REAL/COMPLEX array, dimension (LWORK)
On exit, if INFO = 0, WORK(1) returns the optimal LWORK.

LWORK (input) INTEGER
The dimension of the array WORK. $LWORK \geq \max(1,N-1)$. For optimum performance $LWORK \geq (N-1)*NB$, where NB is the optimal block size.

INFO (output) INTEGER
= 0:   successful exit
< 0:   if INFO = $-i$, the ith argument had an illegal value

SORMBR/CUNMBR

```
SUBROUTINE SORMBR( VECT, SIDE, TRANS, M, N, K, A, LDA, TAU, C,
$                  LDC, WORK, LWORK, INFO )
CHARACTER     SIDE, TRANS, VECT
INTEGER       INFO, K, LDA, LDC, LWORK, M, N
REAL          A( LDA, * ), C( LDC, * ), TAU( * ),
$                  WORK( LWORK )

SUBROUTINE CUNMBR( VECT, SIDE, TRANS, M, N, K, A, LDA, TAU, C,
$                  LDC, WORK, LWORK, INFO )
CHARACTER     SIDE, TRANS, VECT
INTEGER       INFO, K, LDA, LDC, LWORK, M, N
COMPLEX       A( LDA, * ), C( LDC, * ), TAU( * ),
$                  WORK( LWORK )
```

Purpose

If VECT = 'Q', SORMBR/CUNMBR overwrites the general real/complex m-by-n matrix C with

	SIDE = 'L'	SIDE = 'R'	
TRANS = 'N':	Q*C	C*Q	
TRANS = 'T':	Q^T*C	C*Q^T	(*SORMBR only*)
TRANS = 'C':	Q^H*C	C*Q^H	(*CUNMBR only*)

If VECT = 'P', SORMBR/CUNMBR overwrites the general real/complex m-by-n matrix C with

	SIDE = 'L'	SIDE = 'R'	
TRANS = 'N':	P*C	C*P	
TRANS = 'T':	P^T*C	C*P^T	(*SORMBR only*)
TRANS = 'C':	P^H*C	C*P^H	(*CUNMBR only*)

Here Q and P^H are the orthogonal/unitary matrices determined by SGEBRD/CGEBRD when reducing a real/complex matrix A to bidiagonal form: $A = Q*B*P^H$. Q and P^H are defined as products of elementary reflectors H_i and G_i respectively.

Let NQ = M if SIDE = 'L' and NQ = N if SIDE = 'R'. Thus NQ is the order of the orthogonal/unitary matrix Q or P^H that is applied.

If VECT = 'Q', A is assumed to have been an nq-by-k matrix: if NQ ≥ K, $Q = H_1 H_2 \cdots H_k$; if NQ < K, $Q = H_1 H_2 \cdots H_{nq-1}$.

If VECT = 'P', A is assumed to have been a k-by-nq matrix: if K < NQ, $P = G_1 G_2 \cdots G_k$; if K ≥ NQ, $P = G_1 G_2 \cdots G_{nq-1}$.

Arguments

VECT   (input) CHARACTER*1
= 'Q': apply Q or Q^H;
= 'P': apply P or P^H.

SIDE   (input) CHARACTER*1
= 'L': apply Q, Q^H, P or P^H from the Left;
= 'R': apply Q, Q^H, P or P^H from the Right.

TRANS   (input) CHARACTER*1
= 'N': No transpose, apply Q or P
= 'T': Transpose, apply Q^T or P^T (*SORMBR only*)
= 'C': Conjugate transpose, apply Q^H or P^H (*CUNMBR only*)

M   (input) INTEGER
The number of rows of the matrix C. M ≥ 0.

N   (input) INTEGER
The number of columns of the matrix C. N ≥ 0.

K   (input) INTEGER
If VECT = 'Q', the number of columns in the original matrix reduced by SGEBRD/CGEBRD. If VECT = 'P', the number of rows in the original matrix reduced by SGEBRD/CGEBRD. K ≥ 0.

A   (input) REAL/COMPLEX array, dimension
(LDA,min(NQ,K)) if VECT = 'Q', or (LDA,NQ) if VECT = 'P'
The vectors which define the elementary reflectors H_i and G_i, whose products determine the matrices Q and P, as returned by SGEBRD/CGEBRD. A is modified by the routine but restored on exit.

LDA   (input) INTEGER
The leading dimension of the array A. If VECT = 'Q', LDA ≥ max(1,NQ); if VECT = 'P', LDA ≥ max(1,min(NQ,K)).

TAU   (input) REAL/COMPLEX array, dimension (min(NQ,K))
TAU(i) must contain the scalar factor of the elementary reflector H_i or G_i, which determines Q or P, as returned by SGEBRD/CGEBRD in the array argument TAUQ or TAUP.

C   (input/output) REAL/COMPLEX array, dimension (LDC,N)
On entry, the m-by-n matrix C.
On exit, C is overwritten by Q*C or Q^H*C or C*Q^H or C*Q or P*C or P^H*C or C*P or C*P^H.

LDC   (input) INTEGER
The leading dimension of the array C. LDC ≥ max(1,M).

WORK   (workspace) REAL/COMPLEX array, dimension (LWORK)
On exit, if INFO = 0, WORK(1) returns the optimal LWORK.

LWORK   (input) INTEGER
The dimension of the array WORK.
If SIDE = 'L', LWORK ≥ max(1,N);
if SIDE = 'R', LWORK ≥ max(1,M).
For optimum performance LWORK ≥ N*NB if SIDE = 'L', and ≥ M*NB if SIDE = 'R', where NB is the optimal block size.

INFO   (output) INTEGER
= 0:   successful exit
< 0:   if INFO = -i, the ith argument had an illegal value

SORMHR/CUNMHR

```
SUBROUTINE SORMHR( SIDE, TRANS, M, N, ILO, IHI, A, LDA, TAU, C,
$                  LDC, WORK, LWORK, INFO )
    CHARACTER     SIDE, TRANS
    INTEGER       IHI, ILO, INFO, LDA, LDC, LWORK, M, N
    REAL          A( LDA, * ), C( LDC, * ), TAU( * ),
$                 WORK( LWORK )
```

```
SUBROUTINE CUNMHR( SIDE, TRANS, M, N, ILO, IHI, A, LDA, TAU, C,
$                  LDC, WORK, LWORK, INFO )
    CHARACTER      SIDE, TRANS
    INTEGER        IHI, ILO, INFO, LDA, LDC, LWORK, M, N
    COMPLEX        A( LDA, * ), C( LDC, * ), TAU( * ),
$                  WORK( LWORK )
```

Purpose

SORMHR/CUNMHR overwrites the general real/complex m-by-n matrix C with

	SIDE = 'L'	SIDE = 'R'	
TRANS = 'N':	$Q*C$	$C*Q$	
TRANS = 'T':	Q^T*C	$C*Q^T$	(*SORMHR only*)
TRANS = 'C':	Q^H*C	$C*Q^H$	(*CUNMHR only*)

where Q is a real/complex orthogonal/unitary matrix of order NQ, with NQ = M if SIDE = 'L' and NQ = N if SIDE = 'R'. Q is defined as the product of IHI–ILO elementary reflectors H_i, as returned by SGEHRD/CGEHRD:

$$Q = H_{ilo} H_{ilo+1} \cdots H_{ihi-1}.$$

Arguments

SIDE   (input) CHARACTER*1
        = 'L': apply Q or Q^H from the Left;
        = 'R': apply Q or Q^H from the Right.

TRANS   (input) CHARACTER*1
        Specifies whether the matrix Q, Q^T, or Q^H is applied to C.
        = 'N': No transpose, apply Q
        = 'T': Transpose, apply Q^T (*SORMHR only*)
        = 'C': Conjugate transpose, apply Q^H (*CUNMHR only*)

M   (input) INTEGER
        The number of rows of the matrix C. M ≥ 0.

N   (input) INTEGER
        The number of columns of the matrix C. N ≥ 0.

ILO, IHI (input) INTEGER
        ILO and IHI must have the same values as in the previous call of SGEHRD/CGEHRD. Q is equal to the unit matrix except in the submatrix Q(ilo+1:ihi,ilo+1:ihi).
        If SIDE = 'L', 1 ≤ ILO and min(M,ILO) ≤ IHI ≤ M;
        if SIDE = 'R', 1 ≤ ILO and min(N,ILO) ≤ IHI ≤ N.

A   (input) REAL/COMPLEX array, dimension
        (LDA,M) if SIDE = 'L', or (LDA,N) if SIDE = 'R'
        The vectors which define the elementary reflectors, as returned by SGEHRD/CGEHRD. A is modified by the routine but restored on exit.

LDA   (input) INTEGER
        The leading dimension of the array A. LDA ≥ max(1,M) if SIDE = 'L'; LDA ≥ max(1,N) if SIDE = 'R'.

TAU   (input) REAL/COMPLEX array, dimension
        (M–1) if SIDE = 'L', or (N–1) if SIDE = 'R'
        TAU(i) must contain the scalar factor of the elementary reflector H_i, as returned by SGEHRD/CGEHRD.

C   (input/output) REAL/COMPLEX array, dimension (LDC,N)
        On entry, the m-by-n matrix C.
        On exit, C is overwritten by Q*C or Q^H*C or $C*Q^H$ or C*Q.

LDC   (input) INTEGER
        The leading dimension of the array C. LDC ≥ max(1,M).

WORK   (workspace) REAL/COMPLEX array, dimension (LWORK)
        On exit, if INFO = 0, WORK(1) returns the optimal LWORK.

LWORK   (input) INTEGER
        The dimension of the array WORK. If SIDE = 'L', LWORK ≥ max(1,N); if SIDE = 'R', LWORK ≥ max(1,M). For optimum performance LWORK ≥ N*NB if SIDE = 'L' and ≥ M*NB if SIDE = 'R', where NB is the optimal block size.

INFO   (output) INTEGER
        = 0: successful exit
        < 0: if INFO = –i, the ith argument had an illegal value

SORMLQ/CUNMLQ

```
SUBROUTINE SORMLQ( SIDE, TRANS, M, N, K, A, LDA, TAU, C, LDC,
$                  WORK, LWORK, INFO )
    CHARACTER      SIDE, TRANS
    INTEGER        INFO, K, LDA, LDC, LWORK, M, N
    REAL           A( LDA, * ), C( LDC, * ), TAU( * ),
$                  WORK( LWORK )

SUBROUTINE CUNMLQ( SIDE, TRANS, M, N, K, A, LDA, TAU, C, LDC,
$                  WORK, LWORK, INFO )
    CHARACTER      SIDE, TRANS
    INTEGER        INFO, K, LDA, LDC, LWORK, M, N
    COMPLEX        A( LDA, * ), C( LDC, * ), TAU( * ),
$                  WORK( LWORK )
```

Purpose

SORMLQ/CUNMLQ overwrites the general real/complex m-by-n matrix C with

	SIDE = 'L'	SIDE = 'R'	
TRANS = 'N':	$Q*C$	$C*Q$	
TRANS = 'T':	Q^T*C	$C*Q^T$	(*SORMLQ only*)
TRANS = 'C':	Q^H*C	$C*Q^H$	(*CUNMLQ only*)

LWORK (input) INTEGER
       The dimension of the array WORK. If SIDE = 'L', LWORK $\geq$ max(1,N); if SIDE = 'R', LWORK $\geq$ max(1,M). For optimum performance LWORK $\geq$ N*NB if SIDE = 'L', and LWORK $\geq$ M*NB if SIDE = 'R', where NB is the optimal block size.

INFO   (output) INTEGER
       = 0: successful exit
       < 0: if INFO = $-i$, the ith argument had an illegal value

---

SORMQL/CUNMQL

```
SUBROUTINE SORMQL( SIDE, TRANS, M, N, K, A, LDA, TAU, C, LDC,
$                  WORK, LWORK, INFO )
CHARACTER          SIDE, TRANS
INTEGER            INFO, K, LDA, LDC, LWORK, M, N
REAL               A( LDA, * ), C( LDC, * ), TAU( * ),
$                  WORK( LWORK )

SUBROUTINE CUNMQL( SIDE, TRANS, M, N, K, A, LDA, TAU, C, LDC,
$                  WORK, LWORK, INFO )
CHARACTER          SIDE, TRANS
INTEGER            INFO, K, LDA, LDC, LWORK, M, N
COMPLEX            A( LDA, * ), C( LDC, * ), TAU( * ),
$                  WORK( LWORK )
```

Purpose

SORMQL/CUNMQL overwrites the general real/complex m-by-n matrix C with

	SIDE = 'L'	SIDE = 'R'
TRANS = 'N':	Q*C	C*Q
TRANS = 'T':	Q^T*C	C*Q^T	(SORMQL only)
TRANS = 'C':	Q^H*C	C*Q^H	(CUNMQL only)

where Q is a real/complex orthogonal/unitary matrix defined as the product of k elementary reflectors H_i

$$Q = H_k \cdots H_2 H_1$$

as returned by SGEQLF/CGEQLF. Q is of order m if SIDE = 'L' and of order n if SIDE = 'R'.

Arguments

SIDE   (input) CHARACTER*1
       = 'L': apply Q or Q^H from the Left;
       = 'R': apply Q or Q^H from the Right.

---

where Q is a real/complex orthogonal/unitary matrix defined as the product of k elementary reflectors H_i

$$Q = H_k \cdots H_2 H_1 \quad (SORMLQ)$$
$$Q = H_k^H \cdots H_2^H H_1^H \quad (CUNMLQ)$$

as returned by SGELQF/CGELQF. Q is of order m if SIDE = 'L' and of order n if SIDE = 'R'.

Arguments

SIDE   (input) CHARACTER*1
       = 'L': apply Q or Q^H from the Left;
       = 'R': apply Q or Q^H from the Right.

TRANS (input) CHARACTER*1
       = 'N': No transpose, apply Q
       = 'T': Transpose, apply Q^T (SORMLQ only)
       = 'C': Conjugate transpose, apply Q^H (CUNMLQ only)

M   (input) INTEGER
       The number of rows of the matrix C. M $\geq$ 0.

N   (input) INTEGER
       The number of columns of the matrix C. N $\geq$ 0.

K   (input) INTEGER
       The number of elementary reflectors whose product defines the matrix Q. If SIDE = 'L', M $\geq$ K $\geq$ 0; if SIDE = 'R', N $\geq$ K $\geq$ 0.

A   (input) REAL/COMPLEX array, dimension
       (LDA,M) if SIDE = 'L', or (LDA,N) if SIDE = 'R'.
       The ith row must contain the vector which defines the elementary reflector H_i, for i = 1,2,...,k, as returned by SGELQF/CGELQF in the first k rows of its array argument A. A is modified by the routine but restored on exit.

LDA   (input) INTEGER
       The leading dimension of the array A. LDA $\geq$ max(1,K).

TAU   (input) REAL/COMPLEX array, dimension (K)
       TAU(i) must contain the scalar factor of the elementary reflector H_i, as returned by SGELQF/CGELQF.

C   (input/output) REAL/COMPLEX array, dimension (LDC,N)
       On entry, the m-by-n matrix C.
       On exit, C is overwritten by Q*C or Q^H*C or C*Q^H or C*Q.

LDC   (input) INTEGER
       The leading dimension of the array C. LDC $\geq$ max(1,M).

WORK   (workspace) REAL/COMPLEX array, dimension (LWORK)
       On exit, if INFO = 0, WORK(1) returns the optimal LWORK.

TRANS   (input) CHARACTER*1
= 'N':   No transpose, apply Q
= 'T':   Transpose, apply Q^T (SORMQL only)
= 'C':   Conjugate transpose, apply Q^H (CUNMQL only)

M   (input) INTEGER
The number of rows of the matrix C. $M \geq 0$.

N   (input) INTEGER
The number of columns of the matrix C. $N \geq 0$.

K   (input) INTEGER
The number of elementary reflectors whose product defines the matrix Q. If SIDE = 'L', $M \geq K \geq 0$; if SIDE = 'R', $N \geq K \geq 0$.

A   (input) REAL/COMPLEX array, dimension (LDA,K)
The ith column must contain the vector which defines the elementary reflector H_i, for i = 1,2,...,k, as returned by SGEQLF/CGEQLF in the last k columns of its array argument A. A is modified by the routine but restored on exit.

LDA   (input) INTEGER
The leading dimension of the array A. If SIDE = 'L', LDA $\geq$ max(1,M); if SIDE = 'R', LDA $\geq$ max(1,N).

TAU   (input) REAL/COMPLEX array, dimension (K)
TAU(i) must contain the scalar factor of the elementary reflector H_i, as returned by SGEQLF/CGEQLF.

C   (input/output) REAL/COMPLEX array, dimension (LDC,N)
On entry, the m-by-n matrix C.
On exit, C is overwritten by Q*C or Q^H*C or $C*Q^H$ or C*Q.

LDC   (input) INTEGER
The leading dimension of the array C. LDC $\geq$ max(1,M).

WORK   (workspace) REAL/COMPLEX array, dimension (LWORK)
On exit, if INFO = 0, WORK(1) returns the optimal LWORK.

LWORK   (input) INTEGER
The dimension of the array WORK. If SIDE = 'L', LWORK $\geq$ max(1,N); if SIDE = 'R', LWORK $\geq$ max(1,M). For optimum performance LWORK $\geq$ N*NB if SIDE = 'L', and LWORK $\geq$ M*NB if SIDE = 'R', where NB is the optimal block size.

INFO   (output) INTEGER
= 0:   successful exit
< 0:   if INFO = -i, the ith argument had an illegal value

SORMQR/CUNMQR

```
SUBROUTINE SORMQR( SIDE, TRANS, M, N, K, A, LDA, TAU, C, LDC,
$                  WORK, LWORK, INFO )
    CHARACTER      SIDE, TRANS
    INTEGER        INFO, K, LDA, LDC, LWORK, M, N
    REAL           A( LDA, * ), C( LDC, * ), TAU( * ),
$                  WORK( LWORK )

SUBROUTINE CUNMQR( SIDE, TRANS, M, N, K, A, LDA, TAU, C, LDC,
$                  WORK, LWORK, INFO )
    CHARACTER      SIDE, TRANS
    INTEGER        INFO, K, LDA, LDC, LWORK, M, N
    COMPLEX        A( LDA, * ), C( LDC, * ), TAU( * ),
$                  WORK( LWORK )
```

Purpose

SORMQR/CUNMQR overwrites the general real/complex m-by-n matrix C with

	SIDE = 'L'	SIDE = 'R'
TRANS = 'N':	Q*C	C*Q
TRANS = 'T':	Q^T*C	$C*Q^T$	(SORMQR only)
TRANS = 'C':	Q^H*C	$C*Q^H$	(CUNMQR only)

where Q is a real/complex orthogonal/unitary matrix defined as the product of k elementary reflectors H_i:

$$Q = H_1 H_2 \cdots H_k$$

as returned by SGEQRF/CGEQRF. Q is of order m if SIDE = 'L' and of order n if SIDE = 'R'.

Arguments

SIDE   (input) CHARACTER*1
= 'L':   apply Q or Q^H from the Left;
= 'R':   apply Q or Q^H from the Right.

TRANS   (input) CHARACTER*1
= 'N':   No transpose, apply Q
= 'T':   Transpose, apply Q^T (SORMQR only)
= 'C':   Conjugate transpose, apply Q^H (CUNMQR only)

M   (input) INTEGER
The number of rows of the matrix C. $M \geq 0$.

N   (input) INTEGER
The number of columns of the matrix C. $N \geq 0$.

K   (input) INTEGER
The number of elementary reflectors whose product defines the matrix Q. If SIDE = 'L', $M \geq K \geq 0$; if SIDE = 'R', $N \geq K \geq 0$.

A   (input) REAL/COMPLEX array, dimension (LDA,K)
The ith column must contain the vector which defines the elementary reflector H_i, for $i = 1,2,\ldots,k$, as returned by SGEQRF/CGEQRF in the first k columns of its array argument A. A is modified by the routine but restored on exit.

LDA   (input) INTEGER
The leading dimension of the array A. If SIDE = 'L', LDA $\geq$ max(1,M); if SIDE = 'R', LDA $\geq$ max(1,N).

TAU   (input) REAL/COMPLEX array, dimension (K)
TAU(i) must contain the scalar factor of the elementary reflector H_i, as returned by SGEQRF/CGEQRF.

C   (input/output) REAL/COMPLEX array, dimension (LDC,N)
On entry, the m-by-n matrix C.
On exit, C is overwritten by Q*C or Q^H*C or C*Q^H or C*Q.

LDC   (input) INTEGER
The leading dimension of the array C. LDC $\geq$ max(1,M).

WORK   (workspace) REAL/COMPLEX array, dimension (LWORK)
On exit, if INFO = 0, WORK(1) returns the optimal LWORK.

LWORK   (input) INTEGER
The dimension of the array WORK. If SIDE = 'L', LWORK $\geq$ max(1,N); if SIDE = 'R', LWORK $\geq$ max(1,M). For optimum performance LWORK $\geq$ N*NB if SIDE = 'L' and $\geq$ M*NB if SIDE = 'R', where NB is the optimal block size.

INFO   (output) INTEGER
= 0: successful exit
< 0: if INFO = $-i$, the ith argument had an illegal value

SORMRQ/CUNMRQ

```
SUBROUTINE SORMRQ( SIDE, TRANS, M, N, K, A, LDA, TAU, C, LDC,
$                  WORK, LWORK, INFO )
CHARACTER          SIDE, TRANS
INTEGER            INFO, K, LDA, LDC, LWORK, M, N
REAL               A( LDA, * ), C( LDC, * ), TAU( * ),
$                  WORK( LWORK )

SUBROUTINE CUNMRQ( SIDE, TRANS, M, N, K, A, LDA, TAU, C, LDC,
$                  WORK, LWORK, INFO )
CHARACTER          SIDE, TRANS
INTEGER            INFO, K, LDA, LDC, LWORK, M, N
COMPLEX            A( LDA, * ), C( LDC, * ), TAU( * ),
$                  WORK( LWORK )
```

Purpose

SORMRQ/CUNMRQ overwrites the general real/complex m-by-n matrix C with

	SIDE = 'L'	SIDE = 'R'	
TRANS = 'N':	Q*C	C*Q	
TRANS = 'T':	Q^T*C	C*Q^T	(SORMRQ only)
TRANS = 'C':	Q^H*C	C*Q^H	(CUNMRQ only)

where Q is a real/complex orthogonal/unitary matrix defined as the product of k elementary reflectors H_i

$Q = H_1 H_2 \ldots H_k$ (SORMRQ)

$Q = H_1{}^H H_2{}^H \ldots H_k{}^H$ (CUNMRQ)

as returned by SGERQF/CGERQF. Q is of order m if SIDE = 'L' and of order n if SIDE = 'R'.

Arguments

SIDE   (input) CHARACTER*1
= 'L': apply Q or Q^H from the Left;
= 'R': apply Q or Q^H from the Right.

TRANS   (input) CHARACTER*1
= 'N': No transpose, apply Q
= 'T': Transpose, apply Q^T (SORMRQ only)
= 'C': Conjugate transpose, apply Q^H (CUNMRQ only)

M   (input) INTEGER
The number of rows of the matrix C. M $\geq$ 0.

N   (input) INTEGER
The number of columns of the matrix C. N $\geq$ 0.

K   (input) INTEGER
The number of elementary reflectors whose product defines the matrix Q. If SIDE = 'L', M $\geq$ K $\geq$ 0; if SIDE = 'R', N $\geq$ K $\geq$ 0.

A   (input) REAL/COMPLEX array, dimension (LDA,M) if SIDE = 'L', or (LDA,N) if SIDE = 'R'
The ith row must contain the vector which defines the elementary reflector H_i, for $i = 1,2,\ldots,k$, as returned by SGERQF/CGERQF in the last k rows of its array argument A. A is modified by the routine but restored on exit.

LDA   (input) INTEGER
The leading dimension of the array A. LDA $\geq$ max(1,K).

TAU   (input) REAL/COMPLEX array, dimension (K)
TAU(i) must contain the scalar factor of the elementary reflector H_i, as returned by SGERQF/CGERQF.

C　(input/output) REAL/COMPLEX array, dimension (LDC,N)
On entry, the m-by-n matrix C.
On exit, C is overwritten by $Q*C$ or Q^H*C or $C*Q^H$ or $C*Q$.

LDC　(input) INTEGER
The leading dimension of the array C. LDC $\geq$ max(1,M).

WORK　(workspace) REAL/COMPLEX array, dimension (LWORK)
On exit, if INFO = 0, WORK(1) returns the optimal LWORK.

LWORK　(input) INTEGER
The dimension of the array WORK. If SIDE = 'L', LWORK $\geq$ max(1,N); if SIDE = 'R', LWORK $\geq$ max(1,M). For optimum performance LWORK $\geq$ N*NB if SIDE = 'L' and LWORK $\geq$ M*NB if SIDE = 'R', where NB is the optimal block size.

INFO　(output) INTEGER
= 0: successful exit
< 0: if INFO = $-i$, the ith argument had an illegal value

SORMTR/CUNMTR

```
SUBROUTINE SORMTR( SIDE, UPLO, TRANS, M, N, A, LDA, TAU, C, LDC,
$                  WORK, LWORK, INFO )
    CHARACTER         SIDE, TRANS, UPLO
    INTEGER           INFO, LDA, LDC, LWORK, M, N
    REAL              A( LDA, * ), C( LDC, * ), TAU( * ),
$                     WORK( LWORK )

SUBROUTINE CUNMTR( SIDE, UPLO, TRANS, M, N, A, LDA, TAU, C, LDC,
$                  WORK, LWORK, INFO )
    CHARACTER         SIDE, TRANS, UPLO
    INTEGER           INFO, LDA, LDC, LWORK, M, N
    COMPLEX           A( LDA, * ), C( LDC, * ), TAU( * ),
$                     WORK( LWORK )
```

Purpose

SORMTR/CUNMTR overwrites the general real/complex m-by-n matrix C with

	SIDE = 'L'	SIDE = 'R'	
TRANS = 'N':	$Q*C$	$C*Q$	
TRANS = 'T':	Q^T*C	$C*Q^T$	(SORMTR only)
TRANS = 'C':	Q^H*C	$C*Q^H$	(CUNMTR only)

where Q is a real/complex orthogonal/unitary matrix of order NQ, with NQ = M if SIDE = 'L' and NQ = N if SIDE = 'R'. Q is defined as the product of NQ−1 elementary reflectors H_i, as returned by SSYTRD/CHETRD:

if UPLO = 'U', $Q = H_{nq-1} \cdots H_2 H_1$;

if UPLO = 'L', $Q = H_1 H_2 \cdots H_{nq-1}$.

Arguments

SIDE　(input) CHARACTER*1
= 'L': apply Q or Q^H from the Left;
= 'R': apply Q or Q^H from the Right.

UPLO　(input) CHARACTER*1
= 'U': Upper triangle of A contains elementary reflectors from SSYTRD/CHETRD;
= 'L': Lower triangle of A contains elementary reflectors from SSYTRD/CHETRD.

TRANS　(input) CHARACTER*1
= 'N': No transpose, apply Q
= 'T': Transpose, apply Q^T (SORMTR only)
= 'C': Conjugate transpose, apply Q^H (CUNMTR only)

M　(input) INTEGER
The number of rows of the matrix C. M $\geq$ 0.

N　(input) INTEGER
The number of columns of the matrix C. N $\geq$ 0.

A　(input) REAL/COMPLEX array, dimension (LDA,M) if SIDE = 'L', or (LDA,N) if SIDE = 'R'
The vectors which define the elementary reflectors, as returned by SSYTRD/CHETRD. A is modified by the routine but restored on exit.

LDA　(input) INTEGER
The leading dimension of the array A. LDA $\geq$ max(1,M) if SIDE = 'L'; LDA $\geq$ max(1,N) if SIDE = 'R'.

TAU　(input) REAL/COMPLEX array, dimension (M−1) if SIDE = 'L', or (N−1) if SIDE = 'R'
TAU(i) must contain the scalar factor of the elementary reflector H_i, as returned by SSYTRD/CHETRD.

C　(input/output) REAL/COMPLEX array, dimension (LDC,N)
On entry, the m-by-n matrix C.
On exit, C is overwritten by $Q*C$ or Q^H*C or $C*Q^H$ or $C*Q$.

LDC　(input) INTEGER
The leading dimension of the array C. LDC $\geq$ max(1,M).

WORK　(workspace) REAL/COMPLEX array, dimension (LWORK)
On exit, if INFO = 0, WORK(1) returns the optimal LWORK.

LWORK　(input) INTEGER
The dimension of the array WORK. If SIDE = 'L', LWORK $\geq$ max(1,N); if SIDE = 'R', LWORK $\geq$ max(1,M). For optimum performance LWORK $\geq$ N*NB if SIDE = 'L' and $\geq$ M*NB if SIDE = 'R', where NB is the optimal block size.

INFO　(output) INTEGER

= 0: successful exit
< 0: if INFO = -i, the ith argument had an illegal value

SPBCON/CPBCON

```
SUBROUTINE SPBCON( UPLO, N, KD, AB, LDAB, ANORM, RCOND, WORK,
$                   IWORK, INFO )
    CHARACTER         UPLO
    INTEGER           INFO, KD, LDAB, N
    REAL              ANORM, RCOND
    INTEGER           IWORK( * )
    REAL              AB( LDAB, * ), WORK( * )

SUBROUTINE CPBCON( UPLO, N, KD, AB, LDAB, ANORM, RCOND, WORK,
$                   RWORK, INFO )
    CHARACTER         UPLO
    INTEGER           INFO, KD, LDAB, N
    REAL              ANORM, RCOND
    REAL              RWORK( * )
    COMPLEX           AB( LDAB, * ), WORK( * )
```

Purpose

SPBCON/CPBCON estimates the reciprocal of the condition number (in the 1-norm) of a real/complex symmetric/Hermitian positive definite band matrix using the Cholesky factorization $A = U^H*U$ or $A = L*L^H$ computed by SPBTRF/CPBTRF.

An estimate is obtained for $||A^{-1}||$, and the reciprocal of the condition number is computed as RCOND = $1/(||A||.||A^{-1}||)$.

Arguments

UPLO   (input) CHARACTER*1
        = 'U':   Upper triangular factor stored in AB;
        = 'L':   Lower triangular factor stored in AB.

N   (input) INTEGER
        The order of the matrix A. N ≥ 0.

KD   (input) INTEGER
        The number of superdiagonals of the matrix A if UPLO = 'U', or the number of subdiagonals if UPLO = 'L'. KD ≥ 0.

AB   (input) REAL/COMPLEX array, dimension (LDAB,N)
        The triangular factor U or L from the Cholesky factorization $A = U^H*U$ or $A = L*L^H$ of the band matrix A, stored in the first kd+1 rows of the array. The jth column of U or L is stored in j^{th} column of the array AB as follows:
        if UPLO ='U', AB(kd+1+i-jj) = U(ij) for max(1,j-kd)≤i≤j;
        if UPLO ='L', AB(1+i-jj) = L(ij) for j≤i≤min(n,j+kd).

LDAB   (input) INTEGER
        The leading dimension of the array AB. LDAB ≥ KD+1.

ANORM   (input) REAL
        The 1-norm (or infinity-norm) of the symmetric/Hermitian band matrix A.

RCOND   (output) REAL
        The reciprocal of the condition number of the matrix A, computed as RCOND = $1/(||A||.||A^{-1}||)$.

WORK   SPBCON (workspace) REAL array, dimension (3*N)
        CPBCON (workspace) COMPLEX array, dimension (2*N)

IWORK   SPBCON only (workspace) INTEGER array, dimension (N)

RWORK   CPBCON only (workspace) REAL array, dimension (N)

INFO   (output) INTEGER
        = 0: successful exit
        < 0: if INFO = -i, the ith argument had an illegal value

SPBEQU/CPBEQU

```
SUBROUTINE SPBEQU( UPLO, N, KD, AB, LDAB, S, SCOND, AMAX, INFO )
    CHARACTER         UPLO
    INTEGER           INFO, KD, LDAB, N
    REAL              AMAX, SCOND
    REAL              AB( LDAB, * ), S( * )

SUBROUTINE CPBEQU( UPLO, N, KD, AB, LDAB, S, SCOND, AMAX, INFO )
    CHARACTER         UPLO
    INTEGER           INFO, KD, LDAB, N
    REAL              AMAX, SCOND
    REAL              S( * )
    COMPLEX           AB( LDAB, * )
```

Purpose

SPBEQU/CPBEQU computes row and column scalings intended to equilibrate a symmetric/Hermitian positive definite band matrix A and reduce its condition number (with respect to the two-norm). S contains the scale factors, $S(i) = 1/\sqrt{(A(i,i))}$, chosen so that the scaled matrix B with elements $B(i,j) = S(i)*A(i,j)*S(j)$ has ones on the diagonal. This choice of S puts the condition number of B within a factor N of the smallest possible condition number over all possible diagonal scalings.

Arguments

UPLO (input) CHARACTER*1
= 'U': Upper triangle of A is stored;
= 'L': Lower triangle of A is stored.

N (input) INTEGER
The order of the matrix A. $N \geq 0$.

KD (input) INTEGER
The number of superdiagonals of the matrix A if UPLO = 'U', or the number of subdiagonals if UPLO = 'L'. $KD \geq 0$.

AB (input) REAL/COMPLEX array, dimension (LDAB,N)
The upper or lower triangle of the symmetric/Hermitian band matrix A, stored in the first kd+1 rows of the array. The jth column of A is stored in the jth column of the array AB as follows:
if UPLO = 'U', AB(kd+1+i-j,j) = A(i,j) for max(1,j-kd)$\leq i \leq j$;
if UPLO = 'L', AB(1+i-j,j) = A(i,j) for $j \leq i \leq$ min(n,j+kd).

LDAB (input) INTEGER
The leading dimension of the array A. LDAB $\geq$ KD+1.

S (output) REAL array, dimension (N)
If INFO = 0, S contains the scale factors for A.

SCOND (output) REAL
If INFO = 0, S contains the ratio of the smallest S(i) to the largest S(i). If SCOND $\geq$ 0.1 and AMAX is neither too large nor too small, it is not worth scaling by S.

AMAX (output) REAL
Absolute value of largest matrix element. If AMAX is very close to overflow or very close to underflow, the matrix should be scaled.

INFO (output) INTEGER
= 0: successful exit
< 0: if INFO = −i, the ith argument had an illegal value.
> 0: if INFO = i, the ith diagonal element is nonpositive.

SPBRFS/CPBRFS

```
SUBROUTINE SPBRFS( UPLO, N, KD, NRHS, AB, LDAB, AFB, LDAFB, B,
$                  LDB, X, LDX, FERR, BERR, WORK, IWORK, INFO )
      CHARACTER    UPLO
      INTEGER      INFO, KD, LDAB, LDAFB, LDB, LDX, N, NRHS
      INTEGER      IWORK( * )
      REAL         AB( LDAB, * ), AFB( LDAFB, * ), B( LDB, * ),
$                  BERR( * ), FERR( * ), WORK( * ), X( LDX, * )
```

```
SUBROUTINE CPBRFS( UPLO, N, KD, NRHS, AB, LDAB, AFB, LDAFB, B,
$                  LDB, X, LDX, FERR, BERR, WORK, RWORK, INFO )
      CHARACTER    UPLO
      INTEGER      INFO, KD, LDAB, LDAFB, LDB, LDX, N, NRHS
      REAL         BERR( * ), FERR( * ), RWORK( * )
      COMPLEX      AB( LDAB, * ), AFB( LDAFB, * ), B( LDB, * ),
$                  WORK( * ), X( LDX, * )
```

Purpose

SPBRFS/CPBRFS improves the computed solution to a system of linear equations when the coefficient matrix is symmetric/Hermitian positive definite and banded, and provides error bounds and backward error estimates for the solution.

Arguments

UPLO (input) CHARACTER*1
= 'U': Upper triangle of A is stored;
= 'L': Lower triangle of A is stored.

N (input) INTEGER
The order of the matrix A. $N \geq 0$.

KD (input) INTEGER
The number of superdiagonals of the matrix A if UPLO = 'U', or the number of subdiagonals if UPLO = 'L'. $KD \geq 0$.

NRHS (input) INTEGER
The number of right hand sides, i.e., the number of columns of the matrices B and X. NRHS ≥ 0.

AB (input) REAL/COMPLEX array, dimension (LDAB,N)
The upper or lower triangle of the symmetric/Hermitian band matrix A, stored in the first kd+1 rows of the array. The jth column of A is stored in the jth column of the array AB as follows:
if UPLO = 'U', AB(kd+1+i-j,j) = A(i,j) for max(1,j-kd)$\leq i \leq j$;
if UPLO = 'L', AB(1+i-j,j) = A(i,j) for $j \leq i \leq$ min(n,j+kd).

LDAB (input) INTEGER
The leading dimension of the array AB. LDAB $\geq$ KD+1.

AFB (input) REAL/COMPLEX array, dimension (LDAFB,N)
The triangular factor U or L from the Cholesky factorization $A = U^H*U$ or $A = L*L^H$ of the band matrix A as computed by SPBTRF/CPBTRF, in the same storage format as A (see AB).

LDAFB (input) INTEGER
The leading dimension of the array AFB. LDAFB $\geq$ KD+1.

B (input) REAL/COMPLEX array, dimension (LDB,NRHS)
The right hand side matrix B.

LDB (input) INTEGER
The leading dimension of the array B. LDB $\geq$ max(1,N).

L is a lower triangular band matrix, with the same number of superdiagonals or subdiagonals as A. The factored form of A is then used to solve the system of equations A*X = B.

Arguments

UPLO (input) CHARACTER*1
= 'U': Upper triangle of A is stored.
= 'L': Lower triangle of A is stored.

N (input) INTEGER
The number of linear equations, i.e., the order of the matrix A. $N \geq 0$.

KD (input) INTEGER
The number of superdiagonals of the matrix A if UPLO = 'U', or the number of subdiagonals if UPLO = 'L'. $KD \geq 0$.

NRHS (input) INTEGER
The number of right hand sides, i.e., the number of columns of the matrix B. $NRHS \geq 0$.

AB (input/output) REAL/COMPLEX array, dimension (LDAB,N)
On entry, the upper or lower triangle of the symmetric/Hermitian band matrix A, stored in the first kd+1 rows of the array. The jth column of A is stored in the jth column of the array AB as follows:
if UPLO = 'U', $AB(kd+1+i-jj) = A(i,j)$ for $\max(1,j-kd) \leq i \leq j$;
if UPLO = 'L', $AB(1+i-jj) = A(i,j)$ for $j \leq i \leq \min(n,j+kd)$.
On exit, if INFO = 0, the triangular factor U or L from the Cholesky factorization $A = U^H * U$ or $A = L*L^H$, in the same storage format as A.

LDAB (input) INTEGER
The leading dimension of the array AB. $LDAB \geq KD+1$.

B (input/output) REAL/COMPLEX array, dimension (LDB,NRHS)
On entry, the n-by-nrhs right hand side matrix B.
On exit, if INFO = 0, the n-by-nrhs solution matrix X.

LDB (input) INTEGER
The leading dimension of the array B. $LDB \geq \max(1,N)$.

INFO (output) INTEGER
= 0: successful exit
< 0: if INFO = −i, the ith argument had an illegal value
> 0: if INFO = i, the leading minor of order i of A is not positive definite, so the factorization could not be completed, and the solution has not been computed.

X (input/output) REAL/COMPLEX array, dimension (LDX,NRHS)
On entry, the solution matrix X, as computed by SPBTRS/CPBTRS.
On exit, the improved solution matrix X.

LDX (input) INTEGER
The leading dimension of the array X. $LDX \geq \max(1,N)$.

FERR (output) REAL array, dimension (NRHS)
The estimated forward error bound for each solution vector X(j) (the jth column of the solution matrix X). If XTRUE is the true solution corresponding to X(j), FERR(j) bounds the magnitude of the largest element in (X(j) − XTRUE) divided by the magnitude of the largest element in X(j). The quality of the error bound depends on the quality of the estimate of $\|A^{-1}\|$ computed in the code; if the estimate of $\|A^{-1}\|$ is accurate, the error bound is guaranteed.

BERR (output) REAL array, dimension (NRHS)
The componentwise relative backward error of each solution vector X(j) (i.e., the smallest relative change in any element of A or B that makes X(j) an exact solution).

WORK SPBRFS (workspace) REAL array, dimension (3*N)
CPBRFS (workspace) COMPLEX array, dimension (2*N)

IWORK SPBRFS only (workspace) INTEGER array, dimension (N)

RWORK CPBRFS only (workspace) REAL array, dimension (N)

INFO (output) INTEGER
= 0: successful exit
< 0: if INFO = −i, the ith argument had an illegal value

SPBSV/CPBSV

```
SUBROUTINE SPBSV( UPLO, N, KD, NRHS, AB, LDAB, B, LDB, INFO )
CHARACTER    UPLO
INTEGER      INFO, KD, LDAB, LDB, N, NRHS
REAL         AB( LDAB, * ), B( LDB, * )

SUBROUTINE CPBSV( UPLO, N, KD, NRHS, AB, LDAB, B, LDB, INFO )
CHARACTER    UPLO
INTEGER      INFO, KD, LDAB, LDB, N, NRHS
COMPLEX      AB( LDAB, * ), B( LDB, * )
```

Purpose

SPBSV/CPBSV computes the solution to a real/complex system of linear equations A*X = B, where A is an n-by-n symmetric/Hermitian positive definite band matrix and X and B are n-by-nrhs matrices.

The Cholesky decomposition is used to factor A as $A = U^H * U$, if UPLO = 'U', or $A = L*L^H$, if UPLO = 'L', where U is an upper triangular band matrix and

SPBSVX/CPBSVX

```
SUBROUTINE SPBSVX( FACT, UPLO, N, KD, NRHS, AB, LDAB, AFB, LDAFB,
$                   EQUED, S, B, LDB, X, LDX, RCOND, FERR, BERR,
$                   WORK, IWORK, INFO )
    CHARACTER      EQUED, FACT, UPLO
    INTEGER        INFO, KD, LDAB, LDAFB, LDB, LDX, N, NRHS
    REAL           RCOND
    INTEGER        IWORK( * )
    REAL           AB( LDAB, * ), AFB( LDAFB, * ), B( LDB, * ),
$                   BERR( * ), FERR( * ), S( * ), WORK( * ),
$                   X( LDX, * )

SUBROUTINE CPBSVX( FACT, UPLO, N, KD, NRHS, AB, LDAB, AFB, LDAFB,
$                   EQUED, S, B, LDB, X, LDX, RCOND, FERR, BERR,
$                   WORK, RWORK, INFO )
    CHARACTER      EQUED, FACT, UPLO
    INTEGER        INFO, KD, LDAB, LDAFB, LDB, LDX, N, NRHS
    REAL           RCOND
    REAL           BERR( * ), FERR( * ), RWORK( * ), S( * )
    COMPLEX        AB( LDAB, * ), AFB( LDAFB, * ), B( LDB, * ),
$                   WORK( * ), X( LDX, * )
```

Purpose

SPBSVX/CPBSVX uses the Cholesky factorization $A = U^H*U$ or $A = L*L^H$ to compute the solution to a real/complex system of linear equations $A*X = B$, where A is an n-by-n symmetric/Hermitian positive definite band matrix and X and B are n-by-nrhs matrices.

Error bounds on the solution and a condition estimate are also provided.

Description

The following steps are performed:

1. If FACT = 'E', real scaling factors are computed to equilibrate the system:

   $$\text{diag}(S)*A*\text{diag}(S)*(\text{diag}(S))^{-1}*X = \text{diag}(S)*B$$

   Whether or not the system will be equilibrated depends on the scaling of the matrix A, but if equilibration is used, A is overwritten by $\text{diag}(S)*A*\text{diag}(S)$ and B by $\text{diag}(S)*B$.

2. If FACT = 'N' or 'E', the Cholesky decomposition is used to factor the matrix A (after equilibration if FACT = 'E') as
   $A = U^H*U$, if UPLO = 'U', or
   $A = L*L^H$, if UPLO = 'L',
   where U is an upper triangular band matrix, L is a lower triangular band matrix.

3. The factored form of A is used to estimate the condition number of the matrix A. If the reciprocal of the condition number is less than machine precision, steps

4. The system of equations is solved for X using the factored form of A.

5. Iterative refinement is applied to improve the computed solution vectors and calculate error bounds and backward error estimates for them.

6. If FACT = 'E' and equilibration was used, the vectors X are premultiplied by diag(S) so that they solve the original system before equilibration.

Arguments

FACT   (input) CHARACTER*1
          Specifies whether or not the factored form of the matrix A is supplied on entry, and if not, whether the matrix A should be equilibrated before it is factored.
          = 'F':   On entry, AFB contains the factored form of A. AB and AFB will not be modified.
          = 'N':   The matrix A will be copied to AFB and factored.
          = 'E':   The matrix A will be equilibrated if necessary, then copied to AFB and factored.

UPLO   (input) CHARACTER*1
          = 'U':   Upper triangle of A is stored.
          = 'L':   Lower triangle of A is stored.

N   (input) INTEGER
          The number of linear equations, i.e., the order of the matrix A. $N \geq 0$.

KD   (input) INTEGER
          The number of superdiagonals of the matrix A if UPLO = 'U', or the number of subdiagonals if UPLO = 'L'. $KD \geq 0$.

NRHS   (input) INTEGER
          The number of right hand sides, i.e., the number of columns of the matrices B and X. $NRHS \geq 0$.

AB   (input/output) REAL/COMPLEX array, dimension (LDAB,N)
          On entry, the upper or lower triangle of the symmetric/Hermitian band matrix A, stored in the first kd+1 rows of the array. The jth column of A is stored in the jth column of the array AB as follows:
          if UPLO = 'U', $AB(kd+1+i-j,j) = A(i,j)$ for $\max(1,j-kd) \leq i \leq j$;
          if UPLO = 'L', $AB(1+i-j,j) = A(i,j)$ for $j \leq i \leq \min(n,j+kd)$.
          On exit, if EQUED = 'Y', A is replaced by $\text{diag}(S)*A*\text{diag}(S)$.

LDAB   (input) INTEGER
          The leading dimension of the array A. $LDAB \geq KD+1$.

AFB   (input or output) REAL/COMPLEX array, dimension (LDAFB,N)
          If FACT = 'F', then AFB is an input argument and on entry contains the triangular factor U or L from the Cholesky factorization $A = U^H*U$ or $A = L*L^H$, in the same storage format as A (see AB).
          If FACT = 'N', then AFB is an output argument and on exit returns the triangular factor U or L from the Cholesky factorization $A = U^H*U$

or $A = L*L^H$ of the original matrix A. If FACT = 'E', then AFB is an output argument and on exit returns the triangular factor U or L from the Cholesky factorization $A = U^H*U$ or $A = L*L^H$ of the equilibrated matrix A (see the description of A for the form of the equilibrated matrix).

LDAFB   (input) INTEGER
        The leading dimension of the array AFB. LDAFB ≥ KD+1.

EQUED   (output) CHARACTER*1
        Specifies the form of equilibration that was done.
        = 'N': No equilibration (always true if FACT = 'F' or 'N').
        = 'Y': Equilibration was done, i.e., A has been replaced by diag(S)*A*diag(S).

S   (output) REAL array, dimension (N)
        The scale factors for A. Not assigned if FACT = 'F' or 'N'.

B   (input/output) REAL/COMPLEX array, dimension (LDB,NRHS)
        On entry, the n-by-nrhs right hand side matrix B.
        On exit, if EQUED = 'N', B is not modified; if EQUED = 'Y', B is overwritten by diag(S)*B.

LDB   (input) INTEGER
        The leading dimension of the array B. LDB ≥ max(1,N).

X   (output) REAL/COMPLEX array, dimension (LDX,NRHS)
        If INFO = 0, the n-by-nrhs solution matrix X to the original system of equations. Note that if EQUED = 'Y', A and B are modified on exit, and the solution to the equilibrated system is $(\text{diag}(S))^{-1}*X$.

LDX   (input) INTEGER
        The leading dimension of the array X. LDX ≥ max(1,N).

RCOND   (output) REAL
        The estimate of the reciprocal condition number of the matrix A. If RCOND is less than the machine precision (in particular, if RCOND = 0), the matrix is singular to working precision. This condition is indicated by a return code of INFO > 0, and the solution and error bounds are not computed.

FERR   (output) REAL array, dimension (NRHS)
        The estimated forward error bound for each solution vector X(j) (the jth column of the solution matrix X). If XTRUE is the true solution corresponding to X(j), FERR(j) bounds the magnitude of the largest element in (X(j) − XTRUE) divided by the magnitude of the largest element in X(j). The quality of the error bound depends on the quality of the estimate of $||A^{-1}||$ computed in the code; if the estimate of $||A^{-1}||$ is accurate, the error bound is guaranteed.

BERR   (output) REAL array, dimension (NRHS)
        The componentwise relative backward error of each solution vector X(j) (i.e., the smallest relative change in any element of A or B that makes X(j) an exact solution).

WORK   SPBSVX (workspace) REAL array, dimension (3*N)
        CPBSVX (workspace) COMPLEX array, dimension (2*N)

IWORK   SPBSVX only (workspace) INTEGER array, dimension (N)

RWORK   CPBSVX only (workspace) REAL array, dimension (N)

INFO   (output) INTEGER
        = 0: successful exit
        < 0: if INFO = −i, the ith argument had an illegal value
        > 0: if INFO = i, and i is
        ≤ N: if INFO = i, the leading minor of order i of A is not positive definite, so the factorization could not be completed, and the solution and error bounds could not be computed.
        = N+1: RCOND is less than machine precision. The factorization has been completed, but the matrix is singular to working precision, and the solution and error bounds have not been computed.

SPBTRF/CPBTRF

```
SUBROUTINE SPBTRF( UPLO, N, KD, AB, LDAB, INFO )
CHARACTER        UPLO
INTEGER          N, KD, LDAB, INFO
REAL             AB( LDAB, * )
```

```
SUBROUTINE CPBTRF( UPLO, N, KD, AB, LDAB, INFO )
CHARACTER        UPLO
INTEGER          N, KD, LDAB, INFO
COMPLEX          AB( LDAB, * )
```

Purpose

SPBTRF/CPBTRF computes the Cholesky factorization of a real/complex symmetric/Hermitian positive definite band matrix A.

The factorization has the form $A = U^H*U$, if UPLO = 'U', or $A = L*L^H$, if UPLO = 'L', where U is an upper triangular matrix and L is lower triangular.

Arguments

UPLO   (input) CHARACTER*1
        = 'U': Upper triangle of A is stored;
        = 'L': Lower triangle of A is stored.

N   (input) INTEGER
        The order of the matrix A. N ≥ 0.

KD   (input) INTEGER
        The number of superdiagonals of the matrix A if UPLO = 'U', or the number of subdiagonals if UPLO = 'L'. KD ≥ 0.

AB   (input/output) REAL/COMPLEX array, dimension (LDAB,N)
          On entry, the upper or lower triangle of the symmetric/Hermitian band matrix A, stored in the first kd+1 rows of the array. The jth column of matrix A is stored in the jth column of the array AB as follows:
          if UPLO = 'U', $AB(kd+1+i-j,j) = A(i,j)$ for $\max(1,j-kd)\leq i\leq j$;
          if UPLO = 'L', $AB(1+i-j,j) = A(i,j)$ for $j\leq i\leq\min(n,j+kd)$.
          On exit, if INFO = 0, the triangular factor U or L from the Cholesky factorization $A = U^H*U$ or $A = L*L^H$ of the band matrix A, in the same storage format as A.

LDAB   (input) INTEGER
          The leading dimension of the array AB. LDAB $\geq$ KD+1.

INFO   (output) INTEGER
          = 0: successful exit
          < 0: if INFO = −i, the ith argument had an illegal value
          > 0: if INFO = i, the leading minor of order i is not positive definite, and the factorization could not be completed.

SPBTRS/CPBTRS

```
SUBROUTINE SPBTRS( UPLO, N, KD, NRHS, AB, LDAB, B, LDB, INFO )
CHARACTER      UPLO
INTEGER        INFO, KD, LDAB, LDB, N, NRHS
REAL           AB( LDAB, * ), B( LDB, * )

SUBROUTINE CPBTRS( UPLO, N, KD, NRHS, AB, LDAB, B, LDB, INFO )
CHARACTER      UPLO
INTEGER        INFO, KD, LDAB, LDB, N, NRHS
COMPLEX        AB( LDAB, * ), B( LDB, * )
```

Purpose

SPBTRS/CPBTRS solves a system of linear equations $A*X = B$ with a symmetric/Hermitian positive definite band matrix A using the Cholesky factorization $A = U^H*U$ or $A = L*L^H$ computed by SPBTRF/CPBTRF.

Arguments

UPLO   (input) CHARACTER*1
          = 'U': Upper triangular factor stored in AB;
          = 'L': Lower triangular factor stored in AB.

N   (input) INTEGER
          The order of the matrix A. N $\geq$ 0.

KD   (input) INTEGER
          The number of superdiagonals of the matrix A if UPLO = 'U', or the number of subdiagonals if UPLO = 'L'. KD $\geq$ 0.

NRHS   (input) INTEGER
          The number of right hand sides, i.e., the number of columns of the matrix B. NRHS $\geq$ 0.

AB   (input) REAL/COMPLEX array, dimension (LDAB,N)
          The triangular factor U or L from the Cholesky factorization $A = U^H*U$ or $A = L*L^H$ of the band matrix A, stored in the first kd+1 rows of the array. The jth column of U or L is stored in the jth column of the array AB as follows:
          if UPLO ='U', $AB(kd+1+i-j,j) = U(i,j)$ for $\max(1,j-kd)\leq i\leq j$;
          if UPLO ='L', $AB(1+i-j,j) = L(i,j)$ for $j\leq i\leq\min(n,j+kd)$.

LDAB   (input) INTEGER
          The leading dimension of the array AB. LDAB $\geq$ KD+1.

B   (input/output) REAL/COMPLEX array, dimension (LDB,NRHS)
          On entry, the right hand side matrix B.
          On exit, the solution matrix X.

LDB   (input) INTEGER
          The leading dimension of the array B. LDB $\geq$ max(1,N).

INFO   (output) INTEGER
          = 0: successful exit
          < 0: if INFO = −i, the ith argument had an illegal value

SPOCON/CPOCON

```
SUBROUTINE SPOCON( UPLO, N, A, LDA, ANORM, RCOND, WORK, IWORK,
$                  INFO )
CHARACTER      UPLO
INTEGER        INFO, LDA, N
REAL           ANORM, RCOND
INTEGER        IWORK( * )
REAL           A( LDA, * ), WORK( * )

SUBROUTINE CPOCON( UPLO, N, A, LDA, ANORM, RCOND, WORK, RWORK,
$                  INFO )
CHARACTER      UPLO
INTEGER        INFO, LDA, N
REAL           ANORM, RCOND
REAL           RWORK( * )
COMPLEX        A( LDA, * ), WORK( * )
```

Purpose

SPOCON/CPOCON estimates the reciprocal of the condition number (in the 1-norm) of a real/complex symmetric/Hermitian positive definite matrix using the Cholesky factorization $A = U^H*U$ or $A = L*L^H$ computed by SPOTRF/CPOTRF.

Arguments

JOBZ (input) CHARACTER*1
  = 'N': Compute eigenvalues only;
  = 'V': Compute eigenvalues and eigenvectors.

N (input) INTEGER
  The order of the matrix A. $N \geq 0$.

D (input/output) REAL array, dimension (N)
  On entry, the n diagonal elements of the tridiagonal matrix A.
  On exit, if INFO = 0, D contains the eigenvalues in ascending order. If INFO > 0, the eigenvalues are correct for indices 1, 2, $\cdots$, INFO-1, but they are unordered and may not be the smallest eigenvalues of the matrix.

E (input/output) REAL array, dimension (N-1)
  On entry, the (n-1) subdiagonal elements of the tridiagonal matrix A, stored in elements 1 to N-1 of E; E(N) need not be set, but is used by the routine.
  On exit, the contents of E are destroyed.

Z (output) REAL array, dimension (LDZ,N)
  If JOBZ = 'V', then if INFO = 0, Z contains the orthonormal eigenvectors of the matrix A, with the ith column of Z holding the eigenvector associated with the eigenvalue returned in D(i); if INFO > 0, the first INFO-1 columns of Z contain the eigenvectors associated with those eigenvalues which have been computed.
  If JOBZ = 'N', then Z is not referenced.

LDZ (input) INTEGER
  The leading dimension of the array Z. LDZ $\geq$ 1, and if JOBZ = 'V', LDZ $\geq$ max(1,N).

WORK (workspace) REAL array, dimension (max(1,2*N-2))
  If JOBZ = 'N', WORK is not referenced.

INFO (output) INTEGER
  = 0: successful exit
  < 0: if INFO = $-i$, the ith argument had an illegal value
  > 0: if INFO = i, the algorithm failed to converge after finding only i-1 eigenvalues.

SSTEVX

```
SUBROUTINE SSTEVX( JOBZ, RANGE, N, D, E, VL, VU, IL, IU, ABSTOL,
$                  M, W, Z, LDZ, WORK, IWORK, IFAIL, INFO )
    CHARACTER       JOBZ, RANGE
    INTEGER         IL, INFO, IU, LDZ, M, N
    REAL            ABSTOL, VL, VU
    INTEGER         IFAIL( * ), IWORK( * )
    REAL            D( * ), E( * ), W( * ), WORK( * ), Z( LDZ, * )
```

Purpose

SSTEVX computes selected eigenvalues and, optionally, eigenvectors of a real symmetric tridiagonal matrix A. Eigenvalues and eigenvectors can be selected by specifying either a range of values or a range of indices for the desired eigenvalues.

Arguments

JOBZ (input) CHARACTER*1
  = 'N': Compute eigenvalues only;
  = 'V': Compute eigenvalues and eigenvectors.

RANGE (input) CHARACTER*1
  = 'A': all eigenvalues will be found.
  = 'V': all eigenvalues in the half-open interval (VL,VU] will be found.
  = 'I': the ILth through IUth eigenvalues will be found.

N (input) INTEGER
  The order of the matrix A. $N \geq 0$.

D (input/output) REAL array, dimension (N)
  On entry, the n diagonal elements of the tridiagonal matrix A.
  On exit, D may be multiplied by a constant factor chosen to avoid over/underflow in computing the eigenvalues.

E (input/output) REAL array, dimension (N-1)
  On entry, the (n-1) subdiagonal elements of the tridiagonal matrix A, stored in elements 1 to N-1 of E; E(N) need not be set.
  On exit, E may be multiplied by a constant factor chosen to avoid over/underflow in computing the eigenvalues.

VL (input) REAL
  If RANGE='V', the lower bound of the interval to be searched for eigenvalues.
  Not referenced if RANGE = 'A' or 'I'.

VU (input) REAL
  If RANGE='V', the upper bound of the interval to be searched for eigenvalues. VU > VL.
  Not referenced if RANGE = 'A' or 'I'.

IL (input) INTEGER
  If RANGE='I', the index (from smallest to largest) of the smallest eigen-

SSYCON/CSYCON/CHECON

```
SUBROUTINE SSYCON( UPLO, N, A, LDA, IPIV, ANORM, RCOND, WORK,
$                   IWORK, INFO )
   CHARACTER      UPLO
   INTEGER        INFO, LDA, N
   REAL           ANORM, RCOND
   INTEGER        IPIV( * ), IWORK( * )
   REAL           A( LDA, * ), WORK( * )

SUBROUTINE CSYCON( UPLO, N, A, LDA, IPIV, ANORM, RCOND, WORK,
$                   INFO )
   CHARACTER      UPLO
   INTEGER        INFO, LDA, N
   REAL           ANORM, RCOND
   INTEGER        IPIV( * )
   COMPLEX        A( LDA, * ), WORK( * )

SUBROUTINE CHECON( UPLO, N, A, LDA, IPIV, ANORM, RCOND, WORK,
$                   INFO )
   CHARACTER      UPLO
   INTEGER        INFO, LDA, N
   REAL           ANORM, RCOND
   INTEGER        IPIV( * )
   COMPLEX        A( LDA, * ), WORK( * )
```

Purpose

SSYCON/CSYCON estimates the reciprocal of the condition number (in the 1-norm) of a real/complex symmetric matrix A using the factorization $A = U*D*U^T$ or $A = L*D*L^T$ computed by SSYTRF/CSYTRF.

CHECON estimates the reciprocal of the condition number of a complex Hermitian matrix A using the factorization $A = U*D*U^H$ or $A = L*D*L^H$ computed by CHETRF.

An estimate is obtained for $||A^{-1}||$, and the reciprocal of the condition number is computed as $RCOND = 1/(||A|| \cdot ||A^{-1}||)$.

Arguments

UPLO   (input) CHARACTER*1
    Specifies whether the details of the factorization are stored as an upper or lower triangular matrix.
    = 'U': Upper triangular, form is $A = U*D*U^T$ (SSYCON/CSYCON) or $A = U*D*U^H$ (CHECON);
    = 'L': Lower triangular, form is $A = L*D*L^T$ (SSYCON/CSYCON) or $A = L*D*L^H$ (CHECON).

N   (input) INTEGER
    The order of the matrix A. N ≥ 0.

A   (input) REAL/COMPLEX/COMPLEX array, dimension (LDA,N)

---

value to be returned. IL ≥ 1.
Not referenced if RANGE = 'A' or 'V'.

IU   (input) INTEGER
    If RANGE='I', the index (from smallest to largest) of the largest eigenvalue to be returned. min(IL,N) ≤ IU ≤ N.
    Not referenced if RANGE = 'A' or 'V'.

ABSTOL   (input) REAL
    The absolute error tolerance for the eigenvalues. An approximate eigenvalue is accepted as converged when it is determined to lie in an interval [a,b] of width less than or equal to ABSTOL + EPS*max(|a|,|b|), where EPS is the machine precision. If ABSTOL is less than or equal to zero, then $EPS*||A||_1$ will be used in its place.

M   (output) INTEGER
    The total number of eigenvalues found. 0 ≤ M ≤ N.

W   (output) REAL array, dimension (N)
    The first M elements contain the selected eigenvalues in ascending order.

Z   (output) REAL array, dimension (LDZ,N)
    If JOBZ = 'V', then if INFO = 0, the first M columns of Z contain the orthonormal eigenvectors of the matrix A corresponding to the selected eigenvalues, with the ith column of Z holding the eigenvector associated with W(i). If an eigenvector fails to converge (INFO > 0), then that column of Z contains the latest approximation to the eigenvector, and the index of the eigenvector is returned in IFAIL.
    If JOBZ = 'N', then Z is not referenced.

LDZ   (input) INTEGER
    The leading dimension of the array Z. LDZ ≥ 1, and if JOBZ = 'V', LDZ ≥ max(1,N).

WORK   (workspace) REAL array, dimension (4*N)

IWORK   (workspace) INTEGER array, dimension (5*N)

IFAIL   (output) INTEGER array, dimension (N)
    If JOBZ = 'V', then if INFO = 0, the first M elements of IFAIL are zero; if INFO > 0, then IFAIL contains the indices of the eigenvectors that failed to converge.
    If JOBZ = 'N', then IFAIL is not referenced.

INFO   (output) INTEGER
    = 0: successful exit
    < 0: if INFO = -i, the ith argument had an illegal value.
    > 0: if INFO = i, then i eigenvectors failed to converge. Their indices are stored in array IFAIL.

The block diagonal matrix D and the multipliers used to obtain the factor U or L as computed by SSYTRF/CSYTRF/CHETRF.

LDA
(input) INTEGER
The leading dimension of the array A. LDA ≥ max(1,N).

IPIV
(input) INTEGER array, dimension (N)
Details of the interchanges and the block structure of D as determined by SSYTRF/CSYTRF/CHETRF.

ANORM
(input) REAL
The 1-norm of the original matrix A.

RCOND
(output) REAL
The reciprocal of the condition number of the matrix A, computed as $RCOND = 1/(\|A\| \cdot \|A^{-1}\|)$.

WORK
(workspace) REAL/COMPLEX/COMPLEX array, dimension (2*N)

IWORK
SSYCON only (workspace) INTEGER array, dimension (N)

INFO
(output) INTEGER
= 0:   successful exit
< 0:   if INFO = $-i$, the ith argument had an illegal value

SSYEV/CHEEV

```
SUBROUTINE SSYEV( JOBZ, UPLO, N, A, LDA, W, WORK, LWORK, INFO )
CHARACTER        JOBZ, UPLO
INTEGER          INFO, LDA, LWORK, N
REAL             A( LDA, * ), W( * ), WORK( * )
SUBROUTINE CHEEV( JOBZ, UPLO, N, A, LDA, W, WORK, LWORK, RWORK,
$                 INFO )
CHARACTER        JOBZ, UPLO
INTEGER          INFO, LDA, LWORK, N
REAL             RWORK( * ), W( * )
COMPLEX          A( LDA, * ), WORK( * )
```

Purpose

SSYEV/CHEEV computes all the eigenvalues and, optionally, eigenvectors of a real/complex symmetric/Hermitian matrix.

Arguments

JOBZ
(input) CHARACTER*1
= 'N':   Compute eigenvalues only;
= 'V':   Compute eigenvalues and eigenvectors.

UPLO
(input) CHARACTER*1
= 'U':   Upper triangle of A is stored;
= 'L':   Lower triangle of A is stored.

N
(input) INTEGER
The order of the matrix A. N ≥ 0.

A
(input/output) REAL/COMPLEX array, dimension (LDA,N)
On entry, the symmetric/Hermitian matrix A. If UPLO = 'U', the leading n-by-n upper triangular part of A contains the upper triangular part of the matrix A. If UPLO = 'L', the leading n-by-n lower triangular part of A contains the lower triangular part of the matrix A.
On exit, if JOBZ = 'V', then if INFO = 0, A contains the orthonormal eigenvectors of the matrix A, with the ith column of A holding the eigenvector associated with W(i); if INFO > 0, the first INFO−1 columns of A contain the eigenvectors associated with those eigenvalues which have been computed.
If JOBZ = 'N', then on exit the upper triangle (if UPLO = 'U') or the lower triangle (if UPLO='L') of A, including the diagonal, is destroyed.

LDA
(input) INTEGER
The leading dimension of the array A. LDA ≥ max(1,N).

W
(output) REAL array, dimension (N)
If INFO = 0, W contains the eigenvalues in ascending order. If INFO > 0, the eigenvalues are correct for indices 1, 2, ..., INFO−1, but they are unordered and may not be the smallest eigenvalues of the matrix.

WORK
(workspace) REAL/COMPLEX array, dimension (LWORK)
On exit, if INFO = 0, WORK(1) returns the optimal LWORK.

LWORK
(input) INTEGER
The length of the array WORK.
SSYEV
LWORK ≥ max(1,3*N−1).   For optimal efficiency, LWORK ≥ (NB+2)*N, where NB is the block size for SSYTRD returned by ILAENV.
CHEEV
LWORK ≥ max(1,2*N−1).   For optimal efficiency, LWORK ≥ (NB+1)*N, where NB is the block size for CHETRD returned by ILAENV.

RWORK
CHEEV only (workspace) REAL array, dimension (max(1,3*N−2))

INFO
(output) INTEGER
= 0:   successful exit
< 0:   if INFO = −i, the ith argument had an illegal value
> 0:   if INFO = i, the algorithm failed to converge after finding only i−1 eigenvalues.

SSYEVX/CHEEVX

```
SUBROUTINE SSYEVX( JOBZ, RANGE, UPLO, N, A, LDA, VL, VU, IL, IU,
$                   ABSTOL, M, W, Z, LDZ, WORK, LWORK, IWORK,
$                   IFAIL, INFO )
    CHARACTER     JOBZ, RANGE, UPLO
    INTEGER       IL, INFO, IU, LDA, LDZ, LWORK, M, N
    REAL          ABSTOL, VL, VU
    INTEGER       IFAIL( * ), IWORK( * )
    REAL          A( LDA, * ), W( * ), WORK( * ), Z( LDZ, * )

SUBROUTINE CHEEVX( JOBZ, RANGE, UPLO, N, A, LDA, VL, VU, IL, IU,
$                   ABSTOL, M, W, Z, LDZ, WORK, LWORK, RWORK,
$                   IWORK, IFAIL, INFO )
    CHARACTER     JOBZ, RANGE, UPLO
    INTEGER       IL, INFO, IU, LDA, LDZ, LWORK, M, N
    REAL          ABSTOL, VL, VU
    INTEGER       IFAIL( * ), IWORK( * )
    REAL          RWORK( * ), W( * )
    COMPLEX       A( LDA, * ), WORK( * ), Z( LDZ, * )
```

Purpose

SSYEVX/CHEEVX computes selected eigenvalues and, optionally, eigenvectors of a real/complex symmetric/Hermitian matrix A. Eigenvalues and eigenvectors can be selected by specifying either a range of values or a range of indices for the desired eigenvalues.

Arguments

JOBZ   (input) CHARACTER*1
        = 'N':   Compute eigenvalues only;
        = 'V':   Compute eigenvalues and eigenvectors.

RANGE   (input) CHARACTER*1
        = 'A':   all eigenvalues will be found.
        = 'V':   all eigenvalues in the half-open interval (VL,VU] will be found.
        = 'I':   the ILth through IU^{th} eigenvalues will be found.

UPLO   (input) CHARACTER*1
        = 'U':   Upper triangle of A is stored;
        = 'L':   Lower triangle of A is stored.

N   (input) INTEGER
        The order of the matrix A. $N \geq 0$.

A   (input/output) REAL/COMPLEX array, dimension (LDA,N)
        On entry, the symmetric/Hermitian matrix A. If UPLO = 'U', the lead-
        ing n-by-n upper triangular part of A contains the upper triangular part
        of the matrix A. If UPLO = 'L', the leading n-by-n lower triangular part
        of A contains the lower triangular part of the matrix A.
        On exit, the upper triangle (if UPLO='U') or the lower triangle (if
        UPLO='L') of A, including the diagonal, is destroyed.

LDA   (input) INTEGER
        The leading dimension of the array A. $LDA \geq \max(1,N)$.

VL   (input) REAL
        If RANGE='V', the lower bound of the interval to be searched for eigen-
        values.
        Not referenced if RANGE = 'A' or 'I'.

VU   (input) REAL
        If RANGE='V', the upper bound of the interval to be searched for
        eigenvalues. VU > VL.
        Not referenced if RANGE = 'A' or 'I'.

IL   (input) INTEGER
        If RANGE='I', the index (from smallest to largest) of the smallest eigen-
        value to be returned. $IL \geq 1$.
        Not referenced if RANGE = 'A' or 'V'.

IU   (input) INTEGER
        If RANGE='I', the index (from smallest to largest) of the largest eigen-
        value to be returned. $\min(IL,N) \leq IU \leq N$.
        Not referenced if RANGE = 'A' or 'V'.

ABSTOL (input) REAL
        The absolute error tolerance for the eigenvalues. An approximate eigen-
        value is accepted as converged when it is determined to lie in an interval
        [a,b] of width less than or equal to ABSTOL + EPS*max(|a|,|b|), where
        EPS is the machine precision. If ABSTOL is less than or equal to zero,
        then $EPS*\|T\|_1$ will be used in its place, where T is the tridiagonal
        matrix obtained by reducing A to tridiagonal form.

M   (output) INTEGER
        The total number of eigenvalues found. $0 \leq M \leq N$.

W   (output) REAL array, dimension (N)
        The first M elements contain the selected eigenvalues in ascending order.

Z   (output) REAL/COMPLEX array, dimension (LDZ,N)
        If JOBZ = 'V', then if INFO = 0, the first M columns of Z contain the
        orthonormal eigenvectors of the matrix A corresponding to the selected
        eigenvalues, with the ith column of Z holding the eigenvector associated
        with W(i). If an eigenvector fails to converge (INFO > 0), then that
        column of Z contains the latest approximation to the eigenvector, and
        the index of the eigenvector is returned in IFAIL.
        If JOBZ = 'N', then Z is not referenced.

LDZ   (input) INTEGER
        The leading dimension of the array Z. $LDZ \geq 1$, and if JOBZ = 'V',
        $LDZ \geq \max(1,N)$.

WORK   (workspace) REAL/COMPLEX array, dimension (LWORK)
        On exit, if INFO = 0, WORK(1) returns the optimal LWORK.

LWORK   (input) INTEGER
        The length of the array WORK.

ITYPE   (input) INTEGER
= 1: compute $(U^H)^{-1}*A*U^{-1}$ or $L^{-1}*A*(L^H)^{-1}$;
= 2 or 3: compute $U*A*U^H$ or L^H*A*L.

UPLO   (input) CHARACTER*1
= 'U': Upper triangle of A is stored and B is factored as U^H*U;
= 'L': Lower triangle of A is stored and B is factored as $L*L^H$.

N   (input) INTEGER
The order of the matrices A and B. $N \geq 0$.

A   (input/output) REAL/COMPLEX array, dimension (LDA,N)
On entry, the symmetric/Hermitian matrix A. If UPLO = 'U', the leading n-by-n upper triangular part of A contains the upper triangular part of the matrix A, and the strictly lower triangular part of A is not referenced. If UPLO = 'L', the leading n-by-n lower triangular part of the matrix A contains the lower triangular part of the matrix A, and the strictly upper triangular part of A is not referenced.
On exit, if INFO = 0, the transformed matrix, stored in the same format as A.

LDA   (input) INTEGER
The leading dimension of the array A. $LDA \geq \max(1,N)$.

B   (input) REAL/COMPLEX array, dimension (LDB,N)
The triangular factor from the Cholesky factorization of B, as returned by SPOTRF/CPOTRF.

LDB   (input) INTEGER
The leading dimension of the array B. $LDB \geq \max(1,N)$.

INFO   (output) INTEGER
= 0: successful exit
< 0: if INFO = -i, the ith argument had an illegal value.

SSYGV/CHEGV

```
SUBROUTINE SSYGV( ITYPE, JOBZ, UPLO, N, A, LDA, B, LDB, W, WORK,
$                 LWORK, INFO )
          CHARACTER      JOBZ, UPLO
          INTEGER        INFO, ITYPE, LDA, LDB, LWORK, N
          REAL           A( LDA, * ), B( LDB, * ), W( * ), WORK( * )
SUBROUTINE CHEGV( ITYPE, JOBZ, UPLO, N, A, LDA, B, LDB, W, WORK,
$                 LWORK, RWORK, INFO )
          CHARACTER      JOBZ, UPLO
          INTEGER        INFO, ITYPE, LDA, LDB, LWORK, N
          REAL           RWORK( * ), W( * )
          COMPLEX        A( LDA, * ), B( LDB, * ), WORK( * )
```

SSYGV/CHEGV

SSYEVX
LWORK $\geq \max(1,7*N)$. For optimal efficiency, LWORK $\geq (NB+3)*N$, where NB is the block size for SSYTRD returned by ILAENV.
CHEEVX
LWORK $\geq \max(1,2*N-1)$. For optimal efficiency, LWORK $\geq (NB+1)*N$, where NB is the block size for CHETRD returned by ILAENV.

RWORK   *CHEEVX only*   (workspace) REAL array, dimension (7*N)

IWORK   (workspace) INTEGER array, dimension (5*N)

IFAIL   (output) INTEGER array, dimension (N)
If JOBZ = 'V', then if INFO = 0, the first M elements of IFAIL are zero; if INFO > 0, then IFAIL contains the indices of the eigenvectors that failed to converge.
If JOBZ = 'N', then IFAIL is not referenced.

INFO   (output) INTEGER
= 0: successful exit
< 0: if INFO = -i, the ith argument had an illegal value.
> 0: if INFO = i, then i eigenvectors failed to converge. Their indices are stored in array IFAIL.

SSYGST/CHEGST

```
SUBROUTINE SSYGST( ITYPE, UPLO, N, A, LDA, B, LDB, INFO )
          CHARACTER      UPLO
          INTEGER        INFO, ITYPE, LDA, LDB, N
          REAL           A( LDA, * ), B( LDB, * )
SUBROUTINE CHEGST( ITYPE, UPLO, N, A, LDA, B, LDB, INFO )
          CHARACTER      UPLO
          INTEGER        INFO, ITYPE, LDA, LDB, N
          COMPLEX        A( LDA, * ), B( LDB, * )
```

Purpose

SSYGST/CHEGST reduces a real/complex symmetric/Hermitian definite generalized eigenproblem to standard form.

If ITYPE = 1, the problem is $A*x = \lambda*B*x$, and A is overwritten by $(U^H)^{-1}*A*U^{-1}$ or $L^{-1}*A*(L^H)^{-1}$

If ITYPE = 2 or 3, the problem is $A*B*x = \lambda*x$ or $B*A*x = \lambda*x$, and A is overwritten by $U*A*U^H$ or L^H*A*L.

B must have been previously factorized as U^H*U or $L*L^H$ by SPOTRF/CPOTRF.

Purpose

SSYGV/CHEGV computes all the eigenvalues and, optionally, eigenvectors of a real/complex generalized symmetric/Hermitian definite eigenproblem, of the form

$$A*x=\lambda*B*x, \quad A*Bx=\lambda*x, \quad \text{or} \quad B*A*x=\lambda*x.$$

Here A and B are assumed to be symmetric/Hermitian and B is also positive definite.

Arguments

ITYPE (input) INTEGER
Specifies the problem type to be solved:
= 1: $A*x = \lambda*B*x$
= 2: $A*B*x = \lambda*x$
= 3: $B*A*x = \lambda*x$

JOBZ (input) CHARACTER*1
= 'N': Compute eigenvalues only;
= 'V': Compute eigenvalues and eigenvectors.

UPLO (input) CHARACTER*1
= 'U': Upper triangles of A and B are stored;
= 'L': Lower triangles of A and B are stored.

N (input) INTEGER
The order of the matrices A and B. $N \geq 0$.

A (input/output) REAL/COMPLEX array, dimension (LDA,N)
On entry, the symmetric/Hermitian matrix A. If UPLO = 'U', the leading n-by-n upper triangular part of A contains the upper triangular part of the matrix A. If UPLO = 'L', the leading n-by-n lower triangular part of A contains the lower triangular part of the matrix A.
On exit, if JOBZ = 'V', then if INFO = 0, A contains the matrix Z of eigenvectors, with the ith column of A holding the eigenvector associated with W(i); if $0 < INFO \leq N$, the first INFO-1 columns of A contain the eigenvectors associated with those eigenvalues which have been computed. The eigenvectors are normalized as follows:
if ITYPE = 1 or 2, $Z^H*B*Z = I$;
if ITYPE = 3, $Z^H*B^{-1}*Z = I$.
If JOBZ = 'N', then on exit the upper triangle (if UPLO='U') or the lower triangle (if UPLO='L') of A, including the diagonal, is destroyed.

LDA (input) INTEGER
The leading dimension of the array A. $LDA \geq max(1,N)$.

B (input/output) REAL/COMPLEX array, dimension (LDB,N)
On entry, the symmetric/Hermitian positive definite matrix B. If UPLO = 'U', the leading n-by-n upper triangular part of B contains the upper triangular part of the matrix B. If UPLO = 'L', the leading n-by-n lower triangular part of B contains the lower triangular part of the matrix B.
On exit, if $INFO \leq N$, the part of B containing the matrix is overwritten by the triangular factor U or L from the Cholesky factorization $B = U^H*U$ or $B = L*L^H$.

LDB (input) INTEGER
The leading dimension of the array B. $LDB \geq max(1,N)$.

W (output) REAL array, dimension (N)
If INFO = 0, W contains the eigenvalues in ascending order. If $0 < INFO \leq N$, the eigenvalues are correct for indices 1, 2, ..., INFO-1, but they are unordered and may not be the smallest eigenvalues of the matrix.

WORK (workspace) REAL/COMPLEX array, dimension (LWORK)
On exit, if INFO = 0, WORK(1) returns the optimal LWORK.

LWORK (input) INTEGER
The length of the array WORK.
SSYGV
$LWORK \geq max(1,3*N-1)$. For optimal efficiency, $LWORK \geq (NB+2)*N$, where NB is the block size for SSYTRD returned by ILAENV.
CHEGV
$LWORK \geq max(1,2*N-1)$. For optimal efficiency, $LWORK \geq (NB+1)*N$, where NB is the block size for CHETRD returned by ILAENV.

RWORK *CHEGV only* (workspace) REAL array, dimension $(max(1,3*N-2))$

INFO (output) INTEGER
= 0: successful exit
< 0: if INFO = $-i$, the ith argument had an illegal value
> 0: SPOTRF/CPOTRF or SSYEV/CHEEV returned an error code:
$\leq N$: if INFO = i, then SSYEV/CHEEV failed to converge after finding only i-1 eigenvalues.
$> N$: if INFO = N + i, for $1 \leq i \leq N$, then the leading minor of order i of B is not positive definite. The factorization of B could not be completed and no eigenvalues or eigenvectors were computed.

SSYRFS/CSYRFS/CHERFS

```
      SUBROUTINE SSYRFS( UPLO, N, NRHS, A, LDA, AF, LDAF, IPIV, B, LDB,
     $                   X, LDX, FERR, BERR, WORK, IWORK, INFO )
      CHARACTER     UPLO
      INTEGER       INFO, LDA, LDAF, LDB, LDX, N, NRHS
      INTEGER       IPIV( * ), IWORK( * )
      REAL          A( LDA, * ), AF( LDAF, * ), B( LDB, * ),
     $              BERR( * ), FERR( * ), WORK( * ), X( LDX, * )
```

```
SUBROUTINE CSYRFS( UPLO, N, NRHS, A, LDA, AF, LDAF, IPIV, B, LDB,
$                  X, LDX, FERR, BERR, WORK, RWORK, INFO )
    CHARACTER       UPLO
    INTEGER         INFO, LDA, LDAF, LDB, LDX, N, NRHS
    INTEGER         IPIV( * )
    REAL            BERR( * ), FERR( * ), RWORK( * )
    COMPLEX         A( LDA, * ), AF( LDAF, * ), B( LDB, * ),
$                   WORK( * ), X( LDX, * )

SUBROUTINE CHERFS( UPLO, N, NRHS, A, LDA, AF, LDAF, IPIV, B, LDB,
$                  X, LDX, FERR, BERR, WORK, RWORK, INFO )
    CHARACTER       UPLO
    INTEGER         INFO, LDA, LDAF, LDB, LDX, N, NRHS
    INTEGER         IPIV( * )
    REAL            BERR( * ), FERR( * ), RWORK( * )
    COMPLEX         A( LDA, * ), AF( LDAF, * ), B( LDB, * ),
$                   WORK( * ), X( LDX, * )
```

Purpose

SSYRFS/CSYRFS/CHERFS improves the computed solution to a system of linear equations when the coefficient matrix is real/complex/complex symmetric/symmetric/Hermitian indefinite, and provides error bounds and backward error estimates for the solution.

Arguments

UPLO (input) CHARACTER*1
= 'U': Upper triangle of A is stored;
= 'L': Lower triangle of A is stored.

N (input) INTEGER
The order of the matrix A. $N \geq 0$.

NRHS (input) INTEGER
The number of right hand sides, i.e., the number of columns of the matrices B and X. $NRHS \geq 0$.

A (input) REAL/COMPLEX/COMPLEX array, dimension (LDA,N)
The symmetric/symmetric/Hermitian matrix A. If UPLO = 'U', the leading n-by-n upper triangular part of A contains the upper triangular part of the matrix A, and the strictly lower triangular part of A is not referenced. If UPLO = 'L', the leading n-by-n lower triangular part of the matrix A, and the strictly upper triangular part of A is not referenced.

LDA (input) INTEGER
The leading dimension of the array A. $LDA \geq \max(1,N)$.

AF (input) REAL/COMPLEX/COMPLEX array, dimension (LDAF,N)
The factored form of the matrix A. AF contains the block diagonal matrix D and the multipliers used to obtain the factor U or L from the factorization $A = U*D*U^T$ or $A = L*D*L^T$ as computed by

SSYTRF/CSYTRF or the factorization $A = U*D*U^H$ or $A = L*D*L^H$ as computed by CHETRF.

LDAF (input) INTEGER
The leading dimension of the array AF. $LDAF \geq \max(1,N)$.

IPIV (input) INTEGER array, dimension (N)
Details of the interchanges and the block structure of D as determined by SSYTRF/CSYTRF/CHETRF.

B (input) REAL/COMPLEX/COMPLEX array, dimension (LDB,NRHS)
The right hand side matrix B.

LDB (input) INTEGER
The leading dimension of the array B. $LDB \geq \max(1,N)$.

X (input/output) REAL/COMPLEX/COMPLEX array, dimension (LDX,NRHS)
On entry, the solution matrix X, as computed by SSYTRS/CSYTRS/CHETRS.
On exit, the improved solution matrix X.

LDX (input) INTEGER
The leading dimension of the array X. $LDX \geq \max(1,N)$.

FERR (output) REAL array, dimension (NRHS)
The estimated forward error bound for each solution vector X(j) (the jth column of the solution matrix X). If XTRUE is the true solution corresponding to X(j), FERR(j) bounds the magnitude of the largest element in (X(j) − XTRUE) divided by the magnitude of the largest element in X(j). The quality of the error bound depends on the quality of the estimate of $\|A^{-1}\|$ computed in the code; if the estimate of $\|A^{-1}\|$ is accurate, the error bound is guaranteed.

BERR (output) REAL array, dimension (NRHS)
The componentwise relative backward error of each solution vector X(j) (i.e., the smallest relative change in any element of A or B that makes X(j) an exact solution).

WORK SSYRFS (workspace) REAL array, dimension (3*N)
CSYRFS/CHERFS (workspace) COMPLEX array, dimension (2*N)

IWORK SSYRFS only (workspace) INTEGER array, dimension (N)

RWORK CSYRFS/CHERFS only (workspace) REAL array, dimension (N)

INFO (output) INTEGER
= 0: successful exit
< 0: if INFO = −i, the ith argument had an illegal value

SSYSV/CSYSV/CHESV

```
SUBROUTINE SSYSV( UPLO, N, NRHS, A, LDA, IPIV, B, LDB, WORK,
$                 LWORK, INFO )
   CHARACTER     UPLO
   INTEGER       INFO, LDA, LDB, LWORK, N, NRHS
   INTEGER       IPIV( * )
   REAL          A( LDA, * ), B( LDB, * ), WORK( LWORK )

SUBROUTINE CSYSV( UPLO, N, NRHS, A, LDA, IPIV, B, LDB, WORK,
$                 LWORK, INFO )
   CHARACTER     UPLO
   INTEGER       INFO, LDA, LDB, LWORK, N, NRHS
   INTEGER       IPIV( * )
   COMPLEX       A( LDA, * ), B( LDB, * ), WORK( LWORK )

SUBROUTINE CHESV( UPLO, N, NRHS, A, LDA, IPIV, B, LDB, WORK,
$                 LWORK, INFO )
   CHARACTER     UPLO
   INTEGER       INFO, LDA, LDB, LWORK, N, NRHS
   INTEGER       IPIV( * )
   COMPLEX       A( LDA, * ), B( LDB, * ), WORK( LWORK )
```

Purpose

SSYSV/CSYSV/CHESV computes the solution to a real/complex/complex system of linear equations $A*X = B$, where A is an n-by-n symmetric/symmetric/Hermitian matrix and X and B are n-by-nrhs matrices.

The diagonal pivoting method is used to factor A as

$A = U*D*U^T$ or $A = L*D*L^T$ (SSYSV/CSYSV) or

$A = U*D*U^H$ or $A = L*D*L^H$ (CHESV),

where U (or L) is a product of permutation and unit upper (lower) triangular matrices, and D is symmetric (SSYSV/CSYSV) or Hermitian (CHESV) and block diagonal with 1-by-1 and 2-by-2 diagonal blocks. The factored form of A is then used to solve the system of equations $A*X = B$.

Arguments

UPLO   (input) CHARACTER*1
        = 'U':   Upper triangle of A is stored.
        = 'L':   Lower triangle of A is stored.

N   (input) INTEGER
        The number of linear equations, i.e., the order of the matrix A. $N \geq 0$.

NRHS   (input) INTEGER
        The number of right hand sides, i.e., the number of columns of the matrix B. $NRHS \geq 0$.

A   (input/output)
        REAL/COMPLEX/COMPLEX array, dimension (LDA,N)
        On entry, the symmetric/symmetric/Hermitian matrix A. If UPLO = 'U', the leading n-by-n upper triangular part of A contains the upper triangular part of the matrix A, and the strictly lower triangular part of A is not referenced. If UPLO = 'L', the leading n-by-n lower triangular part of A contains the lower triangular part of the matrix A, and the strictly upper triangular part of A is not referenced.
        On exit, if INFO = 0, the block diagonal matrix D and the multipliers used to obtain the factor U or L from the factorization $A = U*D*U^T$ or $A = L*D*L^T$ as computed by SSYTRF/CSYTRF or the factorization $A = U*D*U^H$ or $A = L*D*L^H$ as computed by CHETRF.

LDA   (input) INTEGER
        The leading dimension of the array A. $LDA \geq \max(1,N)$.

IPIV   (output) INTEGER array, dimension (N)
        Details of the interchanges and the block structure of D, as determined by SSYTRF/CSYTRF/CHETRF. If IPIV(k) > 0, then rows and columns k and IPIV(k) were interchanged, and D(k,k) is a 1-by-1 diagonal block. If UPLO = 'U' and IPIV(k) = IPIV(k-1) < 0, then rows and columns k-1 and -IPIV(k) were interchanged and D(k-1:k,k-1:k) is a 2-by-2 diagonal block. If UPLO = 'L' and IPIV(k) = IPIV(k+1) < 0, then rows and columns k+1 and -IPIV(k) were interchanged and D(k:k+1,k:k+1) is a 2-by-2 diagonal block.

B   (input/output)
        REAL/COMPLEX/COMPLEX array, dimension (LDB,NRHS)
        On entry, the n-by-nrhs right hand side matrix B.
        On exit, if INFO = 0, the n-by-nrhs solution matrix X.

LDB   (input) INTEGER
        The leading dimension of the array B. $LDB \geq \max(1,N)$.

WORK   (workspace)
        REAL/COMPLEX/COMPLEX array, dimension (LWORK)
        On exit, if INFO = 0, WORK(1) returns the optimal LWORK.

LWORK   (input) INTEGER
        The length of the array WORK. $LWORK \geq 1$, and for best performance $LWORK \geq N*NB$, where NB is the optimal block size for SSYTRF/CSYTRF/CHETRF.

INFO   (output) INTEGER
        = 0:   successful exit
        < 0:   if INFO = -i, the ith argument had an illegal value
        > 0:   if INFO = i, D(i,i) is exactly zero. The factorization has been completed, but the block diagonal matrix D is exactly singular, and the solution could not be computed.

SSYSVX/CSYSVX/CHESVX

```
SUBROUTINE SSYSVX( FACT, UPLO, N, NRHS, A, LDA, AF, LDAF, IPIV, B,
$                  LDB, X, LDX, RCOND, FERR, BERR, WORK, LWORK,
$                  IWORK, INFO )
     CHARACTER      FACT, UPLO
     INTEGER        INFO, LDA, LDAF, LDB, LDX, LWORK, N, NRHS
     REAL           RCOND
     INTEGER        IPIV( * ), IWORK( * )
     REAL           A( LDA, * ), AF( LDAF, * ), B( LDB, * ),
$                  BERR( * ), FERR( * ), WORK( * ), X( LDX, * )

SUBROUTINE CSYSVX( FACT, UPLO, N, NRHS, A, LDA, AF, LDAF, IPIV, B,
$                  LDB, X, LDX, RCOND, FERR, BERR, WORK, LWORK,
$                  RWORK, INFO )
     CHARACTER      FACT, UPLO
     INTEGER        INFO, LDA, LDAF, LDB, LDX, LWORK, N, NRHS
     REAL           RCOND
     INTEGER        IPIV( * )
     REAL           BERR( * ), FERR( * ), RWORK( * )
     COMPLEX        A( LDA, * ), AF( LDAF, * ), B( LDB, * ),
$                  WORK( * ), X( LDX, * )

SUBROUTINE CHESVX( FACT, UPLO, N, NRHS, A, LDA, AF, LDAF, IPIV, B,
$                  LDB, X, LDX, RCOND, FERR, BERR, WORK, LWORK,
$                  RWORK, INFO )
     CHARACTER      FACT, UPLO
     INTEGER        INFO, LDA, LDAF, LDB, LDX, LWORK, N, NRHS
     REAL           RCOND
     INTEGER        IPIV( * )
     REAL           BERR( * ), FERR( * ), RWORK( * )
     COMPLEX        A( LDA, * ), AF( LDAF, * ), B( LDB, * ),
$                  WORK( * ), X( LDX, * )
```

Purpose

SSYSVX/CSYSVX/CHESVX uses the diagonal pivoting factorization to compute the solution to a real/complex system of linear equations $A*X = B$, where A is an n-by-n symmetric (SSYSVX/CSYSVX) or Hermitian (CHESVX) matrix and X and B are n-by-nrhs matrices.

Error bounds on the solution and a condition estimate are also computed.

Description

The following steps are performed:

1. If FACT = 'N', the diagonal pivoting method is used to factor A. The form of the factorization is

$A = U*D*U^T$ or $A = L*D*L^T$ (SSYSVX/CSYSVX) or

$A = U*D*U^H$ or $A = L*D*L^H$ (CHESVX),

where U (or L) is a product of permutation and unit upper (lower) triangular matrices, and D is symmetric (SSYSVX/CSYSVX) or Hermitian (CHESVX) and block diagonal with 1-by-1 and 2-by-2 diagonal blocks.

2. The factored form of A is used to estimate the condition number of the matrix A. If the reciprocal of the condition number is less than machine precision, steps 3 and 4 are skipped.

3. The system of equations is solved for X using the factored form of A.

4. Iterative refinement is applied to improve the computed solution vectors and calculate error bounds and backward error estimates for them.

Arguments

FACT   (input) CHARACTER*1
        Specifies whether or not the factored form of the matrix A is supplied on entry.
        = 'F': On entry, AF and IPIV contain the factored form of A. A, AF and IPIV will not be modified.
        = 'N': The matrix A will be copied to AF and factored.

UPLO   (input) CHARACTER*1
        = 'U': Upper triangle of A is stored.
        = 'L': Lower triangle of A is stored.

N   (input) INTEGER
        The number of linear equations, i.e., the order of the matrix A. $N \geq 0$.

NRHS   (input) INTEGER
        The number of right hand sides, i.e., the number of columns of the matrices B and X. $NRHS \geq 0$.

A   (input) REAL/COMPLEX/COMPLEX array, dimension (LDA,N)
        The symmetric/symmetric/Hermitian matrix A. If UPLO = 'U', the leading n-by-n upper triangular part of A contains the upper triangular part of the matrix A, and the strictly lower triangular part of A is not referenced. If UPLO = 'L', the leading n-by-n lower triangular part of A contains the lower triangular part of the matrix A, and the strictly upper triangular part of A is not referenced.

LDA   (input) INTEGER
        The leading dimension of the array A. $LDA \geq \max(1,N)$.

AF   (input or output)
        REAL/COMPLEX/COMPLEX array, dimension (LDAF,N)
        If FACT = 'F', then AF is an input argument and on entry contains the block diagonal matrix D and the multipliers used to obtain the factor U or L from the factorization $A = U*D*U^T$ or $A = L*D*L^T$ as computed by SSYTRF/CSYTRF or the factorization $A = U*D*U^H$ or $A = L*D*L^H$ as computed by CHETRF.
        If FACT = 'N', then AF is an output argument and on exit returns the

block diagonal matrix D and the multipliers used to obtain the factor U or L from the factorization.

LDAF (input) INTEGER
The leading dimension of the array AF. LDAF $\geq$ max(1,N).

IPIV (input or output) INTEGER array, dimension (N)
If FACT = 'F', then IPIV is an input argument and on entry contains details of the interchanges and the block structure of D, as determined by SSYTRF/CSYTRF/CHETRF. If IPIV(k) > 0, then rows and columns k and IPIV(k) were interchanged and D(k,k) is a 1-by-1 diagonal block. If UPLO = 'U' and IPIV(k) = IPIV(k-1) < 0, then rows and columns k-1 and -IPIV(k) were interchanged and D(k-1:k,k-1:k) is a 2-by-2 diagonal block. If UPLO = 'L' and IPIV(k) = IPIV(k+1) < 0, then rows and columns k+1 and -IPIV(k) were interchanged and D(k:k+1,k:k+1) is a 2-by-2 diagonal block.
If FACT = 'N', then IPIV is an output argument and on exit contains details of the interchanges and the block structure of D, as determined by SSYTRF/CSYTRF/CHETRF.

B (input) REAL/COMPLEX/COMPLEX array, dimension (LDB,NRHS)
The n-by-nrhs right hand side matrix B.

LDB (input) INTEGER
The leading dimension of the array B. LDB $\geq$ max(1,N).

X (output)
REAL/COMPLEX/COMPLEX array, dimension (LDX,NRHS)
If INFO = 0, the n-by-nrhs solution matrix X.

LDX (input) INTEGER
The leading dimension of the array X. LDX $\geq$ max(1,N).

RCOND (output) REAL
The estimate of the reciprocal condition number of the matrix A. If RCOND is less than the machine precision (in particular, if RCOND = 0), the matrix is singular to working precision. This condition is indicated by a return code of INFO > 0, and the solution and error bounds are not computed.

FERR (output) REAL array, dimension (NRHS)
The estimated forward error bound for each solution vector X(j) (the jth column of the solution matrix X). If XTRUE is the true solution corresponding to X(j), FERR(j) bounds the magnitude of the largest element in (X(j) − XTRUE) divided by the magnitude of the largest element in X(j). The quality of the error bound depends on the quality of the estimate of $\|A^{-1}\|$ computed in the code; if the estimate of $\|A^{-1}\|$ is accurate, the error bound is guaranteed.

BERR (output) REAL array, dimension (NRHS)
The componentwise relative backward error of each solution vector X(j) (i.e., the smallest relative change in any element of A or B that makes X(j) an exact solution).

WORK (workspace)
REAL/COMPLEX/COMPLEX array, dimension (LWORK)
On exit, if INFO = 0, WORK(1) returns the optimal LWORK.

LWORK (input) INTEGER
The length of the array WORK.
SSYSVX
LWORK $\geq$ 3*N, and for best performance LWORK $\geq$ N*NB, where NB is the optimal block size for SSYTRF.
CSYSVX/CHESVX
LWORK $\geq$ 2*N, and for best performance LWORK $\geq$ N*NB, where NB is the optimal block size for CSYTRF/CHETRF.

IWORK *SSYSVX only* (workspace) INTEGER array, dimension (N)

RWORK *CSYSVX/CHESVX only* (workspace) REAL array, dimension (N)

INFO (output) INTEGER
= 0:   successful exit
< 0:   if INFO = −i, the ith argument had an illegal value
> 0:   if INFO = i, and i is
   $\leq$ N: D(i,i) is exactly zero. The factorization has been completed, but the block diagonal matrix D is exactly singular, and the solution and error bounds could not be computed.
   = N+1: the block diagonal matrix D is nonsingular, but RCOND is less than machine precision. The factorization has been completed, but the matrix is singular to working precision, and the solution and error bounds have not been computed.

SSYTRD/CHETRD

```
SUBROUTINE SSYTRD( UPLO, N, A, LDA, D, E, TAU, WORK, LWORK, INFO )
   CHARACTER        UPLO
   INTEGER          INFO, LDA, LWORK, N
   REAL             A( LDA, * ), D( * ), E( * ), TAU( * ),
  $                 WORK( * )

SUBROUTINE CHETRD( UPLO, N, A, LDA, D, E, TAU, WORK, LWORK, INFO )
   CHARACTER        UPLO
   INTEGER          INFO, LDA, LWORK, N
   REAL             D( * ), E( * )
   COMPLEX          A( LDA, * ), TAU( * ), WORK( * )
```

Purpose

SSYTRD/CHETRD reduces a real/complex symmetric/Hermitian matrix A to real symmetric tridiagonal form T by an orthogonal/unitary similarity transformation: $Q^H * A * Q = T$.

```
SUBROUTINE SSYTRF( UPLO, N, A, LDA, IPIV, WORK, LWORK, INFO )
    CHARACTER    UPLO
    INTEGER      INFO, LDA, LWORK, N
    INTEGER      IPIV( * )
    REAL         A( LDA, * ), WORK( LWORK )

SUBROUTINE CSYTRF( UPLO, N, A, LDA, IPIV, WORK, LWORK, INFO )
    CHARACTER    UPLO
    INTEGER      INFO, LDA, LWORK, N
    INTEGER      IPIV( * )
    COMPLEX      A( LDA, * ), WORK( LWORK )

SUBROUTINE CHETRF( UPLO, N, A, LDA, IPIV, WORK, LWORK, INFO )
    CHARACTER    UPLO
    INTEGER      INFO, LDA, LWORK, N
    INTEGER      IPIV( * )
    COMPLEX      A( LDA, * ), WORK( LWORK )
```

Purpose

SSYTRF/CSYTRF/CHETRF computes the factorization of a real/complex/complex symmetric/symmetric/Hermitian matrix A, using the diagonal pivoting method. The form of the factorization is

$$A = U*D*U^T \text{ or } A = L*D*L^T \text{ (SSYTRF/CSYTRF) or}$$

$$A = U*D*U^H \text{ or } A = L*D*L^H \text{ (CHETRF)},$$

where U (or L) is a product of permutation and unit upper (lower) triangular matrices, and D is symmetric (SSYTRF/CSYTRF) or Hermitian (CHETRF) and block diagonal with 1-by-1 and 2-by-2 diagonal blocks.

Arguments

UPLO   (input) CHARACTER*1
        = 'U': Upper triangle of A is stored;
        = 'L': Lower triangle of A is stored.

N   (input) INTEGER
        The order of the matrix A. N $\geq$ 0.

A   (input/output)
        REAL/COMPLEX/COMPLEX array, dimension (LDA,N)
        On entry, the symmetric/symmetric/Hermitian matrix A. If UPLO =
        'U', the leading n-by-n upper triangular part of A contains the upper
        triangular part of the matrix A, and the strictly lower triangular part of
        A is not referenced. If UPLO = 'L', the leading n-by-n lower triangular
        part of A contains the lower triangular part of the matrix A, and the
        strictly upper triangular part of A is not referenced.
        On exit, the block diagonal matrix D and the multipliers used to obtain
        the factor U or L.

Arguments

UPLO   (input) CHARACTER*1
        = 'U': Upper triangle of A is stored;
        = 'L': Lower triangle of A is stored.

N   (input) INTEGER
        The order of the matrix A. N $\geq$ 0.

A   (input/output) REAL/COMPLEX array, dimension (LDA,N)
        On entry, the symmetric/Hermitian matrix A. If UPLO = 'U', the lead-
        ing n-by-n upper triangular part of A contains the upper triangular part
        of the matrix A, and the strictly lower triangular part of A is not ref-
        erenced. If UPLO = 'L', the leading n-by-n lower triangular part of
        A contains the lower triangular part of the matrix A, and the strictly
        upper triangular part of A is not referenced.
        On exit, if UPLO = 'U', the diagonal and first superdiagonal of A are
        overwritten by the corresponding elements of the tridiagonal matrix T,
        and the elements above the first superdiagonal, with the array TAU,
        represent the orthogonal/unitary matrix Q as a product of elementary
        reflectors; if UPLO = 'L', the diagonal and first subdiagonal of A are
        overwritten by the corresponding elements of the tridiagonal matrix
        T, and the elements below the first subdiagonal, with the array TAU,
        represent the orthogonal/unitary matrix Q as a product of elementary
        reflectors. .

LDA   (input) INTEGER
        The leading dimension of the array A. LDA $\geq$ max(1,N).

D   (output) REAL array, dimension (N)
        The diagonal elements of the tridiagonal matrix T: D(i) = A(i,i).

E   (output) REAL array, dimension (N−1)
        The off-diagonal elements of the tridiagonal matrix T: E(i) = A(i,i+1)
        if UPLO = 'U', E(i) = A(i+1,i) if UPLO = 'L'.

TAU   (output) REAL/COMPLEX array, dimension (N)
        The scalar factors of the elementary reflectors.

WORK   (workspace) REAL/COMPLEX array, dimension (LWORK)
        On exit, if INFO = 0, WORK(1) returns the optimal LWORK.

LWORK   (input) INTEGER
        The length of the array WORK. LWORK $\geq$ 1, and for optimum per-
        formance LWORK $\geq$ N*NB, where NB is the optimal block size.

INFO   (output) INTEGER
        = 0: successful exit
        < 0: if INFO = −i, the ith argument had an illegal value.

Purpose

SSYTRI/CSYTRI/CHETRI computes the inverse of a real/complex/complex symmetric/symmetric/Hermitian indefinite matrix A using the factorization $A = U*D*U^T$ or $A = L*D*L^T$ computed by SSYTRF/CSYTRF or the factorization $A = U*D*U^H$ or $A = L*D*L^H$ computed by CHETRF.

Arguments

UPLO   (input) CHARACTER*1
Specifies whether the details of the factorization are stored as an upper or lower triangular matrix.
= 'U': Upper triangular, form is $A = U*D*U^T$ (SSYTRI/CSYTRI) or $A = U*D*U^H$ (CHETRI);
= 'L': Lower triangular, form is $A = L*D*L^T$ (SSYTRI/CSYTRI) or $A = L*D*L^H$ (CHETRI)

N   (input) INTEGER
The order of the matrix A. N ≥ 0.

A   (input/output)
REAL/COMPLEX/COMPLEX array, dimension (LDA,N)
On entry, the block diagonal matrix D and the multipliers used to obtain the factor U or L as computed by SSYTRF/CSYTRF/CHETRF.
On exit, if INFO = 0, the (symmetric/symmetric/Hermitian) inverse of the original matrix. If UPLO = 'U', the upper triangular part of the inverse is formed and the part of A below the diagonal is not referenced; if UPLO = 'L' the lower triangular part of the inverse is formed and the part of A above the diagonal is not referenced.

LDA   (input) INTEGER
The leading dimension of the array A. LDA ≥ max(1,N).

IPIV   (input) INTEGER array, dimension (N)
Details of the interchanges and the block structure of D as determined by SSYTRF/CSYTRF/CHETRF.

WORK   SSYTRI (workspace) REAL array, dimension (N)
CSYTRI/CHETRI (workspace) COMPLEX array, dimension (2*N)

INFO   (output) INTEGER
= 0: successful exit
< 0: if INFO = -i, the ith argument had an illegal value
> 0: if INFO = i, D(i,i) = 0; the matrix is singular and its inverse could not be computed.

LDA   (input) INTEGER
The leading dimension of the array A. LDA ≥ max(1,N).

IPIV   (output) INTEGER array, dimension (N)
Details of the interchanges and the block structure of D. If IPIV(k) > 0, then rows and columns k and IPIV(k) were interchanged and D(k,k) is a 1-by-1 diagonal block. If UPLO = 'U' and IPIV(k) = IPIV(k-1) < 0, then rows and columns k-1 and -IPIV(k) were interchanged and D(k-1:k,k-1:k) is a 2-by-2 diagonal block. If UPLO = 'L' and IPIV(k) = IPIV(k+1) < 0, then rows and columns k+1 and -IPIV(k) were interchanged and D(k:k+1,k:k+1) is a 2-by-2 diagonal block.

WORK   (workspace)
REAL/COMPLEX/COMPLEX array, dimension (LWORK)
On exit, if INFO = 0, WORK(1) returns the optimal LWORK.

LWORK   (input) INTEGER
The length of the array WORK. LWORK ≥ 1, and for best performance LWORK ≥ N*NB, where NB is the block size returned by ILAENV.

INFO   (output) INTEGER
= 0: successful exit
< 0: if INFO = -i, the ith argument had an illegal value
> 0: if INFO = i, D(i,i) is exactly zero. The factorization has been completed, but the block diagonal matrix D is exactly singular, and division by zero will occur if it is used to solve a system of equations.

SSYTRI/CSYTRI/CHETRI

```
SUBROUTINE SSYTRI( UPLO, N, A, LDA, IPIV, WORK, INFO )
CHARACTER     UPLO
INTEGER       INFO, LDA, N
INTEGER       IPIV( * )
REAL          A( LDA, * ), WORK( * )

SUBROUTINE CSYTRI( UPLO, N, A, LDA, IPIV, WORK, INFO )
CHARACTER     UPLO
INTEGER       INFO, LDA, N
INTEGER       IPIV( * )
COMPLEX       A( LDA, * ), WORK( * )

SUBROUTINE CHETRI( UPLO, N, A, LDA, IPIV, WORK, INFO )
CHARACTER     UPLO
INTEGER       INFO, LDA, N
INTEGER       IPIV( * )
COMPLEX       A( LDA, * ), WORK( * )
```

SSYTRS/CSYTRS/CHETRS

```
SUBROUTINE SSYTRS( UPLO, N, NRHS, A, LDA, IPIV, B, LDB, INFO )
CHARACTER        UPLO
INTEGER          INFO, LDA, LDB, N, NRHS
INTEGER          IPIV( * )
REAL             A( LDA, * ), B( LDB, * )

SUBROUTINE CSYTRS( UPLO, N, NRHS, A, LDA, IPIV, B, LDB, INFO )
CHARACTER        UPLO
INTEGER          INFO, LDA, LDB, N, NRHS
INTEGER          IPIV( * )
COMPLEX          A( LDA, * ), B( LDB, * )

SUBROUTINE CHETRS( UPLO, N, NRHS, A, LDA, IPIV, B, LDB, INFO )
CHARACTER        UPLO
INTEGER          INFO, LDA, LDB, N, NRHS
INTEGER          IPIV( * )
COMPLEX          A( LDA, * ), B( LDB, * )
```

Purpose

SSYTRS/CSYTRS/CHETRS solves a system of linear equations $A*X = B$ with a real/complex symmetric/symmetric/Hermitian matrix A using the factorization $A = U*D*U^T$ or $A = L*D*L^T$ computed by SSYTRF/CSYTRF or the factorization $A = U*D*U^H$ or $A = L*D*L^H$ computed by CHETRF.

Arguments

UPLO   (input) CHARACTER*1
Specifies whether the details of the factorization are stored as an upper or lower triangular matrix.
= 'U': Upper triangular, form is $A = U*D*U^T$ (SSYTRS/CSYTRS)
or $A = U*D*U^H$ (CHETRS);
= 'L': Lower triangular, form is $A = L*D*L^T$ (SSYTRS/CSYTRS)
or $A = L*D*L^H$ (CHETRS).

N   (input) INTEGER
The order of the matrix A. $N \geq 0$.

NRHS   (input) INTEGER
The number of right hand sides, i.e., the number of columns of the matrix B. $NRHS \geq 0$.

A   (input) REAL/COMPLEX/COMPLEX array, dimension (LDA,N)
The block diagonal matrix D and the multipliers used to obtain the factor U or L as computed by SSYTRF/CSYTRF/CHETRF.

LDA   (input) INTEGER
The leading dimension of the array A. $LDA \geq \max(1,N)$.

IPIV   (input) INTEGER array, dimension (N)
Details of the interchanges and the block structure of D as determined by SSYTRF/CSYTRF/CHETRF.

B   (input/output)
REAL/COMPLEX/COMPLEX array, dimension (LDB,NRHS)
On entry, the right hand side matrix B.
On exit, the solution matrix X.

LDB   (input) INTEGER
The leading dimension of the array B. $LDB \geq \max(1,N)$.

INFO   (output) INTEGER
= 0:   successful exit
< 0:   if INFO = $-i$, the ith argument had an illegal value

STBCON/CTBCON

```
SUBROUTINE STBCON( NORM, UPLO, DIAG, N, KD, AB, LDAB, RCOND, WORK,
$                  IWORK, INFO )
CHARACTER        DIAG, NORM, UPLO
INTEGER          INFO, KD, LDAB, N
REAL             RCOND
INTEGER          IWORK( * )
REAL             AB( LDAB, * ), WORK( * )

SUBROUTINE CTBCON( NORM, UPLO, DIAG, N, KD, AB, LDAB, RCOND, WORK,
$                  RWORK, INFO )
CHARACTER        DIAG, NORM, UPLO
INTEGER          INFO, KD, LDAB, N
REAL             RCOND
REAL             RWORK( * )
COMPLEX          AB( LDAB, * ), WORK( * )
```

Purpose

STBCON/CTBCON estimates the reciprocal of the condition number of a triangular band matrix A, in either the 1-norm or the infinity-norm.

The norm of A is computed and an estimate is obtained for $||A^{-1}||$, then the reciprocal of the condition number is computed as $RCOND = 1/(||A|| \cdot ||A^{-1}||)$.

Arguments

NORM   (input) CHARACTER*1
Specifies whether the 1-norm condition number or the infinity-norm condition number is required:
= '1' or 'O': 1-norm;
= 'I': Infinity-norm.

UPLO   (input) CHARACTER*1
= 'U': A is upper triangular;
= 'L': A is lower triangular.

DIAG (input) CHARACTER*1
= 'N': A is non-unit triangular;
= 'U': A is unit triangular.

N (input) INTEGER
The order of the matrix A. N ≥ 0.

KD (input) INTEGER
The number of superdiagonals or subdiagonals of the triangular band matrix A. KD ≥ 0.

AB (input) REAL/COMPLEX array, dimension (LDAB,N)
The upper or lower triangular band matrix A, stored in the first kd+1 rows of the array. The jth column of A is stored in the jth column of the array AB as follows:
if UPLO = 'U', AB(kd+1+i−j,j) = A(i,j) for $\max(1,j-kd)\le i\le j$;
if UPLO = 'L', AB(1+i−j,j) = A(i,j) for $j\le i\le \min(n,j+kd)$.
If DIAG = 'U', the diagonal elements of A are not referenced and are assumed to be 1.

LDAB (input) INTEGER
The leading dimension of the array AB. LDAB ≥ KD+1.

RCOND (output) REAL
The reciprocal of the condition number of the matrix A, computed as RCOND = $1/(\|A\|\cdot\|A^{-1}\|)$.

WORK *STBCON* (workspace) REAL array, dimension (3*N)
CTBCON (workspace) COMPLEX array, dimension (2*N)

IWORK *STBCON only* (workspace) INTEGER array, dimension (N)

RWORK *CTBCON only* (workspace) REAL array, dimension (N)

INFO (output) INTEGER
= 0:   successful exit
< 0:   if INFO = −i, the ith argument had an illegal value

STBRFS/CTBRFS

```
SUBROUTINE STBRFS( UPLO, TRANS, DIAG, N, KD, NRHS, AB, LDAB, B,
$                  LDB, X, LDX, FERR, BERR, WORK, IWORK, INFO )
CHARACTER          DIAG, TRANS, UPLO
INTEGER            INFO, KD, LDAB, LDB, LDX, N, NRHS
INTEGER            IWORK( * )
REAL               AB( LDAB, * ), B( LDB, * ), BERR( * ),
$                  FERR( * ), WORK( * ), X( LDX, * )
```

```
SUBROUTINE CTBRFS( UPLO, TRANS, DIAG, N, KD, NRHS, AB, LDAB, B,
$                  LDB, X, LDX, FERR, BERR, WORK, RWORK, INFO )
CHARACTER          DIAG, TRANS, UPLO
INTEGER            INFO, KD, LDAB, LDB, LDX, N, NRHS
REAL               BERR( * ), FERR( * ), RWORK( * )
COMPLEX            AB( LDAB, * ), B( LDB, * ), WORK( * ),
$                  X( LDX, * )
```

Purpose

STBRFS/CTBRFS provides error bounds and backward error estimates for the solution to a system of linear equations with a triangular band coefficient matrix.

The solution vectors X must be computed by STBTRS/CTBTRS or some other means before entering this routine. STBRFS/CTBRFS does not do iterative refinement because doing so cannot improve the backward error.

Arguments

UPLO (input) CHARACTER*1
= 'U': A is upper triangular;
= 'L': A is lower triangular.

TRANS (input) CHARACTER*1
Specifies the form of the system of equations:
= 'N': $A*X = B$ (No transpose)
= 'T': $A^T*X = B$ (Transpose)
= 'C': $A^H*X = B$ (Conjugate transpose)

DIAG (input) CHARACTER*1
= 'N': A is non-unit triangular;
= 'U': A is unit triangular.

N (input) INTEGER
The order of the matrix A. N ≥ 0.

KD (input) INTEGER
The number of superdiagonals or subdiagonals of the triangular band matrix A. KD ≥ 0.

NRHS (input) INTEGER
The number of right hand sides, i.e., the number of columns of the matrices B and X. NRHS ≥ 0.

AB (input) REAL/COMPLEX array, dimension (LDAB,N)
The upper or lower triangular band matrix A, stored in the first kd+1 rows of the array. The jth column of A is stored in the jth column of the array AB as follows:
if UPLO = 'U', AB(kd+1+i−j,j) = A(i,j) for $\max(1,j-kd)\le i\le j$;
if UPLO = 'L', AB(1+i−j,j) = A(i,j) for $j\le i\le \min(n,j+kd)$.
If DIAG = 'U', the diagonal elements of A are not referenced and are assumed to be 1.

LDAB (input) INTEGER
The leading dimension of the array AB. LDAB ≥ KD+1.

Purpose

STBTRS/CTBTRS solves a triangular system of the form $A*X = B$, $A^T*X = B$, or $A^H*X = B$, where A is a triangular band matrix of order n, and B is an n-by-nrhs matrix. A check is made to verify that A is nonsingular.

Arguments

UPLO   (input) CHARACTER*1
= 'U': A is upper triangular;
= 'L': A is lower triangular.

TRANS   (input) CHARACTER*1
Specifies the form of the system of equations:
= 'N': $A*X = B$ (No transpose)
= 'T': $A^T*X = B$ (Transpose)
= 'C': $A^H*X = B$ (Conjugate transpose)

DIAG   (input) CHARACTER*1
= 'N': A is non-unit triangular;
= 'U': A is unit triangular.

N   (input) INTEGER
The order of the matrix A. $N \geq 0$.

KD   (input) INTEGER
The number of superdiagonals or subdiagonals of the triangular band matrix A. $KD \geq 0$.

NRHS   (input) INTEGER
The number of right hand sides, i.e., the number of columns of the matrix B. $NRHS \geq 0$.

AB   (input) REAL/COMPLEX array, dimension (LDAB,N)
The upper or lower triangular band matrix A, stored in the first kd+1 rows of AB. The jth column of A is stored in the jth column of the array AB as follows:
if UPLO = 'U', $AB(kd+1+i-jj) = A(ij)$ for $max(1,j-kd) \leq i \leq j$;
if UPLO = 'L', $AB(1+i-jj) = A(ij)$ for $j \leq i \leq min(n,j+kd)$.
If DIAG = 'U', the diagonal elements of A are not referenced and are assumed to be 1.

LDAB   (input) INTEGER
The leading dimension of the array AB. $LDAB \geq KD+1$.

B   (input/output) REAL/COMPLEX array, dimension (LDB,NRHS)
On entry, the right hand side matrix B.
On exit, if INFO = 0, the solution matrix X.

LDB   (input) INTEGER
The leading dimension of the array B. $LDB \geq max(1,N)$.

INFO   (output) INTEGER
= 0:   successful exit
< 0:   if INFO = $-i$, the ith argument had an illegal value

---

STBTRS/CTBTRS

```
SUBROUTINE STBTRS( UPLO, TRANS, DIAG, N, KD, NRHS, AB, LDAB, B,
$                  LDB, INFO )
    CHARACTER        DIAG, TRANS, UPLO
    INTEGER          INFO, KD, LDAB, LDB, N, NRHS
    REAL             AB( LDAB, * ), B( LDB, * )

SUBROUTINE CTBTRS( UPLO, TRANS, DIAG, N, KD, NRHS, AB, LDAB, B,
$                  LDB, INFO )
    CHARACTER        DIAG, TRANS, UPLO
    INTEGER          INFO, KD, LDAB, LDB, N, NRHS
    COMPLEX          AB( LDAB, * ), B( LDB, * )
```

B   (input) REAL/COMPLEX array, dimension (LDB,NRHS)
The right hand side matrix B.

LDB   (input) INTEGER
The leading dimension of the array B. $LDB \geq max(1,N)$.

X   (input) REAL/COMPLEX array, dimension (LDX,NRHS)
The solution matrix X.

LDX   (input) INTEGER
The leading dimension of the array X. $LDX \geq max(1,N)$.

FERR   (output) REAL array, dimension (NRHS)
The estimated forward error bound for each solution vector X(j) (the jth column of the solution matrix X). If XTRUE is the true solution corresponding to X(j), FERR(j) bounds the magnitude of the largest element in $(X(j) - XTRUE)$ divided by the magnitude of the largest element in X(j). The quality of the error bound depends on the quality of the estimate of $||A^{-1}||$ computed in the code; if the estimate of $||A^{-1}||$ is accurate, the error bound is guaranteed.

BERR   (output) REAL array, dimension (NRHS)
The componentwise relative backward error of each solution vector X(j) (i.e., the smallest relative change in any element of A or B that makes X(j) an exact solution).

WORK   STBRFS (workspace) REAL array, dimension (3*N)
CTBRFS (workspace) COMPLEX array, dimension (2*N)

IWORK   STBRFS only (workspace) INTEGER array, dimension (N)

RWORK   CTBRFS only (workspace) REAL array, dimension (N)

INFO   (output) INTEGER
= 0:   successful exit
< 0:   if INFO = $-i$, the ith argument had an illegal value

---

STBRFS/CTBRFS

> 0:   if INFO = i, the ith diagonal element of A is zero, indicating that the matrix is singular and the solutions X have not been computed.

STPCON/CTPCON

```
SUBROUTINE STPCON( NORM, UPLO, DIAG, N, AP, RCOND, WORK, IWORK,
$                  INFO )
   CHARACTER    DIAG, NORM, UPLO
   INTEGER      INFO, N
   REAL         RCOND
   INTEGER      IWORK( * )
   REAL         AP( * ), WORK( * )

SUBROUTINE CTPCON( NORM, UPLO, DIAG, N, AP, RCOND, WORK, RWORK,
$                  INFO )
   CHARACTER    DIAG, NORM, UPLO
   INTEGER      INFO, N
   REAL         RCOND
   REAL         RWORK( * )
   COMPLEX      AP( * ), WORK( * )
```

Purpose

STPCON/CTPCON estimates the reciprocal of the condition number of a packed triangular matrix A, in either the 1-norm or the infinity-norm.

The norm of A is computed and an estimate is obtained for $\|A^{-1}\|$, then the reciprocal of the condition number is computed as RCOND = $1/(\|A\| \cdot \|A^{-1}\|)$.

Arguments

NORM   (input) CHARACTER*1
        Specifies whether the 1-norm condition number or the infinity-norm condition number is required.
        = '1' or 'O': 1-norm
        = 'I': Infinity-norm

UPLO   (input) CHARACTER*1
        = 'U': A is upper triangular;
        = 'L': A is lower triangular.

DIAG   (input) CHARACTER*1
        = 'N': A is non-unit triangular;
        = 'U': A is unit triangular.

N   (input) INTEGER
        The order of the matrix A. N ≥ 0.

AP   (input) REAL/COMPLEX array, dimension (N*(N+1)/2)
        The upper or lower triangular matrix A, packed columnwise in a linear array. The jth column of A is stored in the array AP as follows:
        if UPLO = 'U', AP(i + (j−1)*j/2) = A(i,j) for 1≤i≤j;
        if UPLO = 'L', AP(i + (j−1)*(2n−j)/2) = A(i,j) for j≤i≤n.
        If DIAG = 'U', the diagonal elements of A are not referenced and are assumed to be 1.

RCOND   (output) REAL
        The reciprocal of the condition number of the matrix A, computed as RCOND = $1/(\|A\| \cdot \|A^{-1}\|)$.

WORK   STPCON (workspace) REAL array, dimension (3*N)
        CTPCON (workspace) COMPLEX array, dimension (2*N)

IWORK   STPCON *only* (workspace) INTEGER array, dimension (N)

RWORK   CTPCON *only* (workspace) REAL array, dimension (N)

INFO   (output) INTEGER
        = 0:   successful exit
        < 0:   if INFO = −i, the ith argument had an illegal value

---

STPRFS/CTPRFS

```
SUBROUTINE STPRFS( UPLO, TRANS, DIAG, N, NRHS, AP, B, LDB, X, LDX,
$                  FERR, BERR, WORK, IWORK, INFO )
   CHARACTER    DIAG, TRANS, UPLO
   INTEGER      INFO, LDB, LDX, N, NRHS
   INTEGER      IWORK( * )
   REAL         AP( * ), B( LDB, * ), BERR( * ), FERR( * ),
$               WORK( * ), X( LDX, * )

SUBROUTINE CTPRFS( UPLO, TRANS, DIAG, N, NRHS, AP, B, LDB, X, LDX,
$                  FERR, BERR, WORK, RWORK, INFO )
   CHARACTER    DIAG, TRANS, UPLO
   INTEGER      INFO, LDB, LDX, N, NRHS
   REAL         BERR( * ), FERR( * ), RWORK( * )
   COMPLEX      AP( * ), B( LDB, * ), WORK( * ), X( LDX, * )
```

Purpose

STPRFS/CTPRFS provides error bounds and backward error estimates for the solution to a system of linear equations with a triangular packed coefficient matrix.

The solution vectors X must be computed by STPTRS/CTPTRS or some other means before entering this routine. STPRFS/CTPRFS does not do iterative refinement because doing so cannot improve the backward error.

Arguments

UPLO (input) CHARACTER*1
= 'U': A is upper triangular;
= 'L': A is lower triangular.

TRANS (input) CHARACTER*1
Specifies the form of the system of equations:
= 'N': $A*X = B$ (No transpose)
= 'T': $A^T*X = B$ (Transpose)
= 'C': $A^H*X = B$ (Conjugate transpose)

DIAG (input) CHARACTER*1
= 'N': A is non-unit triangular;
= 'U': A is unit triangular.

N (input) INTEGER
The order of the matrix A. $N \geq 0$.

NRHS (input) INTEGER
The number of right hand sides, i.e., the number of columns of the matrices B and X. $NRHS \geq 0$.

AP (input) REAL/COMPLEX array, dimension $(N*(N+1)/2)$
The upper or lower triangular matrix A, packed columnwise in a linear array. The jth column of A is stored in the array AP as follows:
if UPLO = 'U', $AP(i + (j-1)*j/2) = A(i,j)$ for $1 \leq i \leq j$;
if UPLO = 'L', $AP(i + (j-1)*(2n-j)/2) = A(i,j)$ for $j \leq i \leq N$.
If DIAG = 'U', the diagonal elements of A are not referenced and are assumed to be 1.

B (input) REAL/COMPLEX array, dimension (LDB,NRHS)
The right hand side matrix B.

LDB (input) INTEGER
The leading dimension of the array B. $LDB \geq \max(1,N)$.

X (input) REAL/COMPLEX array, dimension (LDX,NRHS)
The solution matrix X.

LDX (input) INTEGER
The leading dimension of the array X. $LDX \geq \max(1,N)$.

FERR (output) REAL array, dimension (NRHS)
The estimated forward error bound for each solution vector X(j) (the jth column of the solution matrix X). If XTRUE is the true solution corresponding to X(j), FERR(j) bounds the magnitude of the largest element in $(X(j) - XTRUE)$ divided by the magnitude of the largest element in X(j). The quality of the error bound depends on the quality of the estimate of $\|A^{-1}\|$ computed in the code; if the estimate of $\|A^{-1}\|$ is accurate, the error bound is guaranteed.

BERR (output) REAL array, dimension (NRHS)
The componentwise relative backward error of each solution vector X(j) (i.e., the smallest relative change in any element of A or B that makes X(j) an exact solution).

WORK STPRFS (workspace) REAL array, dimension (3*N)
CTPRFS (workspace) COMPLEX array, dimension (2*N)

IWORK STPRFS only (workspace) INTEGER array, dimension (N)

RWORK CTPRFS only (workspace) REAL array, dimension (N)

INFO (output) INTEGER
= 0:   successful exit
< 0:   if INFO = −i, the ith argument had an illegal value

STPTRI/CTPTRI

```
SUBROUTINE STPTRI( UPLO, DIAG, N, AP, INFO )
CHARACTER        DIAG, UPLO
INTEGER          INFO, N
REAL             AP( * )

SUBROUTINE CTPTRI( UPLO, DIAG, N, AP, INFO )
CHARACTER        DIAG, UPLO
INTEGER          INFO, N
COMPLEX          AP( * )
```

Purpose

STPTRI/CTPTRI computes the inverse of a real/complex upper or lower triangular matrix A stored in packed format.

Arguments

UPLO (input) CHARACTER*1
= 'U': A is upper triangular;
= 'L': A is lower triangular.

DIAG (input) CHARACTER*1
= 'N': A is non-unit triangular;
= 'U': A is unit triangular.

N (input) INTEGER
The order of the matrix A. $N \geq 0$.

AP (input/output) REAL/COMPLEX array, dimension $(N*(N+1)/2)$
On entry, the upper or lower triangular matrix A, packed columnwise in a linear array. The jth column of A is stored in the array AP as follows:
if UPLO = 'U', $AP(i + (j-1)*j/2) = A(i,j)$ for $1 \leq i \leq j$;
if UPLO = 'L', $AP(i + (j-1)*(2n-j)/2) = A(i,j)$ for $j \leq i \leq n$.
If DIAG = 'U', the diagonal elements of A are not referenced and are assumed to be 1.
On exit, the (triangular) inverse of the original matrix, in the same packed storage format.

INFO   (output) INTEGER
= 0: successful exit
< 0: if INFO = -i, the ith argument had an illegal value
> 0: if INFO = i, A(i,i) is exactly zero. The triangular matrix is singular and its inverse cannot be computed.

STPTRS/CTPTRS

```
SUBROUTINE STPTRS( UPLO, TRANS, DIAG, N, NRHS, AP, B, LDB, INFO )
CHARACTER    DIAG, TRANS, UPLO
INTEGER      INFO, LDB, N, NRHS
REAL         AP( * ), B( LDB, * )
SUBROUTINE CTPTRS( UPLO, TRANS, DIAG, N, NRHS, AP, B, LDB, INFO )
CHARACTER    DIAG, TRANS, UPLO
INTEGER      INFO, LDB, N, NRHS
COMPLEX      AP( * ), B( LDB, * )
```

Purpose

STPTRS/CTPTRS solves a triangular system of the form $A*X = B$, $A^T*X = B$, or $A^H*X = B$, where A is a triangular matrix of order n stored in packed format, and B is an n-by-nrhs matrix. A check is made to verify that A is nonsingular.

Arguments

UPLO   (input) CHARACTER*1
= 'U': A is upper triangular;
= 'L': A is lower triangular.

TRANS   (input) CHARACTER*1
Specifies the form of the system of equations:
= 'N': $A*X = B$ (No transpose)
= 'T': $A^T*X = B$ (Transpose)
= 'C': $A^H*X = B$ (Conjugate transpose)

DIAG   (input) CHARACTER*1
= 'N': A is non-unit triangular;
= 'U': A is unit triangular.

N   (input) INTEGER
The order of the matrix A. $N \geq 0$.

NRHS   (input) INTEGER
The number of right hand sides, i.e., the number of columns of the matrix B. $NRHS \geq 0$.

AP   (input) REAL/COMPLEX array, dimension (N*(N+1)/2)
The upper or lower triangular matrix A, packed columnwise in a linear array. The jth column of A is stored in the array AP as follows:

if UPLO = 'U', $AP(i + (j-1)*j/2) = A(i,j)$ for $1 \leq i \leq j$;
if UPLO = 'L', $AP(i + (j-1)*(2n-j)/2) = A(i,j)$ for $j \leq i \leq n$.
If DIAG = 'U', the diagonal elements of A are not referenced and are assumed to be 1.

B   (input/output) REAL/COMPLEX array, dimension (LDB,NRHS)
On entry, the right hand side matrix B.
On exit, if INFO = 0, the solution matrix X.

LDB   (input) INTEGER
The leading dimension of the array B. $LDB \geq \max(1,N)$.

INFO   (output) INTEGER
= 0: successful exit
< 0: if INFO = -i, the ith argument had an illegal value
> 0: if INFO = i, the ith diagonal element of A is zero, indicating that the matrix is singular and the solutions x have not been computed.

STRCON/CTRCON

```
SUBROUTINE STRCON( NORM, UPLO, DIAG, N, A, LDA, RCOND, WORK,
$                   IWORK, INFO )
CHARACTER          DIAG, NORM, UPLO
INTEGER            INFO, LDA, N
REAL               RCOND
INTEGER            IWORK( * )
REAL               A( LDA, * ), WORK( * )
SUBROUTINE CTRCON( NORM, UPLO, DIAG, N, A, LDA, RCOND, WORK,
$                   RWORK, INFO )
CHARACTER          DIAG, NORM, UPLO
INTEGER            INFO, LDA, N
REAL               RCOND
REAL               RWORK( * )
COMPLEX            A( LDA, * ), WORK( * )
```

Purpose

STRCON/CTRCON estimates the reciprocal of the condition number of a triangular matrix A, in either the 1-norm or the infinity-norm.

The norm of A is computed and an estimate is obtained for $||A^{-1}||$, then the reciprocal of the condition number is computed as $RCOND = 1/(||A|| \cdot ||A^{-1}||)$.

Arguments

NORM   (input) CHARACTER*1
Specifies whether the 1-norm condition number or the infinity-norm

condition number is required:
= '1' or 'O': 1-norm;
= 'I': Infinity-norm.

UPLO   (input) CHARACTER*1
      = 'U': A is upper triangular;
      = 'L': A is lower triangular.

DIAG   (input) CHARACTER*1
      = 'N': A is non-unit triangular;
      = 'U': A is unit triangular.

N   (input) INTEGER
      The order of the matrix A. $N \geq 0$.

A   (input) REAL/COMPLEX array, dimension (LDA,N)
      The triangular matrix A. If UPLO = 'U', the leading n-by-n upper triangular part of the array A contains the upper triangular matrix, and the strictly lower triangular part of A is not referenced. If UPLO = 'L', the leading n-by-n lower triangular part of the array A contains the lower triangular matrix, and the strictly upper triangular part of A is not referenced. If DIAG = 'U', the diagonal elements of A are also not referenced and are assumed to be 1.

LDA   (input) INTEGER
      The leading dimension of the array A. $LDA \geq \max(1,N)$.

RCOND (output) REAL
      The reciprocal of the condition number of the matrix A, computed as $RCOND = 1/(||A||\cdot||A^{-1}||)$.

WORK   *STRCON only* (workspace) REAL array, dimension (3*N)
      CTRCON only (workspace) COMPLEX array, dimension (2*N)

IWORK *STRCON only* (workspace) INTEGER array, dimension (N)

RWORK *CTRCON only* (workspace) REAL array, dimension (N)

INFO   (output) INTEGER
      = 0: successful exit
      < 0: if INFO = −i, the ith argument had an illegal value

STREVC/CTREVC

```
      SUBROUTINE STREVC( JOB, HOWMNY, SELECT, N, T, LDT, VL, LDVL, VR,
     $                   LDVR, MM, M, WORK, INFO )
      CHARACTER          HOWMNY, JOB
      INTEGER            INFO, LDT, LDVL, LDVR, N, MM, M
      LOGICAL            SELECT( * )
      REAL               T( LDT, * ), VL( LDVL, * ), VR( LDVR, * ),
     $                   WORK( * )
```

```
      SUBROUTINE CTREVC( JOB, HOWMNY, SELECT, N, T, LDT, VL, LDVL, VR,
     $                   LDVR, MM, M, WORK, RWORK, INFO )
      CHARACTER          HOWMNY, JOB
      INTEGER            INFO, LDT, LDVL, LDVR, N, MM, M
      LOGICAL            SELECT( * )
      REAL               RWORK( * )
      COMPLEX            T( LDT, * ), VL( LDVL, * ), VR( LDVR, * ),
     $                   WORK( * )
```

Purpose

STREVC/CTREVC computes all or some right and/or left eigenvectors of a real/complex upper quasi-triangular/triangular matrix T.

The right eigenvector x and the left eigenvector y are defined by:

$$T*x = w*x, \quad y^H*T = w*y^H.$$

The routine may either return the matrices X and/or Y of right or left eigenvectors of T, or the products Q*X and/or Q*Y, where Q is an input orthogonal/unitary matrix. If T was obtained from the real-Schur/Schur factorization of an original matrix $A = Q*T*Q^H$, then Q*X and/or Q*Y are the matrices of right or left eigenvectors of A.

STREVC only

T must be in Schur canonical form (as returned by SHSEQR), that is, block upper triangular with 1-by-1 and 2-by-2 diagonal blocks; each 2-by-2 diagonal block has its diagonal elements equal and its off-diagonal elements of opposite sign.

Arguments

JOB   (input) CHARACTER*1
      = 'R': compute right eigenvectors only;
      = 'L': compute left eigenvectors only;
      = 'B': compute both right and left eigenvectors.

HOWMNY (input) CHARACTER*1
      = 'A': compute all right and/or left eigenvectors;
      = 'O': compute all right and/or left eigenvectors, multiplied on the left by an input (generally orthogonal/unitary) matrix;
      = 'S': compute some right and/or left eigenvectors, specified by the logical array SELECT.

SELECT *STREVC* (input/output) LOGICAL array, dimension (N)
      CTREVC (input) LOGICAL array, dimension (N)
      If HOWMNY = 'S', SELECT specifies the eigenvectors to be computed.
      If HOWMNY = 'A' or 'O', SELECT is not referenced.
      STREVC
      To select the real eigenvector corresponding to a real eigenvalue W(j), SELECT(j) must be set to .TRUE.. To select the complex eigenvector corresponding to a complex conjugate pair w(j) and w(j+1), either SELECT(j) or SELECT(j+1) must be set to .TRUE.; then on exit

SELECT(j) is .TRUE. and SELECT(j+1) is .FALSE..
CTREVC
To select the eigenvector corresponding to the jth eigenvalue, SELECT(j) must be set to .TRUE..

N (input) INTEGER
The order of the matrix T. N ≥ 0.

T (input) REAL array, dimension (LDT,N)
STREVC
The upper quasi-triangular matrix T in Schur canonical form.
CTREVC
The upper triangular matrix T. T is modified by the routine, but restored on exit.

LDT (input) INTEGER
The leading dimension of the array T. LDT ≥ max(1,N).

VL (input/output) REAL/COMPLEX array, dimension (LDVL,MM)
On entry, if JOB = 'L' or 'B' and HOWMNY = 'O', VL must contain an n-by-n matrix Q (usually the orthogonal/unitary matrix Q of Schur vectors returned by SHSEQR/CHSEQR).
On exit, if JOB = 'L' or 'B', VL contains:
if HOWMNY = 'A', the matrix Y of left eigenvectors of T;
if HOWMNY = 'O', the matrix Q*Y;
if HOWMNY = 'S', the left eigenvectors of T specified by SELECT, stored consecutively in the columns of VL, in the same order as their eigenvalues.
If JOB = 'R', VL is not referenced.
STREVC only
A complex eigenvector corresponding to a complex eigenvalue is stored in two consecutive columns, the first holding the real part, and the second the imaginary part.

LDVL (input) INTEGER
The leading dimension of the array VL. LDVL ≥ max(1,N).

VR (input/output) REAL/COMPLEX array, dimension (LDVR,MM)
On entry, if JOB = 'R' or 'B' and HOWMNY = 'O', VR must contain an n-by-n matrix Q (usually the orthogonal/unitary matrix Q of Schur vectors returned by SHSEQR/CHSEQR).
On exit, if JOB = 'R' or 'B', VR contains:
if HOWMNY = 'A', the matrix X of right eigenvectors of T;
if HOWMNY = 'O', the matrix Q*X;
if HOWMNY = 'S', the right eigenvectors of T specified by SELECT, stored consecutively in the columns of VR, in the same order as their eigenvalues.
If JOB = 'L', VR is not referenced.
STREVC only
A complex eigenvector corresponding to a complex eigenvalue is stored in two consecutive columns, the first holding the real part and the second the imaginary part.

LDVR (input) INTEGER
The leading dimension of the array VR. LDVR ≥ max(1,N).

MM (input) INTEGER
The number of columns in the arrays VL and/or VR. MM ≥ M.

M (output) INTEGER
The number of columns in the arrays VL and/or VR actually used to store the eigenvectors. If HOWMNY = 'A' or 'O', M is set to N.
STREVC
Each selected real eigenvector occupies one column and each selected complex eigenvector occupies two columns.
CTREVC
Each selected eigenvector occupies one column.

WORK (workspace) REAL array, dimension (3*N)
CTREVC (workspace) COMPLEX array, dimension (2*N)

RWORK *CTREVC only* (workspace) REAL array, dimension (N)

INFO (output) INTEGER
= 0: successful exit
< 0: if INFO = −i, the ith argument had an illegal value

STREXC/CTREXC

```
SUBROUTINE STREXC( COMPQ, N, T, LDT, Q, LDQ, IFST, ILST, WORK,
$                  INFO )
CHARACTER          COMPQ
INTEGER            IFST, ILST, INFO, LDQ, LDT, N
REAL               Q( LDQ, * ), T( LDT, * ), WORK( * )

SUBROUTINE CTREXC( COMPQ, N, T, LDT, Q, LDQ, IFST, ILST, INFO )
CHARACTER          COMPQ
INTEGER            IFST, ILST, INFO, LDQ, LDT, N
COMPLEX            Q( LDQ, * ), T( LDT, * )
```

Purpose

STREXC/CTREXC reorders the real-Schur/Schur factorization of a real/complex matrix $A = Q*T*Q^H$, so that the diagonal block/element of T with row index IFST is moved to row ILST.

The real-Schur/Schur form T is reordered by an orthogonal/unitary similarity transformation Z^H*T*Z, and optionally the matrix Q of Schur vectors is updated by postmultiplying it with Z.

STREXC only
T must be in Schur canonical form (as returned by SHSEQR), that is, block upper triangular with 1-by-1 and 2-by-2 diagonal blocks; each 2-by-2 diagonal block has its diagonal elements equal and its off-diagonal elements of opposite sign.

Arguments

COMPQ (input) CHARACTER*1
= 'V': update the matrix Q of Schur vectors;
= 'N': do not update Q.

N (input) INTEGER
The order of the matrix T. N $\geq$ 0.

T (input/output) REAL/COMPLEX array, dimension (LDT,N)
STREXC
On entry, the upper quasi-triangular matrix T, in Schur canonical form.
On exit, the reordered upper quasi-triangular matrix, again in Schur canonical form.
CTREXC
On entry, the upper triangular matrix T.
On exit, the reordered upper triangular matrix.

LDT (input) INTEGER
The leading dimension of the array T. LDT $\geq$ max(1,N).

Q (input/output) REAL/COMPLEX array, dimension (LDQ,N)
On entry, if COMPQ = 'V', the matrix Q of Schur vectors.
On exit, if COMPQ = 'V', Q has been postmultiplied by the orthogonal/unitary transformation matrix Z which reorders T.
If COMPQ = 'N', Q is not referenced.

LDQ (input) INTEGER
The leading dimension of the array Q. LDQ $\geq$ max(1,N).

IFST *STREXC* (input/output) INTEGER
CTREXC (input) INTEGER

ILST *STREXC* (input/output) INTEGER
CTREXC (input) INTEGER
Specify the reordering of the diagonal blocks/elements of T. The block/element with row index IFST is moved to row ILST by a sequence of transpositions between adjacent blocks/elements.
$1 \leq$ IFST $\leq$ N; $1 \leq$ ILST $\leq$ N.
STREXC only
On exit, if IFST pointed on entry to the second row of a 2-by-2 block, it is changed to point to the first row; ILST always points to the first row of the block in its final position (which may differ from its input value by ± 1).

WORK *STREXC only* (workspace) REAL array, dimension (N)

INFO (output) INTEGER
= 0: successful exit
< 0: if INFO = $-i$, the i-th argument had an illegal value
= 1: (*STREXC only*) two adjacent blocks were too close to swap (the problem is very ill-conditioned); T has been partially reordered, and ILST points to the first row of the current position of the block being moved.

STRRFS/CTRRFS

```
SUBROUTINE STRRFS( UPLO, TRANS, DIAG, N, NRHS, A, LDA, B, LDB, X,
$                   LDX, FERR, BERR, WORK, IWORK, INFO )
CHARACTER         DIAG, TRANS, UPLO
INTEGER           INFO, LDA, LDB, LDX, N, NRHS
INTEGER           IWORK( * )
REAL              A( LDA, * ), B( LDB, * ), BERR( * ), FERR( * ),
$                 WORK( * ), X( LDX, * )

SUBROUTINE CTRRFS( UPLO, TRANS, DIAG, N, NRHS, A, LDA, B, LDB, X,
$                   LDX, FERR, BERR, WORK, RWORK, INFO )
CHARACTER         DIAG, TRANS, UPLO
INTEGER           INFO, LDA, LDB, LDX, N, NRHS
REAL              BERR( * ), FERR( * ), RWORK( * )
COMPLEX           A( LDA, * ), B( LDB, * ), WORK( * ),
$                 X( LDX, * )
```

Purpose

STRRFS/CTRRFS provides error bounds and backward error estimates for the solution to a system of linear equations with a triangular coefficient matrix.

The solution vectors X must be computed by STRTRS/CTRTRS or some other means before entering this routine. STRRFS/CTRRFS does not do iterative refinement because doing so cannot improve the backward error.

Arguments

UPLO (input) CHARACTER*1
= 'U': A is upper triangular;
= 'L': A is lower triangular.

TRANS (input) CHARACTER*1
Specifies the form of the system of equations:
= 'N': $A*X = B$ (No transpose)
= 'T': $A^T*X = B$ (Transpose)
= 'C': $A^H*X = B$ (Conjugate transpose)

DIAG (input) CHARACTER*1
= 'N': A is non-unit triangular;
= 'U': A is unit triangular.

N (input) INTEGER
The order of the matrix A. N $\geq$ 0.

NRHS (input) INTEGER
The number of right hand sides, i.e., the number of columns of the matrices B and X. NRHS $\geq$ 0.

A   (input) REAL/COMPLEX array, dimension (LDA,N)
The triangular matrix A. If UPLO = 'U', the leading n-by-n upper triangular part of the array A contains the upper triangular matrix, and the strictly lower triangular part of A is not referenced. If UPLO = 'L', the leading n-by-n lower triangular part of the array A contains the lower triangular matrix, and the strictly upper triangular part of A is not referenced. If DIAG = 'U', the diagonal elements of A are also not referenced and are assumed to be 1.

LDA   (input) INTEGER
The leading dimension of the array A. LDA ≥ max(1,N).

B   (input) REAL/COMPLEX array, dimension (LDB,NRHS)
The right hand side matrix B.

LDB   (input) INTEGER
The leading dimension of the array B. LDB ≥ max(1,N).

X   (input) REAL/COMPLEX array, dimension (LDX,NRHS)
The solution matrix X.

LDX   (input) INTEGER
The leading dimension of the array X. LDX ≥ max(1,N).

FERR   (output) REAL array, dimension (NRHS)
The estimated forward error bound for each solution vector X(j) (the jth column of the solution matrix X). If XTRUE is the true solution corresponding to X(j), FERR(j) bounds the magnitude of the largest element in (X(j) − XTRUE) divided by the magnitude of the largest element in X(j). The quality of the error bound depends on the quality of the estimate of $\|A^{-1}\|$ computed in the code; if the estimate of $\|A^{-1}\|$ is accurate, the error bound is guaranteed.

BERR   (output) REAL array, dimension (NRHS)
The componentwise relative backward error of each solution vector X(j) (i.e., the smallest relative change in any element of A or B that makes X(j) an exact solution).

WORK   *STRRFS* (workspace) REAL array, dimension (3∗N)
CTRRFS (workspace) COMPLEX array, dimension (2∗N)

IWORK *STRRFS only* (workspace) INTEGER array, dimension (N)

RWORK *CTRRFS only* (workspace) REAL array, dimension (N)

INFO   (output) INTEGER
= 0:   successful exit
< 0:   if INFO = −i, the ith argument had an illegal value

STRSEN/CTRSEN

    SUBROUTINE STRSEN(JOB, COMPQ, SELECT, N, T, LDT, Q, LDQ, WR, WI,
   $ M, S, SEP, WORK, LWORK, IWORK, LIWORK, INFO)
    CHARACTER   COMPQ, JOB
    INTEGER   INFO, LDQ, LDT, LIWORK, LWORK, M
    REAL   S, SEP
    LOGICAL   SELECT(*)
    INTEGER   IWORK(*)
    REAL   Q(LDQ, *), T(LDT, *), WI(*), WORK(*),
   $ WR(*)

    SUBROUTINE CTRSEN(JOB, COMPQ, SELECT, N, T, LDT, Q, LDQ, W, M, S,
   $ SEP, WORK, LWORK, INFO)
    CHARACTER   COMPQ, JOB
    INTEGER   INFO, LDQ, LDT, LWORK, M
    REAL   S, SEP
    LOGICAL   SELECT(*)
    COMPLEX   Q(LDQ, *), T(LDT, *), W(*), WORK(*)

Purpose

STRSEN/CTRSEN reorders the real-Schur/Schur factorization of a real/complex matrix $A = Q*T*Q^H$, so that a selected cluster of eigenvalues appears in the leading blocks/elements on the diagonal of the upper quasi-triangular/triangular matrix T, and the leading columns of Q form an orthonormal basis of the corresponding right invariant subspace.

Optionally, the routine computes the reciprocal condition numbers of the cluster of eigenvalues and/or the invariant subspace.

STRSEN only
T must be in Schur canonical form (as returned by SHSEQR), that is, block upper triangular with 1-by-1 and 2-by-2 diagonal blocks; each 2-by-2 diagonal block has its diagonal elements equal and its off-diagonal elements of opposite sign.

Arguments

JOB   (input) CHARACTER∗1
Specifies whether condition numbers are required for the cluster of eigenvalues (S) or the right invariant subspace (SEP):
= 'N':   none;
= 'E':   for eigenvalues only (S);
= 'V':   for invariant subspace only (SEP);
= 'B':   for both eigenvalues and invariant subspace (S and SEP).

COMPQ (input) CHARACTER∗1
= 'V': update the matrix Q of Schur vectors;
= 'N': do not update Q.

SELECT (input) LOGICAL array, dimension (N)
SELECT specifies the eigenvalues in the selected cluster.

STRSEN
To select a real eigenvalue w(j), SELECT(j) must be set to .TRUE.. To select a complex conjugate pair of eigenvalues w(j) and w(j+1), corresponding to a 2-by-2 diagonal block, either SELECT(j) or SELECT(j+1) or both must be set to .TRUE.; a complex conjugate pair of eigenvalues must be either both included in the cluster or both excluded.

CTRSEN
To select the jth eigenvalue, SELECT(j) must be set to .TRUE..

N (input) INTEGER
The order of the matrix T. $N \geq 0$.

T (input/output) REAL/COMPLEX array, dimension (LDT,N)
STRSEN
On entry, the upper quasi-triangular matrix T, in Schur canonical form. On exit, T is overwritten by the reordered matrix T, again in Schur canonical form, with the selected eigenvalues in the leading diagonal blocks.
CTRSEN
On entry, the upper triangular matrix T.
On exit, T is overwritten by the reordered matrix T, with the selected eigenvalues as the leading diagonal elements.

LDT (input) INTEGER
The leading dimension of the array T. $LDT \geq max(1,N)$.

Q (input/output) REAL/COMPLEX array, dimension (LDQ,N)
On entry, if COMPQ = 'V', the matrix Q of Schur vectors.
On exit, if COMPQ = 'V', Q has been postmultiplied by the orthogonal/unitary transformation matrix which reorders T; the leading M columns of Q form an orthonormal basis for the specified invariant subspace.
If COMPQ = 'N', Q is not referenced.

LDQ (input) INTEGER
The leading dimension of the array Q. $LDQ \geq 1$; and if COMPQ = 'V', $LDQ \geq N$.

WR, WI   *STRSEN only*   (output) REAL array, dimension (N)
The real and imaginary parts, respectively, of the reordered eigenvalues of T. The eigenvalues are stored in the same order as on the diagonal of T, with WR(i) = T(i,i) and, if T(ii+1,ii+1) is a 2-by-2 diagonal block, WI(i) > 0 and WI(i+1) = −WI(i). Note that if a complex eigenvalue is sufficiently ill-conditioned, then its value may differ significantly from its value before reordering.

W   *CTRSEN only*   (output) COMPLEX array, dimension (N)
The reordered eigenvalues of T, in the same order as they appear on the diagonal of T.

M (output) INTEGER
The dimension of the specified invariant subspace ($0 \leq M \leq N$).

S (output) REAL
If JOB = 'E' or 'B', S is a lower bound on the reciprocal condition number of the selected cluster of eigenvalues. S cannot underestimate the true reciprocal condition number by more than a factor of sqrt(N).
If M = 0 or N, S = 1.
If JOB = 'N' or 'V', S is not referenced.

SEP (output) REAL
If JOB = 'V' or 'B', SEP is the estimated reciprocal condition number of the specified invariant subspace. If M = 0 or N, SEP = $\|T\|$.
If JOB = 'N' or 'E', SEP is not referenced.

WORK (workspace) REAL/COMPLEX array, dimension (LWORK)
CTRSEN only
If JOB = 'N', WORK is not referenced.

LWORK (input) INTEGER
The dimension of the array WORK.
If JOB = 'N', $LWORK \geq max(1,N)$; (*STRSEN only*)
if JOB = 'N', $LWORK \geq 1$; (*CTRSEN only*)
if JOB = 'E', $LWORK \geq max(1,M*(N-M))$;
if JOB = 'V' or 'B', $LWORK \geq max(1,2*M*(N-M))$.

IWORK   *STRSEN only*   (workspace) INTEGER array, dimension (LIWORK)
If JOB = 'N' or 'E', IWORK is not referenced.

LIWORK   *STRSEN only*   (input) INTEGER
The dimension of the array IWORK.
If JOB = 'N' or 'E', $LIWORK \geq 1$;
if JOB = 'V' or 'B', $LIWORK \geq max(1,M*(N-M))$.

INFO (output) INTEGER
= 0:   successful exit
< 0:   if INFO = −i, the ith argument had an illegal value
= 1:   (*STRSEN only*) reordering of T failed because some eigenvalues are too close to separate (the problem is very ill-conditioned); T may have been partially reordered, and WR and WI contain the eigenvalues in the same order as in T; S and SEP (if requested) are set to zero.

STRSNA/CTRSNA

```
SUBROUTINE STRSNA( JOB, HOWMNY, SELECT, N, T, LDT, VL, LDVL, VR,
$                  LDVR, S, SEP, MM, M, WORK, LDWORK, IWORK,
$                  INFO )
CHARACTER          HOWMNY, JOB
INTEGER            INFO, LDVL, LDVR, LDT, LDWORK, M, MM, N
LOGICAL            SELECT( * )
INTEGER            IWORK( * )
REAL               VL( LDVL, * ), VR( LDVR, * ), S( * ), SEP( * ),
$                  T( LDT, * ), WORK( LDWORK, * )

SUBROUTINE CTRSNA( JOB, HOWMNY, SELECT, N, T, LDT, VL, LDVL, VR,
$                  LDVR, S, SEP, MM, M, WORK, LDWORK, RWORK,
$                  INFO )
CHARACTER          HOWMNY, JOB
INTEGER            INFO, LDVL, LDVR, LDT, LDWORK, M, MM, N
LOGICAL            SELECT( * )
REAL               RWORK( * ), S( * ), SEP( * )
COMPLEX            VL( LDVL, * ), VR( LDVR, * ), T( LDT, * ),
$                  WORK( LDWORK, * )
```

Purpose

STRSNA/CTRSNA estimates reciprocal condition numbers for specified eigenvalues and/or right eigenvectors of a real/complex upper quasi-triangular/triangular matrix T (or of any matrix $A = Q*T*Q^H$ with Q orthogonal/unitary).

STRSNA only
T must be in Schur canonical form (as returned by SHSEQR), that is, block upper triangular with 1-by-1 and 2-by-2 diagonal blocks; each 2-by-2 diagonal block has its diagonal elements equal and its off-diagonal elements of opposite sign.

Arguments

JOB   (input) CHARACTER*1
Specifies whether condition numbers are required for eigenvalues (S) or eigenvectors (SEP):
= 'E':   for eigenvalues only (S);
= 'V':   for eigenvectors (SEP);
= 'B':   for both eigenvalues and eigenvectors (S and SEP).

HOWMNY (input) CHARACTER*1
= 'A':   compute condition numbers for all eigenpairs;
= 'S':   compute condition numbers only for those eigenpairs specified by the array SELECT.

SELECT (input) LOGICAL array, dimension (N)
If HOWMNY = 'S', SELECT specifies the eigenpairs for which condition numbers are required.
If HOWMNY = 'A', SELECT is not referenced.
STRSNA

To select condition numbers for the eigenpair corresponding to a real eigenvalue W(j), SELECT(j) must be set to .TRUE.. To select condition numbers corresponding to a complex conjugate pair of eigenvalues W(j) and W(j+1), either SELECT(j) or SELECT(j+1) or both must be set to .TRUE..
CTRSNA
To select condition numbers for the jth eigenpair, SELECT(j) must be set to .TRUE..

N   (input) INTEGER
The order of the matrix T. N ≥ 0.

T   (input) REAL/COMPLEX array, dimension (LDT,N)
STRSNA
The upper quasi-triangular matrix T, in Schur canonical form.
CTRSNA
The upper triangular matrix T.

LDT   (input) INTEGER
The leading dimension of the array T. LDT ≥ max(1,N).

VL   (input) REAL/COMPLEX array, dimension (LDVL,MM)
If JOB = 'E' or 'B', VL must contain left eigenvectors of T (or of any matrix $Q*T*Q^H$ with Q orthogonal/unitary), corresponding to the eigenpairs specified by HOWMNY and SELECT. The eigenvectors must be stored in consecutive columns of VL, as returned by STREVC/CTREVC or SHSEIN/CHSEIN.
If JOB = 'V', VL is not referenced.

LDVL (input) INTEGER
The leading dimension of the array VL. LDVL ≥ 1; and if JOB = 'E' or 'B', LDVL ≥ N.

VR   (input) REAL/COMPLEX array, dimension (LDVR,MM)
If JOB = 'E' or 'B', VR must contain right eigenvectors of T (or of any matrix $Q*T*Q^H$ with Q orthogonal/unitary), corresponding to the eigenpairs specified by HOWMNY and SELECT. The eigenvectors must be stored in consecutive columns of VR, as returned by STREVC/CTREVC or SHSEIN/CHSEIN.
If JOB = 'V', VR is not referenced.

LDVR (input) INTEGER
The leading dimension of the array VR. LDVR ≥ 1; and if JOB = 'E' or 'B', LDVR ≥ N.

S   (output) REAL array, dimension (MM)
If JOB = 'E' or 'B', the reciprocal condition numbers of the selected eigenvalues, stored in consecutive elements of the array. Thus S(j), SEP(j), and the jth columns of VL and VR all correspond to the same eigenpair (but not in general the jth eigenpair unless all eigenpairs have been selected).
IF JOB = 'V', S is not referenced.
STRSNA only

Purpose

STRSYL/CTRSYL solves the real/complex Sylvester matrix equation:

$$\mathrm{op}(A)*X \pm X*\mathrm{op}(B) = scale*C,$$

where $\mathrm{op}(A) = A$ or A^H, and A and B are both upper quasi-triangular/triangular. A is m-by-m and B is n-by-n; the right hand side C and the solution X are m-by-n; and scale is an output scale factor, set ≤ 1 to avoid overflow in X.

STRSYL only
A and B must be in Schur canonical form (as returned by SHSEQR), that is, block upper triangular with 1-by-1 and 2-by-2 diagonal blocks; each 2-by-2 diagonal block has its diagonal elements equal and its off-diagonal elements of opposite sign.

Arguments

TRANA   (input) CHARACTER*1
Specifies the option op(A):
= 'N': $\mathrm{op}(A) = A$ (No transpose)
= 'T': $\mathrm{op}(A) = A^T$ (Transpose) (*STRSYL only*)
= 'C': $\mathrm{op}(A) = A^H$ (Conjugate transpose)

TRANB   (input) CHARACTER*1
Specifies the option op(B):
= 'N': $\mathrm{op}(B) = B$ (No transpose)
= 'T': $\mathrm{op}(B) = B^T$ (Transpose) (*STRSYL only*)
= 'C': $\mathrm{op}(B) = B^H$ (Conjugate transpose)

ISGN   (input) INTEGER
Specifies the sign in the equation:
= +1: solve $\mathrm{op}(A)*X+X*\mathrm{op}(B) = scale*C$
= -1: solve $\mathrm{op}(A)*X-X*\mathrm{op}(B) = scale*C$

M   (input) INTEGER
The order of the matrix A, and the number of rows in the matrices X and C. $M \geq 0$.

N   (input) INTEGER
The order of the matrix B, and the number of columns in the matrices X and C. $N \geq 0$.

A   (input) REAL/COMPLEX array, dimension (LDA,M)
STRSYL
The upper quasi-triangular matrix A, in Schur canonical form.
CTRSYL
The upper triangular matrix A.

LDA   (input) INTEGER
The leading dimension of the array A. $LDA \geq \max(1,M)$.

B   (input) REAL/COMPLEX array, dimension (LDB,N)
STRSYL
The upper quasi-triangular matrix B, in Schur canonical form.

For a complex conjugate pair of eigenvalues, two consecutive elements of S are set to the same value.

SEP   (output) REAL array, dimension (MM)
If JOB = 'V' or 'B', the estimated reciprocal condition numbers of the selected right eigenvectors, stored in consecutive elements of the array. If JOB = 'E', SEP is not referenced.
STRSNA only
For a complex eigenvector, two consecutive elements of SEP are set to the same value. If the eigenvalues cannot be reordered to compute SEP(j), SEP(j) is set to zero; this can only occur when the true value would be very small anyway.

MM   (input) INTEGER
The number of elements in the arrays S and SEP. $MM \geq M$.

M   (output) INTEGER
On exit, M is the size of arrays S and SEP actually used to store the estimated condition numbers.

WORK   *STRSNA* (workspace) REAL array, dimension (LDWORK,N+6)
CTRSNA (workspace) COMPLEX array, dimension (LDWORK,N+1)
If JOB = 'E', WORK is not referenced.

LDWORK   (input) INTEGER
The leading dimension of the array WORK. LDWORK $\geq$ 1; and if JOB = 'V' or 'B', LDWORK $\geq$ N.

IWORK   *STRSNA only* (workspace) INTEGER array, dimension (2*(N-1))

RWORK   *CTRSNA only* (workspace) REAL array, dimension (N)
If JOB = 'E', RWORK is not referenced.

INFO   (output) INTEGER
= 0:   successful exit
< 0:   if INFO = -i, the ith argument had an illegal value

STRSYL/CTRSYL

```
SUBROUTINE STRSYL( TRANA, TRANB, ISGN, M, N, A, LDA, B, LDB, C,
$                  LDC, SCALE, INFO )
CHARACTER          TRANA, TRANB
INTEGER            INFO, ISGN, LDA, LDB, LDC, M, N
REAL               SCALE
REAL               A( LDA, * ), B( LDB, * ), C( LDC, * )

SUBROUTINE CTRSYL( TRANA, TRANB, ISGN, M, N, A, LDA, B, LDB, C,
$                  LDC, SCALE, INFO )
CHARACTER          TRANA, TRANB
INTEGER            INFO, ISGN, LDA, LDB, LDC, M, N
REAL               SCALE
COMPLEX            A( LDA, * ), B( LDB, * ), C( LDC, * )
```

CTRSYL
The upper triangular matrix B.

LDB   (input) INTEGER
        The leading dimension of the array B. LDB $\geq$ max(1,N).

C   (input/output) REAL/COMPLEX array, dimension (LDC,N)
        On entry, the m-by-n right hand side matrix C.
        On exit, C is overwritten by the solution matrix X.

LDC   (input) INTEGER
        The leading dimension of the array C. LDC $\geq$ max(1,M).

SCALE   (output) REAL
        The scale factor, scale, set $\leq$ 1 to avoid overflow in X.

INFO   (output) INTEGER
        = 0: successful exit
        < 0: if INFO = $-i$, the ith argument had an illegal value
        = 1: A and B have common or very close eigenvalues; perturbed values were used to solve the equation (but the matrices A and B are unchanged).

A   (input/output) REAL/COMPLEX array, dimension (LDA,N)
        On entry, the triangular matrix A. If UPLO = 'U', the leading n-by-n upper triangular part of the array A contains the upper triangular matrix, and the strictly lower triangular part of A is not referenced. If UPLO = 'L', the leading n-by-n lower triangular part of the array A contains the lower triangular matrix, and the strictly upper triangular part of A is not referenced. If DIAG = 'U', the diagonal elements of A are also not referenced and are assumed to be 1.
        On exit, the (triangular) inverse of the original matrix, in the same storage format.

LDA   (input) INTEGER
        The leading dimension of the array A. LDA $\geq$ max(1,N).

INFO   (output) INTEGER
        = 0: successful exit
        < 0: if INFO = $-i$, the ith argument had an illegal value
        > 0: if INFO = i, A(i,i) is exactly zero. The triangular matrix is singular and its inverse cannot be computed.

STRTRI/CTRTRI

```
SUBROUTINE STRTRI( UPLO, DIAG, N, A, LDA, INFO )
      CHARACTER      DIAG, UPLO
      INTEGER        INFO, LDA, N
      REAL           A( LDA, * )

SUBROUTINE CTRTRI( UPLO, DIAG, N, A, LDA, INFO )
      CHARACTER      DIAG, UPLO
      INTEGER        INFO, LDA, N
      COMPLEX        A( LDA, * )
```

Purpose

STRTRI/CTRTRI computes the inverse of a real/complex upper or lower triangular matrix A.

Arguments

UPLO   (input) CHARACTER*1
        = 'U': A is upper triangular;
        = 'L': A is lower triangular.

DIAG   (input) CHARACTER*1
        = 'N': A is non-unit triangular;
        = 'U': A is unit triangular.

N   (input) INTEGER
        The order of the matrix A. N $\geq$ 0.

STRTRS/CTRTRS

```
SUBROUTINE STRTRS( UPLO, TRANS, DIAG, N, NRHS, A, LDA, B, LDB,
     $                   INFO )
      CHARACTER        DIAG, TRANS, UPLO
      INTEGER          INFO, LDA, LDB, N, NRHS
      REAL             A( LDA, * ), B( LDB, * )

SUBROUTINE CTRTRS( UPLO, TRANS, DIAG, N, NRHS, A, LDA, B, LDB,
     $                   INFO )
      CHARACTER        DIAG, TRANS, UPLO
      INTEGER          INFO, LDA, LDB, N, NRHS
      COMPLEX          A( LDA, * ), B( LDB, * )
```

Purpose

STRTRS/CTRTRS solves a triangular system of the form $A*X = B$, $A^T*X = B$, or $A^H*X = B$, where A is a triangular matrix of order n, and B is an n-by-nrhs matrix. A check is made to verify that A is nonsingular.

Arguments

UPLO   (input) CHARACTER*1
        = 'U': A is upper triangular;
        = 'L': A is lower triangular.

TRANS   (input) CHARACTER*1
        Specifies the form of the system of equations:
        = 'N': $A*X = B$ (No transpose)

= 'T': $A^T*X = B$ (Transpose)
= 'C': $A^H*X = B$ (Conjugate transpose)

DIAG   (input) CHARACTER*1
          = 'N': A is non-unit triangular;
          = 'U': A is unit triangular.

N   (input) INTEGER
          The order of the matrix A. N $\geq$ 0.

NRHS   (input) INTEGER
          The number of right hand sides, i.e., the number of columns of the matrix B. NRHS $\geq$ 0.

A   (input) REAL/COMPLEX array, dimension (LDA,N)
          The triangular matrix A. If UPLO = 'U', the leading n-by-n upper triangular matrix, and the strictly lower triangular part of A is not referenced. If UPLO = 'L', the leading n-by-n lower triangular part of the array A contains the lower triangular matrix, and the strictly upper triangular part of A is not referenced. If DIAG = 'U', the diagonal elements of A are also not referenced and are assumed to be 1.

LDA   (input) INTEGER
          The leading dimension of the array A. LDA $\geq$ max(1,N).

B   (input/output) REAL/COMPLEX array, dimension (LDB,NRHS)
          On entry, the right hand side matrix B.
          On exit, if INFO = 0, the solution matrix X.

LDB   (input) INTEGER
          The leading dimension of the array B. LDB $\geq$ max(1,N).

INFO   (output) INTEGER
          = 0:   successful exit
          < 0:   if INFO = -i, the ith argument had an illegal value
          > 0:   if INFO = i, the ith diagonal element of A is zero, indicating that the matrix is singular and the solutions have not been computed.

This can be regarded as an RQ factorization of A.

The upper trapezoidal matrix A is factorized as

$$A = \begin{bmatrix} R & 0 \end{bmatrix} * Z,$$

where Z is an n-by-n orthogonal matrix and R is an m-by-m upper triangular matrix.

Arguments

M   (input) INTEGER
          The number of rows of the matrix A. M $\geq$ 0.

N   (input) INTEGER
          The number of columns of the matrix A. N $\geq$ M.

A   (input/output) REAL/COMPLEX array, dimension (LDA,N)
          On entry, the leading m-by-n upper trapezoidal part of the array A must contain the matrix to be factorized.
          On exit, the leading m-by-m upper triangular part of A contains the upper triangular matrix R, and elements m+1 to n of the first m rows of A, with the array TAU, represent the orthogonal/unitary matrix Z as a product of m elementary reflectors.

LDA   (input) INTEGER
          The leading dimension of the array A. LDA $\geq$ max(1,M).

TAU   (output) REAL/COMPLEX array, dimension (M)
          The scalar factors of the elementary reflectors.

INFO   (output) INTEGER
          = 0:   successful exit
          < 0:   if INFO = -i, the ith argument had an illegal value

---

STZRQF/CTZRQF

```
SUBROUTINE STZRQF( M, N, A, LDA, TAU, INFO )
INTEGER          INFO, LDA, M, N
REAL             A( LDA, * ), TAU( * )

SUBROUTINE CTZRQF( M, N, A, LDA, TAU, INFO )
INTEGER          INFO, LDA, M, N
COMPLEX          A( LDA, * ), TAU( * )
```

Purpose

STZRQF/CTZRQF reduces the m-by-n (m $\leq$ n) real/complex upper trapezoidal matrix A to upper triangular form by means of orthogonal/unitary transformations.